Information, Technology, and Innovation

Information, Technology, and Innovation

Resources for Growth in a Connected World

JOHN M. JORDAN

WILEY

John Wiley & Sons, Inc.

Published by John Wiley & Sons, Inc., Hoboken, New Jersey.
Published simultaneously in Canada.

For general information on our other products and services or for technical support,
please contact our Customer Care Department within the United States at (800) 762-2974,
outside the United States at (317) 572-3993 or fax (317) 572-4002.

Wiley also publishes its books in a variety of electronic formats. Some content that
appears in print may not be available in electronic books. For more information about
Wiley products, visit our web site at www.wiley.com.

Library of Congress Cataloging-in-Publication Data

Jordan, John M.
    Information, Technology, and Innovation : Resources for Growth in a Connected
World / John M. Jordan.
        pages cm
    Includes index.
    ISBN 978-1-118-15578-3 (hardback); ISBN 978-1-118-22598-1 (ebk);
    ISBN 978-1-118-23930-8 (ebk); 978-1-118-26396-9 (ebk)
        1. Technological innovations.   2. Information technology—Management.   I. Title.
HD30.2.J673 2012
303.48'3—dc23

                                                                        2011048573

Printed in the United States of America
10 9 8 7 6 5 4 3 2 1

For Douglas, Phoebe, and Walker

Contents

Preface

The Outer Banks of North Carolina is a chain of barrier islands located off the eastern shore of the state. Most famous for the Kitty Hawk dunes where the Wright Brothers first achieved powered flight, the Banks have a long, rich history. The pirate Edward "Blackbeard" Teach sailed out of Ocracoke Island, while the treacherous waters offshore have claimed dozens of ships over the centuries. In World War II, German submarines sunk merchant vessels there; divers recovered an Enigma decoder machine from one such German submarine in 1981. Merchant hunters once used massive shotgun-like weapons to down hundreds of duck and geese in a single outing on the 30-mile wide Pamlico Sound.

For hundreds of years, the Banks were remote and hard to get to; this quality, along with the wind and sand, was part of the appeal to the Wrights. The 1960s saw the beginning of a period of rapid growth and discovery by the outside world. Bridges and causeways replaced some of the ferries, world-record marlin were caught by Hatteras Island charter captains, and the rapid growth of such southeastern cities as Atlanta, Raleigh-Durham, Charlotte, and the Washington, DC area helped drive a rapid increase in tourism. Finally, the rise in such adventure sports as surfing, windsurfing, and kiteboarding coincided with the area's unique combination of wind and waves to draw international attention to the area. For all the snowboarder-like attitude, however, fishing—on the sound in a skiff, in the Gulf Stream from a 50-foot "battle wagon," or off the beach— was and remains a massive draw to the area.

Despite the modernization, the islands remain prone to hurricane damage. The fragile barrier islands are continually shifting and extreme storms can breach the thin islands. While the sunshine and miles of white sand beaches, many of them protected from development as part of a national seashore, exert their pull toward escape and relaxation, locals keep a close eye on the weather. Evacuation routes are clearly marked and frequently used. After one hurricane, renters were given flyers asking them to be patient with storekeepers and restaurant waitstaff insofar as some of them had just lost their homes.

The Outer Banks is clearly a unique locale, a barrier island ecosystem with a rich history. Inspired by the Foxfire experiment in oral history begun by a Georgia English teacher in the 1960s, the local high school interviewed longtime residents for an excellent series of recollections. As recently as the 1990s, weather information was displayed in block letters, much like old IBM text-based PCs, on local cable television. Wireline telephone coverage was spotty: some calling cards worked better than others. The *New York Times*, Sunday or otherwise, was impossible to obtain. Renting a house involved a mimeographed list of options and a toll-free telephone call to a property management firm. Being removed from the rat race was part of the Banks' appeal.

The rapid growth of the Sun Belt, combined with the real estate bubble of 1995 to 2008, encouraged building and more building. Houses grew bigger. Pools became the norm, even for oceanfront houses. Real estate firms multiplied, and moved from mimeograph to black-and-white offset printing to thick, slick full-color catalogs. The *Washington Post* and Sunday *New York Times* infiltrated the islands, as did upscale restaurants. Cell phone service improved; high-speed Internet access became a routine feature of the rental properties.

As of 2011, the Outer Banks feels less isolated than ever before. Some property managers have dispensed with paper catalogs altogether, moving instead to online guides that feature Google Earth aerial imagery, video walk-throughs of the properties, and extensive photo galleries. The *New York Times*, the BBC, and Al Jazeera are all equally and easily available. Weather channels and resources have proliferated.

Cell phone coverage can extend up to 20 miles offshore. It's great for the fishing guides but just as useful for making the BlackBerry work. Wi-Fi in many rental houses makes tuning out an act of will rather than a default state of affairs. Anonymity becomes less common: A colleague of ours was on the same island as we were on a recent visit, a fact we discovered through Facebook. His page even told us what music he listened to while there.

Local retailers of everything from books to kiteboard gear to fishing tackle now ship worldwide from online storefronts. Fishing guides and restaurateurs look to Match.com for a social life, claiming that "It's hard to develop a relationship with people who are only here a week at a time." Political organizers have turned to the Web as court decisions to protect nesting birds and sea turtles have restricted beach access for fishing and other recreation. One of the main bridges connecting the islands is in need of substantial repairs, and there are online petitions and other resources devoted to that cause as well.

Relentless improvements in electronic connection have brought many changes to life on these islands. Personal safety during extreme weather, health care, and retail selection, particularly in the off season, have increased by a sizable extent. At the same time, the Outer Banks is no longer unique: In a highly connected world, anyplace can to a degree become everyplace. Getting CNN, and Twitter, and e-mail just as easily in an island paradise as in an airport Hilton also has consequences.

This book attempts to explore the intersection of our connecting technologies and our institutions, and the changes that come to business as a result. For a variety of reasons—not all of them related to the Internet—making a living, finding a partner, and other essential, defining pursuits are changing. Just as with life on the Banks, the changes are happening fast, but often invisibly, particularly for the young. The book began as an undergraduate class on global information technology strategy, an exercise in looking closely at the ways in which information and technology alter the business landscape. My objective is neither to be a cheerleader for IT nor to lament the lost glories of years gone by. Rather, I hope to identify both the imperative and the resources for still-deeper innovation as we extend the impact of the information revolution to more strata of society, more areas of the globe, and ultimately more workers.

This book's argument has five phases. First, some basic facts about technology, management, and economics are examined to set some context. The second section is concerned with how humans organize resources and do work in the changing landscape. Business model disruption and innovation is the focus of seven case studies in Section III. A number of particular technologies that can serve as innovation resources—building blocks, as it were—are discussed in Section IV. Finally, the last section sketches out five broad areas of rapid change in the foreseeable future.

Acknowledgments

Many people have contributed to this book with extraordinary intellectual generosity. It is a pleasure to thank as many of them as I can recall. To anyone I left out, my apologies.

Stu Abraham, Lawrence Baxter, Gary Bolles, Brian Geffert, Raghu Garud, Heather Jordan, Tom McGlaughlin, Dave Robertson, and Don Shemanski each read sections of the book and made helpful suggestions. My students, both current and former, have provided assistance with suggestions, corrections, and fresh insights: in particular, to Chao He, Amanda Hahnel, Jamie Joung, Terrence Kim, Tushar Shanker (who did wonderful work on the graphs), and Mike Waldhier, my sincere appreciation. In the heavy lifting department, Lee Erickson, Dave Hall, John Parkinson, Jamie Taylor, and Richard Weddle made substantial suggestions and/or edits after reading one or more versions of the complete manuscript. Each of you made this project better; where it has flaws, those are mine.

At John Wiley, Tim Burgard got a green light for the project and handed me off to the capable team of Stacey Rivera, Natasha Andrews-Noel and Helen Cho who made the production process feel smooth and positive.

Financial support came from the Smeal College of Business at Penn State, with thanks to my department chair, Gene Tyworth, and to Arvind Rangaswamy, our senior associate dean. Thanks also go to the College of Information Sciences and Technology, also at Penn State, for financial support granted by Dean David Hall.

Foundations

For all the breadth of today's technology and business landscape, a surprisingly small number of general principles underlie many patterns of behavior. These principles, however, derive from several areas of the social and behavioral sciences that are usually considered in parallel rather than jointly. At base, the paradox of information technology lies in how much more potential remains to be explored, particularly in the economic realm.

CHAPTER 1

Introduction

If you watch exponential change for long enough, the effects grow beyond comprehension. In the late 1990s the technology analyst George Gilder was fond of telling the story of "the second half of the chessboard." Here is one version:

> The emperor of China was so excited about the invention of chess that he offered the inventor anything he wanted in the kingdom. The inventor thought for a moment and said, "One grain of rice, Your Majesty." "One grain of rice?" the puzzled emperor asked. "Yes, one grain of rice on the first square, two grains of rice on the second square, four grains of rice on the third square, and so on through the 64 squares on the chessboard." The emperor readily granted that seemingly modest request. Of course, there are two possible outcomes to this story. One is that the emperor goes bankrupt because 2 to the 64th power grains of rice equals 18 million trillion grains of rice, which would cover the entire surface of the earth with rice fields two times over.[1]

The story highlights one of the critical facts of contemporary life: Improvements in digital technologies are possible at scales never experienced in previous domains. As a 2005 advertisement from Intel pointed out, if air travel since 1978 had improved at the pace of Moore's law of microprocessor price/performance (one of Gilder's doubling technologies), a flight from New York to Paris would cost about a penny and take less than one second. Cognitively, physically, and collectively, humanity has no background in mastering change at this scale. Yet it has become the expectation; the list later in this chapter should be persuasive.

Given the changes of the past 40 years—the personal computer, the Internet, Global Positioning Systems (GPS), cell phones, and smartphones—it's not hyperbole to refer to a technological revolution. This book explores the consequences of this revolution, particularly but not exclusively for business. The overriding argument is straightforward:

- Computing and communications technologies change how people view and understand the world, and how they relate to each other.
- Not only the Internet but also such technologies as search, GPS, MP3 file compression, and general-purpose computing create substantial value for their users, often at low or zero cost. Online price comparison engines are an obvious example.
- Even though they create enormous value for their users, however, those technologies do not create large numbers of jobs in western economies. At a time when manufacturing is receding in importance, information industries are not yet filling the gap in employment as economic theory would predict.
- Reconciling these three traits will require major innovations going forward. New kinds of warfare and crime will require changes to law and behavior, the entire notion of privacy is in need of reinvention, and getting computers to generate millions of jobs may be the most pressing task of all. The tool kit of current technologies is an extremely rich resource.

Cognition

Let's take a step back. Every past technological innovation over the past 300-plus years has augmented humanity's domination over the physical world. Steam, electricity, internal combustion engines, and jet propulsion provided power. Industrial chemistry provided new fertilizers, dyes, and medicines. Steel, plastics, and other materials could be formed into skyscrapers, household and industrial items, and clothing. Mass production, line and staff organization, the limited liability corporation, and self-service were among many managerial innovations that enhanced companies' ability to organize resources and bring offerings to market.

The current revolution is different. Computing and communications augment not muscles but our brain and our sociability: Rather than expanding control over the physical world, the Internet and the smartphone can combine to make people more informed and cognitively enhanced, if not wiser. Text messaging, Twitter, LinkedIn, and Facebook allow us to maintain both "strong" and "weak" social ties—each of which matters, albeit in different ways—in new ways and at new scales. Like every technology, the tools are

FIGURE 1.1 Claude Elwood Shannon, 1916–2001
Source: Courtesy MIT Museum.

value neutral and also have a dark side; they can be used to exercise forms of control such as bullying, stalking, surveillance, and behavioral tracking. After about 30 years—the IBM Personal Computer (PC) launched in 1981—this revolution is still too new to reflect on very well, and is of a different sort from its predecessors, making comparisons* only minimally useful.

For a brief moment let us consider the "information" piece of "information technology" (IT), the trigger to that cognitive enhancement. Claude Shannon, the little-known patron saint of the information age (see Figure 1.1), conceived of information mathematically; his fundamental insights gave rise to developments ranging from digital circuit design to the blackjack method popularized in the movie *21*. Shannon made key discoveries, of obvious importance to cryptography but also to telephone engineering, concerning the mathematical relationships between signals and noise. He also disconnected information as it would be understood in the computer age from human uses of it: Meaning was "irrelevant to the

---

*When Al Gore called the Internet the "Information Superhighway" in 1978, it was a perfect example of this disconnect.

engineering problem."[2] This tension between information as engineers see it and information that people generate and absorb is one of the defining dynamics of the era. It is expressed in the Facebook privacy debate, Google's treatment of copyrighted texts, and even hedge funds that mine Twitter data and invest accordingly. Equally important, however, these technologies allow groups to form that can collectively create meaning; the editorial backstory behind every Wikipedia entry, collected with as much rigor as the entry itself, stands as an unprecedented history of meaning-making.

The information revolution has several important side effects. First, it stresses a nation's education system: Unlike twentieth-century factories, many information-driven jobs require higher skills than many members of the workforce can demonstrate. Finland's leadership positions in education and high technology are related. Second, the benefits of information flow disproportionately to people who are in a position to understand information. As the economist Tyler Cowen points out, "a lot of the Internet's biggest benefits are distributed in proportion to our cognitive abilities to exploit them."[3] This observation is true at the individual and collective level. Hence India, with a strong technical university system, has been able to capitalize on the past 20 years in ways that its neighbor Pakistan has not.

Innovation

Much more tangibly, this revolution is different in another regard: It has yet to generate very many jobs, particularly in first-world markets. In a way, it may be becoming clear that there is no free lunch. The Internet has created substantial value for consumers: free music, both illegal and now legal. Free news and other information such as weather. Free search engines. Price transparency. Self-service travel reservations and check-in, stock trades, and driver's license renewals. But the massive consumer surplus created by the Internet comes at some cost: of jobs, shareholder dividends, and tax revenues formerly paid by winners in less efficient markets.[4]

In contrast to a broad economic ecosystem created by the automobile industry—repair shops, drive-in and drive-through restaurants, road-builders, parking lots, dealerships, parts suppliers, and final assembly plants—the headcount at the core of the information industry is strikingly small and doesn't extend out very far. Apple, the most valuable company by market capitalization in the world in 2011, employs roughly 50,000 people, more than half of whom work in the retail operation. Compare Apple's 25,000 nonretail workers to the industrial era, when headcounts at IBM, General Motors, and General Electric all topped 400,000 at one time or another. In addition, the jobs that are created tend to be in a very narrow window of technical and managerial skill. Contrast the hiring at

Microsoft or Facebook to the automobile industry, which in addition to the best and the brightest could also give jobs to semiskilled laborers, toll-booth collectors, used-car salesmen, and low-level managers. That reality of small workforces (along with outsourcing deals and offshore contract manufacturing), high skill requirements, and the frequent need for extensive education may become another legacy of the information age.

In the past 50 years, computers have become ubiquitous in American businesses and in many global ones. IT has contributed to increases in efficiency and productivity through a wide variety of mechanisms, whether self-service Web sites, automated teller machines, or gas pumps; improved decision making supported by data analysis and planning software; or robotics on assembly lines. The challenge now is to move beyond optimization of *known* processes. In order to generate new jobs—most of the old ones aren't coming back—the economy needs to utilize the computing and communications resources to do *new* things: cure suffering and disease with new approaches, teach with new pedagogy, and create new forms of value. Rather than optimization, in short, the technology revolution demands breakthroughs in innovation, which as we will see is concerned with more than just patents.

There are of course winners in the business arena. But in the long run, the companies that can operate at a sufficiently high level of innovation and efficiency to win in brutally transparent and/or low-margin markets are a minority: Amazon, Apple, Caterpillar, eBay, Facebook, and Google are familiar names on a reasonably short list. Even Dell, HP, Microsoft, and Yahoo, leaders just a few years ago, are struggling to regain competitive swagger. Others of yesterday's leaders have tumbled from the top rank: Merrill Lynch was bought; General Motors and Chrysler each declared bankruptcy. Arthur Andersen, Lehman Brothers, and Nortel are gone completely. How could decline happen so quickly?

Given our era's place in the history of technology, it appears that structural changes to work and economics are occurring. To set some context, consider how mechanization changed American agriculture after 1900. Because they allowed fewer people to till the land, tractors and other machines drove increased farm size and migration of spare laborers to cities. Manufacturing replaced agriculture at the core of the economy. Beginning in 1960, computers helped optimize manufacturing. Coincident with the rise of enterprise and then personal computing, services replaced manufacturing as the main employer and value generator in the U.S. economy. In short, *innovation could be to information what mechanization was to agriculture: the agent of its marginalization and the gateway to a new economic era.*

How IT relates to this shift from manufacturing to services and, potentially, a new wave of innovation is still not well understood; to take one example, as Michael Mandel argued in *Bloomberg Businessweek*, a

shortfall of innovation helps explain the misplaced optimism that contributed to the financial crises of the past years.[5] But rather than merely
incant that "innovation is good," I believe that the structure of economic
history has certain limits, and computers' propensity for optimization may
be encountering one such limit. It takes people to innovate, however, and
identifying both the need as well as the capabilities and resources necessary for them to do so may be a partial path out of the structural economic stagnation in which we find ourselves.

Consider Dell, which achieved industry leadership in the 1990s
through optimization of inventory control, demand creation, and the
matching of the two. The 2000s have treated the company less well. Apple,
which like Dell boasts extremely high levels of supply chain performance,
has separated itself from the PC industry through its relentless innovation.
Seeing Apple pull away with the stunning success of the iPhone, Google
in turn mobilized the Android smartphone platform through a different,
but similarly effective, series of technical and organizational innovations.
In contrast to Apple and Google, optimizers like Dell are suffering, and
unsuccessful innovators including Nokia are making desperate attempts
to compete. Successful innovation is no longer a matter of building better mousetraps, however: The biggest winners are the companies that can
innovate at the level of systems, or platforms.

The Macro Picture

At the risk of missing some important nuances, three broad issues—
globalization, the shift from manufacturing to services, and stagnant
middle-class wage growth—need to be considered in tandem with the
technology and associated business changes that serve as the primary
focus of this book. It should be noted at the outset that coincidence does
not imply causation: To assert that the rise of the information era happened in the same period as a transition from manufacturing to services
should not be taken to say one caused the other. In fact, some other
dynamic may have caused both. That said, powerful forces need to be
acknowledged before analyzing the technology sector by itself. We have
more to say about each of the topics in the coming chapters.

Globalization

The rise of globalization (regardless of how it is defined) and the rapid
diffusion of the Internet and mobile phones are neatly aligned in time,
taking off around 1989. Figure 1.2 shows one effort to measure globalization, building on three factors: Economic, social, and political inputs all
inform this index, which was created by KOF, a Swiss think tank.[6] These

are imprecise measures, to be sure, but it is difficult to argue, even anecdotally, that the world is less "global" than it was 20 years ago.

In addition, the developing world in particular is being transformed by extremely rapid adoption of cellular phones and mobile data. We address this phenomenon in more detail in chapter 12, but note the similarity of the curves in Figure 1.3 showing the same effect in disparate countries: Usually after competition is introduced into a market, people

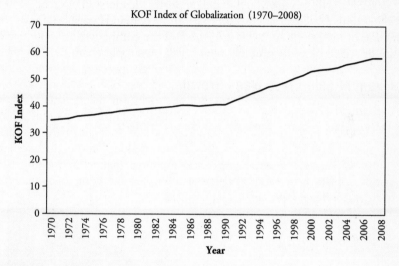

FIGURE 1.2 One Index of Globalization Shows Steady Growth
Data Source: KOF Index of Globalization.

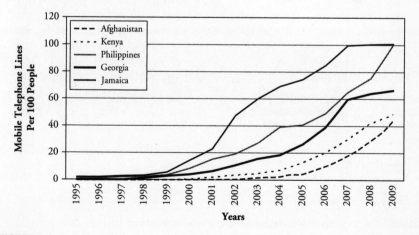

FIGURE 1.3 Mobile Telephone Lines per 100 People: Selected Countries, 1995–2009
Source: UN data.

find a way to either buy or gain access to phones for health, economic, and familial reasons.

Rise of the Services Sector

After about 1950, the manufacturing sector declined as a component of U.S. gross domestic product (GDP). Services, whether provided by banks, retail shops, hairstylists, the health care sector, or professionals such as lawyers for government employees, grew at a stunning rate in both employees and economic impact. As Figure 1.4 illustrates, given that governments lagged private companies in shedding jobs after 2008, government (an additional component of the services sector) was actually larger than goods-producing employment.

Stagnant Middle-Class Wage Growth

In the United States as well as other western nations and Japan, per capita income has remained nearly flat in real dollars since about 1970, as

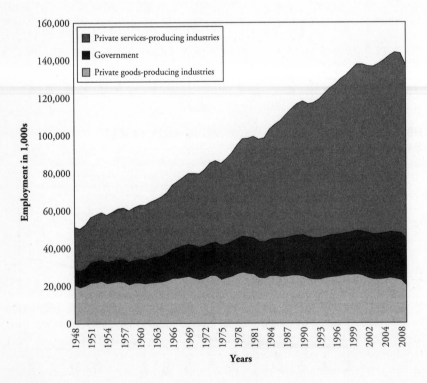

FIGURE 1.4 U.S. Employment by Sector, 1948–2009
Source: U.S. Bureau of Economic Analysis.

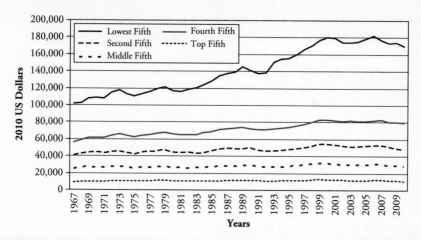

FIGURE 1.5 U.S. Household Income by Quintiles, 1967–2010, in Constant 2010 Dollars
Source: U.S. Census Bureau.

Figure 1.5 shows. Thus, the computer can be argued to have introduced efficiency improvements into the economy, but only the top 20 percent of wage earners harvested the majority of those gains.

In short,

- U.S. workers are competing with producers of goods and services in many lands.
- Most U.S. workers have not seen real wage increases in decades.
- American workers are increasingly unlikely to make things.

Why these things happened at the same time as the rise of computing remains a puzzle.

Earthquakes Every Year

Switching from macro context to the topic at hand, it is a commonplace to state that we live in extraordinary times. Rather than merely assert this, however, it doesn't take a lot of digging to find data: In nearly every year for the past 15, a new industry has been jump-started, an old one crippled, or a new way of looking at the world propagated. Consider a quick timetable that *ignores* such developments as PayPal, Wikipedia, Twitter, Craigslist, AOL, online mapping, or the iPod:

1995   Adoption of the Netscape browser goes from 0 to 38 million users in 18 months, the world's fastest technology take-off to date.

1996   Windows 95 sells 1 million copies in its first four days on the market, many through physical retailers, and later serves as gateway to the Net for millions of users via Internet networking support, CD-ROM, and native modem drivers.

1997   Dell focuses on supply-chain and related innovations as opposed to lab-based research and development, the norm at IBM and or HP. As the world's businesses and households strive to join the online migration, the build-to-order model surges in popularity for desktop configuration. IBM soon exits the business, while such manufacturers as Digital, Compaq, Gateway, and others either fade or get absorbed in consolidations. From an also-ran position in 1996, Dell more than doubled its global market share in five years, becoming the number-one PC producer.[7]

1998   Linux and Apache explode in market share for server operating systems and Web server software respectively. Linux shipments tripled, not counting free downloads; Apache powered the majority of Web sites as sampled by the Netcraft measurement firm,[8] particularly as compared to Microsoft's competing Internet Information Server. The fact that neither product emerged from a traditional development process, from a corporation, or from a monetary transaction stymied many industry observers who contended that the open-source model simply could not work.[9]

1999   Annual DVD player sales quadruple from 1 million to 4 million, an astonishing rate of adoption for a physical product (as opposed to virtual Netscape software downloads).

2000   Shortly after its launch in June 1999, Napster redefined the music landscape. Rather than attempt to use the tool for promotion in the manner of radio, the music industry wanted to shut down all peer-to-peer file sharing. Because it employed a centralized directory structure, Napster was vulnerable to legal action in ways later distributed models were not; much of the enterprise's brief history was spent in or around courtrooms. Twenty-five million users, many of them college students enjoying broadband speeds that few other populations could access, flocked to the service, which shut down in 2001. In a fascinating secondary outcome to the ascendency of MP3 music, manufacturers including Bose, Yamaha, and Harman International witnessed a 93%—*93%!*—drop in sales of stand-alone audio components over the next four years.[10]

2001   After indexing a billion Web documents and contracting with Yahoo to power the latter's search bar in 2000, Google rapidly becomes essential; the American Dialect Society called the verb its "word of the year" for 2002, and the term entered both *Merriam-Webster* and the *Oxford English Dictionary* in 2006. Counting partnerships, Google handled about 85% of all Web searches as of early 2004 before Yahoo pulled out of the agreement and built its own capability. A staggering succession of acquisitions—including Pyra (Blogger), Keyhole (Google Earth), YouTube, GrandCentral, and Hans Rosling's Gapminder—followed, none of which contributed meaningful revenues as compared to the core search business.

2002   According to Instat, wireless local area network shipments rose 65% from 2001 to 2002.[11] Business shipments of 11.6 million units led the way, and with home shipments of 6.8 million units, the total market revenue totaled $2.2 billion. Given that the more familiar term for this technology—Wi-Fi—entered the *Merriam-Webster* dictionary in 2005, it's no surprise that it became a multibillion-dollar industry only three years after launch. Even more significantly, wireless networking entered all those homes and businesses one at a time: There was no "Sputnik moment,"* no tax credit, no policy mandate, no Big Blue[†] or Ma Bell.[‡] Instead, particularly on the consumer side, the rapid adoption represents millions of trips to Best Buy or the equivalent. Combined with wide deployment of cable modems and DSL connections in this same period, lots of U.S. citizens weaned themselves off the acoustic modem in a surprising short period of time, without anyone making much of a fuss.

2003   In yet another quiet transition that was barely remarked on, cell phones surpassed landline connections in the United States, replicating the norm in essentially every other country in the world. At about the same time, digital cameras overtook their analog equivalents (Kodak stopped making film cameras entirely in 2004); shortly afterward, dedicated digital cameras would in turn be usurped by cell phone cameras. In one brief moment, two stable, ubiquitous technologies dating to the late nineteenth century were surpassed by digital counterparts.

2004   No technology can compare to the wireline phone for reach in the United States, where "universal service" is literally the law of the land. After 100 years, more than 97% of households had phone

---

*The Russian orbiting satellite that beat the U.S. into space flight in 1957. President Barack Obama argued that America stood on the verge of a new "Sputnik moment" of innovation and discovery in his January 2011 State of the Union address.
†The nickname for IBM at the height of its dominance in the 1970s and 1980s.
‡The nickname for AT&T, in reference to the Bell system of telephone companies.

service; the average household had 1.3 lines. The 1–2 punch of Voice over Internet Protocol (VoIP; the phone service offered by Vonage, Skype, and cable operators' triple plays) and mobile changed that in a hurry: Wireline penetration is heading south of 40% less than 15 years after peaking. Equities markets took notice of the VoIP take-off and began depressing telecom valuations accordingly, cellular growth notwithstanding. Skype, meanwhile, has grown enormous: As of March 2011, up to 29 million concurrent users are logged in. The total installed base was roughly the same size as Facebook, with 663 million users at the end of 2010, at which time the service accounted for 13 percent of all international calling minutes—on the entire planet. From launch through 2009, users had completed 250 billion minutes of calls.[12]

2005 GPS is another technology that seeped into mainstream adoption without anyone making an editorial point of noting a breakout year, yet its ubiquity cannot be ignored. In 2004, GPS on a mobile phone was successfully proven; it rapidly became a key component of the mobile platform. The original $12 billion investment by the U.S. Department of Defense spawned a commercial market worth $13 billion in 2003 alone; recent estimates predict a $70 billion annual GPS market spend by 2013, with location-based services expected to comprise $10 billion by themselves.[13]

2006 Following its launch in April 2005, YouTube soared from 50 million page views per day after barely six months live to hit 7 billion on several days in August 2006. At the time of its acquisition by Google, 100 million videos had been uploaded. Every one of them had the capacity to reach a worldwide audience for zero distribution cost and minimal, if any, production expense. As of mid-2011, 48 hours of content are uploaded to YouTube every minute of every day. The ability to review, catalog, or analyze such a flood of content still lies in the future.[14]

2007 While Amazon refuses to release unit sales figures for the e-reader launched in 2007, one statistic about electronic books merits mentioning: Kindle book sales in the first quarter of 2011 eclipsed Amazon sales of all print books combined. In other words, a technology dating back nearly to Gutenberg (1398–1468) was eclipsed in market share in less than four years, although it will bear watching to see how much the Kindle converted nonreaders and how much it took market share away from physical media.

2008 According to Morgan Stanley analyst Mary Meeker's statistics, the iPhone (counted along with its Wi-Fi-only iPod Touch sibling) reached 50 million customers faster than any piece of hardware in human history and jump-started the entire smartphone market.

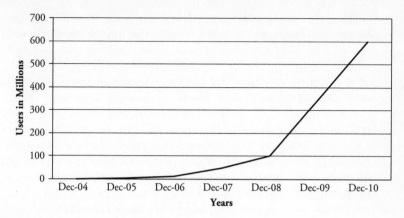

FIGURE 1.6 Facebook User Growth (in millions)

2009 Facebook claimed an incredible 600 million users in roughly six years after launch, as Figure 1.6 illustrates. The breakout year was 2009, as membership doubled off of a substantial base from about 150 million to 350 million.

2010 Apple sold 3 million iPads in less than 90 days. This matches the sales rate of the DVD after five years in the market. Even more telling is the calculation by Deutsche Bank analyst Chris Whitmore that if the iPad counted as a PC, it completely rewrites the laptop market share scoreboard, putting Apple on top by a comfortable margin—after one calendar quarter.[15]

Past Predictions

Given this steady pattern of exponential change, it appears likely that the pace of innovation will not slow and, in fact, should increase still further if more people are to share in the economic benefits of the information revolution. For all that is new, though, there's a sense in which this period is somehow familiar: Many technologies and practices related to them are variations on previous ideas.

- *Cloud computing*, the provision of computing resources to many distributed users, typically over the Internet, is a latter-day version of time sharing, a concept developed by General Electric and others in the 1960s to share centralized computing resources

(continued)

among distributed users. James Goodnight, the widely respected founder and chief executive officer of SAS Institute, an analytics software company, stated that "the cloud is nothing more than a damn big server farm." He elaborated: "Google [and] Amazon had these huge server farms that they had to have to store all the data and they got all these CPUs [central processing units] that aren't that terribly busy. Why not try to sell them off? Sell some of the time," he said. "What we're talking about here is a concept called time sharing. That's all it is. We'll sell you a piece of our hardware if you give us X number of dollars. In this case, it's real cheap. But that's all it is, time-sharing."[16]

- The notion of a device with access to one's *personal library of facts, history, and other information* was foretold by Massachusetts Institute of Technology engineering dean Vannever Bush in a device he called a memex, which seemingly supercharged the microfilm reader*:

Consider a future device for individual use, which is a sort of mechanized private file and library. It needs a name, and to coin one at random, "memex" will do. A memex is a device in which an individual stores all his books, records, and communications, and which is mechanized so that it may be consulted with exceeding speed and flexibility. It is an enlarged intimate supplement to his memory.

It consists of a desk, and while it can presumably be operated from a distance, it is primarily the piece of furniture at which he works. On the top are slanting translucent screens, on which material can be projected for convenient reading. There is a keyboard, and sets of buttons and levers. Otherwise it looks like an ordinary desk.[17]

- For as much attention as the *iPad* and other tablets are receiving, the original design brief can in some ways be traced to Alan Kay, who has been associated with fundamental inventions in object-oriented computing and the windowing behavior of the modern graphical user interface. Explained in a 1972 paper, Kay's

---

*A mid-twentieth-century technology for storing magazines, newspapers, and PhD dissertations on long reels of black-and-white film that was magnified in a hood the size of a small doghouse.

Dynabook was tablet size but was targeted primarily at children, not as a toy but a tool for learning programming. Kay was an Apple fellow during Steve Jobs's first tenure at the Cupertino company so Jobs undoubtedly had intimate knowledge of the concept.[18]

- *Text messaging* includes as a basic feature community-driven innovations in spelling and abbreviation. But in about 1850, Alfred Vail*—an American co-inventor, with Samuel F. B. Morse, of the telegraph—suggested saving words and concealing messages through the use of agreed-upon code phrases that feel strikingly familiar:

    shf   Stocks have fallen
    mhii My health is improving
    gmlt Give my love to[19]

- Conceiving of *music* migrating from vinyl or polycarbonate platters, to bits on a local hard drive, then to an account in the computational cloud seems very current in 2011; Amazon, Google, and Apple are working on such programs while Spotify is just becoming available in the United States after finding success in parts of Europe. The idea is not entirely new, however: In 1876, music was sent from a centralized location over a telephone wire. Both Alexander Graham Bell and his competitor Elisha Gray thought the market for person-to-person communication was smaller than the chance to bring concert halls to people rather than the other way around.

- Mark Twain, he of *Huckleberry Finn*, foretold *social networking*. In a little-known short story from 1898, he wrote of an invention called the "telectroscope," a data-centric extension of the then-brand-new telephone system: "The improved 'limitless-distance' telephone was presently introduced, and the daily doings of the globe made visible to everybody, and audibly discussable too, by witnesses separated by any number of leagues . . . day by day, and night by night, he called up one corner of the globe after another, and looked upon its life, and studied its strange sights, and spoke with its people, and realized that by grace of this marvellous instrument he was almost as free as the birds of the air."[20]

---

*Vail's cousin Theodore became the first president of AT&T and a significant figure in the history of American business.

Themes

For the purposes of understanding the changes that matter for business, four broad themes inform this book.

Time and Place

As we will see in multiple contexts, the *speed of change* is newsworthy. Innovation breakthroughs that formerly took decades to reach mass audiences now diffuse in mere months. Some consequences of this extreme speed crop up repeatedly, affecting economics, personal life, and the competitive business landscape.

Although the *Economist*'s Frances Cairncross announced "the death of distance" back in the 1990s, we continue to see innovations in the definition and *redefinition of place and space*. There are times when the square meter I occupy on the earth's surface is decisive or meaningful, and there are times when my identity is purely a function of networked bit streams. The interesting zone is of course the middle where physical and virtual locations interact in often peculiar ways.

Finally, it becomes clear that as the *New York Times* columnist Thomas Friedman has asserted on many occasions,[21] *globalization* and the computing/communications landscape are intertwined. The Internet itself; offshoring and the rise of India in particular; the Arab Spring; cyberwarfare; Somali piracy; global capital flows; complex derivatives and other financial instruments; Skype, e-mail, text messaging, and other low-cost international communications tools; and long, complex supply chains: All of these intermingle globalization and the IT revolution. The year 1989 marks a convenient start to the modern era, punctuated as it was by the fall of the Berlin Wall, Tiananmen Square, and the take-off of cellular telephony. Also in that year, a British computer scientist named Tim Berners-Lee drafted the proposal that, once implemented beginning in 1991, became the World Wide Web. Thus, modern globalization represents a complex convergence of technology, geopolitics, and popular expectation.

To take only a few examples of the intersection of globalization and technology, consider these:

- Global stock exchanges are increasingly correlated.[22] Large multinationals use the same networked accounting software packages and audit firms, global financial firms invest in multiple markets using similar algorithms, and markets themselves are better interconnected than ever.
- Whether using air freight or container ships, global logistics networks rely on substantial and innovative investments in information and communications technologies. Real-time package tracking for even

low-value parcels has become the expectation, no matter the origin of the shipment. UPS, which moves and tracks 15 million packages per day, describes itself as "a technology company that just happens to have trucks."[23]

- While it could be said 20 years ago that half the planet had never made a phone call, earth's overall teledensity—number of telephones divided by the number of people, per 100 people—is now greater than 100: There are more phones, most of them mobile, than there are humans. The poorest and most remote locales, with very few exceptions, are getting connected: Even Afghanistan has 41 mobile phones for every 100 inhabitants, according to the International Telecommunications Union.[24]

Systems

As a network of networks, the Internet helps enable social and technical systems to be connected at low cost and nearly infinite reach. Accordingly, *systems thinking* is becoming essential: Seeing how individual and collective entities interact, and how unexpected side effects can surprise all concerned, has become more important than ever. In part this impact relates to the speed with which events can unfold. As more people join various facets of the global information grid, formerly separate domains (including security, identity, work, and others) now interact, often at a deep level. When systems design is good, hardware, software, content, and experience converge in a powerfully coherent phenomenon like the iPod. Much more often, disconnected entities combine to form dysfunctionally connected fragments, as with many government Web sites: "You can't get here from here" often sums up the experience. Mere connection does not a system make.

The other primary impact of today's systems of systems is incredible complexity. An old saying borne of frustration goes something like this: "To err is human, but to really screw things up requires a computer." Given the intricacy of today's systems, errors of malice, incompetence, or plain bad luck can quickly scale out of control; an example would be the Wall Street "flash crash" of 2010 in which equities values oscillated wildly, driven in part by automated trading algorithms. Complexity compromises usability, security, and system performance, yet simplification is often difficult to design in. What some scientists refer to as "emergence"— unexpected outcomes of simple, uncoordinated actions—is reaching new extremes at the level of the global Internet: Such emergent phenomena as the formation of sand dune ridges or bird flocking are orders of magnitude smaller than global financial or information flows, and the science is still catching up. It also appears that twentieth-century structures—traditional bureaucracies—cannot manage really large systems, so an important aspect of tomorrow's innovation will be organizational and managerial.

Organizations

As events from Finland (the home of the Angry Birds game, Linux, and Nokia), to China, to Egypt testify, the influence of the current technology toolbox on organizational possibility is significant. In particular, the decrease in coordination costs made possible by mobility, social networking, and automated information flows is resulting in the emergence of *new organizational forms*. Wikipedia serves as a powerful example: No corporation or think tank or club, the organizational form of the global information resource is in fact the wiki, a peer-generated editorial platform. Getting people across time and distance to contribute a lot or a little to some larger purpose has never been easier. Two implications of this capability relate to risk and strategic possibility.

Speaking of old-style bureaucracies in particular (since it's too soon to see how Linux will age, for example), most every organization pursues self-preservation as a core value. At the same time that new models of collaboration and coordination are possible, risks to organizations are advancing with frightening speed. *Risk changes shape*. When ubiquitous connection becomes possible, the implications of bad news, threats, and honest mistakes can spread blindingly fast. The definitions of *prudence*, *preparation*, and *protection* are all in transition. Social media enable dispersed people to coordinate responses to perceived danger but also to plan crimes, spread rumors, and scam one another.

Time and again, old foundations of *strategic thought and action*—including barriers to entry, preservation of profit margin, building of market share, and the pursuit of growth—are being rewritten by new business practices, social dynamics, and external forces. What are the benefits and liabilities of scale, for example, in light of recalibrated coordination costs? What are the strategic responses to zero as a practical price point for certain categories of goods? What constitutes an industry, or a barrier? What sector is Amazon really in? eBay took on some capabilities of a bank by buying PayPal; Microsoft, after buying Skype and aligning with Nokia, now feels something like a phone company.

Perhaps the most important legacy of this revolution will be its facilitation of *decentralization*: In the absence of paper, long time lags in business processes, and the imperative for physical colocation, what really is the role of a headquarters? If speed in response to volatile markets and other conditions is becoming more important than organizational mass, can large firms adapt quickly enough? Is "too big to fail" more like a euphemism for "too big to get out of its own way"?

That decentralization can be put to many uses: As longtime Internet commentator Clay Shirky points out, the infrastructure is value neutral. Thus, the same potential for collaboration outside corporations that drives mass efforts to find Steve Fossett's downed aircraft allows terrorist and criminal groups to perform better. They can mount attacks of considerable sophistication, as in Mumbai in November 2008, or strike institutions responsible for the well-being of many people without leaving meaningful evidence. The playing field is more level than in recent memory, but the rules of the game and the nature of the players are changing as well.

Workers

As every piece of information, whether a grocery list or a 3D movie, is reduced to digital form, able to be infinitely copied and instantaneously moved across the globe, *exchanges of economic value* are challenging idea creators in particular. As it gets harder to get paid to be a musician, for example, or a newspaper reporter, some commentators argue that quality in those realms is declining.[25] So-called user-generated content— amateur news video, blog posts, Twitter dispatches—alter the role of professional news gatherers, pundits, and performers. Every content industry faces basic challenges to its twentieth-century existence.

In manufacturing, meanwhile, the increasing role of *digitization is raising the skills required of the workforce.* Whether with robotics, enterprise software systems, global sourcing and distribution, or increased software content of manufactured products (such as refrigerators or garage door openers with Internet access), the manufacturing workforce must deliver high levels of computer literacy. At a time of high unemployment and increasing wealth disparity, the road ahead for people without such skills is not promising.

At the same time, a college education is no longer a guarantee of lifetime middle-class status. While some skills, such as nursing, remain in high demand, such tasks as bookkeeping and even legal and equity research are being shifted to lower-wage locales. Other skills, such as engineering and management, can become outdated relatively quickly unless people learned how to learn at the time of their primary training. While the information revolution pays an education premium, it does not do so uniformly or perpetually.

We've Seen This Movie Before

Every generation appears to be fond of calling its experiences unprecedented. But for all of the amazing statistics compiled over the past 15 years, moments of technology disruption and economic transformation are remarkably predictable. Carlota Perez, currently an economic historian at the Technological University of Tallinn in Estonia, studied the persistent patterns underlying five techno-economic eras. Table 1.1 is adapted from her work.[26]

Each of these sometimes-overlapping periods has followed a rough sequence of four phases: A new technology appears in the market, often disrupting existing arrangements. There's a period of rapid, often silly adoption from which a bubble emerges. Bubbles burst; for infotech, that happened in 2000. After the speculative excesses burn off, the economic potential of the new technology is explored and exploited, pervading everyday life. Note that the truly substantial transformations occur *after* the bubble. Once the market matures and the transformative potential is largely exhausted, historically a given technology phase is replaced by a new technology paradigm.

TABLE 1.1 Technological Revolutions Follow a Stable Pattern

Revolution	Key Technologies	Begins	Bubble Bursts	Postbubble Changes
Industrial revolution	British cotton factories	1771	1793	Rise of U.S. South as world cotton supplier; Lowell mills integrate spinning and weaving
Steam and railways	Steam engines	1829	1848	U.S. transcontinental railroad; westward U.S. population migration
Steel, electricity, and heavy engineering	Cheap steel; electrical generation	1875	1893	Mass electrification, rise of AT&T, tank warfare
Oil, cars, and mass production	Mass-produced automobiles; home electrical appliances	1908	1929	Interstate highways, growth of suburbs, GM becomes world's largest company
Information and communications technologies	Integrated circuit; software	1971	2000	Facebook, global cell phone adoption, Wikipedia

Source: Adapted from Carlota Perez, *Technological Revolutions and Financial Capital: The Dynamics of Bubbles and Golden Ages* (Northampton, MA: Elgar, 2002).

Such a model puts us squarely in what Perez calls the third, or synergy, phase, in which technology change is merely part of the fabric of everyday life. Bubble valuations are still possible, as Facebook, Groupon, and Twitter suggest. But consider the iPad: Nobody can name the processor or processor speed, hard drive capacity, recommended software configuration, or most any other standard specification of the PC era. Instead, much like a blender whose revolutions per minute are unknown to essentially all consumers, the iPad "just works" to deliver movies, articles, games, weather, and other information. Consumer and employee expectations of technology are rising accordingly, and devices with poor usability will get harder to sell.

The very power of our computational context is raising the standard of execution, however: For the integration of technology to reshape other areas, such as health, public safety, and education, will require innovation at a structural level. (The stance of teachers' unions relative to online learning as practiced at Khan Academy is one telling example of a failure to innovate.[27]) That is, Perez's model of synergy makes sense in terms of historical patterns, but both the economic slowdown and the limited areas of transformation suggest that much is left to be done before this phase of technology diffusion slows down. The good news is that for innovators and entrepreneurs, there are a wealth of opportunities to put the information revolution to work in the service of customers, investors, and employees.

We turn next to a look at the demographic most at home with the new computing and communications landscape, those under 30. To what degree will their lives and careers be dominated by the tools that have become so much a part of everyday life?

Notes

1. George Gilder, "Regulating the Telecosm," Cato Institute, www.cato.org/pubs/policy_report/cpr-19n5-1.html.
2. Shannon quoted in James Gleick, *The Information: A History, a Theory, a Flood* (New York: Pantheon, 2011), p. 416.
3. Tyler Cowen, *The Great Stagnation: How America Ate All the Low-Hanging Fruit of Modern History, Got Sick, and Will (Eventually) Feel Better* (New York: Dutton, 2011), Amazon Kindle edition, location 464.
4. For more see ibid.
5. Michael Mandel, "The Failed Promise of Innovation in the U.S." *Bloomberg Businessweek*, June 3, 2009, www.businessweek.com/magazine/content/09_24/b4135000953288.htm?chan=top+news_top+news+index+-+temp_top+story
6. KOF Index of Globalization, http://globalization.kof.ethz.ch/.
7. "Gartner Dataquest Says 2001 Is a Year Battered PC Vendors Would Rather Forget," Gartner Press Release, January 17, 2002.
8. Nathan Wallace, "Web Server Popularity," May 13, 1999, www.e-gineer.com/v1/articles/web-server-popularity.htm.

9. John Roberts, "Thurownomics 101," September 22, 2000, CRN.com, www.crn .com/news/channel-programs/18834629/thurownomics-101.htm.

10. *Financial Times,* November 16, 2003.

11. In-Stat press release, www.instat.com/press.asp?ID=541&sku=IN020181LN, February 12, 2003.

12. Om Malik, "Skype by the Numbers: It's Really Big," Gigaom.com April 20, 2010, http://gigaom.com/2010/04/20/skype-q4-2009-number/.

13. "World GPS Market Forecast to 2013," July 2011, pdf.marketpublishers. com/584/world_gps_market_forecast_to_2013.pdf.

14. "Great Scott! Over 35 Hours of Video Uploaded Every Minute to YouTube," November 10, 2010, http://youtube-global.blogspot.com/2010/11/great-scott-over-35-hours-of-video.html.

15. Tim Carmody, "Apple Is No. 1 Computer Seller—If You Count iPads," October 18, 2010, www.wired.com/gadgetlab/2010/10/count-ipads-as-pcs-and-apple-is-number-one-in-us/.

16. Tom Steinert-Threlkeld, "Memo to Google & Amazon: 'Cloud Computing' Really Is Time-Sharing," March 23, 2009, www.zdnet.com/blog/btl/memo-to-google-amazon-cloud-computing-really-is-time-sharing-next-will-punch-cards-make-a-comeback/15096.

17. Vannevar Bush, "As We May Think," *Atlantic Monthly* (July 1945). www .theatlantic.com/magazine/archive/1945/07/as-we-may-think/3881/.

18. See also Wolfgang Gruener, "Did Steve Jobs Steal the iPad? Genius Inventor Alan Kay Reveals All," *Tom's Hardware US*, April 17, 2010, www.tomshardware .com/news/alan-kay-steve-jobs-ipad-iphone,10209.html.

19. Gleick, *The Information*, p. 154.

20. Crawford Kilian, "Mark Twain, Father of the Internet," *The Tyee*, January 8, 2007. http://thetyee.ca/Books/2007/01/08/MarkTwain/. (Thanks to John Parkinson for this obscure reference.)

21. See, for example, "A Theory of Everything (Sort of)," *New York Times*, August 13, 2011, www.nytimes.com/2011/08/14/opinion/sunday/Friedman-a-theory-of-everyting-sort-of.html?_r=1.

22. "All in the Same Boat," *The Economist*, September 10, 2011, www.economist .com/node/21528640.

23. "A Tech Company with Trucks," *Sacramento Business Journal*, December 10, 2010, www.bizjournals.com/sacramento/print-edition/2010/12/10/a-tech-company-with-trucks.html.

24. www.itu.int/ITU-D/ict/statistics/index.html.

25. See, for example, Jaron Lanier, *You Are Not a Gadget: A Manifesto* (New York: Knopf, 2010).

26. Carlota Perez, *Technological Revolutions and Financial Capital: The Dynamics of Bubbles and Golden Ages* (Northampton, MA: Elgar, 2002). See especially pp. 14 and 57.

27. See, for example, Alex Wagner, "Can Sal Khan Reform Education In America?" *Huffington Post*, April 4, 2011, www.huffingtonpost.com/2011/04/04/the-khan-academy-and-educ_n_844390.html.

CHAPTER 2

Demographics

The rise of social networking (including social games), smartphones, and text messaging can be attributed in large measure to the behavior of "digital natives" whose skills, personas, and expectations have been shaped by a lifetime of exposure to the Internet and its accompanying technologies. How these technologies shape people, and vice versa, is fascinating to watch, given such a real-life and real-time case study. For businesses, employing and selling to this population present particular challenges and opportunities.

It would be difficult, and at any rate artificial, to try to argue chickens and eggs in questions of demographic change and technological change. Given the magnitude of what has happened in the past 20 years, it's appropriate to begin by asking a few questions about radical shifts in who is using information technologies and where they are doing so.

A number of commentators have noted how quickly the young pick up on such things as electronic games, text messaging, MP3 music, and other tools.[1] Whether they are called *oyayubizoku* ("clan of the thumb") in Japan, "digital natives," or the "net generation," people currently under 30 are argued to access, process, and understand information in markedly different ways from their predecessors.[2] The implications of this change vary.

For starters, people facile with such tools are changing the workplace. Second, in the realm of politics, this group played a decisive role in the 2008 U.S. elections, utilizing blogs, online video, social networks, and text messaging to motivate, communicate, and coordinate. Not long afterward, the same tools played a central role in India's elections. Third, outside of work and the civic sphere, that generation is also changing personal relationships and dating, though as we will see, older people tend to follow suit quickly in this regard. Finally, many facets of recreation (with online gaming, fantasy sports leagues, and poker, in particular) play out differently by generation. All of these changes will be discussed throughout the book.

While we will have much more to say in regard to the world outside the OECD* when we discuss mobility in Chapter 27, it's worth mentioning here how mobile phones and data devices are changing entire countries and, indeed, continents. While in the developed world mobility and broadband connections have a wide range of uses, many of them recreational, in India, Africa, and elsewhere, the life-changing aspects of mobile telephony tend to be more essential: Is there a market for my catch or crop? Is my Haitian daughter alive after the earthquake? Based on this picture of a tumor or broken limb, how soon must I travel to a doctor? Thus, demography is being reshaped by technology: Standards of living and life expectancy are projected to improve in ways that dams and other infrastructure investment have yet to drive.

Is There a "Net Generation"?

The Canadian consultant Don Tapscott has, for well over a decade, been focusing attention on what he calls "the net generation."[3] He identifies eight norms to describe people born in the 1980s as they diverge from their elders:

1. Freedom and freedom of choice
2. Customization
3. Collaboration
4. Scrutiny of outsiders
5. Integrity
6. Fun, including at school and work
7. Speed
8. Innovation

All of these traits are readily evident when one spends time with educated, generally affluent people under 30. To call them a generation, however, overreaches the evidence. Tapscott relied on an online survey instrument that suffers from considerable self-selection bias: Active net users found the survey and proceeded to discuss how actively they used and internalized various facets of the net. Based in large measure on the behavior of his admittedly talented, bright, and insightful children and

---

*The countries of the Organization for Economic Cooperation and Development include the U.S., western Europe, and other rich countries. The public health and data visualization expert Hans Rosling referred to it as "the country club of the United Nations."

their friends, Tapscott says in his most recent book in the ongoing study that he "came [in 1996] to the conclusion that *the defining characteristic of an entire generation* was that they were the first to be 'growing up digital'"[4] (emphasis added).

That statement is problematic for any number of reasons; let's list five:

1. *Ethnicity.* Middle-class white and Asian young people, such as those in big-city U.S. and Canadian locales like Tapscott's Toronto, absolutely exhibit some of those eight traits from time to time. They are not, however, a "generation": According to the Pew Hispanic Center in 2010, only 42% of Latinos without a high school degree (that group counts for 42% of the total ethnic constituency) go online.[5] Given that the U.S. Latin population is large, fast growing, and less educated than whites, it cannot be bundled into Tapscott's "generation" without qualification.

2. *Heterogeneous online behavior.* Just as offline, the online world is hardly homogeneous. To connect any two users of various elements of the Internet only on that basis makes as much sense as to say that everybody who drives, or watches television, is a generation. Danah Boyd's observations on social class differences between Facebook and MySpace users are instructive here (and absent from Tapscott's bibliography).[6] Video watchers and file-sharing uploaders are at least two different species, as are flame warriors versus lurkers, or Columbine-searchers versus Amazon shoppers. Web 2.0—the tendency of user-powered Web sites such as Flickr and Facebook to build off "civilian" energy, and Tapscott's pole star—is an undeniably powerful force, but it is not yet universally embraced by members of any broad demographic, not even the 20-somethings. Apple, eBay, Amazon, and even Google still retain elements of older, content-driven business models and are only minimally participatory.

3. *Ethics.* As far as "integrity" being a generational attribute, think about the business school students at Duke: Ten percent of the class of 2008 was caught cheating despite honor code posters prominently posted in the building and multiple adjustments to the curriculum in that direction. A separate study of 54 universities found that 56% of MBA students admitted to cheating; how many more cheaters lied?[7] In 2005, dozens of applicants to Harvard Business School tried to view acceptance letters before they were mailed by poking around in the school's Web site after a security hole was reported. The school denied admission to all 119 net-savvy snoopers.[8]

4. *Too soon to tell.* This cadre is still young. To define a generation, before they reach 30, by a set of technology artifacts embraced in different ways to various degrees by only some of them feels premature if nothing else. How many of the Paris/Chicago/Prague 1968

generation similarly embraced "fun" or "freedom" as core values back in the age of typewriters? Short of World War II, at any time has an American generation been defined (to the extent that a generation can be defined) before they reached 30?

5. *Reversing expectations.* We're enduring a prolonged global recession, and the results could well consign the first generation in memory, if not American history, to economic prospects worse than those of their parents.[9] According to the 2010 Census, the U.S. poverty level hit 15%. Forty percent of people in their 20s live at home at some point.[10] That is, if the net generation experiences widespread downward social mobility, that will be considerably more defining than the fact that some of them like to blog or watch funny videos at work.

At the same time, any technology change that can drive redesigns in something as essential as people's clothing needs to be noted: Cable-routing systems for earbud wires are standard in many backpacks, most skiwear, and some exercise apparel. Even if Tapscott overstates the size of the cadre, millions of people are behaving from a network-centric, digital orientation: Facebook organizes their social world, iPods or iPhones their music and movies, GPS their travels, and Hulu their television viewing.

Digital Natives

A more nuanced view of the online young comes from John Palfrey and Urs Gasser in their book *Born Digital*. First, unlike Tapscott, they recognize how people in the whole world are online, so they refer to their digital natives as a global population rather than a generation.[11] The book is filled with subtle understandings of work, safety, and creativity. A key point is made early, in regard to identity: "Digital Natives live much of their lives online, without distinguishing between the online and the offline. Instead of thinking of their digital identity and their real-space identity as separate things, they just have an identity (with representations in two, or three, or more different spaces)."[12]

Digital Natives also treat research as almost exclusively the province of Google searches, sometimes with few tools for assessing the quality of various results. Physical space can become inconsequential: "Friends" of multiple sorts without linguistic differentiation can exist, and move, essentially anywhere. Like Tapscott, Palfrey and Gasser demonstrate concern over some people's data hygiene habits, worrying that offhand utterances, photos, or connections will come back to embarrass, or do worse to, the natives' later adult selves. If stalkers wanted to devise a perfect technology for their craft, they could do worse than Facebook.

Millennials at Work

A number of consulting firms appear to have found a profitable market in training white-collar managers to cope with "millennials," "Gen Y," or whatever one calls these people, who are different in large measure because of their facility with technology. This divergence in communication tools and styles is already having dramatic effects, according to 40- and 50-something peers of mine, particularly in knowledge-driven industries such as advertising, accounting, and consulting. Although I frequently see generational differences working with university students, from the reports of many colleagues, the sharp differences in communications platforms across generations are radically complicating the task of management. It's not unheard of for senior executives to have administrative assistants print off their e-mails, and voicemail remains the medium of choice in some firms. At the other demographic extreme, teens often disregard e-mail in favor of some combination of Twitter, text messaging, PC-based instant messaging (Google Chat), Skype, and social-network message tools.[13]

It's too soon to tell what exactly is happening, but a trend in real estate appears to be toward tighter quarters. According to the *Los Angeles Times*, the norm in the 1970s for American corporate office space was 500 to 700 square feet per employee. The average in 2010 was just over 200 square feet per person, and the space allocation could fall to as little as 50 square feet by 2015, according to Peter Miscovich, a real estate broker at Jones Lang LaSalle.[14] Part of this can of course be attributed to expense control, but teams in some industries are growing closer and more collaborative; some people *like* closer proximity to coworkers. Finally, laptops, videoconferencing, and mobile phones mean that desks no longer serve the same function they formerly did.

In addition, people who grew up with a Web-centric social sensibility often communicate rather more freely than their elders (or regulators, in some cases) would prefer. The enterprise information services (IS) organization has the unenviable task of logging all material communications, and sometimes of turning off some of the most powerful Web 2.0 exemplars. The aforementioned middle-age managers, meanwhile, must communicate across an increasingly wide variety of technologies, each with particularities of convenience, cultural norms, interoperability, and security and privacy. Add to this cultural dynamic the technical incompatibilities among communications tools. It feels a bit like the 1980s days of the CompuServe versus Prodigy online services: My Facebook message won't cross over to your LinkedIn profile.

The locus of work will be addressed later, but for now we can note that both managers and managed are still adjusting to expectations of a seven-day, 24-hour workweek, made possible by BlackBerries, PCs, and the like. The workplace is increasingly located wherever the person and his or her tools are. The fact that the tools are always on and used for both work and private tasks, and are both personal and invisibly intimate has implications for relationships, for personal health and well-being, and for the basic employment contract, both specified and implied.

Behavior and Expectations

Several behavioral dynamics of the digital natives are pertinent. First, the ease of online collaboration and interaction has lowered coordination costs: Organizing a group of 3 or of 3,000 has never been easier.[15] If the underlying assumption is that because people are reachable, they can be counted on, they will be repeatedly invited to contribute in some way to a project they care about. Mobilizing people, whether for a party or a cause, is now primarily a matter of desire, not logistical hurdles. Text-based interactions are so comfortable that the line between friend, acquaintance, and stranger becomes easily blurred. Digital privacy and trust are very much in flux.

Second, speed matters. Having to wait on a modem-grade connection causes nearly physical pain, as witnessed by the public outrage toward AT&T for poor iPhone connections. Multitasking is common, to the point where the need to prohibit texting and driving is motivating legislation in many states. The speed of change is very real to the digital natives. Within a single family, for example, the ages at which children get mobile phones or Facebook accounts will invariably drop as younger siblings come of age.

Looking Ahead

Technology is driving in the young (and now young adults) new understandings and expectations of time, of intimacy, of productivity, of property rights, of work, of location, and of choice. Laws and norms are slow to adapt, but change is under way in these domains as well. Any institution one can name—from public schools and libraries to bars and clubs to policing—must react. Much of what follows in this book will be read very differently by a 20-year-old as compared to his or her parent, wherever each may live. The point is not to catalog the ways this population is different—that has been capably done elsewhere—but rather to highlight the particular ways that demography is driving sociotechnical change. At the same time, the converse is true: The generation with the longest to live in the aftermath of the global recession is also the one with potentially the most powerful set of tools for living that have ever been developed.

When Millennials Come to Work

Many 20-something new hires come to corporate workplaces immersed in technology only to find themselves frustrated by the seemingly arbitrary and archaic rules governing the use of computing on the job. Four areas appear to be particular stress points:

1. *Millennials are mobile; enterprises are fixed.* Having lived on laptops, iPods, and smartphones from a young age, 20-somethings frequently are stymied by the 8:00-to-5:00 precepts of many organizations. Flexible working hours, working from home, and enterprise support for smartphones and tablets are the expectation, yet all three can be blocked by rules, infrastructure, and custom. Voicemail might be a foreign concept, particularly if it cannot be forwarded to the device and platform of choice.

   In response, change is happening one company and one manager at a time. In particular, some IS organizations are experimenting with flexible architectures that allow employees to bring whatever edge device they see fit to the corporate system. This notion of "bring your own device" (BYOD) challenges security practices, to be sure, but, done right, can build workplace morale and allows sales forces, in particular, to push the envelope with technologies (such as tablets in particular) that increase customer involvement. At the same time, given the speed of technology change, BYOD does not rely on the organization to pick winners in turbulent markets.

2. *Enterprise systems are hard to learn.* Customer relationship management software, big enterprise packages such as SAP and Oracle, and custom applications built in-house can all be daunting to understand and typically are not particularly user-friendly at the interface layer. Once people master the systems, they often perform with a certain level of disappointment inherent in the experience. For people used to instantaneous responses from a Google search, sensory involvement with a console game, or full Facebook functionality on a smartphone, the real-world strengths and weaknesses of enterprise software can be intensely frustrating. The fact that enterprise systems usually run only on desktops rather than on mobile platforms can compound the alienation.

   Some organizations are experimenting with mentors who informally teach new recruits both the cultural norms of the company

   (continued)

and the tricks of the trade in terms of taming the beast that is enterprise software. For their part, software vendors and systems integrators are consciously trying to improve usability, sometimes by incorporating gaming elements in software design. Support for mobile platforms is a front-burner priority across the industry.

3. *For millennials, software is social.* A particular flashpoint often relates to the use of Facebook on company time. Many firms block the service at the firewall, which simply drives the behavior to the smartphone; in most cases even prisons cannot interfere with the cellular signal. The reality is that social networking can be an enormous waste of time, and managers' concern about lost productivity has roots in fact. At the same time, more and more companies are encouraging social behavior in working environments, whether in marketing teams that use online chat for customer interaction, collaborative spaces in forecasting or research and development, or efforts to judge market sentiment on the basis of macro-level social data in the form of Facebook "likes" or Twitter mentions. Millennials' native comfort with social software can be leveraged for corporate benefit in many such deployments. In the final analysis, however, it's still a balancing act for employees not to abuse the window on the outside world at the same time that managers set expectations and trust employees to manage their time, networks, and assets responsibly.

4. *Self-service trumps formal training.* Many 20-somethings are quite adept with many technologies: video editing, complex game consoles, wireless networking, distributed storage, music mixes, and so on. When they encounter technology roadblocks on the job, many prefer to try to troubleshoot the issue themselves rather than wait in the queue of trouble tickets being addressed by the IS group. Of course, the downside of such behavior is the potential for making the situation worse. The thought of sitting through corporate technology training, meanwhile, can be depressing, especially when the same manager who required the training asks the new hire for help setting up a ringtone or fixing the printer.

One promising development is in text-based technical support, which has the benefit of being able to be done remotely (potentially in India) and utilizing the employee's mobile phone rather than the compromised PC under repair. It also allows the conversation to occur in the 20-somethings' native environment while allowing tech support to multitask.

Notes

1. See Rich Ling, *New Tech, New Ties* (Cambridge, MA: MIT Press, 2008).
2. For useful data on a subset of this group, see Aaron Smith, Lee Rainie, and Kathryn Zickuhr, "College Students and Technology," Pew Internet and American Life project, July 19, 2011, http://pewinternet.org/Reports/2011/College-students-and-technology.aspx.
3. Don Tapscott, *Grown Up Digital* (New York: McGraw-Hill, 2009). See also his *Growing Up Digital: The Rise of the Net Generation* (New York: McGraw-Hill, 1999).
4. Tapscott, *Grown Up Digital*, p. 2.
5. Gretchen Livingston, "Latinos and Digital Technology, 2010," Pew Hispanic Center, February 9, 2011, http://pewhispanic.org/reports/report.php?ReportID=134.
6. Danah Boyd, "Viewing American Class Divisions through Facebook and MySpace," *Apophenia Blog Essay,* June 24, 2007. www.danah.org/papers/essays/ClassDivisions.html.
7. Della Bradshaw, "MBA Students Are 'Biggest Cheats,'" *Financial Times*, September 20, 2006.
8. Linda Rosencrance, "Harvard Rejects Business-School Applicants Who Hacked Site," *Computerworld,* March 8, 2005, www.computerworld.com/s/article/print/100261/Harvard_rejects_business_school_applicants_who_hacked_site.
9. See, for example, Catherine Ramell, "Are You Better Off Than Your Parents Were?" *New York Times* Economix blog, February 10, 2010, http://economix.blogs.nytimes.com/2010/02/10/are-you-better-off-than-your-parents-were/.
10. Robin Marantz Henig, "What Is It about 20-Somethings?" *New York Times Sunday Magazine*, August 18, 2010, www.nytimes.com/2010/08/22/magazine/22Adulthood-t.html.
11. John Palfrey and Urs Gasser, *Born Digital: Understanding the First Generation of Digital Natives* (New York: Perseus, 2008), p. 14.
12. Ibid., p. 4.
13. See Frank Bruni, "Sorry, Wrong In-box," *New York Times*, August 31, 2011, www.nytimes.com/2011/09/01/opinion/sorry-wrong-in-box.html?_r=1&src=me&ref=general.
14. Roger Vincent, "Office Walls Are Closing in on Corporate Workers," *Los Angeles Times*, December 15, 2010, http://articles.latimes.com/2010/dec/15/business/la-fi-office-space-20101215/.
15. Clay Shirky has been stressing this point for years. See, for example, his *Cognitive Surplus: Creativity and Generosity in a Connected Age* (New York: Penguin, 2010), pp. 65 ff.

CHAPTER 3

Behavioral Economics

Why do people do what they do? In the twentieth-century West, neoclassical economics asserted that rational people want more of most things and will act to achieve this goal. The assumption is embedded in virtually every economics course taught in western universities and operationalized from there onward. One implication of said rationality is that one way to motivate people is to promise them more of something (typically money) in return for more of a desired behavior. Both the bonus culture of Wall Street, so much in the news after 2008, and the debate over competing views of chief executive compensation silently embed this set of assumptions. In the laboratory and in the wild, however, people don't actually do the rational thing all that often. The discovery of reliable behavioral patterns that defy neoclassical rationality aligns closely with a broad range of technology-related phenomena.

Challenges to Economic Man

Beginning in the 1960s, psychologists and economists began to employ theories of human motivation to explain certain decisions and other economic actions. Previously, market behavior had been theorized in neoclassical economics to be the outcome of a) rational actors b) who have identified preferences that can be associated with a value c) acting independently with access to full and relevant information d) to improve their utility as individuals or profits as firms.[1] Economic man turns out to be more complex than was previously thought, however, and sometimes he goes missing entirely.

Rational actors are hard to find; all of us employ "irrational" tools to make decisions. Many factors go into our preferences, not all of them conscious and many of them not clearly valued. Information about our options is rarely full and even more rarely perfect. Finally, we act for many reasons, not only to maximize our utility.

First, people internalize "irrational" elements (such as past experience, rules of thumb, and verbal framing mechanisms, such as the recited order of a list) as they make choices. The myth of "the hot hand" in basketball, for example, was debunked in 1985: Making a shot changes the player's *prediction* of the next shot's success but not the actual chances of its going in. In short, we frequently see patterns where there are none.[2] This influence can be quite subtle: Experimental subjects who are asked the last digits of their social security number then go on to use those random numbers to "anchor" an unrelated operation, such as a bid on a product or a guess on an obscure fact.[3] In technical terms, people can reliably be found to hold biases and employ rules of thumb while making choices.

Second, the neoclassical assumptions regarding preferences have been tested in many ways. Daniel Kahneman, a coauthor (with the late Amos Tversky) of some seminal papers in the field, won the 2002 Nobel Prize in economics "for having integrated insights from psychological research into economic science, especially concerning human judgment and decision-making under uncertainty."[4] A few years later, the then–University of Chicago legal scholar Cass Sunstein wrote a book with longtime behavioral economist Richard Thaler called *Nudge*, on "choice architectures": The structure in which choices are presented to people changes what they choose.[5] Sunstein is currently working in the Obama administration. Other mainstream authors include Duke's Dan Ariely, whose *Predictably Irrational* includes a chapter on the power of "free" or apparently free prices that reliably lead people to make "irrational" choices.[6]

Third, imperfect information, which had long been acknowledged, was found to come in many forms, with many outcomes. In a classic paper, George Akerlof showed how the market for used cars was shaped by buyers' overwhelming perception that sellers generally intended to hide defects: Information asymmetry can have the effect of crippling entire categories of transactions. It is a case of "all other things being equal" not holding true, and people behaving accordingly.[7]

Finally, empirical experiments and theoretical constructs found people valued fairness rather than maximizing their utility at the cost of another, visible human. Here's a deft telling of a landmark experiment from George Mason University's Center for the Study of Neuroeconomics:

> *Take two people and tell them they have the opportunity to split $10. Furthermore, tell one person that, as first mover, they get to make a one time offer, and tell the other person that, as second mover, they get the opportunity to either accept or reject this offer.*

> *If the offer is rejected they both go home with zero. This stylized negotiation was first studied by experimental economists in [a 1982 paper] and economists got a surprise. Game theory predicts an unequal split favoring the person who gets to make the offer. After all if I offer a ($9, $1) split where you only get $1 you should take it since a dollar is better than nothing, but instead a majority of the offers are to split equally.*[8]

As Clay Shirky, currently a professor of media studies at New York University, noted, "[P]eople behave [in the experiment] as if their relationship matters, even when they are told it doesn't."[9] Fairness does not square with the maximization assumptions so common before the turn of the twenty-first century.

Not only in matters of fairness but also in the realm of motivation, people maximize things other than economic utility. Repeated and well-designed studies have found cognitive tasks have intrinsic satisfactions, so much so that people actually do *worse* at brainstorming and other jobs when incentives are raised. Instead, for brain work, extensive research suggests people are rewarded with three intangibles:

1. *Mastery.* Getting better at something difficult (whether golf, coding, or a foreign language) for the sake of being able to do it better, or well.
2. *Autonomy.* People who solve hard problems (and lots of other people as well) want to be left alone in the process of doing so. The rise of professionalism in law and medicine relates directly to this motivation.[10]
3. *Purpose.* Working in the pursuit of some purpose larger than the self and beyond the paycheck is coming to the fore for many students entering the workforce. Some firms, such as Zappos and Deloitte, are capitalizing on this desire in their recruiting by emphasizing nonmonetary rewards, such as an authentic firm mission or explicit ways of "giving back."[11]

Behavioral Economics in a Networked Age

What is the place of behavioral economics in the landscape of information technology? First of all, as work can be accomplished outside firms because of the power of self-organization, some scholars have invoked the lessons of behavioral economics to explain the behavior of people who contribute, without monetary compensation, to such formidable efforts as Linux or Wikipedia. In the former case, roughly 8,000 programmer-years were estimated to be invested as of 2001;[12] Wikipedia has nearly

500 million edits. The lack of monetary pay is an existence case, not a hypothetical, and both examples operate at a large enough scale that motivation must be explained somehow. Mastery, autonomy, and purpose do that job quite well, it would appear.

Second, the behavior exhibited by participants in large-scale social networks (such as Facebook, but also online games) is showing extensive investment of both play and work time for no apparent (external) reward. Behavioral "locks and keys," as game developer Jesse Schell put it,[13] are at work all around the technology landscape:

- When DARPA (Defense Advanced Research Projects Agency, the Department of Defense research and development group behind the Internet) wanted to celebrate the Internet's fortieth birthday in 2009, they conducted a fascinating experiment. Ten red weather balloons were tethered in plain view in different U.S. locations, and the first team to submit the correct coordinates of all 10 won $40,000. MIT's team won, in large measure because they devised a clever incentive model to grow the network of observers: The $4,000 per balloon was divided between referring parties and the observer him- or herself, leading to increased participation. Other fascinating developments included the spoofing of competing teams with Photoshopped fake balloons. Open networks, operating on Twitter for instance, performed quite well.[14]
- Why do people watch different movies in the streamed Netflix than they put into their queues of mailed DVDs? In part, it's because people are aspirational: In the future, the logic goes, I really should watch something redeeming. When Friday comes, however, the lowbrow option wins out and *Schindler's List* stays in the envelope. Given that every streaming decision is made in the moment, the aspirations disappear.[15]
- Online dating is clearly a huge business, but the rules of engagement are still being sorted out. The desire to attract appealing candidates with one's description leads to the temptation to lie. Researchers at Cornell and Michigan State looked at daters' actual height, weight, and age, then compared those to online representations.[16] Unlike purely virtual environments, online dating ideally leads to face-to-face meeting, so the ability to lie is tempered by the possibility of real-world confirmation. Men lied about height and, infrequently, about age more than women did, while both sexes lied almost equally, and in the majority of cases, about weight. As the researchers concluded, "The pattern of the deceptions, frequent but slight, suggests that deception on online dating profiles is strategic. Participants balanced the tension between appearing as attractive as possible while also being perceived as honest."

- In life and technology broadly considered, the power of default settings is coming to be more fully understood. Facebook's default privacy settings, for example, are most favorable to Facebook, not the person joining the service. Google tracks an individual's search history unless she turns off the setting deep in a complex menu of choices. So-called opt-out versus opt-in defaults are only one example: audible notifications, color schemes, units of measurement, and countless other options are extremely frequently left on the "factory" settings. Given this inertia, the noted technology commentator Kevin Kelly has noted how much the power lies in the hands of those who set the defaults.[17]

- Behavioral economics has many insights to contribute to this domain. stickK.com was founded by three Yale professors who saw the application of behavioral economics to personal aspiration. The model is simple: People select a goal, set the stakes, get a referee, and build a network of friends for moral support. Whether for weight loss, smoking cessation, or dissertation writing, there is evidence to suggest small, symbolically powerful incentives affect behavior much more than substantial financial rewards.

- Symbolic rewards, paradoxically, can get people to spend real money. The business models of many online games feature large inflows of revenue for upgraded game elements (swords, shields, real estate). Disney's Club Penguin gives away game points but charges $6 per month for players to redeem the points.

- Foursquare was one of the hot companies at the SXSW culture and technology gathering in 2010, following Twitter's breakout there a few years earlier. In Foursquare, people "check in" to the real-world places they visit via mobile phone, announcing their presence to friends and proprietor alike. It turns out you can check in to a place you are not visiting: To make a point, one man became mayor (one of Foursquare's honorary titles) of the North Pole. Foursquare's founder replied to that effort in a blog comment by asking "We often wonder why people 'cheat' when there's really nothing to win—it's not like we're giving away trips to Hawaii or Ford Fiestas over here. But I guess the combo of mayorships, local recognition and, hey, maybe a free slice of pizza is a little too much for some people to live without."[18]

- Facebook games like FarmVille, with extremely limited graphics and plotlines, contrast vividly with PlayStation 3 titles with massive visual horsepower but steep learning curves. In addition, FarmVille invites investment of time and attention, which creates a form of lock-in. (Leaderboards at console game sites perform a similar function.) Females especially appear to be gravitating to Facebook games because of the social aspect rather than a skills challenge, and they previously helped drive the Wii to the top of console market share; Microsoft and Sony are responding by mimicking Nintendo's simple but gesture-driven platform. The shift hit home hard at game firm Electronic Arts, which bought a social network game company (Playfish) for $275 million in cash the same day that the firm laid off 1,500 console-supporting employees.

Looking Ahead

Several tendencies appear to be emerging. First, the barrier between real life and play life can get fuzzy. In 2008, two Dutch youths were convicted of stealing virtual goods from an online gamer by beating him up at school and coercing him into transferring the goods. A Chinese gamer was murdered over the sale of an online sword artifact. The Wii bowler uses a real arm motion to hurl a virtual ball toward virtual pins. People's FarmVille opponents are their real-world friends. In addition, people are powerfully motivated by symbols, just as they are elsewhere, whether those artifacts are military service ribbons, flags, or luxury cars. Finally, as always, people work assiduously to game every system, whether of grades or Facebook friend counts or stickK weight-loss programs. Leaderboards matter, whether of financial accumulation, imaginary milestones, or athletic performances, and with competition invariably comes a testing of the limits of the contest.

Given that people can work and connect from anywhere, and that fewer and fewer jobs rely on fixed physical infrastructure, corporations are no longer the assumed unit of organization. As groups grow easier to form, they can accomplish many kinds of work, and a key consideration in pursuit of a goal becomes motivating the right people rather than forming the organization. Money is no longer assumed to be the only way to drive behavior, especially cognitive effort, so new kinds of organizations are challenging the primacy of companies, schools and universities, and traditional non-profits, as we will see in Chapters 9 and 11.

Both the degree of portability and the global scale are new here: Ten years ago, no one could play Scrabble with hundreds of people while sitting on a bus. Now that we can, what comes next? With so many games now resident in the computational cloud, how will people remember or re-create them in the future? How will human relationships, whether intense or trivial, scale in these virtually physical or physically virtual settings particularly?

Finally, how will other systems, currently driven by other incentive programs, be transformed by the permeation of game and other group dynamics? Schell points to education as an obvious target, but corporate human resources, aging, personal fitness, and retirement savings are just as likely. As a result, nearly every field of endeavor could be affected by the clever application of behavioral carrots and sticks via new electronic media. Social engineering, in short, appears to be supplanting—or at any rate joining—technical engineering in the vanguard of innovation.

Notes

1. For one summary of the neoclassical position, see www.econlib.org/library/Enc1/NeoclassicalEconomics.html.
2. Thomas Gilovich, Robert Vallone, and Amos Tversky, "The Hot Hand in Basketball: On the Misperception of Random Sequences," *Cognitive Psychology* 17 (1985): 295–314.
3. Amos Tversky and Daniel Kahneman, "Judgment under Uncertainty: Heuristics and Biases," *Science* 185 (1974): 1124–1130.
4. Nobel Prize citation at http://nobelprize.org/nobel_prizes/economics/laureates/2002/press.html.
5. Richard Thaler and Cass R. Sunstein, *Nudge: Improving Decisions about Health, Wealth, and Happiness* (New Haven, CT: Yale University Press, 2009).
6. Dan Ariely, *Predictably Irrational: The Hidden Forces That Shape Our Decisions* (New York: HarperCollins, 2008).
7. George A. Akerlof, "The Market for 'Lemons': Quality Uncertainty and the Market Mechanism," *Quarterly Journal of Economics* 84, no. 3 (1970): 488–500.
8. The original paper is Werner Güth, Rolf Schmittberger, and Bernd Schwarze, "An Experimental Analysis of Ultimatum Bargaining," *Journal of Economic Behavior and Organization* 3, no. 4 (December 1982): 367–388; the summary is at http://neuroeconomics.typepad.com/neuroeconomics/2003/09/what_is_the_ult.html.
9. Clay Shirky, *Cognitive Surplus: Creativity And Generosity In A Connected Age* (New York: Penguin, 2010), p. 107.
10. Paul Starr, *The Social Transformation of American Medicine: The Rise of a Sovereign Profession and the Making of a Vast Industry* (New York: Basic Books, 1984).
11. Dan Pink, *Drive: The Surprising Truth about What Motivates Us* (New York: Riverhead, 2009).
12. David A. Wheeler, "Counting Source Lines of Code," www.dwheeler.com/sloc/.
13. Jesse Schell, DICE conference presentation, http://g4tv.com/videos/44277/dice-2010-design-outside-the-box-presentation/.
14. Lance Whitney, "MIT Floats Ideas in DARPA Balloon Challenge," *C\|Net*, December 8, 2009, http://news.cnet.com/8301-1023_3-10411211-93.html. See also John C. Tang, Manuel Cebrian, Nicklaus A. Giacobe, Hyun-Woo Kim, Taemie Kim, and Douglas "Beaker" Wickert, "Reflecting on the DARPA Red Balloon Challenge," *Communications of the ACM* 54, no. 4 (April 2011): 78–85.

15. Dan Ariely, "Gamed: How Online Companies Get You to Share More and Spend More," *Wired* (July 2011), www.wired.com/magazine/2011/06/ff_gamed/.
16. Jeffrey T. Hancock, Catalina Toma, and Nicole Ellison, "The Truth about Lying in Online Dating Profiles," *Proceedings of the SIGCHI Conference on Human Factors in Computing Systems* (New York: ACM, 2007), pp. 449–452.
17. "Triumph of the Default," www.kk.org/thetechnium/archives/2009/06/triumph_of_the.php.
18. Jim Bumgardner, "Mayor of the North Pole," blog post and comments at www.krazydad.com/blog/2010/02/mayor-of-the-north-pole/.

CHAPTER 4

Information Economics

In the late 1990s, there was talk of a new economy in which old rules like supply and demand no longer applied; key aspects of the economy would be characterized by abundance, by the problems that come from having to allocate surplus.[1] As we all know, whether with iron ore, rice, or water, those scenarios did not come to pass; "too much" is seldom the problem. Throughout the hype, traditionalists held the line: "Durable economic principles can guide you in today's frenetic business environment. Technology changes. Economic laws do not."[2] Information goods include encyclopedias, compact discs, cell phone minutes, or equity analysis, all of which are valued not by what they are but what they convey. The characteristics involved in information economics—particularly network effects, lock-in, and pricing behavior—underlie many of the phenomena in this book.

Very few private-sector companies have chief economists. Investment banks, publicly traded homebuilders, and large healthcare firms all might have need for such a position, but generally few companies hire such individuals. In 1998, two economists from the University of California at Berkeley published *Information Rules*,[3] a neoclassical approach to such issues as technology lock-in (why does everyone still use the demonstrably inferior QWERTY keyboard?), information pricing, and standards wars. Unless otherwise noted, all foundation concepts and some examples noted here come from this source.

In 2002, one of the authors, Hal Varian, began consulting at Google. Shortly thereafter, he took a leave of absence (and eventually retired) from his academic post, moving full time to become Google's chief economist. In that position, Varian's tenure has coincided with the rapid growth of Google's breakthrough AdWords/AdSense pricing mechanism—which is based on complex auction mechanics—as well as the firm's foray into bidding on wireless spectrum.[4] Google has begun to lobby world governments and enter often-complicated agreements with competitors and other entities (in regard to mobile phones or book publishing for two examples). At both the macro/policy and micro/strategy levels, information economics is sufficiently nonintuitive and, at Google's scale, so complex that having such expertise in-house appears to have been well worth the hire.

Information Goods

Goods whose primary value lies in the information they convey (rather than in their physical essence, as with wheat, or their functional use, such as a comb) can behave in unexpected ways. Classic examples of information goods include books, newspapers, stock tickers, and movies/DVDs. The peculiar properties of digital information goods combined with the nature of the Internet and related technologies have led to upheaval in some old industries. In brief, four behaviors of information goods have become relevant in music, news, software, financial analysis, and other sectors, often changing business models or economic viability in the process. These four behaviors are:

1. Sampling
2. First-copy costs
3. Price based on value, not cost
4. Network effects

Sampling

Information goods are experienced and thus need somehow to be sampled before deciding to buy.

The only way to know whether you like a song or movie is to "consume" the information before purchase. Trailers serve this purpose for movies; radio airplay was perfect sampling for recorded music. Third parties become important: Word of mouth, about which we will hear more later, and reviewers are important pieces of the puzzle. Compare news to a car, in which statistics, crash-test results, and other metrics can guide customer choices. Information goods, in other words, cannot easily be understood through standardized representations or objective measurements: Knowing how many actors (or jokes) were in *Airplane* tells the viewer nothing. Counting pages for a book is similarly worthless.

Reputation, whether conveyed by brand, word of mouth, or otherwise, helps overcome the sampling problem. People buy the *Wall Street Journal* a year at a time not because they looked at every day's edition before they bought it but because past performance suggests they will benefit from the kinds of information that will be delivered.

First-Copy Costs

Information goods are expensive to produce and very inexpensive to reproduce and, over the Internet, to distribute.

The shorthand way of saying this relates to commercial software: The first copy of Windows 7 cost billions of dollars in research and development costs, advertising, and testing. The second copy cost under a dollar if physical media are involved, more with logistics costs; for online downloads with essentially free distribution, that second-copy cost drops toward zero. With newspapers, it's a similar model, except that timely physical distribution at scale can be very expensive, particularly as the prices of electricity, ink, and diesel fuel for delivery trucks all typically rise with the cost of crude oil.

Price Based on Value, Not Cost

Because replication and distribution costs for the copies after the original are essentially zero online, the price of information goods is not based on cost but on the value attached to the good by individual customers.

Supply and demand curves multiply: At the extreme, there are as many optimal prices as there are people with value preferences. One important task, then, is to find ways to differentiate the product and capture as much of the market's price tolerance as possible. Economists call this price discrimination, and it is often illegal and usually unpopular. What businesses can do is to offer subtle variations on the basic offering. In addition, consumers have become accustomed to free being a viable price for many information goods.

Network Effects

Externalities (outcomes of trade not accounted for in the transaction) are frequently negative: Traffic and pollution can be used as examples. Network externalities, also called network effects,[5] can also be positive: The behavior of someone else in the network makes me better off without my doing anything. Flu shots are a positive network externality: The more people in my office who get inoculations, the lower my risk of exposure in that sphere of my life. If someone else signs up with my cellular carrier, in-network calls and texts to that subscriber are often free. If more people buy Word after I do, the odds of being able to exchange documents are better the more people are on the platform.

Pricing Information: Versioning and Bundling

Unlike most examples in commercial history, free is a viable price point for digital information goods: Linux is a classic example. Subsidies are often common: Advertisers provide a revenue stream so newspaper readers, television viewers, and Google searchers can enjoy lower priced or no-cost media. Other revenue streams are possible: Some bands allow taping of concerts to increase fan loyalty or to encourage the sale of T-shirts, commercial-quality recordings, or future concert tickets. (See "Software Copying" later in the chapter.)

Pricing information goods to extract as much profit as possible from this cacophony of demand curves, and often in networked scenarios, is a fascinating exercise. In particular, the notion of "versioning" is very appealing. This practice relates to the ways that producers can reconfigure information goods so as to present different market segments with attractively priced versions of the same core product. Basic and deluxe versions of software are frequently very similar under the hood, but the "professional" features included in the platinum version allow the seller to extract premium prices from people who value the good more highly.

Movies are a convenient example. Depending on one's personal preferences, a customer can watch a movie in dozens of ways, each with its own set of costs and benefits, starting with time from original release:

- Opening-night premiere in Hollywood: thousands of dollars if at all available
- Opening week, New York, Friday evening: $20 per seat
- Opening week, Topeka, afternoon matinee: $5 per seat
- IMAX 3D version: $25 per seat
- Second-run theater: $1 with coupon
- Comcast pay-per-view: $5 for a roomful of viewers
- Hotel pay-per-view: $13.95
- Pirated copy of DVD in China: $0.25
- Over-the-air free TV two years after release: commercial interruption
- Netflix: physical DVD rental price varies by plan and activity level
- Director's cut Blu-ray disc with commentary, bloopers, and other extras: $40

For movies, the multitude of distribution and delivery channels makes versioning extremely effective: Blockbuster hits like *Avatar* stay in theaters as long as they can command an audience while duds are pulled after a week or go straight to cable television and/or DVD. Few other offerings can exploit so much of an audience's willingness to spend, although until the ascendency of the Kindle, hardcover books also had longer runs before the paperback release if they sold well.

Versioning can be based on attributes of the *good*: Higher-quality (Blu-ray versus VHS), better documentation, extra content such as directors' commentaries on DVDs, access to relevant archives and data sets, real-time stock quotes versus 20-second delayed. Versioning can also create multiple pricing options based on characteristics of the *buyer*: student discounts, group pricing, or differential pricing by geography.

This practice can backfire, as when Lexicon, a high-end home theater company, repackaged an inexpensive Blu-ray player inside a fancier case and tried to charge a 600% premium.[6] The attributes of a more expensive version (whether in a Lexus compared to a Toyota or in a software package or online dating service) need at once to deliver perceptible value to some segment of the customer base and leverage the investment in the base platform. As customers get savvier and share observations online, maintaining the value perception for the different versions can be difficult, as Lexicon discovered.

Based on some classic observations of human behavior, the *Information Rules* authors recommend adding a third, extremely expensive version of many products that will sell very few copies. The reason for this is the anecdotally familiar notion of extremeness aversion: The best-selling wine in most restaurants is the second cheapest, and buyers typically find comfort in medium sizes, intermediate variants, and other middle options. Having a "diamond" version with extra-special tech support or another apparently worthwhile attribute makes the formerly most expensive "deluxe" version look like prudent middle ground.

Another practice related to addressing the many demand curves for an information good is bundling. While travel presents a classic example in the cruise plus airfare plus hotel plus on-ship amenity credit for a single price, many information goods are bundled:

- Newspapers are bundled by content (sports, entertainment, news, food, classified ads, etc.) and by time: Subscriptions are temporal bundles. As we will see, both of these bundles are being disaggregated by the Internet, with significant implications for news gatherers, citizens, and investors.
- Software is bundled; office software with a word processor, spreadsheet, presentation graphics, and potentially other elements is the typical product.
- Cable television service is bundled, not only in service tiers with access to different groups of channels but also in "triple plays" of TV, Internet, and wired telephony.

- *Encyclopaedia Britannica* was a classic bundled offer, including thousands of entries that the owner would never read.
- Music used to be sold in bundles called albums. Once file-sharing and, later, legal download services made it possible to obtain single songs, the music industry faced the same issues as the news sector. By contrast, few people want only "the best" five minutes of a movie or television show: Dramas and comedies and documentaries do not unbundle in the same way as music. A TV series is a bundle of episodes, but a movie is not a bundle of scenes.

Network Effects

Physical goods can exhibit network effects: Owning a Lotus sports car in an isolated region is made difficult by the lack of trained mechanics, spare parts, or a liquid secondary market for buying and selling these unusual cars. Compare Lotus to Toyota: The more people who own Toyotas in a given geography, the more options an owner has for service. As demand expands, additional dealers move in, providing opportunities for comparison shopping and potentially better service in the presence of competition.

Information goods exhibit many network effects beyond the file-sharing compatibility noted earlier. The English language is an information good with strong network effects, for example: The more people who learn it, the more communications options English speakers have and the easier global travel becomes. VHS versus Betamax and HD-DVD versus Blu-Ray illustrate how standards wars between competing technical systems (and potentially business models), are, at base, stories of network effects. Buyers did not want to own a soon-to-be-obsolete video player/recorder, in part because of the poor selection of prerecorded titles for the losing ecosystem.

Electronic games are perfect examples of network effects. This applies to game platforms (Xbox, Wii, PlayStation) as well as online games and online social networks: As more people flock to a platform, the more valuable and attractive it becomes compared to competing alternatives. Online dating is full of network externalities: The more people who sign up, the better tuned the matching algorithms and the better the selection of potential partners.

The fax machine is a commonly cited example: The first fax machine on earth could have cost $1 million, been gold-plated and encrusted in diamonds, but it would have been worthless for lack of partners. As the technology took hold, every time another fax machine was sold anywhere in the world, the option value of any existing machine rose by a small amount.[7] The same pattern of thought can be applied to Facebook, LinkedIn, and other social networking services. It is not clear that network effects do not have a ceiling, however: The 2 billionth Facebook user might not be as valuable as the 100 millionth.*

As the fax became available in offices all over the world, its network effect helped drive another phenomenon: positive feedback. Because of the importance of standards, defined both by market success (Microsoft Windows) and industry committees (IEEE[†] 802.11 or Wi-Fi), success in a technology can often build future success. The same holds true for gaming platforms: I can't play against you if our controllers and software don't agree. With GPS units, in contrast, brand proliferation is a possibility because of weak network effects: Your unit and my unit have little to do with each other. In some situations, search potentially being one, strong positive feedback leads to winner-take-all markets, or markets with a very small number of entrants protected by high barriers to entry.

Technical standards play a critical role in information economics. The choice of mobile phone standard for a given geography involved billions of dollars in revenue for the suppliers as well as intense frustration when a Verizon CDMA[‡] phone from Louisville would not work in London or Lisbon. Railroad gauges (nonconforming geographies quickly got isolated), alternating current power supply (electric plugs in the United Kingdom are still not uniform), and the locking device used in container shipping[8] (a truly transformative, if invisible, technology standard that helped enable globalization) provide other examples of the long-lasting importance of winning standards battles.

Lock-in

The technology phenomenon known as lock-in can be related to both network effects and winner-take-all positive feedback. As a comparison, consider an automobile. I can drive a Dodge and you a Toyota, but

---

*But as my colleague John Parkinson points out, Facebook's 2 billionth member is the fifth person in some individual's social graph. Networks with power-law characteristics (see Chapter 6) behave in strange ways.

[†]Pronounced "Eye-triple-E", the IEEE is the Institute of Electrical and Electronics Engineers, a global professional body responsible for, among other things, many technical standards in computing and communications.

[‡]For a time the predominant set of cell phone standards used in the United States, but rarely elsewhere, where GSM (Global System for Mobile) dominated. CDMA is shorthand for both CDMAOne and CDMA2000 technologies.

those choices are generally independent. If we were to switch vehicles for whatever reason, I would have access to the same roads and destinations, my driving skills would transfer quickly (except perhaps my ability to find the windshield wiper or headlight controls), and the experience would be generally unremarkable: Switching costs between cars, while not zero—my floor mats and snow tires might not fit the new vehicle—are extremely low.

Now consider software. At the personal level, your documents from Pages on the Mac should be read by my copy of Word on an HP PC. There might be some hiccups, but Mac–PC compatibility is reasonably high (even though that has not always been true). At the enterprise level, things get more complicated: Switching software can be a $100 million proposition as data stored to support billing in Oracle, for example, would likely not be ready to support sales force management in SAP. Users trained on one system face long and sometimes difficult transitions to new software and, sometimes, hardware. Investments in computing hardware, networking equipment, and other infrastructure may or may not be able to support a short-notice switchover.

Switching costs are part of lock-in, but there are other aspects as well. Just as Gillette blades won't fit Schick razors, neither will Dell printer cartridges fit a Xerox unit. Uniqueness in consumables and other modules (ink, video game cartridges, batteries) can impose switching costs or otherwise lock a customer to a product. Training, support, documentation, and other "soft" elements of a system can enforce lock-in; contracts are still another vehicle to achieve the same objective.

Closely related to lock-in (keeping a customer a customer) is *lock-out*: preventing a competitor from entering a market or from converting an existing customer. The same proprietary inkjet cartridge that delivers high profit margins to HP after the printer was sold below cost or even given away in a bundle serves both purposes, lock-in and lock-out, as it prevents customers from moving their supply of ink to a Dell or Xerox machine.

Looking Ahead

The economics of information goods is sufficiently different from other kinds of goods that a wide variety of business decisions, personal behaviors, and legal issues have been affected. We will see the importance of lock-in, of free copy costs, and of the need for sampling in many examples in the forthcoming chapters.

Software Copying

Software copying is truly a problem without precedent. While the Xerox machine did not duplicate the printing (and particularly the binding) process, photocopying did have a major economic impact on at least two subsectors: textbook publishing and sheet music. Even so, these markets are small relative to software, music, movies, and proprietary research. Thus, the business model changes, court cases, and other signs of market adaptation to photocopying do not compare to the issues we face today.

There is surprisingly little literature on the historical arc of this issue. Nevertheless, given the prominence of Napster and its torrenting successors, the world's intellectual property interactions with the Chinese government and market, and the rise to economic power of the gaming sector, technologies of copying and its control have become central issues in a digital economy.

Duplicating a physical artifact requires, at the minimum, having access to both raw materials and skills. Whether that's steel and metalworking, food and cooking, or wood and carpentry, the issue of copying has been nonexistent in some markets and rampant in others. Elsewhere, particularly in branded consumer products such as watches and purses, copying—imitation rather than replication—can be a significant concern. Physicality also implies a moderate barrier to movement: Successful counterfeiters still face the problem of getting merchandise to customers.

The Internet removes the barrier of getting raw materials because code is malleable, easily transported, and closer to idea than infrastructure. The skill involved in copying a file, whether of executable code or data, is minuscule in contrast to what was needed to create either the software artifact or a physical original. Unlike physical counterfeits, which typically lack material quality and/or craftsmanship compared to the original, or analog copies in which successive generations of cassette tapes, photocopies, or faxes rapidly degrade, digital copies are nearly perfect. Furthermore, the means of production (a PC) is inexpensive and ubiquitous, which makes tracing the origin of copies harder than locating activities with heavier infrastructure, such as radio broadcasts and LP record pressing. Finally, the digital distribution channel is not only faster than a physical counterpart, it is instantaneously global.

Owners of digital content have relied on three tactics to combat copying.

(continued)

First, there has been a series of attempts to make computer discs hard or impossible to copy by hiding files, using proprietary formats (such as game cartridges) or doing something called nibbilizing that rearranged the bit sequence of a copy. (Similarly, Macrovision enforced copy protection in analog VHS recorders.) As software distribution goes increasingly online, such measures still have their place, but they have not slowed the spread of copying by a significant margin. An exception is the video DVD (particularly Blu-ray), which can be copied by knowledgeable users but not casual ones: Proprietary protection of the digital bitstream in a DVD player or PC is enforced in hardware.

Second, software publishers can make it hard or impossible to use a copy. Some companies required users to consult a paper manual ("What is the last word on page 67?") to generate crude authentication. One manual used symbols, and the company printed the manual in a color scheme that was impossible to photocopy. Still others relied on a hardware device called a dongle to activate a program in conjunction with the software and a generic PC (which quickly raised the problem of getting multiple dongles to interact gracefully on the same machine). More recently, a program can "phone home" via the Internet to see if software with a given serial number is in use on multiple machines. This approach can be made relatively robust for application software, and a variant called FairPlay prevents unauthorized copying of Apple's iTunes music files. Adobe is including auditing and monitoring of print materials in its LiveCycle Policy Server: If a user forwards an e-mail or file, prints it, or otherwise interacts with it, the originator of the document can be informed. How this extensive reach will affect task design and business processes remains to be determined.

Finally, software owners can lobby legislatures to change laws relating to copyright. The doctrine of fair use has been dramatically altered by both the duplication technologies of the past 100 years and the lobbying of content industries. There have been many unintended consequences: Copying application software off a 5¼-inch floppy onto a USB stick generally would be illegal, but with rapidly outmoded storage technologies, what is the owner of the application to do if she owns a PC without the appropriate outmoded drive? At the enterprise and government level, archiving digital assets often turns into an exercise in curatorship of a technology museum: Successive generations of outmoded hardware and software need to be maintained in the event that a given file or storage format needs to be read. Some estimates put the number of digital formats in the tens of thousands.

The content industry currently tends to reject copying as backup: If I buy an iTunes song (or 500 of them) and my host PC's hard drive dies, until cloud music lockers, I'd generally be out of luck even though all software was purchased and used under the terms of the license. Another example is DVDs: If I have two places of residence and want to watch a movie where I am, why must I buy a second copy of the same software rather than make a single copy for personal use? Once again, copyright law tends to prohibit any copying under blanket provisions. Such a move blurs the distinction between copying and counterfeiting, which are overlapping but not identical concepts. As processor speeds, graphics capability, and bandwidth all improve, content owners have lobbied to engineer copy protection deeper into the computing platform under the guise of anticounterfeiting but also to preclude many activities potentially protected by fair use.

This degree of restriction on customer behavior would be unprecedented. If I want to weld a Ferrari nose onto the front end of a Caterpillar dump truck, Ferrari (or Caterpillar) can't control what is done either with the purchased asset or, more important, an oxyacetylene torch. Governments have engineered protection into color copiers, for example, and it's hard to argue against some degree of action in the public interest to protect the integrity of the money supply. But being able to use small clips of published text in scholarly works, for example, is standard practice—and essential to the expansion of knowledge in law or literary criticism. The parallel action of copying any portion of a movie for personal or scholarly use, however, might be illegal, depending on jurisdiction. Similarly, the study of cryptography is highly regulated: Scholars who decode copyprotection algorithms run the risk of prosecution if they publish their findings.

Herein lies the conundrum. The digital asset copying problem is unprecedented, so new kinds and degrees of measures will be required. At the same time, the legitimacy of certain forms of copying—for preservation, backup, or fair use—means that broad prohibitions, enforced in a general-purpose computing platform, come at an extremely high price to the purchasers and users of software and other digital media. No single answer will apply in every market to every application, but there have been some noteworthy efforts:

(*continued*)

- *Use copying to build an installed base.* Software makers with sufficiently strong cash reserves and long planning horizons can consider letting copies go relatively unpunished to build up a user base. Once a large body of people is trained on the software and file extensions and other conventions are well established, there are high enough switching costs that there may be reason to buy later versions of the product, particularly if the registration process is tightened, the pricing is attractive, and/or competitors have been weakened.
- *Use copying of entertainment to sell other entertainment.* The Grateful Dead's support of tape-swappers who were allowed to record concerts is a widely cited example of allowing amateur copies to thrive as an adjunct to, rather than a substitute for, commercially released products. Other artists have used music downloads as an alternative path around the gatekeepers of radio playlists to build live audiences for concerts—where the T-shirt concession is tightly protected against counterfeiters.[9]
- *Reconsider analog.* Several music labels, faced with plummeting CD sales, have turned to high-quality vinyl releases of both new and back catalog. Some high-end financial newsletters never left paper distribution. So-called three-dimensional printing produces analog physical objects based on digital models.
- *Utilize advertising-supported distribution.* Archives are a perfect example: While a few newspapers have succeeded in charging subscriptions, most are failing to monetize their back issues with clumsy subscription or registration models that often don't support permanent linking from blogs or other sources of traffic. As paper newspapers continue to decline in circulation, the economic models of hybrid (digital + physical) production and distribution are ripe for reinvention. As a former big-city newspaper editor recently noted, this talk about the sky falling on newspaper ad revenues has happened before: In the late 1960s, political advertising moved overwhelmingly to television almost overnight, and the newspaper industry survived.
- *Think of King Gillette and sell blades after giving away razors.*[10] Giving away a multiplayer game title free, or allowing users to copy it without restriction, provides software publishers with a powerful distribution channel. (Back in the day it used to be called "viral.") Recovering the cost can be achieved more effectively by making the proprietary online gaming environment a tightly controlled, for-profit affair, with monthly or annual

renewals: Players will pay for access to other players, not for the plastic disc. Several online gaming environments (including Second Life) have spun off real economies based on cash flowing to merchants of virtual assets.

The list is not exhaustive but should suggest that there are enough viable responses to digital copying such that broad prohibition of all software copying will impose social costs that may outweigh proprietary benefits. It's important that there be open public debate to consider all of these potential costs, benefits, and risks of various courses of action. Copying and piracy, meanwhile, are not one and the same, but the rhetorical landscape tends to make this distinction harder and harder to draw. At the same time, true piracy—illicit DVD pressing plants, for example—should be considered and addressed separately rather than being conceptually lumped in with the many gray areas of fair use.

Notes

1. One example is Kevin Kelly, *New Rules for the New Economy* (New York: Viking, 1998).
2. Carl Shapiro and Hal R. Varian, *Information Rules: A Strategic Guide to the Network Economy* (Boston: Harvard Business School Press, 1999), p. 1.
3. Ibid.
4. See Steven Levy, "Secret of Googlenomics: Data-Fueled Recipe Brews Profitability," *Wired*, May 22, 2009, www.wired.com/culture/culturereviews/magazine/17-06/nep_googlenomics?currentPage=all.
5. For a terminological distinction that argues that if the effect can be internalized by someone (possibly the platform owner), the effect cannot be called an externality, see www.utdallas.edu/~liebowit/palgrave/network.html.
6. Brian Barrett, "Lexicon Charges $3500 for a Repackaged $500 Oppo Blu-ray Player," January 18, 2010, http://gizmodo.com/5450893/lexicon-charges-3500-for-a-repackaged-500-oppo-blu+ray-player.
7. See, for example, Michael Katz and Carl Shapiro, "Systems Competition and Network Effects," *Journal of Economic Perspectives* 8, no. 2 (Spring 1994): 93–115.
8. On railroad gauges, see Varian and Shapiro, *Information Rules*, p. 208. An excellent source on the shipping container is Marc Levinson, *The Box: How the Shipping Container Made the World Smaller and the World Economy Bigger* (Princeton, NJ: Princeton University Press, 2008).

9. See, for example, Joshua Green, "Management Secrets of the Grateful Dead," *Atlantic Monthly* (March 2010), www.theatlantic.com/magazine/archive/2010/03/management-secrets-of-the-grateful-dead/7918/.

10. The history of this innovation is less straightforward than often reported. See Alan Elliott, "Gillette, The King Of Razors," *Investors Business Daily*, October 18, 2010. http://news.investors.com/Article/550711/201010181705/Gillette-The-King-Of-Razors.htm.

CHAPTER 5

Platforms

Given that one, if not the, byword of today's technological landscape is "connectedness," much attention has been focused on how systems of networked or related devices evolve. Whether the connection is obvious, as in mobile phones or Facebook friends, or less direct, as in unrelated people who all use Windows and Microsoft Office, the notion of platforms is central to any understanding of this world. Winning in a platform market can be a multibillion-dollar outcome but can involve speculative investments of the same scale. Such household names as Apple, Google, Intel, Nokia, and Sony need to be understood at least in part through the platform lens.

What do we mean by the term "platform"? A few definitions are in order. Platforms are foundational technologies, building blocks upon which an entire industry might develop. Michael Cusumano of MIT and his then-graduate student Annabelle Gawer were plainspoken in their essential study of the topic: A platform is "an evolving system made of interdependent pieces that can each be innovated upon."[1] That's concise but dense, and worth playing out: Platforms have to evolve, which presents challenging issues around innovation, return on investment, and other strategic decisions. Platforms are the product of multiple actors: Even Microsoft, a dominant company if ever there was one, relied on both a powerful network of software developers to build applications on the foundation technology and a myriad of hardware companies. Platforms are systems, not merely products: Their interdependent aspects can create prisoner's dilemma and other game theory scenarios, as when developers must choose where to focus their innovation and programming efforts. For these individuals and companies, betting on Microsoft in 1990 was a good move, as was aligning with the Apple App Store in 2008.

Harvard's Thomas Eisenmann and his colleagues Geoffrey Parker and Marshall Van Alstyne focus on the networks that rise up in the presence of a platform; these scholars account for the actors as much as the technologies:

> *A platform-mediated network is comprised of users whose transactions are subject to direct and/or indirect network effects, along with one or more intermediaries that facilitate users' transactions. . . . Rules are used to coordinate network participants' activities. They include standards that ensure compatibility among different components, protocols that govern information exchange, policies that constrain user behavior, and contracts that specify terms of trade and the rights and responsibilities of network participants.*[2]

Most of these aspects are straightforward, but for now, the role of rules should be highlighted. Whether in the form of government regulations, technical standards, or copyright or patent protection, these rules can become exceedingly complicated, expensive to create and enforce, and difficult to time with regard to the market. The right rule set can accelerate time to broad adoption; the wrong set can stall innovation in committees, litigation, or market uncertainty. Notable failed platforms include the 3DO video game, Super Audio Compact Disc (SACD) music format, and IBM's OS/2 computer operating system.

Recently, a strand of scholarship has been focusing on ways that a platform can be either one-sided or two-sided.[3] In the former case, there are sellers and there are purchaser/users: In wireline telephony, the Bell company or companies were on one side and "subscribers" were on the other. Innovation was minimal, and the system, while closed, was exceptionally profitable and predictable. AT&T was a monopoly provider, from the handsets all the way through the infrastructure and voice services. By contrast, we now see examples of one-sided platforms with multiple firms, beginning with mobile telephony: Person A with a Samsung phone on T-Mobile can seamlessly call person B who has a Motorola phone operating on the Sprint network. Standards and protocols make such behavior possible.

Two-sided markets are exemplified by a credit card company: Before consumers will carry the card, they want to know that it will be accepted by many merchants. Merchants, for their part, want to know that enough consumers will use the card to justify the expenses of vendor adoption. Getting both sides of the platform to invest, especially in the early stages, can be challenging but extremely advantageous once the "flywheel effect" kicks in: One side of the interaction often subsidizes the other. More recently, Apple's nurturing of application developers on one side and end users on the other has worked extremely well: A large app selection enhances the iPhone's market appeal just as large user markets attract more developers. Shopping malls, health maintenance organizations, and video game console manufacturers also operate in two-sided markets.[4]

A wide range of strategic decisions is involved in platform success, none more important than opening or closing the platform. (This may or may not involve opening the source code: Linux is both open source and an open platform. The terms can be confusing.) eBay is a closed platform in the sense that user identities and reputational profiles work only within the auction site. For several years in the United States, Apple's iPhone worked only on AT&T's network. Apple imposes standards of content appropriateness and performance on third-party apps that Google's Android platform does not. Every DVD player's price includes royalties to the platform's creators, and all players are strictly defined in their features and performance. Closed platforms benefit from interoperability at the expense of innovation; for open platforms, the reverse is usually the case. Android users might need to run antivirus software on their smartphones but do not face the limits Apple places on the iPhone ecosystem.

In contrast, any 120-volt electrical appliance should work in any U.S. state. ISO* standards govern shipping containers, which will fit on any ship in any port. Closed platforms such as video games keep all profit within a small number of partner companies, while open platforms (such as 802.11 or Wi-Fi, not to mention the Internet itself) can grow exceptionally large, sometimes exhibiting literally global network effects along with coordination and compatibility issues.

Platforms can be controlled by one or more companies in two dimensions: who controls the platform, usually through patents, and who delivers it to the market? Sony owns the PlayStation intellectual property (IP), licenses the rights to build games for it to outside firms, and handles console design and manufacturing in-house. Industry consortia such as the one behind Orbitz may have multiple entities that own the IP, even though there is a single channel to market. The DVD standard, by contrast, is owned by a small number of firms and delivered to the market by hundreds.[5]

Until Linux proved otherwise, conventional wisdom held that platforms needed proprietary control: Microsoft Windows, the AT&T phone network, and the compact disc owned by Sony and Philips are familiar examples. The following exchange between the widely respected MIT

---

*The International Organization for Standardization, a non-governmental organization, is the world's largest developer and publisher of international standards.

economist Lester Thurow and *Computer Reseller News*, a major trade publication, illustrated a widely held skepticism:

> *CRN: Do you think the Linux operating system will be successful?*
> *THUROW: It can't possibly work. It's open architecture. People change it, and the changes aren't compatible. Look at Unix. There are now 18 different incompatible versions. That started out as one system with open architecture. The only way [software] can be compatible is if one company owns it.*[6]

At the same time that Linux and other fully open platforms are enjoying great success, Apple is building a series of mobile platforms that, while in some ways are closed, are also extremely profitable. According to Morgan Stanley's Mary Meeker, the iPhone and iPod Touch surpassed 50 million units shipped in nine quarters after launch.[7] Netscape Navigator reportedly had 38 million downloads in 18 months, but that could include double and triple counting. In addition, Netscape's Internet distribution model allowed it a substantial advantage over conventional logistics while Apple physically moved all those devices.

The iPhone and Android platforms have spurred a vast ecosystem of software developers. Hundreds of thousands of applications for each platform are available. While about 400,000 are free and the average selling price is $1.44 for paid apps, GPS add-ons from TomTom sell for $50. Other top sellers include mobile editions of both conventional board games such as Uno and electronic games like Madden.

Thus, the iPhone neatly illustrates the interdependent aspects of a platform. Those applications are helping drive truly staggering demands on bandwidth. Researchers at the giant networking company Cisco Systems estimate that global mobile bandwidth demand will increase 66 *times* in the four years following 2009. Based on AT&T's experience, that number is fully believable: Mobile data traffic increased 4,962% (essentially 50 times) in the three years following the iPhone launch, but time will tell. The wide dissatisfaction with iPhone performance was often blamed on AT&T's network, but provisioning that kind of growth would tax any organization. In addition, as much as the iPhone has stressed the cellular network, the picture would be far worse if Wi-Fi, which is essentially ten times faster, had not picked up so much of the load.

Strategic Levers

The key themes of Gawer and Cusumano's case study of Intel are interdependency and innovation, both of which involve players operating outside the traditional vertically integrated firm yet that need to be managed.

While the tech sector is obviously characterized by these dynamics, the authors point out that more and more industries have this structure, in part because of the increasing software content outside computers. As the Intel story unfolds, many of the lessons—about openness, about competition, about internal friction—do in fact translate far beyond the world of semiconductor design and fabrication.

Gawer and Cusumano assert that firms have four basic "levers" they can pull to influence the direction of a platform that typically is not owned by any one firm.[8] These levers are:

1. *Scope of the firm.* This is a macroscopic view of the buy/build decision: What gets done inside, or outside, or in both places? How are changes to these priorities and competencies decided and navigated?
2. *Product technology.* In particular, how are decisions made and executed with regard to architecture, interfaces, and intellectual property? How modular is a product or subunit? How open are the interface technologies* used to integrate third-party innovation?
3. *Relationships with external complementors.* Does a platform leader follow Intel, which in the 1990s professed not to want to drive companies out of business? Or is the model closer to Microsoft, which repeatedly did so by swallowing software functionality introduced by competitors, typically into the operating system?
4. *Internal organization.* Intel is a huge, powerful company with the usual fiefdoms and internal competitiveness. How are these delimited and ruled in such a way as to support innovation of interdependent pieces? How are culture and process managed? Perhaps most critically, how are long-term industry efforts (such as the USB standard) accounted for in quarterly financial reporting and performance measurements?

The Intel Architecture Lab was a critically important piece of computing history during the boom of the 1990s, a place that embodied the paradox of "coopetition": Secrets were shared (in the form of forthcoming Intel architectures and specifications), interoperability was assured (usually) on equal terms, and new markets were invaded (in the case of the incursion of the PCI[†] bus on IBM territory). The stated goal was to sell more processors not by stealing share as a primary tactic but by increasing the vitality of the entire PC industry.

---

*A classic example is the application programming interface, or API, which sets the rules of the road for different software components to interact with each other.
[†]A bus is a subsystem, something like a switch in the lay sense, that transfers data between components inside a computer. IBM owned several bus standards (including ISA) in the early 1990s that were superseded by an Intel-led consortium that developed the royalty-free, technically superior PCI specifications.

Related to this type of position, platform owners must be aware of a particular competitive dynamic known as platform envelopment.[9] As opposed to traditional firm-based competition (Coke versus Pepsi), platform ecosystems can win or lose somewhat independently of any given company's strategy or execution. 3-D television is one example. For existing platforms, the business model often can be undermined by the incorporation of a platform inside a larger system: Microsoft was fought in court by Real Networks over the nature of Windows-based media players that replicated Real's functionality. Western Union's telegraph business was rendered obsolete by e-mail, a business outcome for which no strategic response (lowering prices, mergers or acquisitions, entry into new markets) would have been adequate. Thus, competition in the age of platforms concerns new kinds of strategic constraints and possibilities.

Finally, because of the highly connected and interconnected nature of the technology landscape, corporate competition may now be less central than platform competition. Consider the long list of contemporary platforms, some not directly competing with any others yet all a product of the Internet age:

- Adobe Flash
- Adobe pdf
- Amazon Kindle
- Amazon Web Services
- Apple iTunes/App Store
- eBay
- Facebook
- Google AdWords/AdSense
- Google Android
- Google Chrome
- Google Maps
- GPS
- LinkedIn
- Linux
- Microsoft Xbox
- Microsoft Windows
- Nintendo Wii
- Salesforce.com
- PayPal
- SAP
- Sony PlayStation
- Twitter
- Wi-Fi
- YouTube

Looking Ahead

The companies, entities, and standards just listed will be key to understanding the next 25 years. As opposed to being the age of the great railroads, or AT&T, or Wal-Mart, American business success will increasingly be defined by platform dynamics: innovation, revenue capture, ecosystem health and development, and lock-in and lock-out. Next we turn to the issue of what kinds of markets will emerge to engage these platforms.

Notes

1. Annabelle Gawer and Michael Cusumano, *Platform Leadership: How Intel, Microsoft, and Cisco Drive Industry Innovation* (Boston: Harvard Business School Press, 2002), p. 2.
2. Thomas R. Eisenmann, Geoffrey Parker, and Marshall Van Alstyne, "Opening Platforms: How, When, and Why?" Harvard Business School Working Paper 09-030, p. 3., 2008.
3. J. Rochet and J. Tirole, "Platform Competition in Two-Sided Markets," *Journal of the European Economic Association* 1, no. 4 (2003): 990–1029.
4. On two-sided markets, see David S. Evans and Richard Schmalensee, *Catalyst Code* (Boston: Harvard Business School Press, 2007) as well as Thomas Eisenmann, Geoffry Parker, and Marshall Van Alstyne, "Strategies for Two-Sided Markets," *Harvard Business Review* (October 2006). http://hbr.org/2006/10/strategies-for-two-sided-markets/ar/1.
5. Eisenmann et al., "Opening Platforms," p. 5.
6. John Roberts, "Thurownomics 101," *Computer Reseller News*, September 22, 2000, www.crn.com/news/channel-programs/18834629/thurownomics-101.htm.
7. Mary Meeker, Scott Devitt, Liang Wu, "Economy + Internet Trends," presentation to Web 2.0 Summit, October 20, 2009, San Francisco www.morganstanley.com/institutional/techresearch/internet_ad_trends102009.html.
8. Gawer and Cusumano, *Platform Leadership*, p. 40.
9. Thomas Eisenmann, Geoffrey Parker, and Marshall Van Alstyne, "Platform Envelopment," Harvard Business School Working Paper 07-104., 2007.

CHAPTER 6

Power Laws and Their Implications

While many people are accustomed to seeing bell curves explaining many facets of everyday reality, these statistical distributions do an extremely poor job of explaining information, or risk, or social network landscapes. Instead, power laws explain both the leviathans of the Internet—Facebook or Google—and the millions of YouTube videos that apparently nobody watches. The behavior of systems that conform to these curves is both predictable and new as compared to scenarios involving physical widgets sold through physical stores in local markets.

A Bit of History

Back at the turn of the century, the Internet sector was in the middle of a momentous slide in market capitalization. Priceline went from nearly $500 a share to single digits in three quarters. CDnow fell from $23 to $3.40 in about nine months ending in March 2000. Corvis, Music Maker, Dr. Koop—2000 was a meltdown the likes of which few investors had ever seen or imagined. Science was invoked to explain this new world of Internet business.

Bernardo Huberman, then at Xerox's Palo Alto Research Center (PARC), and others found that the proportion of Web sites that got the bulk of the traffic fell far from standard market share metrics: As of December 1, 1997, the top 1% of the Web site population accounted for over 55% of all traffic.[1] This kind of distribution was not new, as it turned out. A Harvard linguist with the splendid name of George Zipf counted words and found that a tiny percentage of the English language accounts for a disproportionate share of usage. A Zipf distribution, plotted on a log-log scale, is a straight line from upper left to lower right. In linear scale, it plunges from the top left and then goes flat for the characteristic long tail of the distribution: Twosies and then onesies occupy most of the x-axis, as seen in Figure 6.1.

Given such "scientific" logic, investors began to argue that the Internet was a new kind of market, with high barriers to entry that made incumbents' positions extremely secure. Michael Mauboussin, then at CS First Boston and now at Legg Mason, wrote a paper in late 1999 called "Absolute Power."[2] In it he asserted that "power laws . . . strongly support the view that on-line markets are winner-take-all." But winners don't take all: Since that time, Google has challenged and surpassed Yahoo, weblogs have markedly deteriorated traffic to online news sites, and MySpace lost its early lead in social networking. Is the Zipf distribution somehow changing? Were power laws wrongly applied or somehow misunderstood?

In 2004, Chris Anderson, editor of *Wired*, had a different reading of the graph. Instead of looking at the few very big winners at the head, he focused on the long tail. In an article that became a book, Anderson explained how a variety of Web businesses have prospered by successfully addressing the very large number of niches in any given market. Jeff Bezos, for instance, at one time estimated that 30% of the books Amazon sold weren't in physical retailers. Unlike Excite, which couldn't make money posting banner ads against the mostly unique queries that came into the site, Google uses Adwords to sell nearly anything to however many people search for something related to it, one search at a time. Netflix carries far more inventory than a neighborhood retailer can and can

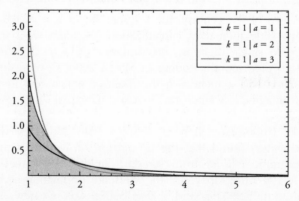

FIGURE 6.1 Generic Power Law Graph
Source: Wolfram Alpha LLC. 2011. Wolfram I Alpha, www.wolframalpha.com.

thus satisfy any film nut's most esoteric request. eBay matches a vast selection of goods with a global audience of both mass and niche customers.

Long-Tail Successes

Amazon, eBay, Google, and Netflix—the four horsemen of the long tail, as it were—share several important characteristics. First, they either offload physical inventory to other parties (in the Netflix case, its warehouse network includes customers' kitchen tables) or have developed best-in-the-world supply chain management (Amazon). Google touches as few invoices as possible and no physical product whatsoever.

Second, each company has invested in matching large, sparse populations of customers to large, sparse populations of products. That investment might take the form of search: AltaVista founder Louis Monier worked at eBay for a time; Amazon tried to make a run at Google in general search with A9 in 2006 before retrenching and innovating in more focused "search inside the book" and mobile/location services. As Netflix showed, other technologies are powerful in the long tail as well: Using collaborative filtering, social reviewing, and audience surveys, both Amazon and Netflix have become expert at predicting future desires based on past behavior.

This sparseness, combined with the Internet's vast scale, is the defining characteristic of the long tail. As YouTube illustrates, people are happy to create content for small or even nonexistent audiences. At the same time, producers of distinctive small-market goods (like weblogs, garage demo music, and self-published books) can through a variety of mechanisms reach a paying public. Thus, the news is good for both makers and users, buyers and sellers to the point that libertarian commentator Virginia Postrel has made huge selection a political issue, writing on the virtues of the choice and variety we currently enjoy.[3]

Cautionary Tales

In his hugely influential tandem of books, *The Black Swan* and *Fooled by Randomness*, Nassim Nicholas Taleb raised the contrast between power laws and Gaussian (bell curve) distributions to the level of cultural criticism.[4] He asserted that risk, wealth, fame, and information on networks all fit long-tail distributions, noting that fat-tail risk (global financial meltdown, tsunamis, Hurricane Katrina, etc.) is both always with us and all-too-frequently left unacknowledged by the ubiquitous bell curves employed by financial analysts. The events of 2008 seemed to bear him out, for reasons we will see in Chapter 7 on risk. For our purposes, it is important to focus on the loss of the "average" as a meaningful concept in power law scenarios. We will return to the implications of this fact soon.

The second caution about the long tail comes from a different direction. Dan Frankowski was working on an early social data set at the University of Minnesota: the MovieLens film rating system. He and his coresearchers found that as data got sparser (such as with a large list of movies, many of which got only a handful of votes), it became easier to link a public comment on a message board, for example, with a private data point (a rating on MovieLens or, hypothetically, a rental at Netflix). Whereas rating or commenting on a hit movie at the head of the distribution was reasonably anonymous, moving out onto the tail, especially in conjunction with expressions related to other titles in the sparse space, significantly increased the odds of reidentification.[5] This dynamic is informing many other technologies aimed at finding important relationships in large, noisy data sets.

Facts of Life

Living in a long tail has new costs, opportunities, and risks. Recent research suggests that the long tail is getting both longer and more lucrative. MIT's Erik Brynjolfsson and his colleagues compared Amazon's sales data from 2000 to 2008. After quantitatively rigorous analysis, the conclusions are vivid: "The . . . results provide empirical evidence that Amazon's Long Tail has become longer and fatter in 2008 than in 2000. As sales ranks increase, book sales decline. Such a decline is at a slower pace in 2008 than in 2000."[6]

At about the same time, University of Pennsylvania Professor Serguei Netessine and his colleague Tom F. Tan analyzed movie rental data that was part of the data set made available to Netflix prize* researchers. They came to a similar conclusion comparing customer habits in 2000 versus 2005: There was a marked drop in demand for the top 500 titles, the "knee" of the curve was thicker, and 15% of demand came from titles ranked below 3,000, which is the inventory of a typical physical video store. As Figure 6.2 illustrates, the long tail at Netflix grew both fatter and longer after the year 2000, just as it had at Amazon.[7]

---

*An innovative competition sponsored by the video rental firm: Machine learning and other statistical experts competed for a $1 million prize, along with other bonuses, awarded to teams that improved Netflix's algorithmic matching of user attributes with predicted enjoyment of a given movie title.

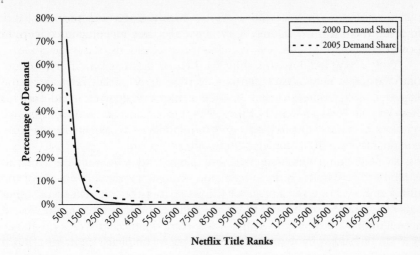

FIGURE 6.2 Changing Power Law Distribution at Netflix
Source: Tom F. Tan and Serguei Netessine, "Is Tom Cruise Threatened? Using Netflix Prize Data to Examine the Long Tail of Electronic Commerce," Wharton working paper. *knowledge .wharton.upenn.edu/papers/1361.pdf.*

Implications

For merchandising, selection can become a basis of competition in ways it could never be in physical stores. Especially for digital goods, such as Kindle books or music and movie downloads, the lack of physical inventory rewrites the rules on competition. Demand planning, production planning, and logistics of getting the right number of units to where demand is expected to materialize are no longer issues. As with app stores for basically the same reason, digital downloads remove much of the risk from the seller, which can pay royalties after sale without up-front investment in inventory.

As we saw, long tails of supply can now be matched more effectively with sparse communities of demand. The net result is that formerly neglected items find larger audiences, and while they may or may not become hits (as in the case of Soulja Boy*), some songs, videos, and eBay items do climb out of the long tail of obscurity. Price and availability will change accordingly: If World War II recruiting posters become popular for

---

*DeAndre Cortez Way created a rap career on the basis of an online video ("Crank That," which reached #1 on the Billboard Hot 100) that spawned countless YouTube tributes and imitations.

whatever reason, people with access to such artifacts will be more likely to bring them to market. Inventory items can thus move up or down the power law curve.

Both eBay and Amazon shift the risk of holding physical inventory onto extensive networks of partners. Netflix, Apple, and Google are striving to become purely digital in their content businesses. Compared to Best Buy or Tower Records of the 1980s, the organizational shape, capital requirements, growth prospects, and hiring needs of a twenty-first-century content business are completely different.

Outside the entertainment realm, Linux and Wikipedia turn out to exhibit long-tail traits on the supply side: A small number of very busy contributors do a huge percentage of the work, but the long tail of contributors of single items turns out to be a significant population as well.[8] Not all contributions are of equal weight: If a solitary contributor writes one piece of code or biography that wouldn't have been completed otherwise, it is a potentially important win for the overall effort. The Internet commentator Clay Shirky makes this point clearly: Traditional organizations cannot afford to have large numbers of contributors who don't contribute much. Pareto reigns, on the logic that "we can have 5% of the population do 85% of the work." Indeed, that would be a fortunate company. But in the connected, global world of voluntary, loose organizational forms, low coordination costs enable the perhaps quirky, perhaps uninspired contributions of the long tail to be harvested at low if any cost.[9]

Looking Ahead

For these reasons, management is changing at places like developer networks, as we will see in Chapter 17: One-tenth of 1% of Google Android applications have more than 50,000 downloads; 79% of titles have reached fewer than 100 people. Because of the app store structure, however, no product planner needs to develop ulcers about slow-selling titles: All the risk is borne by the developers as Apple and Google much prefer to gain market share in hardware.[10] At the same time, managing the entire ecosystem presents new challenges: With low barriers to entry and hundreds of thousands of applications to manage, even something as simple as paying application developers can be a real headache. In addition, maintaining the platform's attractiveness is vitally important but involves many intangibles and competitive pressures, just as product development does, but in a far less constrained space. Long tails also change the possibilities for how people and resources organize to get work done, as we see in the next chapter.

Notes

1. Lada A. Adamic and Bernardo A. Huberman, "The Nature of Markets in the World Wide Web," *Quarterly Journal of Electronic Commerce* 1 (2000): 5–12.
2. www.capatcolumbia.com/Articles/Reports/Grl_260.pdf.
3. Virginia Postrel, "I'm Pro-Choice," *Forbes* magazine, March 28, 2005, http://dynamist.com/articles-speeches/forbes/choice.html.
4. Nassim Nicholas Taleb, *The Black Swan: The Impact of the Highly Improbable* (New York: Random House, 2007), and *Fooled by Randomness: The Hidden Role of Chance in Life and in the Markets* (New York: Random House, 2005).
5. Dan Frankowski, Dan Cosley, Shilad Sen, Loren Terveen, and John Riedl, "You Are What You Say: Privacy Risks of Public Mentions, paper presented at SIGIR '06, August 6–11, 2006, Seattle, Washington, www.cs.cmu.edu/~wcohen/10-802/fixed/Frankowski_et_al._SIGIR_2006.html.
6. Erik Brynjolfsson, Yu (Jeffrey) Hu, Michael D. Smith, "A Longer Tail?: Estimating the Shape of Amazon's Sales Distribution Curve in 2008," 2009 Working Paper, http://pages.stern.nyu.edu/~bakos/wise/papers/wise2009-p10_paper.pdf.
7. Tom F. Tan and Serguei Netessine, "Is Tom Cruise Threatened? Using Netflix Prize Data to Examine the Long Tail of Electronic Commerce," Wharton Working Paper, September 16, 2009, http://knowledge.wharton.upenn.edu/papers/1361.pdf.
8. See Ed H. Chi, Niki Kittur, Bryan Pendleton, Bongwon Suh, "Long Tail Of user Participation in Wikipedia," Xerox PARC blog post, May 15, 2007, http://asc-parc.blogspot.com/2007/05/long-tail-and-power-law-graphs-of-user.html.
9. Clay Shirky, "Institutions versus Collaboration," TED video, 2005, www.ted.com/talks/clay_shirky_on_institutions_versus_collaboration.html.
10. Distimo App Store census, May 2011, www.distimo.com/.

CHAPTER 7

Security and Risk

The task of security has evolved rapidly in an interconnected age. Where previously police and private forces had to protect physical assets with fences, locks, and other tangible efforts, now both threats and assets can be ephemeral and distributed. Networks of networks introduce redundancy (as in a power grid, where the local generating plant no longer constitutes a single point of failure), but they also introduce unprecedented levels of complexity. That complexity underlies all considerations of security, which has moved from obvious efforts to protect things and people from harm (in the ways just mentioned) to become a maze of cost-benefit-risk considerations. Those calculations are complicated by humans' completely predictable inability to assess risk rationally.

Considered as a sociotechnical system of people and technologies interacting in both directions, the discipline of security must be conducted very differently as compared to local efforts of a constabulary or parking lot guard. Thus, our focus here is on the managerial imperatives rather than on the techniques of perimeter protection, intrusion detection, firewall selection and configuration, password resets, and other activities that often constitute the focus of the discipline. In short, mastering the domains of costs (hard and soft), benefits, and risks requires new skills, new metrics, and new attitudes compared to the practice of physical security conducted in local settings.

Landscape

The Internet is increasingly made mobile and connects billions of devices both stationary and in motion, "users" both animate and electronic, and for purposes ranging from deep-space exploration to commercial exploitation of humanity's basest desires. Given such broad span, it presents ample opportunities for people to find trouble. Put simply, humanity has never attempted to manage anything so big, so rapidly evolving, so distributed, or so complicated. A few numbers only hint at the size of the challenge; *the scale is nearly impossible for humans to comprehend*, which is one of the key issues in dealing with security and risk:

- Both Google and Bing estimate 1 trillion Web pages as of mid-2010.
- Out of a global population of more than 7 billion people, roughly 2 billion people are online.
- In the United States alone, mobile devices generate 600 billion geo-tagged messages—each day—accurate to within 10 meters if you're on a Wi-Fi connection.[1]
- Half of Facebook's more than 500 million users check in daily; by itself, the site accounts for one-quarter of all U.S. page views and a third of all online ads.
- Cisco estimates that Internet Protocol (IP) traffic will quadruple between 2009 and 2014.

For anything so sprawling and fast-moving, conventional understandings clearly fail; seeing firewalls as being "like fences," for example, constitutes a cognitive trap. The scale of bad things occurring in information space is similarly difficult to apprehend:

- Symantec, a digital security vendor, observed 14.6 trillion spam messages in the third quarter of 2010, which is approximately 91% of all e-mail traffic. Spam increased 100,000% between 1997 and 2004, according to the IEEE.
- Personal records for 26 million U.S. military veterans were compromised when a single laptop computer went missing in 2008.
- Heartland Payment Systems, a credit card processor, reported a data breach of roughly 130 million records in 2009.
- As of late 2011, more than 2,600 reported U.S. data breaches had exposed more than 500 million records, according to privacyrights.org.
- The Conficker worm alone has infected an estimated 12 million PCs since 2008.
- As of 2010, one thousand credit card numbers could be bought on underground services for $300, only 30 cents per user.
- The Kroxxu bot network had infected over 100,000 Web domains between its launch in 2009 and a year later, as opposed to attacking personal computers as had been previous practice.

Information Space Is Neither Average nor Normal

As discussed in more detail in Chapter 6, information spaces present prime examples of fat-tailed distributions: A few population members for examples are disproportionately huge (Google and Facebook, Harry Potter books, *Avatar* and *Pirates of the Caribbean*), while the curve of the distribution rapidly descends into the famous long tail of onesies and twosies. Thinking of this world in terms of the familiar bell curve conceptualization is impossible: The "average" Web site or information good is a contradiction in terms. If Harry Potter volume 19 sells 5 million copies and a routine academic study of medieval France sells 20 copies, talking about 2.5 million as the average of the two makes no sense whatsoever.

The infrastructure needed to manage an Amazon or a Yahoo! reflects this extremity. Data center buildings run in the hundreds of thousands of square feet, pulling down in excess of an estimated 100-megawatt power feeds. (For comparison, aluminum smelters use between 150 and 450 megawatts.) On the output side of the equation, Google served about 3 billion searches per day in late 2009, according to data compiled by market research firm comscore; that's 34,000 per second.[2]

In such a world, threats to information are not random or average. In a power-law scenario, one example (a Harry Potter or Warren Buffett, in wealth) can alter the entire landscape; in a bell curve assumption, however, large sample sizes guarantee curve smoothing: No one instance of human height or focus-group preference can reshape the landscape. In other words, Bill Gates can be 10 billion times richer than a random Kenyan, but nobody can eat 10 billion times more cherry Pop-Tarts than another customer. Nobody can stand even 1 order of magnitude taller than her neighbor.

This potential for extremity has significant implications for risk management: Very, very bad things can happen in hypernetworked environments. Whether in regard to the spread of rumors or malware, the speed and scale of today's networks drive risk skyward. For example, in 2003 the Slammer worm (technologically simple compared to the current generation of malware) infected 75,000 machines in 10 minutes.

As Nassim Nicholas Taleb noted in *The Black Swan*, bell curve distributions use averaging across many samples within a finite range to generate certainty.[3] In information and risk space, one instance outside the presumed norm (a BP oil spill, a Hurricane Katrina, a Heartland data breach) can alter the entire landscape. Given extreme interconnection, two consequences emerge: (1) The Internet allows enormous populations (sometimes audiences) to be assembled, and (2) changes can spread across populations extremely rapidly. Both of these realities change fundamental facets of security practice as compared to previous eras.

People Systematically Misestimate Risk

Here's a simple experiment. The following list of hazards to Americans' health is alphabetical, but seeing them listed from riskiest to least risky reveals extreme differences in probability: There are no split hairs. Even when asking a group, where there is some averaging of opinion and pooling of knowledge (a lifeguard knows about sharks while a daughter of a lung cancer survivor may know about that disease), there are invariably big misses: Perception, fear, and reality do not align. Try listing these from the most deaths per year to the least:

- Airplane accidents
- Cancer
- Dog attacks
- Lightning
- Motor vehicle accidents
- Murder
- Residential fires
- Sharks

Invariably, individuals' fears, phobias, and recent experiences color perception of something as intrinsically attention-getting as accidental death. While infrequent events typically are confused, it's also common for people not to realize the most deadly phenomena on the list: Note that number 1 outranks number 2 by well over an order of magnitude (numbers refer to deaths per year), yet precautions against cancer are not ubiquitous:

1. Cancer: 550,000
2. Motor vehicle accidents: 42,000
3. Murder: 16,000
4. Residential fires: 3,500
5. Airplane accidents: 600
6. Lightning: 90
7. Dog attacks: 20
8. Sharks: <1

Why does this confusion about danger matter? Security does not simply involve keeping bad people from doing bad things to me or my organization. Instead, particularly in virtual settings involving often-intangible assets, security is a matter of priority setting, risk–reward trade-offs, and other managerial assessments. If people cannot understand in a very rational way the risk of dying, it takes considerable self-awareness, careful fact finding, and professional judgment to make good decisions regarding risks of less intuitive events on behalf of other people.

As we can see at any U.S. airport, security decisions typically are made by people away from the front lines—as well they should, *provided the senior decision makers are adequately informed*. At the same time, security policies can and often do reflect agendas far removed from actually keeping assets or people safer: The political uses of the Transportation Security Administration threat level colors in the 2004 election stand as an obvious example. The combination of multiple priorities and human logical fallibility relative to risk, however, means that a lot of time, money, and effort can be expended with little measurable impact on security or risk mitigation.

Instead, what security guru Bruce Schneier has called "security theater" often presents visual and dramatic elements that manipulate public perception with little impact on real threats.[4] A few examples should suffice:

- In the 1950s and 1960s, schoolchildren practiced ducking under desks in the event of a nuclear attack.
- After the 9/11 attacks, National Guardsmen patrolled public places carrying automatic weapons. It was never revealed whether all of the weapons were actually loaded, given the danger posed by a nervous, semitrained civilian with such a powerful weapon in a crowded scenario.
- Nail clippers were long banned from aircraft even though any of the soda cans routinely emptied during the flight could be turned into something far more lethal with no tools whatsoever.

In short, "security theater" is a predictable outcome of the normal decision-making process, reflecting the political dimension of organizational behavior rather than a sensible response to an actual threat.

Doing It Right

Many people have written extensively and well on the topic of effective security, not least of all Schneier. Three points bear consideration:

1. *Security involves people.* People are both irrationally afraid of things that pose little risk (sharks) and casual with devices that can be quite

dangerous if used incorrectly: Cars, text messaging, and USB drives each can serve as an example. At the same time, as Cormac Herley of Microsoft Research has shown, users of information systems behave rationally given their personal position on a risk–reward continuum: What systems administrators understand as part of a totality, users often see as hassles or roadblocks to be avoided.[5] He notes that password resets, close inspection of web addresses for phishing threats, and checking digital authentication certificates all take too much time relative to the slim likelihood that such practices will confer a benefit to an individual. In short, private incentives must be managed in the pursuit of organizational objectives.

Effective security thus requires that people be motivated, so behavioral economics, with its emphasis on reward structures and actual actions rather than fictional economic creatures, becomes highly relevant. Logic was not enough to make hospital doctors and other personnel wash their hands, for example, even though the benefits were obvious and dramatic. Similarly, more sophisticated designs for enterprise security will balance rewards and punishments in original and clever ways rather than simply having administrators dictating official procedure and expecting (or demanding) compliance.

2. *Security involves systems.* Much like usability, to which security is obviously related, security is too seldom seen as a system or, more typically in a connected world, a system of systems. Designing systems (network security) is much more difficult than designing products (firewalls). Policies and procedures span organizational boundaries, become brittle with time, and must interact in the pursuit of various purposes. (The same employee ID that gets you past the security guard announces your name and perhaps other information to potential intruders who take careful notes while you go out for lunch wearing the badge.)

Getting systems to be usable, evolving, robust against multiple types of threat, and affordable is extremely difficult. Because systems transcend organizations, and because security is effective only when nothing happens, budgeting against risk is difficult. Who pays, who benefits, and who is inconvenienced frequently misalign. Interfaces between systems are particularly hard to get right, not least because organizational authority must be managed across various gaps. Parking lots are problematic for this reason: Building or store security and the door locks on the automobile are both effective, but at the interface, attackers exploit various weaknesses that fall between organizational mandates.

Designing Usable Systems

Why is it so hard to get usability right? As Don Norman, one of the heroic figures in modern usability studies, puts it, complex products are not merely things; they provide services: "[A]lthough a camera is thought of as a product, its real value is the service it offers to its owner: Cameras provide memories. Similarly, music players provide a service: the enjoyment of listening."[6] In this light, the product must be considered as part of a system that supports experience, and systems thinking is hard, complicated, and difficult to accomplish in functionally siloed organizations.

The ubiquitous iPod makes his point perfectly.

> *The iPod is a story of systems thinking, so let me repeat the essence for emphasis. It is not about the iPod; it is about the system. Apple was the first company to license music for downloading. It provides a simple, easy to understand pricing scheme. It has a first-class website that is not only easy to use but fun as well. The purchase, downloading the song to the computer and thence to the iPod are all handled well and effortlessly. And the iPod is indeed well designed, well thought out, a pleasure to look at, to touch and hold, and to use. Then there is the Digital Rights Management system, invisible to the user, but that both satisfies legal issues and locks the customer into lifelong servitude to Apple (this part of the system is undergoing debate and change). There is also the huge number of third-party add-ons that help increase the power and pleasure of the unit while bringing a very large, high-margin income to Apple for licensing and royalties. Finally, the "Genius Bar" of experts offering service advice freely to Apple customers who visit the Apple stores transforms the usual unpleasant service experience into a pleasant exploration and learning experience. There are other excellent music players. No one seems to understand the systems thinking that has made Apple so successful.*

One of the designers of the iPod interface, Paul Mercer of Pixo, affirms that systems thinking shaped the design process: "The iPod is very simple-minded, in terms of at least what the device does. It's very smooth in what it does, but the screen is low-resolution, and it

(continued)

really doesn't do much other than let you navigate your music. That tells you two things. It tells you first that the simplification that went into the design was very well thought through, and second that the capability to build it is not commoditized."[7] Thus, more *complex* management and design vision are prerequisites for user *simplification*.

Because it requires systems thinking and complex organizational behavior to achieve, usability is often last on the list of design criteria, behind such considerations as manufacturability or modular assembly, materials costs, packaging, skill levels of the factory employees, and so on. The hall of shame for usability issues is far longer than the list of successes. For every garage door opener, LEGO brick, or Amazon Kindle, there are multiple BMW iDrives, Windows ribbons, European faucets, or inconsistent anesthesia machines: Doctors on a machine from company A turned the upper right knob clockwise to increase the flow rate but had to go counterclockwise on company B's machine in the next operating room over. Fortunately, the industry has standardized the control interface, with a resulting decline in human endangerment.[8]

3. *Security involves trade-offs*. Here we return to the crux of why risk management is too often both ineffective and overly expensive. While many security measures involve *technical* expertise, sometimes expensive and/or extensive, the *managerial* process of counterbalancing goals, objectives, resources, costs, and consequences can be mightily complex. The technical skills involved in perimeter protection, fraud detection, or antishoplifting measures can be esoteric, to be sure, but effective security is not a technical battle; it's a *management* problem. The trade-offs have much less to do with the hardware elements of the relevant systems than with the power relationships and competing agendas of the people involved.

   Bruce Schneier gets the last word here. He proposes a simple five-step rubric for assessing a security solution that can expose some of these agendas to scrutiny and reasoned discussion:
   a. What assets are you trying to protect? This question is often less obvious than it may appear.
   b. What are the risks to those assets?
   c. How well does the security solution mitigate those risks?
   d. What other risks does the security solution cause? Unintended consequences proliferate in these situations: Bank vaults did not need to be blown open when kidnapping the manager's spouse

was an option; time locks were the countermeasure to the countermeasure.
e. What costs and trade-offs does the security solution impose?[9]

Everything important is addressed in this process: A $5,000 door lock to protect $200 worth of property would be exposed, as would soft costs, such as inconvenience or false positives. Too often the features and functionality of the door lock or other technology become the focal point rather than their being weighed in rational fashion alongside the other four facets of the proposed solution.

Looking Ahead

Unfortunately, few security measures are introduced in this considered fashion, so we continue to live with unnecessary vulnerabilities, excessive expense, and intrusive and/or obnoxious measures that impose excessive costs on users and bystanders. Unfortunately, given the nature of both today's threats and institutions, the situation is unlikely to improve dramatically any time soon.

Notes

1. Jeff Jonas, "Your Movements Speak for Themselves: Space-Time Travel Data Is Analytic Super-Food!" August 16, 2009, http://jeffjonas.typepad.com/jeff_jonas/2009/08/your-movements-speak-for-themselves-spacetime-travel-data-is-analytic-superfood.html.
2. comStore, "comScore Reports Global Search Market Growth of 46 Percent in 2009," Press Release, January 22, 2010, www.comscore.com/Press_Events/Press_Releases/2010/1/Global_Search_Market_Grows_46_Percent_in_2009.
3. Nassim Nicholas Taleb, *The Black Swan: The Impact of the Highly Improbable* (New York: Random House, 2007), pp. 229 ff.
4. Bruce Schneier, *Beyond Fear: Thinking Sensibly about Security in an Uncertain World* (New York: Copernicus, 2003), p. 38.
5. Cormac Herley, "So Long, and No Thanks for the Externalities: The Rational Rejection of Security Advice by Users," New Security Paradigms Workshop, April 20, 2009, http://research.microsoft.com/apps/pubs/?id=80436.
6. Don Norman, "Systems Thinking: A Product Is More than the Product," *Interactions* vol 16 issue 5, http://jnd.org/dn.mss/systems_thinking_a_product_is_more_than_the_product.html.
7. Mercer quoted in Bill Moggridge, *Designing Interactions* (Cambridge, MA: MIT Press, 2007), p. 315.
8. See Atul Gawande, *Complications: A Surgeon's Notes on an Imperfect Science* (New York: Macmillan, 2003).
9. Schneier, *Beyond Fear*, p. 14.

Work and Organization

Given new capability, people will put it to use. Before looking at ways technology is changing the process of making money in Section III, we will examine different ways today's technology changes are reshaping how resources are organized and how people create value within old and new forms of coordinated effort.

CHAPTER 8

A Brief History
of Organizational Innovation

To set the context for the new organizational possibilities being created at the juncture of computing and communications, it's worth looking at a series of prior ideas and practices that explained functions, companies, corporations, and the markets in which they interacted. Where facilities were located, how much things cost, and who created them all derived from often-unspoken assumptions that the current period sometimes calls into question.

In our era, many elements of organizational life are in transition or are being subjected to multiplying possibilities:

- Where does work happen?
- Who tells people what to do?
- How is performance assessed, and by whom?
- Why do organizations exist?
- How is value created, stored, and exchanged?

Before we can understand how the computing and communications revolutions of the past quarter century are changing the shape of groups that perform work, it's useful to see how those groups have been understood over time.

1776: Division of Labor

Adam Smith's description of pin making is borrowed from a French and perhaps dated source. Nevertheless, the notion of taking an industrial process and letting un- or semiskilled individuals focus on discrete process steps was clearly a step away from craft work, in which a relatively skilled individual was responsible for more or perhaps all operations.

> *One man draws out the wire, another straights it, a third cuts it, a fourth points it, a fifth grinds it at the top for receiving the head; to make the head requires two or three distinct operations; to put it on, is a peculiar business, to whiten the pins is another; it is even a trade by itself to put them into the paper; and the important business of making a pin is, in this manner, divided into about eighteen distinct operations, which, in some manufactories, are all performed by distinct hands, though in others the same man will sometimes perform two or three of them.*[1]

Smith asserted that 10 men could make 48,000 pins per day in contrast to an individual working alone, who might make between 1 and 20: a theoretical gain of 2,400%, at minimum.

1860–1890: Railroads and the Rise of Administration

A little less than a century later, railroads posed an entirely new set of business challenges. The broad geographic coverage of railroads necessitated new institutions of both centralized control and distributed execution. As one scholar put it, "The major railroad companies pioneered the organizational structure that has become known as 'Big Business' in the decades between 1860 and 1890, which was the organizational analogue of the physical infrastructure."[2] The telegraph, a powerful network in its own right, was essential for the many coordination tasks of railroad management, and the two technologies grew in tandem, often sharing rights of way.

Railroads literally invented much of modern management practice. Local "solar" time was impractical for system timetables, so standardized time zones were instituted in the 1880s. The scale of capital that had to be raised was so vast that ownership, often in joint-stock corporations, was separated from management, which had many specific and technically sophisticated variations. Railroad management became a career track, entirely separate from both manual labor and the classic professions of the ministry, medicine, or law.[3]

1910: Scientific Management and the Further Division of Labor

In an age characterized by labor strife, ethnic tension, and rapid industrial expansion in both Europe and the United States, Frederick Winslow Taylor helped initiate a movement with far-reaching consequences. A respected authority who was invited to lecture at the newly formed Harvard Business School, Taylor believed that the interests of labor and capital could be harmonized if three root causes were addressed:

1. Workers slowed their pace ("soldiered") and limited output to protect their jobs.
2. Management techniques were defective, forcing labor into an adversarial posture.
3. The inefficiency of rule-of-thumb planning and production methods limited material output.

In response, Taylor separated task conception from its execution: Management's job was to find the "one best way" of doing a job (usually through time-and-motion studies in which task elements were broken down and timed with the infamous stopwatch), then to teach unskilled laborers that particular method. In this way, labor became fungible, and what later became known as "best practices" could be more uniformly applied. As Taylor wrote in 1911,

> to work according to scientific laws, the management must take over and perform much of the work which is now left to the men; almost every act of the workman should be preceded by one or more preparatory acts of the management which enable him to do his work better and quicker than he otherwise could. And each man should daily be taught by and receive the most friendly help from those who are over him, instead of being, at the one extreme, driven or coerced by his bosses, and at the other left to his own unaided devices.[4]

One key to aligning the interests of labor and capital was the piece-rate system, in which output correlated to compensation. Such a system could be, and was, frequently gamed, particularly by management; "speed-ups" and recalibration of wage scales in the face of increased performance were common. To see the lasting impact of Taylorism, one need only step into a McDonald's, where all cooking skill is engineered into the infrastructure, albeit without the piecework pay scheme.

1930s: Alfred Sloan at General Motors

On its way to becoming the world's largest industrial corporation, General Motors grew rapidly, primarily through acquisition in the early years. Coordination among the many operating entities was minimal as the entrepreneurial heads maintained owner-manager roles. At the scale of a loosely organized huge corporation, levels of spending could rise to potentially dangerous levels. In a precursor to Cisco's record-setting $2 billion write-down of excess networking inventory in 2001, GM suffered inventory losses of more than $83 million—more than $1 billion in 2010 dollars—in 1921–1922.

In response, an engineer/entrepreneur named Alfred Sloan (who later became the company's chief executive officer) helped create the divisional structure. GM automobile brands, including Cadillac, Oldsmobile, and Chevrolet, were structured by market price point, then allowed to operate relatively autonomously to coordinate supply and demand. Planning and forecasting grew in importance, and consumption data, in the form of R. L. Polk collections of automobile registrations,* was tied to production. GM became closely identified with an organizational structure built on line (day-to-day operational), staff (analysis and oversight), and general (headquarters) management. Sloan added an additional refinement: interdivisional committees for such activities as new product development or sales. These committees themselves had full-time staffs.[5]

1937–1981: Transaction Costs

Why do firms exist? Beginning with Ronald Coase in the 1930s and continuing through the work of Oliver Williamson, both Nobel laureates, a school of thought has focused on when internally organized resources at a firm (such as an office supply cabinet) are preferable to going to the market (a trip to the store to buy pencils). Traditional notions of price mechanisms do not apply to behavior inside a firm: "Within a firm, these market transactions are eliminated and in place of the complicated market structure with exchange transactions is substituted the

---

*Polk remains an important information provider 140 years after its founding. Previously focused on city directories, Polk branched out into collections of automobile registrations in the 1920s. Polk later participated in the computerization of Vehicle Identification Numbers and most recently acquired the Carfax used-vehicle information reporting service.

entrepreneur-co-ordinator, who directs production."[6] Instead, a variety of transaction costs apply to firms, which eventually came to be defined as being related to:

- Search and information (location of supplier and required inventory, price, etc.)
- Bargaining costs, including both negotiation and formal contracting
- Policing and enforcement of the terms of the transaction[7]

Yet Coase's emphasis on an entrepreneur was already dated; the railroads had separated capital from management many decades earlier, and Sloan was then introducing at GM an extremely complex model that relied on various species of managers. Those managers had as their goal not always the profitability of the firm but the preservation of their position, a trait noticed by the German sociologist Max Weber in *Economy and Society* (1922) well before Coase wrote.

The notion of transaction cost economics does have important implications for the modern organization, however. If technologies can lower the cost of dealing with the market, as in a browser-based self-service travel site, firm-based travel resources can be freed up. At the same time, the distance of most bureaucracies from the market, and from that "entrepreneur-coordinator" role, can lead to slow decisions, non-value-adding effort, and other traits that inhibit firm performance.

1980s: Economies of Scope and Core Competencies

Economies of scale are familiar: The more a producer makes of a single item, the lower the cost of raw materials, production facilities and expertise, and perhaps sales channels. But what happens if the producer sells two or more items? Here economies of scope may apply: In the words of one of the seminal articles of the period, "if economies of scope are based upon the common and recurrent use of proprietary knowhow [*sic*] or the common and recurrent use of a specialized and indivisible physical asset, then multiproduct enterprise (diversification) is an efficient way of organizing economic activity."[8]

In other words, there may be economic logic in favor of a bus company with large parking lots and a crew of diesel mechanics starting a heavy-truck rental business that utilizes some of the same assets. If Procter & Gamble already has a sales force and distribution channel to grocery and discount department stores in place for cleaning supplies, buying Gillette and its Duracell battery brand should build on the existing capabilities and infrastructure.

Shortly after this justification for diversification came into circulation, however, business school professors Gary Hamel and C. K. Prahalad asserted the notion of core competencies, the handful of deep proficiencies that separate a firm from its competitors.[9] In the best-case scenario, a core competency is difficult to copy, can be applied across multiple product lines or geographies, and is experienced as a valued attribute by the customer. Core competencies take years or decades to develop and ideally become part of the organization's culture and identity. Developing the depth of expertise needed for core competency, and the need for a long-term view, can be difficult to balance against the urge to acquire or otherwise diversify in pursuit of the oft-cited but seldom realized quality of "synergy."

1995: Linux as "Commons-Based Peer Production"

The Harvard legal scholar Yochai Benkler contrasts the organizational model behind Linux, and later Wikipedia, against those of both individuals in markets and employees in firms working for managers. His 2002 paper "Coase's Penguin" bridges the worlds of software development and economic theory, explaining the paper's mission succinctly:

> Commons-based peer production . . . has particular advantages as an information process for identifying and allocating human creativity available to work on information and cultural resources. It depends on very large aggregations of individuals [who] self-identify for tasks and perform them for a variety of motivational reasons that I discuss at some length.[10]

According to Benkler, altruism is irrelevant to any discussion of why people contribute their labor, credibility, and other resources to such efforts: Commons-based peer production allows people to self-identify for informational or cultural questions, and the management problem that challenges most organizations becomes instead an exercise in editorial filtering:

> Peer production provides a framework within which individuals who have the best information available about their own fit for a task can self-identify for the task. This provides an information gain over firms and markets, but only if the system develops some mechanism to filter out mistaken judgments that agents make about themselves. This is why practically all successful peer production systems have a robust mechanism for peer review or

statistical weeding out of contributions from agents who misjudge themselves.[11]

2000: Offshore

In an industrial age, manufacturing facilities needed to be placed at a nexus of labor, capital, and raw materials. Thus, waterpower helped establish New England as a center for textiles and shoemaking for a time, Pittsburgh became the center of steel making, and Detroit emerged at the core of the U.S. auto industry. As economies rely more on services, no longer do factories have to close in search of labor arbitrage and access to emerging markets for jobs to be exported. Rather, some kinds of services can be delivered through a wire (call centers and computer programming are familiar examples) while other services, such as nursing, truck driving, and the proverbial haircut, are destined to be delivered in person.

The line between personal and impersonal services, as the Princeton economist Alan Blinder has named them, does not follow class lines, as factory closings did. High-wage equity analysis, radiology interpretation, and new-product design can move to offshore locales just as easily as manufacturing, call center, and transcription services, each a traditionally low-wage position. As Blinder noted in 2006:

> *The fraction of service jobs in the United States and other rich countries that can potentially be moved offshore is certain to rise as technology improves and as countries such as China and India continue to modernize, prosper, and educate their work forces. Eventually, the number of service-sector jobs that will be vulnerable to competition from abroad will likely exceed the total number of manufacturing jobs. Thus, coping with foreign competition, currently a concern for only a minority of workers in rich countries, will become a major concern for many more.[12]*

Looking Ahead

The evolution reflected in these few readings has wide-ranging implications for every facet of every modern society. The logic of factory location is completely different from that of universities, venture capital firms, or data centers. Education for a lifetime of abstract cognitive work must coexist with practical training for hotel and restaurant management or elementary school teaching. The life expectancy of a manual laborer, particularly in the presence of toxins, may or may not be different from that of office

workers in the same country, particularly if the latter tend to be seden-
tary. The long-term, possibly career-long, implicit employment contract that
held true for union automobile workers, for example, is fading to be a distant memory. Tax revenues, the lifeblood of every community, every state,
and every major nation, are changing as a result of new work practices
(outsourcing), wage scales, and value delivery arrangements (self-service).
Finally, people are essentially social animals and now have at their disposal
a variety of technologies that augment and ideally enhance that sociability.

Notes

1. Adam Smith, *An Inquiry into the Nature and Causes of the Wealth of Nations,*
   section   I.1.3,   www.econlib.org/library/Smith/smWN1.html#B.I,%20Ch.1,%
   20Of%20the%20Division%20of%20Labor.
2. Amy Friedlander, *Emerging Infrastructure: The Growth of Railroads* (Reston,
   VA: Corporation for National Research Initiatives, 1994), p. 7.
3. Alfred D. Chandler, *The Visible Hand: The Managerial Revolution in American
   Business* (Cambridge, MA: Harvard Belknap Press, 1977), pp. 87–89.
4. Frederick Winslow Taylor, *The Principles of Scientific Management* (1911;
   reprint, Norton, 1967), p. 8. See also John M. Jordan, *Machine-Age Ideology:
   Social Engineering and American Liberalism, 1911–1939* (Chapel Hill:
   University of North Carolina Press, 1994), pp. 39 ff.
5. Chandler, *Visible Hand,* pp. 456–463.
6. Ronald Coase, "The Nature of the Firm," *Economica* 4, no. 16 (1937): 388.
7. Carl Dahlman, "The Problem of Externality," *Journal of Law and Economics*
   21, no. 2 (1979): 141–162.
8. David J. Teece, "Economies of Scope and the Scope of the Enterprise,"
   Journal of Economic Behavior & Organization 1, no. 3 (September 1980):
   223–247. See also John Panzar and Robert Willig, "Economies of Scale in
   Multi-Output Production," *Quarterly Journal of Economics* 91, no. 3 (August
   1977): 481–493.
9. See C. K. Prahalad and Gary Hamel, "The Core Competence of the
   Corporation," *Harvard Business Review* (May 1990): 79–91, and Gary Hamel
   and C. K. Prahalad, *Competing for the Future* (Boston: Harvard Business
   School Press, 1994).
10. Yochai Benkler, "Coase's Penguin, or, Linux and the Nature of the Firm," *Yale
    Law Journal* 112, no. 3 (2002), pp. 375–376.
11. Ibid. 376.
12. Alan S. Blinder, "Offshoring: The Next Industrial Revolution?" *Foreign Affairs*
    85 no. 1 (March/April 2006): 119.

CHAPTER 9

Firms, Ecosystems, and Collaboratives

The Internet and mobility are changing how resources can be organized to do work. The limited liability joint stock corporation remains useful for assembling capital at scale, which helps build railroads, steel mills, and other industrial facilities. With manufacturing less important in the U.S. economy in the past 50 years and new tools facilitating coordination and collaboration at scale without need for twentieth-century firms, we are witnessing some fascinating new sizes, shapes, and types of organizations. As MIT professor Erik Brynolfsson noted in the *Sloan Management Review*, we need to rethink the very nature of firms, beginning with Ronald Coase's famous theory: "The traditionally sharp distinction between markets and firms is giving way to a multiplicity of different kinds of organizational forms that don't necessarily have those sharp boundaries."[1]

Emerging Nonfirm Models

Rather than try to construct a typology or theory of nonfirm entities, I give a series of examples in which people can get things done outside traditional governmental and company settings. Each of these relies on some combination of connectedness, mobility, data access and interrogation, and other attributes of the contemporary landscape.

Kickstarter.com

How do art and creativity find funding? The answers have varied tremendously throughout human history: rich patrons, family, credit card debt, and many forms of government funding. David Bowie issued an asset-backed security with the future revenue streams of the albums he recorded before 1990 as collateral.[2] Given the decline in the audience for buying recorded music, Moody's downgraded the $55 million in debt to one step above junk bonds. Prudential, the buyer of the notes, looks to be the loser here while Bowie was either smart or lucky (but hasn't created much art of note since 1997, when the transaction occurred).

In 2009, a new model emerged. Kickstarter allows artists and other creators to post projects to which donors (not lenders) can commit. If I want to make an independent film, or catalog the works of a graffiti artist, or write a book, I can post the project, and any special rewards to funders, on the site. Donors and artists alike are protected by a threshold requirement: If the required sum is not raised, the project never launches. Kickstarter takes 5% of the funds, and Amazon payments cost another 5%. Once completed, the works are permanently archived on the site. The site attracted some notice in 2010 when a user-controlled alternative to Facebook, called Diaspora, raised $200,000.

Donors might receive a signed copy of the finished work, or pdf updates while the work is in process, or tickets to the film's premiere, or other reciprocation. While it's too early to judge the longevity or scope of the model, *TIME* magazine named it one of the 50 best inventions of 2010.

Software Developer Networks

Microsoft enjoyed a huge competitive advantage in software developer networks in the 1990s. As of 2002, one worldwide estimate showed about 10 million developers in the Microsoft camp.[3] None of these men and women was an employee but was often trained, certified, and equipped with tool sets by Microsoft. The developers, in turn, could sense market demand for applications large and small and build solutions in the Windows environments for customers conditioned to seek out the Windows branding in the service provider.

More recently, the App Store model has attracted developers who seek a more direct path to monetization. Apple has hundreds of thousands of applications for the iPhone and iPad; Google's Android platform has nearly as many, depending on counting methodology. Tools are still important, but rather than certification programs, the App Store model relies on the market for validation of an application. Obviously dry cleaners and other small businesses need accounting programs, or whatever, and Google can't compete with Microsoft for this slice of the business. Even so, enterprise software vendors such as Adobe, Autodesk, Oracle, and SAP must navigate new territory as the app store model, along with software as a service (see Chapter 26), make such competitors as Salesforce.com and its Force.com developer program a new kind of market entrant. Much like Apple, Force. com allows developers to go direct to market rather than have to team up with conventional vendors.

The app store developers aren't really a network in any meaningful sense of the word: They don't meet, don't know each other, don't exist in a directory of members, affiliates, or prospects. There are developer conferences, of course, but not in the same form that Microsoft pioneered. The networks, particular the app store developers, certainly aren't even remotely an extension of Apple's, Google's, or HTC's corporate organization: The market model is much more central than any organizational chart can be.

Not all of these developer networks play inside the lines, as it were. Despite robust security technologies, Sony PlayStations and Apple iPhones have been unlocked by third-party teams. The iPhone Dev Team, described by the *Wall Street Journal* as "a loose-knit but exclusive group of highly-skilled technologists who are considered to be the leaders among iPhone hackers,"[4] has contributed a steady stream of software kits for Apple customers to "jailbreak" their devices. The procedure is not illegal but can void certain warranty provisions. The benefit to the user is greater control over the device, access to software not necessarily approved by Apple, and sometimes features not supported by the official operating system.

The iPhone Dev Team is so loosely organized that it functioned quite effectively, solving truly difficult technical challenges in elegant ways, even though its members did not physically meet until they were invited to a German hackers' conference in 2008.

Kiva.org

Founded in 2005, Kiva.org is a nonprofit microlending effort. The organization, headquartered in San Francisco, recruits both lenders and entrepreneurial organizations around the world. The Internet connects the individuals and groups that lend money to roughly 125 lending partners (intermediaries) in developing countries and in the United States, and the lending partners disburse and collect the loans. Kiva does not charge any interest, but the independent field partner for each loan can charge interest.

After six years, Kiva has loaned more than $200 million, with a repayment rate of 98.65%. More than 500,000 donations have come in and nearly 300,000 loans have been initiated, at an average size of slightly under $400. While the recipients often are featured on the Kiva Web site, lenders can no longer choose who will receive their loan, as was formerly the case. Still, the transparency of seeing the effect of money for a farmer's seeds, or a fishing boat repair, or a village water pump is strong encouragement to donors, so most money that people give to Kiva is reloaned multiple times.[5]

Kiva and other microfinance organizations challenge the conventional wisdom of economic development, as embodied in large capital projects funded by the World Bank and similar groups. Instead of massive dams, for example, Kiva works at the individual or small-group level, with high success rates that relate in part to the emotional and economic investment of the people rather than a country's elites, the traditional point of contact for the large aid organizations. At the same time, the scale of the macro aid organizations is truly substantial, and Kiva has never billed itself as a replacement for traditional economic development.

Even given its successes, Kiva faces substantial challenges:

- The quality of the local lending partners
- Currency risk
- Balancing supply and demand for microcredit at a global scale
- Transparency into lending partners' practices

Still, the point for our purposes relates to $200 million in loans to the world's poorest, with low overhead and emotional linkages between donors and recipients. Fifteen years ago such a model would have been impossible even to conceive.

Internet Engineering Task Force

More than a decade ago, the *Boston Globe*'s economics editor (yes, daily newspapers once had economics editors) David Warsh contrasted Microsoft's pursuit of features to the Internet Engineering Task Force (IETF), the unique organization behind the network of networks. In the article, the IETF was personified by Harvard University's Scott Bradner, a true übergeek who embraces a minimalist, functionalist perspective. "Which system of development," Warsh asked, "[Bill] Gates's or Bradner's, has been more advantageous to consumers? . . . Which technology has benefited you more?"[6] Bradner contends that, like the *Oxford English Dictionary*, the IETF serves admirably as a case study in open-source methodology, though the people making the model work didn't call it that at the time.

Companies in any realm of intellectual property, especially, should consider Warsh's conclusion:

> *Simpler standards [in contrast to those coming from governmental or other bureaucratic entities that can get snarled in ego battles or*

lowest-common-denominator consensus, and in contrast to many proprietary standards that emphasize features over function] mean greater success. And it was the elegant standards of the IETF, simply written and speedily established, that have made possible the dissemination of innovations such as the World Wide Web and its browsers.

As stated on its website, the IETF's structure and mission are straightforward and refreshingly apolitical:

The IETF's mission is "to make the Internet work better," but it is the Internet Engineering Task Force, so this means: make the Internet work better from an engineering point of view. We try to avoid policy and business questions, as much as possible. If you're interested in these general aspects, consider joining the Internet Society.

A famous aspect of its mission statement commits the group to "rough consensus and running code." That is, the IETF makes "standards based on the combined engineering judgment of our participants and our real-world experience in implementing and deploying our specifications."[7] The IETF has meetings, to be sure, and a disciplined process for considering and implementing proposed changes, but, remarkably, such a powerful and dynamic global communications network is not "owned" by any corporation, government, or individual.

eBird.org

Species migration provides crucial scientific data in many realms, not least of which is climate change. Bird-watchers can play a valuable role here, pursuing their hobby but sharing observational data with larger databases that can generate large-scale pattern recognition. Cornell's Lab of Ornithology and the National Audubon Society teamed up in 2002 to build an online tool for information collection and dissemination related to the abundance and distribution of avian species across time and space. In January 2010 alone, 1.5 million bird observations were submitted in North America. A birder can keep his or her personal log on the site and use tools for visualization and other forms of analysis. Multiple languages are supported. Unusually and usefully, regional bird experts review all submissions to maintain a high level of data quality. eBird in turn supports still larger efforts, such as the Global Biodiversity Information Facility.[8]

Distributed Capital

One day a few years ago, I was having trouble with my VPN connection to the corporate e-mail server and the weather was unseasonably warm, so I took the dog for a walk around the block while the network hairball cleared. I did a rough count of people on the street in our small town outside Boston and was stunned to conclude that, not counting the retirees, more people had "alternative" work arrangements than conventional ones. Changing the names, here are the people who lived on our street:

- Keith has a PhD in operations research and is employed by a Wall Street bank doing quantitative analysis from his home office. He was hard-wired into the mothership via a dedicated T1 line. His wife, Karin, ran a nonprofit.
- Tina was and is a personal fitness trainer.
- Natalie ran a software company from her home. Two people worked for her there.
- Brian was a professor of engineering and grew fruit that he sold at his farm stand.
- Jim and Stephanie worked for moviemakers building sets in their barn/workshop and scouting locations for movie shoots.
- Rich left the dot-com world and sold musical instruments to schools.
- Greg was another sales executive, working for a technology hardware vendor.

Observations

First, I make no claim for this being an "average" neighborhood—the Boston metro area is pretty expensive to live in, and our town had grown more affluent than many. Even so, as a "weak signal," this employment pattern is indicative of larger trends. It may be happening here earlier than elsewhere, and probably to a greater degree, but we're not unique.

Second, just on our street there's a wide spread among the service businesses and occupations represented. While there are a lot of classic "knowledge workers," with six PhDs on the street, there are other occupational types represented as well: personal training and carpentry, for two. The sales reps are another interesting category, and we have a classic entrepreneur who doesn't hold an advanced degree.

Third, there's a split between those who need the Internet to do what they do and those who could get along without it.

Finally, I realized that the difference between working at home and telecommuting to work somewhere else is blurring. Professors are home most of the day and have summers off, and while they couldn't teach without a classroom in 2005, online learning is growing extremely fast, so location matters for education less than it formerly did. In addition, the fitness trainer's "shop" is wherever she is at a given time.

Getting aggregate numbers for these kinds of workers is difficult—nobody has a good count of American distributed workers, nor is much international data reliable; even the label is problematic. Anecdotally, the trend seems to have accelerated since 1995, and it's happening in many types of businesses. Because service work is often brain work, and because the Internet allows those people to work remotely or in a home-based business, one outcome is that the means of production are getting more decentralized. As more factories move offshore, as companies reevaluate their real estate holdings in an attempt to manage costs, and as retirees from conventional jobs find new types of employment after age 60 or so, this tendency will likely accelerate. This decentralization of the inputs to economic output will compound the already fuzzy problem of measuring services productivity, as we see in Chapter 14.

The impact of this decentralization will be far-reaching. For example, the best way to reduce traffic congestion is not to build bigger roads but to reduce the need to drive, whether to work or elsewhere. Similarly, the explosion of interest in home-schooling can be attributed in part to the availability of online resources and community for families who opt to home-school their children. According to a study done by the U.S. Census Bureau in 2007, there are roughly 1.5 million students doing home-schooling, and the annual growth rate of this student population appears to be in the neighborhood of 15%. Finally, the availability of online information is changing the role and function of libraries—and librarians. The bottom line is that most of the people working away from offices are not one-person shops.

Implications

There are several varieties of fallout from this overall line of thinking.

MEASUREMENT First, a warning flag should go up when talking about abstractions called "productivity" or "the workplace." Services are often delivered in highly decentralized arrangements in some ways closer to the craft or guild model that applied before industrialization (and then mass production) changed the scale of economic production. Measuring the *inputs* to service output, particularly when they are decentralized, is difficult and perhaps impossible. Quantifying services *output*, meanwhile, remains controversial.[9]

INFRASTRUCTURE The emergence of powerful information networks is shifting the load traditionally borne by public or other forms of infrastructure.

The power grid, roads, schools, Internet service providers (ISPs)—all will be utilized differently as the capital base further decentralizes. In addition, given contract manufacturing, offshore programming, cloud computing, and more and more examples of software as a service, the infrastructure requirements for starting a venture have plummeted: Leadership, talent, and a few laptops and smartphones are often sufficient.

RETHINKING SIZE The importance of scale can at times be diminished. For example, Jeff Vinik didn't need the resources of Fidelity Investments to run his hedge fund after he quit managing the giant Magellan mutual fund. In the 1950s, one reason a hotel investor would affiliate with Holiday Inn was for access to the brand and, later, the reservations network. Now small inns and other lodging providers can work word-of-mouth and other referral channels and be profitable standing alone. The question is how and where dispersal can work and what the center, if there is one, looks like.

TALENT As Linux and other developer networks grow in stature and viability, managing the people who remain in traditional organizations will likely become more difficult. What management writer Dan Pink reasonably calls "the purpose motive"[10] is a powerful spur to hard work: As grand challenges have shown, people will work for free on hard, worthy problems. Outside of those settings, bureaucracies are not known for proving either worthy challenges or worthy purposes.

One defining fact of many successful start-ups—Netflix, Zappos, and Skype come to mind—is their leaders' ability to put profitability in the context of doing something "insanely great," in the famous phrasing of Steve Jobs. Given alternatives to purpose-challenged cubicle-dwelling, more and more attractive job candidates will opt out of traditional large organizations. Harvard Business School and other institutions are seeing strong growth of a cadre of students who resist traditional employment and, more important, traditional motivation.[11] Both nonprofits and start-ups are challenging investment banking and consulting as destinations for ambitious, capable leaders of the next generation.

Looking Ahead

In the end, the purpose of a firm, to be an alternative to market transactions, is being rescaled, rethought, and redefined. Firms will always be an option, to be sure, but as the examples have shown, no longer are they a default for delivering value. One major hint points to the magnitude of the shift that is well under way: Contrasted to "firm," the English vocabulary lacks good words to describe Wikipedia, Linux, Skype, and other networked entities that can do much of what commercial firms might once have been formed to undertake.

Notes

1. "Beyond Enterprise 2.0, An Interview with Erik Brynjolfsson and Andrew McAfee," *Sloan Management Review* (Spring 2007): 55.
2. Karen Richardson, "Bankers Hope for a Reprise of 'Bowie Bonds,'" *Wall Street Journal*, August 23, 2005, http://online.wsj.com/public/article/SB112476043457720240-Tvpthd07S8mCqCxLFNKIPnWWY9g_20060823.html.
3. http://answers.google.com/answers/threadview/id/43891.html.
4. Yukari Iwatani Kane, "The iPhone 3GS Hacking Debate," WSJ Blogs, July 6, 2009. http://blogs.wsj.com/digits/2009/07/06/the-iphone-3gs-hacking-debate/.
5. www.kiva.org/about.
6. David Warsh column, *Boston Globe,* November 28, 1999.
7. www.ietf.org/about/mission.html.
8. http://ebird.org/content/ebird/about. Thanks to Lee Erickson for pointing me to this effort.
9. For a prominent example, see Zev Griliches, "Introduction to 'Output Measurement in the Services Sectors,'" in Griliches, ed., *Output Measurement in the Services Sectors* (Chicago: University of Chicago Press, 1990), pp. 1–22.
10. Daniel H. Pink, *Drive: The Surprising Truth about What Motivates Us* (New York: Riverhead Trade), 2011.
11. See, for example, John A. Byrne, "Harvard MBAs: Putting Goals of Corporate Domination Aside," Fortune.com, May 25, 2011, http://management.fortune.cnn.com/2011/05/25/harvard-mbas-putting-goals-of-corporate-domination-aside/.

CHAPTER 10

Government

Governments have significant interactions with the technology and communications domains. They tax: Wireline telephony used to be a big revenue generator. They regulate: Wireless spectrum is auctioned and regulated by several agencies. They sue: Overly aggressive platforms risk being targeted with antitrust litigation. Finally, they buy: Government is a large but idiosyncratic user of many information technologies. The transition from a manufacturing to services economy in the United States coincides with the rise of computing, with some far-reaching implications.

Isolating how IT has shaped the economy and society turns out to be much less direct than looking for the impact of, say, the automobile. At the macro level, for about a century manufacturing surged at agriculture's expense as the primary locus of employment. From 1950 until 1980, however, while manufacturing employment grew in raw numbers, this growth occurred against the backdrop of the population expansion that followed World War II: as a percentage of total employment, and of economic output, manufacturing was shrinking even as it appeared to grow.

Given that the 1950-to-2000 half century was marked by a precipitous loss of employment as a percentage of the workforce in both agricultural and manufacturing arenas, we know that services have become the dominant economic sector. According to the Central Intelligence Agency's *World Factbook*, "industry" constitutes 20% of the U.S. economy while services add up to 79%. How could this sector grow so big so fast, and what are some of the implications?

For all the rhetoric about becoming a nation of burger-flippers, government has become a much bigger economic entity, a major driver of that services sector: Prison guards, for example, constitute one of this century's fastest-growing occupational categories. As of 2010, there were more government employees—about 22 million at all levels, not counting military personnel—than in all good-producing sectors combined: At 17 million, that group is smaller than it was in 1961 even though gross domestic product is about six times bigger in constant dollars.

Prison guards aside, about 80% of government jobs involve paperwork,* which IT can automate. Thus, it seems safe to suggest that one feature of the economic landscape—a large governmental economic presence as employer, regulator, and collector of taxes—relates closely to the ability of computers to collect and manage large quantities of information.

The impact of the computer on the U.S. economy can be partially attributed to its automation of government tasks. Those tasks, many of which escape measurement in standard indexes of economic output, are another legacy of the computer: If paperwork gets easier to do, more of it will be generated.

The Biggest Employer

Ever since World War II, the federal government has been increasing as an employer, either directly or indirectly. For example, seven new cabinet departments (plus the noncabinet Environmental Protection Agency, founded in 1970) date from the computer age and reflect the growing scope of government:

1. Housing and Urban Development (1966)
2. Transportation (1966)
3. Energy (1977)
4. Health and Human Services (1979)
5. Education (1979)
6. Veterans Affairs (1989)
7. Homeland Security (2003)

Note that numbers 4 and 5 were broken out of the Department of Health Education and Welfare.

Headcount at these agencies is significant: By itself, the Department of Veterans Affairs employs about 280,000 people, making it both the biggest single federal nonmilitary organization and about the same size, by headcount, as General Electric.

---

*According to the Bureau of Labor Statistics, management, professional, and administrative support jobs represented 80.4% of federal jobs as of 2008.

In the aggregate, the U.S. federal government employed more than 2 million people in 2010. That's about the same employment as UPS, IBM, McDonald's, Target, and Kroger combined, which means that the federal government, excluding armed services, employs about as many people as Wal-Mart. As big as the Beltway may seem in the public imagination, however, only about 1 in 6 federal jobs is located in the Washington, DC, metro area.

Finding government employment information at the state level is frustrating, particularly given the use of contractors. A Kentucky legislator introduced a bill in 2010 that would require the state to tally merit, nonmerit, and contract employees: Currently the information is difficult or impossible to obtain in many states, not to even mention the various local layers. All told, it is extremely difficult to count government and government-related workers in the aggregate.

"Government" can be an abstract term, so I looked for concrete data closer to home. As a state, Pennsylvania is reasonably representative, with a relatively large economy (number 6 out of 50), and a per capita income almost perfectly at the median, ranking twenty-sixth of 50. Agriculture is important but not predominant, and 25 Fortune 500 companies are headquartered here. As of the first quarter of 2010, the biggest employer was the State of Pennsylvania. (No figures were released in the document, compiled by the state Center for Workforce Information & Analysis.) Number 2 was the U.S. government, even after the closing of the Philadelphia naval yard in 1995.

To continue that list of Pennsylvania's top employers, note the paucity of private sector job generators:

3. Wal-Mart
4. City of Philadelphia
5. University of Pennsylvania (roughly 35,000 jobs, including a big medical center)
6. Philadelphia school district
7. Penn State University (not counting the affiliated medical center)
8. Giant Food Stores
9. UPS
10. University of Pittsburgh
11. PNC Bank
12. University of Pittsburgh Medical Center
13. State System of Higher Education (public colleges and universities excluding Penn State, Pittsburgh, and Temple)
14. Weis Supermarkets

All told, 20 of the top 50 employers in Pennsylvania are not businesses in the traditional sense of the word: That's 40% of the leaderboard,

including six of the top seven. More significantly, Pennsylvania is officially a services economy: Only 1 employer (Merck) in the top 25 and 4
in the top 50 make anything. Many kinds of services are represented, with
healthcare in the lead, followed by education, grocery, retail, financial services, and fast food/convenience stores.

The contrast to the intermediate past is shocking. Courtesy of
researchers at the Pennsylvania Department of Labor and Industry, here
are the top 25 employers of 1965 (the earliest year for which records are
available):

1. United States Steel
2. Bethlehem Steel
3. Westinghouse Electric
4. Bell Telephone of Pennsylvania
5. Jones & Laughlin Steel
6. General Electric
7. Sears, Roebuck
8. A&P
9. Acme Markets
10. Western Electric
11. Philco
12. Budd
13. Philadelphia Electric
14. Boeing
15. Crucible Steel
16. Pittsburgh Plate Glass
17. Allegheny Ludlum Steel
18. Sylvania Electric
19. Sun Oil
20. Pittsburgh Steel
21. Armco Steel
22. Aluminum Company of America (Alcoa)
23. RCA
24. Armstrong Cork
25. Rohm and Haas

(Note that the methodology of the 1965 list was not made clear:
Government entities, hospitals, and universities are not listed, but the
absence is unexplained.)

Of the 25, services are represented only by retailers and utilities: No
banks or healthcare providers make the top 40. Seven steelmakers dominate the list, joined by Alcoa. The state's heritage in energy was still
represented by Atlantic Refining in Philadelphia, Sun Oil, and Gulf Oil.

Transportation is more of a factor today, with UPS at 9 and US Airways at 30; in 1965, no railroads made the list, even though their suppliers (Budd and GE) did.

The composition of the 1965 and 2010 lists illustrate several germane points with regard to the recent economic downturn. First, it's hard to stay on top: Almost all companies that at one time appeared to be powerfully untouchable sooner or later fall by the wayside. Bell of Pennsylvania, the number-4 employer in 1965, morphed into Verizon, currently number 28. Among retailers, A&P disappeared, as did Gimbels and G.C. Murphy, while Sears fell from seventh to thirty-second. Second, in the Pennsylvania case at least, the kinds of firms traditionally targeted by economic development agencies—addressing dynamic markets, paying high wages, and anchoring a community or region—are not particularly large employers:

14. Merck
19. The Vanguard Group (headquartered outside Philadelphia)
25. Comcast (headquartered in downtown Philadelphia)
39. GE (which makes railroad locomotives in Erie)

Government Hiring at a Crossroads

After this historical wave of growth in hiring by governments at every level of U.S. society, however, data points from all over converge to announce a time of reckoning:

- According to the Pew Center on the States, the 50 states collectively have $3.3 trillion of *pension obligations*, with about a third, $1 trillion, unfunded.
- In part because the recession has reduced states' revenues, 48 out of 50 states faced *budget shortfalls* in 2009 and 2010; 46 had gaps in 2011. (The exceptions were resource-intensive Alaska and Montana, along with North Dakota and Arkansas.) The 2010 state budget shortfalls totaled $191 billion.
- Illinois, which ranked dead last in pension funding in 2008, was forced to *raise taxes* on individual income a full 75% in 2011. The state legislature also approved the issuance of $3.7 billion in bonds to more adequately fund pension obligations.
- At the University of California at Los Angeles, the dean of the Anderson School of Business is attempting to *privatize a state resource*. State budget cuts leave California's support of Anderson at about 6 cents on the dollar. By withdrawing from the state system,

Anderson can set its own tuition and pay superstar faculty superstar salaries, thus enhancing its ability to attract top talent.[1] In all levels of government in the United States, the *wage differential* of the 1990s has reversed and public sector workers earn, on average, 30% more than private sector counterparts. In addition to being paid more, government workers' healthcare, vacation time, retirement, and other benefits typically are more generous than in industry.

- *Underperformance is seldom addressed* with meaningful action. Firing either incompetent or unaffordable public workers is far more difficult than doing layoffs in the private sector when companies or whole industries face transitions in technology, customer behavior, or competition. (According to *The Economist*, the Los Angeles school district spent $3.5 million trying to fire seven underperforming teachers and succeeded with only five.[2] Insofar as the district's entire teaching force numbers 33,000, the effort was aimed at 1/50th of 1%. By contrast, private sector organizations routinely churn the bottom 10% of performers.)

Inevitable Downsizing

The bills are coming due on these public institutions. In the private sector, the cost of unsustainable labor arrangements, defined as payroll costs out of sync with revenues, is layoffs. While Ford can claim a lot of positive news in 2011, for example, the past decade was tough: Total auto industry layoffs after 2006 were estimated at 200,000 jobs, and tens of thousands of jobs were cut at Ford earlier in the decade as well. As services comprise more of the U.S. economy, manufacturing jobs are changing, and the big labor unions that represented these workers in the steel and auto heyday shrank after 1973, from about a quarter of private sector workers to less than a tenth in 2010.

According to the Bureau of Labor Statistics, however, government employees, a key component of that services workforce, increased in union membership from 23% to roughly 38% in the 20 years following 1973, and that membership percentage has stayed pretty constant even as the sector has grown dramatically. But just as the auto industry painfully discovered after 2000 that it could no longer afford the small-C contract it had agreed to with the unions in the 1950s and 1960s, governments at every level are facing deficits that derive substantially from labor costs (see Figure 10.1): Expensive pensions and expensive current workforces (with expensive healthcare) that often lack performance accountability are and will continue to be unaffordable. UBS Securities estimated in mid-2011 that roughly 750,000 nonfederal government jobs could be cut in 2011–2012.[3]

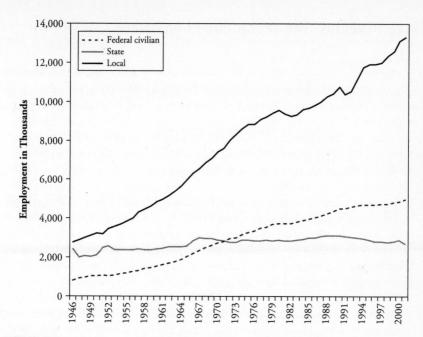

FIGURE 10.1 U.S. Government Employment since World War II
Source: U.S. Census.

In short, given a protracted employment recession (and thus a downturn in both taxable income and taxable spending for revenue generation), governments are facing truly hard choices. At the federal level, conservative legislators are proposing drastic cuts in the defense budget, previously an approach that ideology would not permit. As he confronted a $28 billion deficit, California governor Jerry Brown (like his counterparts elsewhere) proposed deep, politically and humanly painful cuts in the social safety net, in education (the community college budget was proposed to be reduced by $400 million), and in public safety.

U.S. governments at every level are facing their auto industry moment. The Pennsylvania city of Harrisburg teeters on the edge of bankruptcy; it would be the biggest municipal entity to enter that process since Orange County in California lost billions of dollars in pension investments in 1994. While the likelihood of default is higher for some European nations than in most U.S. entities, the prospect of governments in any country defaulting on their obligations is obviously disturbing to markets and individuals alike. Whether it is debt, pensions, or current expenses, governments are being forced to cut spending in bold strokes.

Government on the Technology Landscape

What does government performance have to do with this book's larger argument? The world we are in and entering is not the world that existed when those budgetary assumptions were being formed. The process of resizing government thus needs to begin with a look at what governments can and need to do as well as how they do it. Furthermore, there are tasks that at one time were essential, but technological obsolescence is slow to alter governments. Thus, at least five buckets of questions need to be asked—the topics under each heading are merely suggestive:

1. *What must government do, and how can other entities help deliver necessary services?* This is a big category, obviously, but perhaps not as big as it once was. Funding bridges, inspecting food and oil wells, testing new drugs, defending the nation—lots of government tasks cannot go away and some may need to get bigger. At the same time, for-profit universities and hospitals might be better ways to approach some facets of education and health. At the primary and secondary levels, the National Home Education Research Institute asserts that between 1.5 and 2 million U.S. students are home-schooled. Both schools and homes can have their place as loci of education, but the fact is that in many locales, the schools are no longer good enough, and parents have more resources than ever to meet the need. Some churches have proven effective at delivering social services, though of course issues of evangelization and discrimination can be tricky. Prisons, several types of security services, school cafeterias, and many other functions are outsourced or even privatized; perhaps outsourcing more activities should be considered.

    Crowdsourcing (Internet-enabled coordination of mass volunteer effort; see Chapter 11) can assist government efforts. An excellent example is PeerToPatent.org. This joint effort of the U.S. Patent Office and New York University's law school enlists the power of the masses to assist patent examiners. Specifically, people are asked to submit evidence of "prior art"—evidence that a pending patent is not in fact original and should not be granted protection. Given the current state of U.S. patent law, large-scale reform will be impossible to fund for the foreseeable future, so any leverage generated by the masses will contribute to breaking the logjam.[4]

2. *What can government stop doing entirely?* Agricultural extension agents provided a valuable function in their day. Today, however, if a farmer sees a pest or a leaf condition, his or her first stop is likely to be the Internet. The State of California is attempting to get out of the incarceration business for low-level offenses, shifting responsibility

for these to the local level. Republican legislators are asking, sensibly, about federal support for rail transportation, which is expensive, especially when the benefits are highly localized. Debate is increasing over the necessary population density to support unsubsidized high-speed trains; the United States lacks the crowded regions that make Japan's line between Tokyo and Osaka break even.[5]

Telecommunications regulators were a necessary counterweight to a monopolistic AT&T, but now that wireline telephony participation is dropping and all segments are intensely competitive, the market can do much of what 1 federal and 50 state regulators once did. California, to take one example, administers a billion-dollar universal service fund, dedicated, among other things, to "ensuring basic telephone service remains available and affordable to all Californians regardless of geography, language, cultural, ethnic, physical, or income differences"—even if fewer people than at any time in more than 50 years want that service.

3. *What is the right level of organization?* The size of administrative units is typically a historical accident. Whether those units are currently the right size is, or should be, open for discussion. Water, sewer, fire, police, school, and recreational districts are rarely coherent. How big should a town be? When many towns are contiguous, why does each need a school superintendent (often with only one high school, which has at least one principal), a mayor and/or town manager, a chief of police? What is the optimum size for a school district, a fire department, a state park in a given part of the country? Most important, what government entity can mandate that other units consolidate, disband, or otherwise change shape?

4. *How can interested parties self-organize?* In the afterglow of Wikipedia's tenth birthday, it's worth asking what other efforts formerly undertaken by government might be better accomplished by interested citizens. Mash-ups are one easy example: Given good clean data (the collection of which remains an essential task of government), crimes, potholes, economic opportunity, underperforming schools, and other opportunities for improvement can be identified by the people. Noise measurements (e.g., near wind farms) are being crowdsourced. People can also organize on the revenue side: In Mill Valley, California, a community foundation has existed for nearly 30 years to supplement tax funding. To date the organization has raised more than $14 million—that's a lot of bake sales and charity auctions. Similar parent-run organizations exist in many towns, and one question concerns what mobile coordination and payment platforms will mean for the future of such efforts. Entrepreneurial Girl Scout cookie teams are reportedly using Square (a smartphone add-on) to process credit card transactions, for example.

5. *How can government do what it needs to do, more efficiently?* IT in government remains a sore subject. President Obama's former chief information officer Vivek Kundra recently put forth a 25-step plan to reform federal IT management.[6] Many of the items are broad and seemingly self-evident to anyone familiar with industry ("consolidate data centers" and "develop a strategy for shared services"). The fact is, however, that industry does not follow federal acquisition or implementation practices; getting federal IT to perform at a reasonable fraction of an Amazon or FedEx would be a massive achievement. Many of the most notable IT project failures of the past decade are government implementations: Systems development disasters at the U.S. Census and the Federal Bureau of Investigation are prime examples of the performance gap.

Compared to customer service in travel, banking, shopping, or information businesses (iTunes is an obvious example), finding even basic information on most government Web sites can be painful. Transparency can be difficult to track down. Control of bills passing through legislation is a key perquisite of power, and holding up the process with committee hearings that happen very slowly and/or erratically is common, so clear, open calendars are not always the rule. Like legislatures, regulatory bodies can be opaque, in that budget and headcount information is typically difficult to obtain, unlike the information readily available in a private company's annual report.

If information can be hard to find, the state of online transactions is even more dismal: Compare getting a fishing license or renewing other permits to checking in for an airplane flight. While efficient government looks much better to citizens on the outside than to gainfully employed government workers on the inside of slow-moving bureaucracies with no incentive to improve customer service, perhaps the current crisis can provide the impetus for real change to commence. In a sector that lags private industry by many performance metrics, a combination of new tools and more focused motivation has the promise to improve service, cut costs, increase accountability, and enhance security.

Looking Ahead

As government at the scale of 2010 employment grows less and less affordable (not least of all because of the paperwork costs of healthcare for aging and retired government employees), the challenge to both bureaucrats and citizens will relate to information and technology at multiple levels. How can groups self-organize to accomplish things that used to require formal entities? How can government reorganize and reprioritize in light of 2012 realities of telecommunications, nutrition, and water consumption, to take three examples? How will such cultural norms as trust, aging, ethnic identity, and literacy evolve after mobile phones, after Facebook, after the Kindle, and after WikiLeaks? President Obama spoke of a "Sputnik moment" for the economy at large, but perhaps the challenge could be better and more pointedly addressed to the same government that put a man on the moon in response to the original Sputnik moment.

Notes

1. David A. Kaplan, "UCLA's Plan to Take Its B-school private," *Fortune*, September 20, 2011, http://management.fortune.cnn.com/2011/09/20/uclas-plan-to-take-its-b-school-private/?section=magazines_fortune.
2. "(Government) Workers of the World Unite!" *The Economist*, January 6, 2011, www.economist.com/node/17849199.
3. Reuters, "State and Local Governments May Cut 450,000 jobs in FY2012," May 23, 2011, www.reuters.com/article/2011/05/23/us-markets-municipals-idUSTRE74M60U20110523.
4. www.peertopatent.org/.
5. "A Lost Cause: The High-Speed Rail Race," *Washington Post*, February 16, 2011, www.washingtonpost.com/wp-dyn/content/article/2011/02/16/AR2011021605977.html.
6. "White House Forum on IT Management Reform," www.cio.gov/pages.cfm/page/White-House-Forum-on-IT-Management-Reform.

CHAPTER 11

Crowds

The Internet is remarkable for its ability for convene groups of people. These groups, which we will call crowds for the sake of convenience, can get work done in two basic ways. The first of these, commonly called crowdsourcing, takes big tasks and divides them among a large number of usually voluntary contributors. Examples would be Amazon Mechanical Turk or Flickr's tagging mechanism to generate words to describe photos. The second function of crowds is to process information with market mechanisms. This function was popularized by James Surowiecki's book on the wisdom of crowds.[1]

Crowdsourcing: Group Effort

Perhaps the most extraordinary of Linux founder Linus Torvalds's discoveries was not technical but psychological: Given a suitably hard but interesting problem, distributed communities of people will work on it for free. The first decade of the twenty-first century has witnessed the growth of crowdsourcing to include several defining artifacts of the Internet, including Amazon, Facebook, Flickr, and Wikipedia.

Crowds can do amazing things. England's *Guardian* newspaper was playing catch-up to the rival *Telegraph,* which had a four-week head start analyzing a mass of public records related to an expense-account scandal in the House of Lords. Once it obtained the records, the *Guardian* could not wait for its professional reporters to dig through 2 million pages of documentation and still publish anything meaningful. The solution was to crowdsource the data problem: Let citizen-readers look for nuggets of meaningful information.

Twenty thousand volunteers assisted, digging through more than 170,000 documents in 80 hours. Net cost to the newspaper: £50 for temporary server rental (from Amazon) and less than two person-weeks to build the site. By making the hunt for juicy news bits into a game—complete with leaderboards—and making feedback easy, as well as by spicing up the game by using politicians' headshots, the *Guardian* helped build reader identification with the paper at the same time it found investigative threads for further follow-up.[2]

Recent scholarship has identified four challenges to successful crowdsourcing:

1. How are participants recruited and retained?
2. What contributions do participants make?
3. How are contributions combined into solutions to a given problem?
4. How are users and their contributions evaluated?[3]

By sorting along these dimensions, several buckets of crowdsourcing emerge.

Evaluating

The simplest tactic is to ask people for their opinion. Amazon product reviews were an important step, but then the site went a step further and asked people to review the reviews. Netflix uses viewer feedback to recommend movies for both the reviewer and for people who share similar preferences. eBay's reputational currency—have buyer and seller been trustworthy in past transactions—is a further use of crowds as evaluators. Rotten Tomatoes builds movie reviews off user ratings.

More recently, Digg and Technorati have refined the evaluation function to rate larger bodies of content, including news items. In addition, with the tagging function, Delicious helped pioneer the evaluation as classification: Rather than merely saying I like it, or I like it 6 stars out of 10, tagging uses masses of community input to say, of a photo, that's a sunset, or of a news story, that's about product recalls. Flickr's community had generated 20 million unique tags as of early 2008; by 2011, the site hosted more than 5 billion images. In contrast to rigid, formal taxonomies, such people-powered "folksonomies" are excellent examples of "good-enough" solutions: Unlike the Library of Congress cataloging system, for example, which is costly, authoritative, and cannot scale without expensive people with esoteric skills, there are no "right" or "wrong" tags on Flickr, only more and less common ones. Crowdsourcing scales to absolutely huge sizes, as we see soon. The behavioral patterns, at scale, of anonymous evaluators are also unpredictable and merit considerable further study.

Sharing

Through a variety of platforms, it has become trivially easy to share information with groups of any size, reaching into the hundreds of millions. The original sharing architecture at scale was probably Napster, in which the material that was shared belonged to other people. Since then, YouTube, Flickr, and blogging tools have expanded the range of possibility beyond words to images and video. An incredible 48 hours of video are uploaded to YouTube every minute as of mid-2011, up from half that sum one year prior. On the downstream side, YouTube records 3 billion page views every day.[4]

More substantive knowledge can also be shared. Such idea-gathering and problem-solving sites as Innocentive and NineSigma pose hard business and engineering problems on behalf of such clients as Eli Lilly and Procter & Gamble. The power is in a very small number of people who can speak to the issue, not a mass of worker bees. More recently, Quora launched a question-based site that is hybrid of broad- and narrow-casting: Expertise self-selects and answers are voted up or down by subsequent readers. Anyone can post any question, but getting experts' attention is something of an art form. The richness of the conversations, across an amazing variety of topics, is stunning, and to date no money changes hands.

Creativity is a further category of sharing. Threadless solicits T-shirt design ideas and prints and sells the most popular ones. Quirky crowdsources new product development, soliciting both original ideas and influential changes to those concepts. Both iStockphoto and Flickr get the work of photographers into the hands of massive audiences. In all cases, recognition is one major currency of motivation.

Networking

Compare, for a moment, Facebook to Yahoo of 1998. What, really, does Facebook deliver? In contrast to free e-mail, horoscopes, weather, classified ads, maps, stock quotes, and an abundance of other content, Facebook builds only an empty lattice, to be populated with the life histories, opinions, photos, and interactions of its 600 million-plus members. LinkedIn, MySpace (for a time), Orkut, and the rest of the social networking sites can also be viewed through the lens of crowdsourcing. That is, they answer the four questions with a compelling combination of good engineering, chutzpah (regarding privacy), networked innovation (in games and charitable contributions especially), editorial and related rule setting, and, most crucially, major network effects: The more of my friends who join, the more compelled I am to become a member.

Building

Linux and Wikipedia possess a structure that separates them from other types of sites. By building an "architecture of participation," to use the technical publisher Tim O'Reilly's apt phrase,[5] these efforts have shown the way for what Harvard law professor Yochai Benkler (see Chapter 8) has called "commons-based peer production."[6] Nobody is "in charge," in that tasks are taken up voluntarily in response to self-identified needs. Multiple efforts might be directed at the same issue, making crowdsourcing "wasteful" of resources when viewed from a traditional managerial perspective. As we saw in regard to long tails, however, there is room in these participatory architectures for both heavy contributors and extremely casual ones.

Much like natural selection, competing solutions can be compared or possibly interbred to create "offspring" with the best characteristics of the previous-generation donor ideas. When Darwinian struggle does ensue (check the Wikipedia edits history for some sense of how vigorous these contests can be), the overall intellectual quality of the effort is usually the winner. The quality of Linux, particularly in the domains most valued by its user-builders—robustness and security—testifies to the magic of the crowdsourced approach.

A different approach to writing code is to turn it into a game, specifically a contest. TopCoder takes software tasks and breaks them into chunks, with specific performance criteria. Prize money goes to the top two entries in most cases. Importantly, a subsequent contest for the community, which currently numbers more than 300,000, is to test the winning code. Programmers compete not just for money but also (yet again) peer recognition. In a classic two-sided platform play, TopCoder attracks both talented programmers but also top-shelf clients including NASA, Eli Lilly, and the National Security Agency. Such interest comes because the model works: Defects run well below the industry average while project completion is about 50% faster.[7]

Grunt Work

Finally, crowds can do mundane tasks in networks of undifferentiated contributors. The SETI@home project, in which computing cycles were harvested from screen savers to chug through terabytes of radiotelegraphic space noise in the search for life outside earth, is crowdsourcing of people's computers. The zombie-bot networks of exploited machines that generate spam or denial-of-service attacks constitute a dark-side example of crowdsourcing, albeit involuntary.

Amazon's Mechanical Turk (named for an eighteenth-century chess-playing automaton with a human hidden inside) delegates what it calls

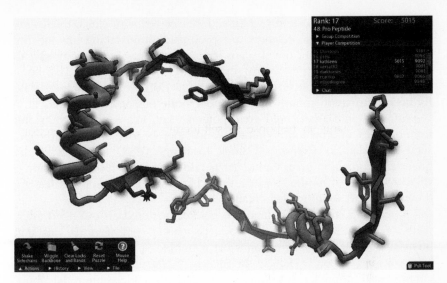

FIGURE 11.1 Foldit: An Online Game that Lets Crowds Try to Solve Biochemical Puzzles
Source: University of Washington Center for Game Science.

HITs: Human Intelligence Tasks. Naming the subjects of a photograph is a classic example, as is scanning aerial photographs for traces of wreckage, as when the noted balloonist and pilot Steve Fossett crashed in Nevada.[8] The *Guardian* example noted earlier shows how random volunteers, needing no special expertise or creativity, can help parse large data sets.

Grunt work can be fun, for the right people. Scientists at the University of Washington have helped create a 3-D online game called Foldit to apply human ingenuity, at a mass scale, to protein folding problems: People, it turns out, are better at spatial reasoning than computers. (See Figure 11.1.) Before drugs can be designed, the crystal structure of the target must be understood. In 2011, the game helped solve the structure of a protein that is related to the AIDS virus. Three different players made key contributions on which the research team could build. The structure of the M-PMV retroviral protease had been a mystery for roughly a decade; the gamers helped solve it in 16 days.[9]

Information Markets and Other Crowd Wisdom

Crowds also can accomplish work through market mechanisms. We've seen markets process information for a long time: When the National Basketball Association addressed the scandal surrounding its referee

Tim Donaghy*, the situation highlighted the secrecy with which the league assigns refs to games. Referees are prohibited from telling anyone but immediate family about travel plans, because the Las Vegas point spread moves if the refereeing crews are revealed ahead of game time. That point spread is a highly nuanced information artifact of a market compensating for new information about relevant inputs to the outcome of a game.

Information markets hold great potential but, like real markets, suffer from bubbles, information asymmetry, and other externalities. Nevertheless, such exemplars as Hollywood Stock Exchange (HSX) (now owned by financial information giant Cantor Fitzgerald), the Iowa Electronic Markets (IEM) for political futures, and start-ups like Fluid Innovation are leading the way toward wider implementation.

It seems clear that U.S. financial markets suffered an extended aftermath of an inflated mortgage-products market, but it turns out that financial scholars can't agree on what a bubble is. According to Cornell University's Maureen O'Hara in the *Review of Financial Studies*,[10] the "less controversial" approach is to follow one scholar's mild assertion that "bubbles are typically associated with dramatic asset price increases, followed by a collapse." Begging the question of what constitutes a collapse, the issue for our purposes concerns the potential for bubble equivalents in information markets. It's worth discussing some of the larger issues.

How Do Crowds Express Wisdom or, to Use a Less Loaded Phrase, Process Information?

Several ways of processing information come to mind. In many cases, crowdsourcing and information markets overlap when enough tags have been contributed, or enough votes tabulated, to give the recommendation the weight of an informal market mechanism:

- *Voting*, whether officially in the process of politics, or unofficially with product reviews, Digg or similar feedback ("Was this review helpful?"). All of these actions are voluntary and unsolicited, making statistical significance a moot point.
- *Surveys*, constructed with elaborate statistical tools and focused on carefully focused questions. Interaction among respondents is usually low, making surveys useful in collecting independent opinions.

---

*Tim Donaghy resigned from his position as a National Basketball Association referee when it was found that he had bet on games he officiated (and whose outcome he presumably affected). He later served time in federal prison for his role in a larger betting scandal.

- *Convened feedback,* a catch-all that includes tagging, blogs and comments, message boards, trackbacks, wikis, and similar vehicles. Once again, the action is voluntary, but the field of play is unconstrained. Compared to the other three categories, convened feedback can contain substantial noise, but its free form allows topics to emerge from the group rather than from the pollster, market maker, or publisher.
- *Betting,* the putting of real (as at IEM) or imagined (at HSX) currency where one's mouth is. Given the right kind of topic and the right kind of crowd, this process can be extremely powerful, albeit with constrained questions. We will focus on the market process for the remainder of our discussion.

What Kinds of Questions Best Lend Themselves to Group Wisdom?

On this topic of targets for collective information processing Surowieki is direct: "Groups are only smart when there is a balance between the information that everyone in the groups shares and the information that each of the members of the group holds privately." Conversely, "what happens when [a] bubble bursts is that the expectations converge."[11] In contests and other group effort scenarios such as those noted earlier, bubbles are less of an issue, but markets as processing mechanisms appear to have this particular weakness.

Cass Sunstein, a University of Chicago law professor when he wrote it, agrees in his book *Infotopia.*[12] He states: "This is the most fundamental limitation of prediction markets: They cannot work well unless investors have dispersed information that can be aggregated." Elsewhere in a blog post he notes that in an informal experiment with University of Chicago law professors, the crowd came extremely close to the weight of the horse that won the Kentucky Derby, did "pretty badly" on the number of lines in Shakespeare's *Antigone,* and performed "horrendously" when asked the number of Supreme Court invalidations of state and federal law. He speculates that markets employ some self-selection bias: "[P]articipants have strong incentives to be right, and won't participate unless they think they have something to gain."[13]

The best questions for prediction markets, then, involve issues about which people have formed independent judgments and on which they are willing to stake a financial and/or reputational investment. It may be that the topics cannot be too close to one's professional interests, as the financial example would suggest, and in line with the accuracy of the HSX Oscar predictions, which traditionally run about 85%.

Where Is Error Introduced?

The French political philosopher Condorcet (1743–1794) originally formulated the jury theorem that explains the wisdom of groups of people, when each individual is more than 50% likely to be right. Bad things happen when people are less than 50% likely to be right, however, at which time crowds then amplify error.

Numerous experiments have shown that group averages suffer when participants start listening to outside authorities or to each other. What Sunstein called "dispersed information" and what Surowiecki contrasts to mob behavior—independence—is more and more difficult to find. Many of the start-ups in idea markets include chat features—they are, after all, often social networking plays—making for yet another category of echo chamber.

Another kind of error comes when predictions ignore randomness. Particularly in thickly traded markets with many actors, the complexity of a given market can expose participants to phenomena for which there is no logical explanation—even though many will be offered. As Nassim Nicholas Taleb pointed out in *The Black Swan*, newswire reports on market movement routinely and fallaciously link events and price changes: It's not uncommon to see the equivalent of both "Dow falls on higher oil prices" and "Dow falls on lower oil prices" headlines during the same day.[14]

Varieties of Market Experience

Some of the many businesses seeking to monetize prediction markets are listed next.

- Newsfutures (now Lumenogic) makes a business-to-business play, building internal prediction markets for the likes of Eli Lilly, the Department of Defense, and Yahoo.
- Spigit sells as enterprise software to support internal innovation and external customer interaction. Communities are formed to collect and evaluate new ideas.
- Intrade is an Irish firm that trades in real money (with a play money sandbox) applied to questions in politics, business (predictions on market share are common), entertainment, and other areas. The business model is built on small transaction fees on every trade.
- Other prediction markets or related efforts focus on sports. YooNew was a futures market in sports tickets that suffered in the aftermath of the 2008 credit crunch. Hubdub used to be a general-purpose prediction market but it has since tightened its focus.

Apart from social networking plays and predictions, seemingly trivial commitments to intellectual positions work elsewhere. Sunstein's more recent book, called *Nudge*, was coauthored with the Chicago behavioral economist Richard Thaler.[15] It points to the value of commitment for such personal behaviors as weight loss or project fulfillment. For example, a PhD candidate, already hired as a lecturer at a substantial discount from an assistant professor's salary, was behind on his dissertation. Thaler made him write a $100 check at the beginning of every month a chapter was due. If the chapter came in on time, the check was ripped up. If the work came in late, the $100 went into a fund for a grad student party to which the candidate would not be invited. The incentive worked, notwithstanding the fact that $400 or $500 was a tiny portion of the salary differential at stake. A Yale economics professor who lost weight under a similar game has cofounded stickK.com, an ad-funded online business designed to institutionalize similar "commitment contracts." These commitments are a particular form of crowdsourcing, to be sure, but the combination of both real and reputational currencies with networked groups represents a consistent thread with more formal market mechanisms.

Looking Ahead

It's clear that crowds can in fact be smart when the members don't listen to each other too closely. It's also clear that financial and/or reputational investment are connected to both good predictions and fulfilled commitments. Several other issues are less obvious. Is there a novelty effect with prediction markets? Will clever people and/or software devise ways to game the system, similar to short-selling in finance or sniping on eBay? What do prediction bubbles look like, and what are their implications? When are crowds good at answering questions and when, if ever, are they good at posing them? (Note that on most markets, individuals can ask questions, not groups.) Can we reliably predict whether a given group will predict wisely?

At a larger level, how do online information markets relate to older forms of group expression, particularly voting? In the United States, the filtration of a state's individual votes through the winner-take-all Electoral College is already controversial (currently only Maine and Nebraska allot their votes proportionately), and so-called National Popular Vote legislation has been in states with 77 electoral votes—not yet enough to overturn the current process. Will some form of prediction market or other crowd wisdom accelerate or obviate this potential change?

Any process that can, under the right circumstances, deliver such powerful results will surely have unintended consequences. The controversy over John Poindexter's Futures Markets Applied to Prediction (FutureMAP) program, which was canceled by DARPA* in July 2003, will certainly not be the last of the tricky issues revolving around this class of tools.[16]

As blogging, social networking, and user-generated content proliferate, we're seeing one manifestation of a larger trend toward delegitimization of received cultural authority. Doctors are learning how to respond to patients with volumes of research, expert and folk opinion, and a desire to dictate rather than receive treatment. Instead of trusting politicians, professional reviewers, or commercial spokespeople, many people across the world are putting trust in each other's opinions: Zagat is a great example of "expert" ratings systems being challenged by masses of uncredentialed, anonymous diners.

Zagat also raises the issue of when crowds can be "wise," cannot possibly be "wise," or generally do not matter one way or the other: For all the masses of opinions coalescing online, at the end of the day, how many serve any purpose beyond amplified venting? At the same time, businesses are getting more skilled in harvesting the wisdom of crowds, so while there will always be anonymous noise, mechanisms are emerging to collect the value of people's knowledge and instincts.

Notes

1. James Surowiecki, *The Wisdom of Crowds: Why the Many Are Smarter Than the Few and How Collective Wisdom Shapes Business, Economies, Societies and Nations* (New York: Doubleday, 2004).
2. Michael Andersen, "Four Crowdsourcing Lessons from the Guardian's (Spectacular) Expenses-Scandal Experiment," Niemen Journalism Lab blog, Harvard University, June 23, 2009, www.niemanlab.org/2009/06/four-crowd sourcing-lessons-from-the-guardians-spectacular-expenses-scandal-experiment/.
3. Anhai Doan, Raghu Ramakrishnam, and Alon Y. Halevy, "Crowdsourcing Systems on the World-Wide Web," *Communications of the ACM* 54 (April 2011): 88.
4. "Thanks, YouTube community, for two BIG gifts on our sixth birthday!" Youtube, May 25, 2011, http://youtube-global.blogspot.com/2011/05/thanks-youtube-community-for-two-big.html.
5. Tim O'Reilly, "The Architecture of Participation," June 2004, http://oreilly.com/pub/a/oreilly/tim/articles/architecture_of_participation.html.

---

*Founded in 1958 in response to Sputnik, the Defense Advanced Research Projects Agency serves as the research and development function for the U.S. Department of Defense. Its work led to GPS, the Internet, both stealth and unmanned aviation technologies, and other still-classified innovations.

6. Yochai Benkler, *The Wealth of Networks: How Social Production Transforms Markets and Freedom* (New Haven, CT: Yale University Press, 206), p. 60.
7. Alpheus Bingham, and Dwayne Spradlin, *The Open Innovation Marketplace: Creating Value in the Challenge-Driven Enterprise* (London: FT Press, 2011), pp. 158–161.
8. Michael Arrington, "Search for Steve Fossett Expands to Amazon's Mechanical Turk," TechCrunch blog, September 8, 2007, http://techcrunch .com/2007/09/08/search-for-steve-fossett-expands-to-amazons-mechanical-turk/.
9. Kyle Niemeyer, "Gamers Discover Protein Structure that Could Help in War on HIV," Ars Technica, September 21, 2011, http://arstechnica.com/science/news/2011/09/gamers-discover-protein-structure-relevant-to-hiv-drugs.ars.
10. Maureen O'Hara, "Bubbles: Some Perspectives (and Loose Talk) from History," *Review of Financial Studies* 21, no. 1 (2008): 11–17. Available at SSRN: http://ssrn.com/abstract=1151603.
11. Surowiecki, *Wisdom of Crowds*, pp. 255–256.
12. Cass R. Sunstein, *Infotopia: How Many Minds Produce Knowledge* (New York: Oxford University Press, 2006), pp. 136–137.
13. "Are Crowds Wise?" Lessig blog post, July 19, 2005, http://lessig.org/blog/2005/07/are_crowds_wise.html.
14. Taleb, *The Black Swan*, p. 74.
15. Thaler and Sunstein, *Nudge: Improving Decisions about Health, Wealth, and Happiness* (New York: Penguin, 2009).
16. www.iwar.org.uk/news-archive/tia/futuremap-program.htm.

CHAPTER 12

Mobility

By looking at the ways that mobile phones and data devices are transforming developing economies, a contrast with more familiar patterns can emerge. While convenience, social needs, and an extension of desktop computing patterns can be observed in the United States and other locales in the Organization for Economic Cooperation and Development (OECD), in Kenya, the devices, payment processes, and application portfolio can differ significantly. In what is being termed "frugal innovation" or "reverse innovation," the developing countries are pioneering new uses and mental frameworks, showing more mature markets the way forward on critical axes such as disaster responsiveness.

Bottom Up

It's easy to look at the worldwide adoption of the mobile phone in quantitative terms and be amazed. The speed with which literally billions of the world's poorest people have gained access to or even possession of mobile telephony and then data services is staggering. In the late 1990s, it was commonplace to say "half the world has never made a phone call." That might have been true in 1985, but by 2000, it was nonsense. Even so, United Nations' Secretary General Kofi Annan said so. So did Al Gore, HP chief executive Carly Fiorina, and AOL founder Steve Case.

As Clay Shirky pointed out in a terrific essay from 2002, however, such assertions ignored truly explosive growth, first in land lines then in cellular: "[H]alf again as many land lines were run in the last 6 years of the 20th century as were run in the whole previous history of telephony."

That's a lot. But mobile phones were growing far faster: a tenfold (1,000%) increase in the five years ending in 2000.[1] That near billion then multiplied another five times in the following 10 years: That's an estimated 5 billion mobile phones on a planet of roughly 6.8 billion. India alone added 128 million subscribers—in one year.[2] The macro situation is summarized in Figure 12.1.

The infrastructure is keeping pace with the handsets: According to the International Telecommunications Union (ITU), 90% of the world's population has cellular coverage. Even Africa, at 50% coverage of the rural population, has grown from 20% only seven years earlier.[3] This is astounding growth: Again according to the ITU, "in 1985, some three billion people, or around half of the world's population, lived in economies with a teledensity (telephone lines per 100 inhabitants) of less than one. The global average teledensity was around seven."[4] Now there are about as many telephone connections as there are people, which is not the same as saying those connections are equally distributed. Even so, the planet has reached 100% teledensity, statistically anyway.

Three key business innovations helped facilitate this rapid growth. First, the lack of credit and banking structures for billions of people precluded adoption of the post-paid model, in which the carrier gives the subscriber credit up front and (ideally) collects bills based on use after the fact. *Prepaid phones* allowed users to pay "by the drink" and reduced credit risk for the carriers. Mom-and-pop convenience stores allow users to top-up minutes, multiplying the reach of the carrier beyond expensive company stores.

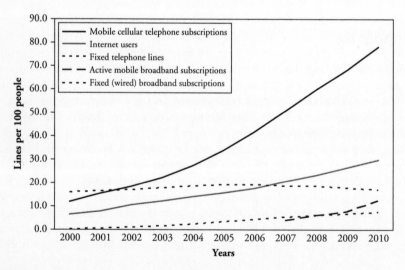

FIGURE 12.1 Mobile Telephones Compared to Other Technologies, 2000–2010
Source: International Telecommunications Union.

Second, the price of handsets was often subsidized in the West by long-term contracts: A Verizon cell phone might be only $40, but the two-year service contract, at (say) $50 per month means that the product/service bundle will cost the customer $1,240 over the life of the contract. That leaves plenty of pricing flexibility to sell the $40 handset at a loss. With the recognition of the size of the prepaid markets in such populous countries as Brazil, India, and Mexico, handset manufacturers were spurred by two factors: the size of the market for low-price phones and tough competition from each other. Motorola, to take one example, lost significant market share to South Korean companies in the early 2000s; Nokia, which sells well in the developing world, lost the smartphone market to Apple and the Google Android coalition a few years later. For both reasons, along with Chinese manufacturing costs and expertise, carriers in the developing world can offer *low-cost handsets* for a reasonable percentage of per capita monthly income. The Chinese firm Huawei also aggressively targeted the carrier equipment market, winning market share from Sweden's Ericsson for cellular transmission equipment.[5]

Finally, monthly subscription or per-minute prepaid charges dropped substantially in the face of *competition.* For many countries accustomed to government-sanctioned (or-run) telecom firms, the introduction of competition involved some cognitive dissonance, but prices in country after country dropped steeply after a second or third wireless carrier entered (or was allowed to enter) the market. Other entrants, in the form of wholesalers, helped lower costs as they helped network owners pay off capital investment as well as serve additional market segments.

But rather than look at teledensity and similar numbers, it's important to understand the *qualitative* differences that this rapid adoption of mobility is introducing. Jenny Aker and Isaac Mbiti undertook a systematic study titled "Mobile Phones and Economic Development in Africa" in 2010. They identify several mechanisms of impact, which I adapt slightly here.

- Mobile phones can improve access to and use of information, thereby reducing search costs, improving coordination among agents, and increasing market efficiency.
- This increased communication should improve firms' productive efficiency by allowing them to better manage their supply chains.
- Mobile phones create new jobs to address demand for mobile-related services, thereby providing income-generating opportunities in rural and urban areas.
- Mobile phones can facilitate communication among social networks in response to shocks, thereby reducing households' exposure to risk.
- Mobile phone-based applications and development projects—sometimes known as m-development—have the potential to facilitate the delivery of financial, agricultural, health, and educational services.[6]

Search Costs

Given the high degree of information asymmetry in the developing world, getting buyers and sellers on the same page can have substantial benefits. For agricultural goods, taking grain to market on foot or over long distances generally precluded bargaining: The price discovery effort was so great that hauling the crop home to wait for a better price was generally impractical. Simply being able to know the price before setting out is a significant advancement. Labor can be hired more efficiently as well, with faster responsiveness to changing conditions than can be achieved through newspapers, for example.

A Harvard economist found far-reaching benefits for the use of mobile phones in Indian sardine markets. Offshore, the fishermen had to commit to a port for fuel reasons without knowing the price or even if a buyer and ice would be available. If the fisherman guessed wrong, fish were dumped into the water at the port. An estimated 5% of the catch was wasted outright, and most fishermen sailed in and out of only one port even though multiple fish markets operated in a nine-mile range.

With the introduction of basic cell phone service around the turn of the twenty-first century, markets worked significantly better. Thirty-five percent of fisherman sailed to alternate ports once they got confirmation of a buyer. Fishermen's profits went up 8% while consumer prices fell 4%, presumably because the surplus fish were not wasted as often. Reduction in information asymmetry resulted in much closer pricing at markets up and down the coast. Better communication made one particular fishery market work better, and similar examples can be found in many developing economies.[7]

Supply Chain Efficiency

When the McKinsey Global Institute sought to explain the extraordinary growth in U.S. productivity between 1995 and 2000, technology in and of itself was difficult to isolate as a driver. Coupled with managerial innovation, however, such technologies as bar code scanning, electronic data interchange, and warehouse management software led to Wal-Mart and its supplier network helping to generate a substantial portion of that productivity increase. With 27% market share in the mid-1990s and a 48% productivity advantage over its peers, Wal-Mart's overall impact moved the aggregate U.S. productivity needle all by itself.[8]

While it's early and the large-scale managerial innovation for developing world supply chains is still primarily in the future, some examples are already showing up:

- In India, mobile phone calls are valuable even when the recipient does not pick up. The "missed call"* message on the phone conveys ample information at no cost since a call was not completed. When a businessman finishes a meeting, for example, he calls the taxi driver who had dropped him and waited, who does not answer but knows to pull the car to the front door of the meeting place.
- DHL, the global logistics firm, is experimenting with social networks as the "last mile" for package delivery in crowded urban environments. If a woman is taking public transit from location X to location Y, would she mind carrying a small parcel along in the trial bring. BUDDY program? Initial indications are positive, particularly in places with high carbon dioxide footprints and strong civic awareness.[9] Given that supply chains in South America include burros to take goods into poor neighborhoods, for example, overlaying social networks with logistics networks might work in some cities.
- Surveys in Africa found that something as simple as ordering replenishment of dwindling supplies via mobile phone should improve the percentage of stockouts in both consumer and business-to-business transactions. In addition, in line with the search costs mentioned earlier, low-cost suppliers are more easily identified, particularly by small business owners. Previously, replenishment often required travel to place an order. Finally in the world of small services business, many types of tradespeople found that 24-hour access was an important facet of their business.[10]

Mobile Phone Industry Impact

Just as the wireline telephone companies were often dominant players in their countries' economies, wireless companies generate noteworthy impact in the countries in which they operate. Wireless providers in Kenya, for example, employ more than 3,000 people directly.[11] In Senegal, while wireless officially employed only 415 people in 2007, 30,000 people worked in Internet cafés, call centers, and the like.[12] In addition, building a wireless network often requires capital investment in power generation and transmission, wireline backhaul networks, roads, rights-of-way, cell towers, billing and switching centers, and/or satellite uplinks. New businesses need legal determinations, business loans, real estate, and other services. The sum of all those categories of impact will

---

*In South Africa, the same practice is called "beeping" and may have different meanings attached to the number of rings that precede the disconnection.

certainly have increased in the intervening years in many developing countries.

Once again, numbers, even when available, do not tell the whole story. Mobile phones are changing the role of women in economies across the world, as when some daring Saudi Arabian women took to the roads in June 2011, driving cars as a form of social protest. Just as groups of women play a leading role in microfinance, they often help organize and run phone-sharing businesses in rural villages.[13] In Bangladesh, 50,000 women were estimated to make their living as "phone ladies" in 2002, a number that grew to 220,000 by 2008.[14]

Even in the poorest countries, a support industry for mobile phones has emerged. Given the low penetration of electricity, for example, enterprising businesses have emerged to charge mobile phones by transporting them to nearly villages or by building charging stations from car batteries or other apparatuses. Repairing is another frequent business opportunity: The hacking skill of a street vendor is often impressive, particularly when many mobile devices are designed not to be repaired, much less by someone who's possibly illiterate, self-taught, and lacks access to factory tools, software, and documentation. Whole physical shopping areas have emerged for a wide variety of mobile-related services in such cities as Kabul, Cairo, Mumbai, and elsewhere.[15]

Risk Mitigation

Aker and Mbiti say little other than that mobility helps reinforce the vitality of kinship networks, which has important roles for both the economy and society of many African countries. Hearing about impending weather would be another example for mobility-conferred advantage for farmers or other people exposed to the elements. Informal reference checks ("Does this person show up for work reliably?" "Does this customer pay her bills on time?") can become practical only in a mobile environment, particularly when written literacy may be limited. Penn State University's WishVast project in Kenya is an example of trying to use mobility to increase trust among potential economic participants who may lack kinship connections but wish to do business.[16]

Kinship networks in migratory cultures use mobility in complex ways. Women who grew accustomed to a certain degree of freedom while male heads of households left home for seasonal work, for example, now often have mobile phones with no balance—and thus no outbound calling—on which they get calls from the physically absent but emotionally very present male.[17] Mobile communications is changing gender relations in many other ways as well, as we will see.

Transparency can do more than help families and householders. The prospect of election monitoring, for example, should decrease corruption, ideally improving the place of the rule of law, enforceability of contracts, and other preconditions for economic advancement. Ushahidi, Swahili for "witness," is an open-source mapping and coordination platform first used in the 2008 Kenyan elections but since adapted to a wide variety of crisis-monitoring applications. In Mexico, for example, it was the basis for a vote fraud-monitoring tool called Cuidemos el Voto, or "Let's protect the vote together." Ushahidi has also been deployed in Haiti, in Japan, and in various countries during the swine flu outbreak. Wired applications would never have had the same impact or the same portability.

Similarly, controversy surrounds the role of mobile phones in the so-called Arab Spring of 2011, when 11 countries experienced major protests, civil uprisings, or a change of regime in the span of only six months or so. The Egyptian unit of Vodafone, through its advertising agency JWT, posted a video claiming it was the catalyst for the uprising that culminated in the removal of President Hosni Mubarak. Egyptian radicals claimed in response that political factors were far more important than any commercial representations of what JWT called "Our Power."[18] The issues are big and complicated, but in short, to say that mobile phones aid in risk mitigation only at the household level understates the case.

Apps for Change*

As *The Economist* clearly pointed out, mobility is making a bigger difference in the developing world than it is in OECD countries, where it is far from trivial. But rather than Facebook, photo-sharing, or Angry Birds, the apps that matter in Africa, India, and elsewhere affect life expectancy, income per household, and the survival of democracy. In these areas, innovation in Africa and elsewhere is actually outpacing what is possible where more established alternatives to mobility—such as clinics, branch banks, or long-standing rule of law—have become part of the landscape. Indeed, a wide body of thought and practice is springing up around the notion of "reverse innovation" or its relative, "frugal innovation," in which new products and services are designed for the special needs of emerging markets rather than being old, stripped-down, or ill-fitting versions of offers first seen in the United States, wealthy parts of Australasia,

---

*I borrow the title from a Nokia-sponsored competition for which I was a judge. The winning idea activated one's social network in the event of need for blood donation.

or Europe.[19] Reverse innovation need not involve telecommunications—important new marketing practices involve smaller packaging for soap, for example—but clearly some exciting possibilities ride on the wireless airwaves.

The entire notion of a semiopen platform on which third-party applications can be developed is new; before 2008, getting software onto a cellular carrier's devices was difficult. Revenue sharing, security, bandwidth limitations, time to market, and a lack of unifying standards meant that few start-ups dared develop for the mobile phone or, more precisely, dozens of them: Button location, screen size and resolution, programming language, and localization of language and currency posed daunting technical problems even before questions of revenue, marketing, sales, and customer service were brought into the discussion.

Even without looking at the smartphone application explosion on Android and Apple, clever use of text messaging and other rudimentary data tools is making possible substantial gains in many areas: Most mobile phones in the developing world lack large screens and powerful data capabilities, as do the carrier networks in the latter instance. Two examples follow.

Mobile Money

Mobile financial applications, commonly known as m-money or m-banking, came to market in 2005 in several developing countries. Specifics vary: The application might come from a mobile carrier, a bank, or a joint effort; it might allow international money transfers or not; payment and storage of value options vary. According to Mobile Money Live, 20 million people in developing countries should have access by 2012.[20]

The basic functionality generally allows mobile subscribers or banking customers to store value in an account accessible by the handset, convert cash in and out of the stored value account, and transfer value between users by using a set of text messages, menu commands, and personal identification numbers (PINs).

As with Ushahidi, Kenya is leading the way. Safaricom's M-Pesa mobile money program launched in 2007,* with rapid uptake: About two years later, roughly 40 percent of Kenyans had already used the service to send or receive money. A popular feature is remittance from Kenyans abroad: M-Pesa allows someone in England, say, to send part of his or her

---

*With help from a U.K. development organization, the Department for International Development; Safaricom is part of U.K.-based Vodafone: www.dfid .gov.uk/Global-Issues/Emerging-policy/Wealth-creation-private-sector/Finance/.

paycheck home, at rates lower than Western Union, with greater coverage. Within Kenya, M-Pesa charged roughly 60% less than the post office for a simple transfer.

According to the carrier, in only two years, the cumulative value of the money transferred via M-Pesa was over $3.7 billion—nearly 10 percent of Kenya's annual gross domestic product. A fascinating question relates to whether M-Pesa is a mobile wallet or a mobile bank: It began as a transfer mechanism but now offers seamless links to interest-paying savings accounts. More questions relate to whether groups or individuals will change their saving or spending habits and whether various forms of fraud might slow the rapid growth of the service. As microfinance evolves, entities such as post offices will likely emerge as partners with carriers, development agencies, and other trusted entities to build capability further.

Side Effects of Mobile Money: Afghanistan

Afghanistan in 2001 had little infrastructure and no banking system; all transactions were conducted in cash at the time that American troops were deployed to the country. As of 2010, 97% of the country remains "unbanked," but mobile money is proving to reduce corruption. The country has a teledensity approaching 50: 12 million cell phones in country of 28 million.

According to two former U.S. Army officers, one of whom served in Afghanistan (the other was in Iraq):

In 2009, the Afghan National Police began a test to pay salaries through mobile telephones rather than in cash. It immediately found that at least 10% of its payments had been going to ghost policemen who didn't exist; middlemen in the police hierarchy were pocketing the difference. Salaries for Afghan police and soldiers are calculated to be competitive with Taliban salaries, but beat cops and deployed soldiers had been receiving only a fraction of the amount paid by U.S. taxpayers because of corruption in the payment system. Most Afghan cops assumed that they had been given a significant raise when, in fact, they simply received their full pay for the first time—over the phone.[21]

Mobile Health

Given the state of healthcare in much of the developing world, replicating western methods will have only limited success. Decentralized approaches, peer-to-peer practices, and remote diagnostics and treatment all show great promise. Thus far, many health initiatives are philanthropically funded, but a new generation of indigenous entrepreneurs is launching a series of home-grown applications in the field of so-called m-health.

Data collection is one prime opportunity. Given the state of health statistics, rapid knowledge of infectious outbreaks, for example, can deliver significant benefits to patients, caregivers, and aid organizations. Basic information provision is another opportunity. HIV-positive patients in several African countries receive text messages reminding them about their medication schedule. University student Josh Nesbit built a simple SMS application for health-delivery workers in Malawi in 2007 that merged with other efforts to become Medic Mobile, an open-source platform helping to provide a management layer for information gathering, patient follow-up, and other nontherapeutic aspects of healthcare: Time savings from not having to walk miles to report symptoms or coordinate treatment amounted to thousands of hours in the pilot tests.[22]

Bright Simons is a Ghanaian entrepreneur who developed mPedigree, a simple text-based system for identifying counterfeit pharmaceuticals. Globally, an estimated 10% to 25% of all drugs sold are fake, but in some developing countries, the number can reach 80%, according to the World Health Organization. With mPedigree, a scratch-off panel on the packaging reveals a number code. The patient texts the number to a validation site, which signals whether the number is legitimate. As of mid-2011, the program was running in Ghana, India, Rwanda, and the Philippines.[23]

Sensors of many shapes and sizes are being coupled to mobile phones for remote diagnosis and monitoring. Mobile instruments able to measure everything from electrocardiograms, to blood slides, to blood pressure are being tested; remote access to even basics such as body weight and temperature has value and represents an improvement over the current situation in which a caregiver can be hundreds of miles away. Just for comparison, Germany has 3.4 doctors for 1,000 citizens; Kenya has 1.4 for every 10,000 people.

Looking Ahead

Mobility in the developing world represents several things. First, it is both an instance of and a platform for frugal innovation. Second, it is emerging in cultural ways that differ from the path to mobility in the OECD countries, given that landlines in many countries were nearly nonexistent. The overlay of cellular networks on top of tribal, kin, and other networks will be fascinating to watch and to learn from. Third, the difference between applications that range from the trivial to the helpful in the West and the truly life-altering possibilities presented by job hunting, agricultural price discovery, and healthcare provision on the mobile net is substantial: Rarely can anyone on a smartphone claim that the device is a matter of life-changing importance, whereas the millions of people connecting for the first time are voting with their precious income on exactly that fact.

Notes

1. Clay Shirky, "Half the World," Clay Shirky's Writings About the Internet, September 3, 2002, www.shirky.com/writings/half_the_world.html.
2. "A Special Report on Telecoms in Emerging Markets: Mobile Marvels," *The Economist*, September 24, 2009, www.economist.com/node/14483896.
3. International Telecommunications Union, 2010 World Telecommunication/ ICT Development Report, www.itu.int/dms_pub/itu-d/opb/ind/D-IND-WTDR-2010-PDF-E.pdf.
4. Tim Kelly, "Twenty Years of Measuring the Missing Link," www.itu.int/osg/ spu/sfo/missinglink/kelly-20-years.pdf.
5. "Huawei Aims to Beat Ericsson in New Gear Orders," *Bloomberg Businessweek*, November 17, 2010, www.businessweek.com/news/2010-11-17/ huawei-aims-to-beat-ericsson-in-new-gear-orders.html.
6. Jenny Aker and Isaac Mbiti, "Mobile Phones and Economic Development in Africa," Center for Global Development Working Paper 211 (June, 1 2010): 8, www.cgdev.org/content/publications/detail/1424175/.
7. Robert Jensen, "The Digital Provide: Information (Technology), Market Performance, and Welfare in the South Indian Fisheries Sector," *The Quarterly Journal of Economics* 122, no. 3 (2007): pp 879–924, http://qje.oxfordjournals .org/content/122/3/879.abstract - fn-1. See also "To Do with the Price of Fish," *The Economist*, May 10, 2007, www.economist.com/node/9149142.
8. McKinsey Global Institute, "US Productivity Growth 1995–2000: Understanding the Contribution of Information Technology Relative to Other Factors," October 2001, www.mckinsey.com/mgi/publications/us/index.asp.
9. www.forbes.com/sites/billbarol/2010/11/26/bring-buddy-dhl-crowdsources-your-grandma/ www.livinglabs-global.com/showcase/showcase/392/bringbuddy.aspx.
10. Jonathan Samuel, Niraj Shah, and Wenona Hadingham, "Mobile Communications in South Africa, Tanzania and Egypt: Results from Community and Business Surveys," *Vodafone Policy Papers Series* no. 3 (March 2005): 44–52.
11. Timothy Waema, Catherine Adeya, and Margaret Nyambura Ndung'u, *Kenya ICT Sector Performance Review 2009–2010*, researchICTAfrica.net, www .researchictafrica.net/publications/Policy_Paper_Series_Towards_Evidence-

based_ICT_Policy_and_Regulation_-_Volume_2/Vol%202%20Paper%2010%20-%20Kenya%20ICT%20Sector%20Performance%20Review%202010.pdf.

12. Mamadou Alhadji LY, *Senegal ICT Sector Performance Review 2009/2010*, researchICTAfrica.net, p. 27, www.researchictafrica.net/publications/Policy_Paper_Series_Towards_Evidence-based_ICT_Policy_and_Regulation_-_Volume_2/Vol_2_Paper_20_-_Senegal_ICT_Sector_Performance_Review_2010_English_Version.pdf.

13. "Grameen Phone—Turning Local Women into Telecom Entrepreneurs," http://social-enterprise.posterous.com/grameen-phone-turning-local-women-into-teleco.

14. Alfred Hermida, "Mobile Money Spinner for Women," *BBC*, October 8, 2002, http://news.bbc.co.uk/2/hi/technology/2254231.stm.

15. For an example, see the work of smartphone ethnographer Jan Chipchase at http://janchipchase.com/2006/10/value-added-services/.

16. http://sites.google.com/site/thewishvastproject/.

17. I am indebted to my student Amanda Hahnel for relating this insight from her internship in India.

18. "Vodafone Denies Using Arab Spring to Sell Phones," Channel 4 news, June 3, 2011, www.channel4.com/news/vodafone-denies-using-arab-spring-to-sell-phones.

19. See, for example, "First Break All the Rules: The Charms of Frugal Innovation," *The Economist*, April 15, 2010, www.economist.com/node/15879359.

20. www.wirelessintelligence.com/mobile-money/.

21. Dan Rice and Guy Filippelli, "One Cell Phone at a Time: Countering Corruption in Afghanistan," September 2, 2010 blog post, http://smallwarsjournal.com/blog/2010/09/one-cell-phone-at-a-time-count/.

22. N. Mahmud, J. Rodriguez, and J. Nesbit, "A Text Message-Based Intervention to Bridge the Healthcare Communication Gap in the Rural Developing World," *Journal of Technology and Health Care* 18, no. 2 (2010): 137–144.

23. www.mpedigree.net/mpedigree/index.php.

CHAPTER 13

Work

What constitutes work, where it happens, who does it, and how it is rewarded are all in flux. Multiple macro-level forces are responsible, and a full treatment of the question is out of our current scope. The interaction between people's work and their technologies has always been important, however, so some attention to the question is in line here.

The Big Picture: Macro Trends

Ever since its founding, the United States has steadily produced more and more economic value. In 1900, U.S. gross domestic product (GDP) per capita, in current dollars, was $268. By 1950, that figure had multiplied seven times to about $2,000. Between 1950 and 2000, the multiple was 18. To put that per capita figure in perspective, *real* GDP rose from $294 billion to $9,817 billion: a 33-fold increase. (The ratio of 18 to 33 suggests that total population nearly doubled, which it did, from 151 million to 281 million.)

The role of agriculture has changed in surprising ways. The number of farms in the United States in 1950 was almost the same as in 1900, a little over five and a half million after having peaked in the mid-1930s. By 2000, the number of farms had dropped to 2.2 million, but the average size, possibly reflecting the rise of organic farms, was actually dropping from its high in 1994. The amount of total acreage in farms reached its peak in 1953: For all the talk of urbanization in the late nineteenth century, it turns out that in 1950, the United States was still robustly rural, in land use terms anyway.

The surprising amount of farm acreage belied a strong population shift, however. In 1900, 41 percent of the U.S. workforce was employed in agriculture. The number fell to 16% in 1945 and to less than 2% in 2000, with most workers part time. Agriculture was less than 1% of GDP by that time, a ninth of what it had been in 1945.[1]

Where did people go when they left the farms, which were mostly located in the Midwest? South and west, of course: The 13 states that constitute the Census Bureau's West region (every state west of Texas) combined to grow from 13% of U.S. population in 1950 to 22.5% 50 years later. Surprisingly, the South increased only from 31% to 36%. Before talking about macroeconomic effects of computing, one has to appreciate the impact of other technologies, such as air conditioning, on where people live: Such fast-growing states as Virginia, Georgia, Texas, and Arizona can be uncomfortable and unhealthy without climate control. Air conditioning in turn raises the importance of electric power, which was still a novelty in the rural South in 1950.

Along with internal migration, the second half of the twentieth century was marked by broad social change: Political and economic involvement by women became broader, in terms of numbers, and deeper, in terms of impact. Women doubled their participation in the workforce, from 30% to 60% (see Figure 13.1, which begins at 1960), and now women often, but not routinely, hold seats as chief executives, senators, Supreme Court justices, and astronauts. Women also constitute well over half of the college population only a generation after having gained admittance to the leading private universities. The United States is also a much older nation than in 1950. Life expectancy at birth has risen from 68 to 77. Both of these trends relate closely to changes in medical technology and, for women, birth control. It will require further study to determine how much the increase in life expectancy relates to computing: Trends in immunization,

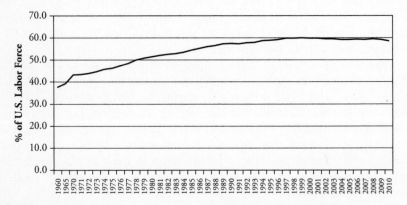

FIGURE 13.1 Female Participation in the U.S. Labor Force, 1960–2010
Source: U.S. Census.

smoking, nutrition, and cardiac interventions are, I suspect, far more important.

In demographic terms, the automobile stands out among technologies with major impact. The pervasiveness of its influence tracks closely with the invention and habitation of the suburb—a term that did not exist at the time of the 1900 census. But from 1910 until 1950, when the percentage of population in suburbs more than tripled, to 23% of the population, the rise of the automobile literally reshaped the landscape. In the 50 years of the information age that constitutes our focus here, the percentage of population in suburbs more than doubled: Fully half the U.S. population now lives in suburbs, a striking testimony to the geographic transition caused by the automobile.

Shifting from residence to occupation, manufacturing grew at agriculture's expense, as the air conditioning—and automobile-related figures would suggest. But while manufacturing employment peaked in 1979 at over 19 million jobs, it had been declining since 1953 as a percentage of total employment: The drop, from 1 job in 3 to 1 in 12, constitutes another defining characteristic of the past half century.

Where

As the world and the North American economy become more virtual, businesses are encountering new layers of the paradox of place. An Internet connection can link two people by voice, text chat, or video almost anywhere in the developed world, with many developing nations catching up fast. As coordination costs drop, work can more easily migrate to low-wage locales. For product work, that migration implies moving factories. More recently, services from radiology, to call centers, to coding have begun to be outsourced and/or offshored. One shorthand prediction calls China the emerging factory to the world, with India its back office. But costs are only one aspect of the tension between place and space.

The dynamics of place affect many business choices. Locating a factory or distribution center near a prime customer, as Dell's suppliers have near Austin, tightens tolerances on deliveries and can support higher levels of customer service. Moving research and development operations near major university centers, as Novartis and other companies have around MIT and Harvard, can impose high wage scales onto employers. For employers outside those sectors that do not require such specialized (and localized) expertise, Massachusetts is undesirable as a new business destination, and high housing prices are noted as a major deterrent to job growth there.

Richard Florida's influential book, *The Rise of the Creative Class*,[2] argued that rather than lobbying with tax breaks and other inducements for large Toyota or Mercedes factories, states and localities in search of jobs should instead seek to attract creative individuals. Because these people can do such tasks as stock picking, screenwriting, or software architecture essentially anywhere, they tend to migrate to places with good music and culture, interesting restaurants and diverse populations, and strong educational institutions. After arriving, they put their skills and networks together and make jobs for themselves and others. Florida's examples—San Francisco, Minneapolis, and Pittsburgh, among many others—appear to support his thesis. But another characteristic joins these places: Essential but noncreative people such as plumbers, police officers, teachers, and support personnel can get priced out of cities that he lists as exemplars.

The commuting distance for the working people who make creative centers work is increasing. These jobs matter for quality of life. Places like Marin County, California, and Greenwich, Connecticut, are undeniably appealing in many ways. But what happens when auto repair shops and dry cleaners can't survive? Many skilled jobs can be performed remotely, to be sure, but how can affluent, attractive locales keep nurses, delivery truck drivers, and other people whose skills are in short supply right now? Societies at all stages of economic development are experiencing the effects of selective job mobility in the aftermath of the Internet and cellular telephony revolutions.

There's another recent phenomenon of skills and place: Workers in skilled jobs (such as information technology) often are trained at academic centers far from an employer base. Kathy Brittain White served as chief information officer at Cardinal Health before founding Rural Sourcing, an American company that seeks to provide the cost savings of displacing work to a lower-cost, lower-wage environment. Her twist to the offshore model is locating programming and support centers in such places as Greenville, North Carolina—home to East Carolina University, which now enrolls more than 20,000 students.

Rural Sourcing uses networks to take relative isolation and turn it into comparative advantage. In a parallel move, Google opened major facilities in New York, Ann Arbor, and Pittsburgh, the latter because of Carnegie Mellon's powerful computer science presence. In the nineteenth century, proximity to water power made New England mill towns economic engines for the shoe and textile industries that were centered there. Detroit built on access to freighter ports that delivered the bulk materials for the auto industry (and on the venture capital provided by timber barons enriched by the need for mass-produced wooden furniture and building supplies).

Today, university towns are vying to attract knowledge-intensive industries, but what are the other sources of advantage for the next

25 years? If home-schooling continues its strong rise in popularity, more people might move to places without demonstrably good school systems. Telemedicine could reduce the urge to live near major medical centers. Long commutes have multiple negative side effects,[3] so towns with light traffic will likely increase in appeal. Online shopping addresses the concern about the lack of quality retailers in a given place. Many such wildcards remain to be played.

Far from the fields that White is cultivating, the place of cities remains contested and important. The public intellectual Jane Jacobs, a powerful voice in twentieth-century American urbanism, lacked academic credentials but argued for the organic aspects of cities. She opposed zoning, for example, reasoning that people should be able to live near their work. Her energy and ideas helped defeat some of the more sweeping "urban renewal" efforts of the 1950s and 1960s as citizen movements began to oppose the bulldozing of neighborhoods that happened to lie in the path of expressways. Criticized for advocating gentrification, she herself was priced out of Greenwich Village in the 1990s and found Toronto more hospitable to her thinking (and financial means) than her adopted New York, which she tended to idealize. Jacobs's crusade served as a reminder that the cost of the suburban model can be measured only partially in fuel consumption or rising commute times.[4]

The best-selling author Thomas Friedman famously asserted that "the world is flat" in his book of that name: Anyone anywhere can participate in the global economy via various connections.[5] Florida replied that, rather than being flat, "the world is spiky" in that concentrations of talent and resources matter more than the ubiquitous access Friedman chronicles. Instead of forcing these two arguments into false opposition, it is useful to use the insights of both to examine how connection is changing work, culture, and economics.

The uncomfortable juxtaposition of globalization and locality is not a new phenomenon—just look at England in the twilight of empire. If people earn money only from local sources but spend it on goods and, increasingly, services from "away," eventually money needs to come back into the locality: Just as a multicrop family farm is no longer a viable option for many, neither is a self-sustaining local economy. Somehow, money needs to come in as well as leave, and the current trade imbalance and federal debt levels both ratchet up that imperative.

Outputs

One of the great but difficult thinkers of the twentieth century, the economist and satirist Thorstein Veblen, wrestled with people's interconnected relationships both to what Karl Marx* named the means of production and to the consumption of mass-produced goods. Veblen attributed a nobility to work that he called the "instinct of workmanship": Man the maker "has a sense of the merit of serviceability or efficiency and of the demerit of futility, waste, or incapacity." By contrast, what Veblen memorably named "conspicuous consumption" was "ceremonial" in that it sorted people by reputation, the basis of an ultimately unwinnable competition.[6]

By mentioning Veblen I raise an unanswerable question. The people who buy mass-produced stuff, often called "consumers," want in some deep-rooted way to shape their environment beyond just piling up purchased goods. How much people want to stand out as unique, and how much they want to create something tangible, is of course impossible to differentiate or quantify, and sometimes an artifact embodies both consumption (or conspicuousness) and workmanship. But the current business landscape provides too many examples for this to be a fad: There's something very potent afoot in the rise of cooking shows, in "maker" culture, and in such phenomena as Habitat for Humanity.

Harvard professor Daniel Bell identified what he called the coming of postindustrial society more than 30 years ago, but it took the Internet for us to feel what it's like to transcend factories the way factories had trumped farming roughly a half-century before he wrote. As information about stuff becomes more valuable than stuff itself, the activities of creation and individualization take on a new shape in both tangible and intangible realms. First, in an economy largely devoted to nonessentials, there exists some (essential?) desire to make meaningful stuff, not just ideas and decisions. Second, we can see a broad-based quest to differentiate oneself by differentiating one's stuff. Finally, there's a sense of entitlement, related to the "affordable luxury" trend embodied by Starbucks, itself a primo customizer: I want the best (of something) made for me because I'm worth it.

Skills

Like many others, I persist in believing that the transformative power of computing lies ahead of us. Whether it's in genome-aware therapeutics, or rich-media self-publishing, or low-cost avionics that make small jets feasible as air taxis, the majority of digital innovations that will remake the

---

*German political philosopher and progenitor of social science, whose ideas underlie modern communism (1818–1883).

economy are as yet uncommercialized. And compared to such landmarks as the invention of the steam engine or the factory system, our 50 years of computing represents enormous change in short time. The daunting fact is that the change to come looms even bigger.

In the interim, the demands of a digital economy contribute to complex and difficult demographic issues: skill- and education-based bifurcation, along with a changing racial composition. In the middle of the twentieth century, factory work paid better than farm work and was widely accessible at the low end. People could leave farms, enter manufacturing with no or few skills and little education, and stay afloat. A further correlate here is decentralization: Factory work collects resources in one place while services industries (and powerful communications networks) disperse them. What are the consequences of the growth of the South and West without a heavy reliance on industrial centers such as Milwaukee, Pittsburgh, or Detroit?

Prior to and during World War II, the internal migration of black Americans from the rural South to the industrial Midwest led to such varied changes as a rebirth of popular music, a power base for the Democratic party, and the rise of a black middle class. Only one or two cultural hops separate Henry Ford from Diana Ross, Lyndon Johnson, and the *Cosby Show*. Look a little closer and you see the Rolling Stones, Magic Johnson's National Basketball Association, and Oprah Winfrey, who was born in Mississippi but made her name in Chicago.

Now the opposite dynamic is at work as manufacturing automation and globalization release workers to take jobs in lower-paying categories, such as hospital food service or big-box retail; in raw numbers, the biggest job creators for several years after 2001 were Home Depot and Lowe's, and of course Wal-Mart's net role in employment remains hotly disputed. Retail and other services often teach their workers how to use automated systems but rarely prepare them to enter a better-paying sector. How the shift to services interrelates with America's racial picture, including of course the emerging Hispanic majority, will be critically important to track.

As the CIA's *World Factbook* puts the issue:

> *The onrush of technology largely explains the gradual develop-*
> *ment of a "two-tier labor market" in which those at the bottom*
> *lack the education and the professional/technical skills of those*
> *at the top and, more and more, fail to get comparable pay raises,*
> *health insurance coverage, and other benefits. Since 1975, practi-*
> *cally all the gains in household income have gone to the top 20%*
> *of households.*[7]

The consequences of such a bifurcated populace touch sociology, politics, economics, and even ethics, so I won't even attempt a summary comment. Perhaps this trend is the result of moving farther and farther from a subsistence economy. One of the things we'll be tracking as this research progresses is the changing composition of the economy away from food, clothing, and shelter to transportation, entertainment, and other luxuries. The interplay of rapid population growth, rapid increase in the amount of livable and available real estate, wider education, suburbanization, and the shift to a services economy all contribute to making the task of assessing information's role highly problematic.

Work

What have computers and the digital revolution done to work? Answers vary considerably. In 1992, Robert Reich (later Bill Clinton's secretary of labor) devised a tripartite schema to classify the workers of the world, seeing global workforces as already having been divided into three groups: routine producers (e.g., call center reps or assembly-line workers), in-person servers (waiters or nurses), and symbolic analysts who manipulate pure information for large profits (Wall Street quants). Digitization in the service of high leverage made the "symbolic analysts" rich and skewed income distribution. Seeing the relation of rich to poor less than 20 years later, Reich may have been onto something crucial, but his tepid solution—training and education—has failed to shift the terms of the debate, partly because school systems change incredibly slowly and require levels (and types) of investment that are for a number of reasons politically impossible in the United States.

A decade later, Richard Florida defined the engine of the new economy as the "creative class," 38 million of whom comprised 30% of the workforce. For the winners, digitization empowers flexible work that gives great meaning:

> *In this new world, it is no longer the organizations we work for, churches, neighborhoods, or even family ties that define us. Instead, we do this ourselves, defining our identities along the varied dimensions of our creativity. Other aspects of our lives— what we consume, new forms of leisure and recreation, efforts at community-building—then organize themselves around this process of identity creation.*[8]

Surely 30% of the workforce can't work at ad agencies or Disney. No, says Florida:

> *I define the core of the Creative Class to include people in sci-*
> *ence and engineering, architecture and design, education, arts,*
> *music and entertainment, whose economic function is to create*
> *new ideas, new technology and/or new creative content. Around*
> *the core, the Creative Class also includes a broader group of cre-*
> *ative professionals in business and finance, law, health care and*
> *related fields.*

The core and the doughnut are linked not by geography or income or skills but by a value set:

> *[A]ll members of the Creative Class—whether they are artists or engi-*
> *neers, musicians or computer scientists, writers or entrepreneurs—*
> *share a common creative ethos that values creativity, individuality,*
> *difference and merit. For the members of the Creative Class, every*
> *aspect and every manifestation of creativity—technological, cultural*
> *and economic—is interlinked and inseparable.*[9]

Whatever its relation to life as most people know it, Florida's book resonated. It led to a thriving consulting business helping cities attempt to become more economically competitive. How? Not with tax incentives for auto plants but by luring more of those 38 million people with more tolerant attitudes, better mass transit, more authentic espresso bars, and the other factors that separate Toronto from Topeka or Minneapolis from Modesto.

In the intervening years, however, much has happened to cast doubt on Florida's vision of the future. What exactly do those creative people do to help the U.S. balance of trade deficit? Movies, mergers and acquisition deals, and Microsoft all contribute to exports, but not to the degree that farm goods do, and none approaches the aerospace sector's international impact. What happens when offshore competition threatens large numbers of those 38 million jobs? Legal research, programming, equity analysis, and even moviemaking and distance learning are already being produced and delivered from afar in lower-wage settings—what will be next?

More fundamentally, just how creative are those 38 million people? Job titles can be deceiving: A good friend of mine was for a time an architect at HOK, the sports division of which has given us such modern monuments as Camden Yards in Baltimore or AT&T Park in San Francisco. What was our young Howard Roark's creative contribution? Bathrooms for the Hong Kong airport.

Matthew Crawford, in a recent book called *Shop Class as Soulcraft*, raises similar doubts.[10] Beginning with the observation that many high schools are dropping shop class because it fails to train people to be symbolic analysts, Crawford challenges the reader to think deeply about the value of work. Because it often lacks real output, modern bureaucratic life, defined largely by office automation, can be unfulfilling. In contrast to the carpenter whose windows can't leak, or the farmer who feeds people with tangible crops or livestock, the office worker (creative or not) lacks physical boundaries to define the real from the artificial or the possible from the impossible.

As Crawford notes, quoting Robert Jackall's *Moral Mazes* (now 20 years old), office memos are crafted to be unincriminating no matter how subsequent events play out. Taking a firm stand is often seen as career limiting, so most eventualities remain unforeclosed; every statement is hedged. Along similar lines, after receiving a PhD from the University of Chicago, Crawford works for a think tank generating position papers that begin not with the facts but with a position, reasoning backward to convenient truths. It is intellectual bad faith of the first order, and he quits. Worse yet, in his circles of occupational hell, are jobs built on teams with their indeterminate appropriation of credit and blame, along with the human resource-driven trust-building games that frequently pass the point of self-parody.

In contrast, the author points to his work as a motorcycle mechanic. No symbolic analyst he, Crawford confronts physical limits every day and pays a steep price for failure. If he drops a washer into a crankcase, at times he must tear down the engine block to retrieve it and cannot in good conscience bill the customer for all of the hours involved. Mistakes, stupid or otherwise, have concrete consequences. On the positive side of the ledger, when he fixes a broken fork, returns a dead bike to life after 10 years off the road, or hears the particular sound of a well-tuned engine, he derives great satisfaction. He also contends that mechanical work can be more intellectually engaging than knowledge work, implicitly challenging Florida's new world order.

In some measure, we are fighting a new stage of the philosophical battle joined by Rene Descartes (1596–1650), who separated thought from emotion and thereby physicality. Craft work (fixing or building things) joins the practice of medicine, certainly, but also full-throated singing as moments where mind and body unite. Sport constitutes another similar realm, as does cooking, the recent enthusiasm for which might be seen as a reassertion of the satisfaction that can come only when head, hands, and palate unite in a primal act—that of feeding another person. Compare the gestalt of today's many cooking shows to the treatment of the modern workplace in current television programming and the contrast is obvious: Julia Child, enshrined at the Smithsonian, is a hero while cubicle America's cultural icon has yet to transcend the comic strip Dilbert.

Shop Class as Soulcraft also makes the pragmatic point that fixing things cannot be offshored; one can make a healthy living as an electrician, for example, or an auto repairman. Last time I was in for an oil change, my mechanic was telling me about one manufacturer's switch to a fiber-optic system bus—he knows more computer networking than I ever will. To service appliances or furnaces today is to have studied hundreds of hours of digital control and monitoring technology. High schools, however, generally operate under the principle that college-bound students will have better careers than those who work in jobs that require mere training. But what economists call the education premium can no longer be assured today, much less in 50 years when today's high school graduates will almost certainly still be working.

There's also the matter of permanence. As Crawford notes, many of today's appliances are built to break and not be repaired. How does today's work give people the opportunity to build something that will last beyond their life span? For teachers, this is one of the true joys of the profession. For most knowledge workers, the answer is less clear. True craftsmen raise a red flag about throw-away work. As Michael Ruhlman, known more for his books on chefs and cooking, reported in a book on wooden boats:

> *I asked Gannon why wooden boats were important to him—why had he devoted his life to them? Ross seemed surprised by my apparent ignorance regarding what to him was plain, and his blazing eyes burned right through me.*
>
> *"Do you want to teach your daughter [then three years old] that what you do, what you care about, is disposable?" he asked. "That you can throw your work away? It doesn't matter?"[11]*

Whether in passing down the family farm or painting "& Sons" on the service van, craft work is often connected to future generations that bureaucracy cannot sustain. This lack of long-term continuity may be another reason why the modern office lacks heroic images in popular culture.

Looking Ahead

Tom Malone of MIT explores the future landscape of work through the lens of its institutions. In his 2004 book, *The Future of Work*, he lays out various scenarios primarily concerned with the coordination and collaborative facets of organizations.[12] He sees the future as more decentralized, less hierarchical, and more democratic. If it comes to pass, Malone's vision foreshadows the demise of *The Office*'s Michael Scott and his kin. Pettiness and incompetence are eternal, however, so it is worth pondering both what will happen to a Michael in a Maloneite world and what manner of successor will emerge instead.

In the end of any analysis, work cannot be categorized with any precision. It is both universal and specifically grounded in time, place, and individual. It offers both rewards and challenges (some of which may overlap), utilizes groups and solo contributors, and defines us in multiple ways. The diversity of the perspectives mentioned here is itself incomplete, missing, for example, the perspective of the Japanese salaryman, the unionized autoworker, or the classic professions of law or clergy (both of which themselves are in the midst of deep change). I have made no mention of wages, which are retreating in many settings. The appeal of Dan Pink's vision of *Free Agent Nation* (2002), for example, has been replaced by the reality of the less glamorous name for continuous partial employment: "temping."

As to the question What have computers done to work?, the answer is probably less clear than it will be in another 25 years, when the changes to economies, workplaces, and individual performance will separate themselves from the end of the oil/automotive/steel age that wound down in the late twentieth century. The exciting news comes in the realization that the future of work is not yet defined, making it contingent on the attitudes and actions of many people.

Notes

1. Carolyn Dimitri, Anne Effland, and Neilson Conklin, "The 20th Century Transformation of U.S. Agriculture and Farm Policy," U.S. Department of Agriculture Economic Research Service Electronic Information Bulletin Number 3, June 2005, www.ers.usda.gov/publications/eib3/eib3.htm.
2. Richard Florida, *The Rise of the Creative Class: and How It's Transforming Work, Leisure, Community and Everyday Life* (New York: Basic Books, 2002).
3. Annie Lowrey, "Your Commute Is Killing You: Long Commutes Cause Obesity, Neck Pain, Loneliness, Divorce, Stress, and Insomnia," *Slate*, May 26, 2011, www.slate.com/id/2295603/.
4. "Jane Jacobs, Anatomiser of Cities, Died on April 24th, aged 89," *The Economist*, May 11, 2006, www.economist.com/node/6910989.
5. Friedman, *The World Is Flat: A Brief History of the Twenty-First Century* (New York: Farrar Strass & Giroux, 2005).
6. For a brief introduction to Veblen, see *The Concise Encyclopedia of Economics* at www.econlib.org/library/Enc/bios/Veblen.html. For more extended treatment, see John Patrick Diggins, *The Bard of Savagery* (New York: Seabury, 1978).

7. CIA *World Factbook*, www.cia.gov/library/publications/the-world-factbook/geos/us.html.

8. Florida, *Rise of the Creative Class*, pp. 7–8.

9. Ibid., p. 8.

10. Matthew B. Crawford, *Shop Class as Soulcraft: An Inquiry Into the Value of Work* (New York: Penguin, 2009).

11. Michael Ruhlman, *Wooden Boats: In Pursuit of the Perfect Craft at an American Boatyard* (New York: Penguin, 2001), p. 7.

12. Thomas W. Malone, *The Future of Work: How the New Order of Business Will Shape Your Organization, Your Management Style and Your Life* (Boston: Harvard Business School Press, 2004).

CHAPTER 14

Productivity

There are some structural issues with our economy, where a lot of businesses have learned to become much more efficient with a lot fewer workers. You see it when you go to a bank and you use an ATM; you don't go to a bank teller.

—President Barack Obama, June 14, 2011

Do computers and similar technologies make economies grow? Do these technologies displace workers? How might information and technology improve economic performance, whether at the firm, sector, or national level? Because previous technologies augmented physical power and mastery, they offer only limited insight into the impact of technologies that expand people's abilities to remember, to know, and to connect.

The debate over the relationship between automating technologies and unemployment is not new, as Adam Smith's famous example of pin making goes back to 1776 (see Chapter 8). Trying to understand services productivity is particularly messy: That automated teller machine does not merely replicate the pin factory or behave like industrial scenarios. Finally, trying to quantify the particular contribution of information technology (IT) to productivity, and thus to the current unemployment scenario, proves particularly difficult. Nevertheless, the question is worth considering closely insofar as multiple shifts are coinciding, making job seeking, managing, investing, and policy formulation difficult, at best, in these challenging times.

Classic Productivity Definitions

At the most basic level, a nation's economic output is divided by the number of workers or the number of hours worked. This model is obviously rough and has two major implications. First, investment (whether in better machinery or elsewhere) does not necessarily map to hours worked. Second, unemployment should drive this measure of productivity up, all other things being equal, merely as a matter of shrinking the denominator in the fraction: Fewer workers producing the same level of output are intuitively more productive. Unemployment, however, is not free.

A more sophisticated metric is called multifactor productivity, or MFP. This indicator attempts to track how efficiently both labor and capital are being utilized. It is calculated as a residual, by looking at hours worked (or some variant thereof) and capital stock (summarizing a nation's balance sheet, as it were, to tally up the things that can produce other things of value for sale). Any rise in economic output not captured in labor or capital will be counted as improved productivity. The problem here is that measuring productive capital at any level of scale is extremely difficult.[1]

MFP, while hard to pin down, does have advantages. One strength is in its emphasis on innovation. In theory, if inventors and innovators are granted monopolies (through patents), their investment in new technologies can be recouped as competitors are prevented from copying the innovation.[2] Skilled labor is an important ingredient in this process: Commercialization is much more difficult if the workforce cannot perform the necessary functions to bring new ideas and products to market. For one estimate of MFP for the United States, see Figure 14.1.

One relevant study took a deep dive into one manufacturing niche: valve assembly. The researchers found three mechanisms by which IT could influence productivity by changing business practices, not merely accelerating current-state activities:

> We find that adoption of new IT-enhanced equipment (1) alters business strategies, moving valve manufacturers away from commodity production based on long production runs to customized production in smaller batches; (2) improves the efficiency of all stages of the production process with reductions in setup times supporting the change in business strategy; and (3) increases the skill requirements of workers while promoting the adoption of new human resource practices.[3]

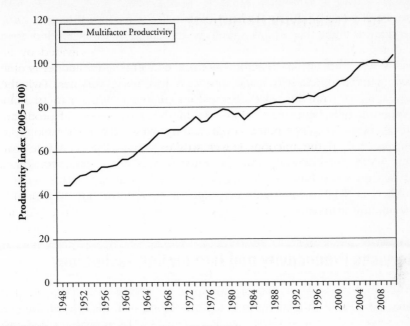

FIGURE 14.1 Multifactor Productivity, 1948–2010
Source: Bureau of Labor Statistics.

Services Productivity

As *The Economist* points out, quoting *Fast Company* from 2004, ATMs did not displace bank tellers. Instead, the rise of self-service coincided with a broad expansion of bank functions and an aging (and growing) American population: Baby boomers started needing lots of car loans, and home mortgages, and tuition loans starting in about 1970, when the first boomers turned 25. People were required to deliver all those financial services:

1985: 60,000 ATMs; 485,000 bank tellers
2002: 352,000 ATMs; 527,000 bank tellers[4]

That a technology advance coincided with a shift in the banking market tells us little about productivity. Did ATMs, or word processors, or BlackBerries increase output per unit of input? Nobody knows: The output of a bank teller, or nurse, or college professor, is notoriously hard to measure. Even at the aggregate level, the measurement problem is significant.

Is a bank's output merely the sum of its teller transactions? Maybe. Other economists argue that a bank should be measured by its balances of loans and deposits.[5]

A key concept in macroeconomics concerns intermediate goods: raw material purchases, work-in-process inventory, and the like. Very few services were included in these calculations, airplane tickets and telephone bills being exceptions. As of the early 1990s, for example, ad agencies and computer programming were not included.[6] Thus, the problem is twofold: Services inputs to certain facets of the economy were not counted, and the output of systems integrators, such as Accenture or Tata Consulting Services, or advertising firms, such as Publicis or WPP, is intuitively very difficult to count in any consistent or meaningful manner.

Services Productivity and Information Technology

In the mid-1990s, a number of prominent economists pointed to roughly three decades of investment in computers along with the related software and services and asked for statistical evidence of IT's improvement of productivity, particularly in the period between 1974 and 1994, when overall productivity stagnated.

Those years coincided with the steep decline in manufacturing's contribution to the U.S. economy. Measuring the productivity of an individual office worker is difficult (as in a performance review), not to mention measuring the productivity of millions of such workers in the aggregate. Services are especially sensitive to labor inputs: Low student–faculty ratios are usually thought to represent quality teaching, not inefficiency. As the economist William Baumol noted, a string quintet still must be played by five musicians; there has been zero increase in productivity over the 300 years since the art form originated.[7]

The late 1990s were marked by the Internet stock market bubble, heavy investment by large firms in enterprise software packages, and business process "reengineering." Alongside these developments, productivity spiked: Manufacturing sectors improved an average of 2.3% annually, but services did even better, at 2.6%. In hotels, however, the effect was less pronounced, possibly reflecting Baumol's "disease" in which high-quality service is associated with high labor content.[8]

Unfortunately, healthcare is another component in the services sector marked by low productivity growth and, until recently, relatively low innovation in the use of it. Measuring the productivity of such a vast, inefficiently organized, and intangibly measured sector is inherently difficult, so it will be hard to assess the impact of self-care, for example: People who research their back spasms on the Internet, try some exercises or heating pads, and avoid a trip to a physician. Such behavior should improve the productivity of the doctor's office, but only in theory can it be counted.

In a systematic review of the IT productivity paradox in the mid-1990s, economist Eric Brynjolfsson and his colleagues at the Massachusetts Institute of Technology investigated what they saw as four explanations for the apparent contradiction.[9] Subsequent history suggests they are correct.

1. *Mismeasurement of outputs and inputs.* Services industries (led by the financial sector) are among the heaviest users of IT, and services outputs are hard to measure. As we saw, productivity statistics in general are complex and not terribly robust.

2. *Lags due to learning and adjustment.* This explanation has grown in influence in the past 15 years. To take one common example, the organizational adjustment to a $50 million to $100 million enterprise software deployment takes years, by which time many other factors will influence productivity: currency fluctuations, mergers or acquisitions, broad economic recessions, and so on.

3. *Redistribution and dissipation of profits.* If a leading firm in a sector uses information effectively, it may steal market share from less effective competitors. The sector at large thus may not appear to gain in productivity. In addition, IT-maximizing firms might be using the technology investment for more effective forecasting, let's say, as opposed to using less labor in order fulfillment. The latter action would theoretically improve productivity. But if the wrong items were being produced relative to the market leader that more accurately sensed demand, profitability would improve at the leading firm even though productivity could go up at the laggard.

4. *Mismanagement of information and technology.* In the early years of computing, paper processes were automated but the basic business design was left unchanged. In the 1990s, however, such companies as Wal-Mart, Dell, Amazon, and Google invented entirely new business processes and in some cases business models building on IT. The revenue per employee at Amazon ($960,000) or Google ($1.2 million) is far higher than at Harley-Davidson or Clorox (both are leanness leaders in their respective categories at about $650,000). "Mismanagement" sounds negative, but it is easy to see, as with every past technology shift, that managers take decades to internalize the capability of a new way of doing work before they can reinvent commerce to exploit the new tools.

Information Technology and Unemployment

Are we in a situation that parallels farming, when tractors reduced the number of men and horses needed to work a given acreage? One way to look at the question involves job losses by industry. Using Bureau of Labor Statistics (BLS) numbers from 2009 (see Table 14.1), I compared the number of layoffs and business closings to the total employment in the sector.[10] Not surprisingly, construction and manufacturing both lost in excess of 10% of total jobs. It's hard to point to IT as a prime factor in either case: The credit crisis and China, respectively, are much more likely explanations. Professional and business services, an extremely broad category, shrank by 8% in one year, which includes consultants among many other titles.

Another analysis can come from looking at jobs that never materialized. Using the BLS 10-year projections of job growth from 2000,[11] the computer and information industry moved in a very different direction from what economists predicted. Applications programmers, for example, rather than being a growth category, actually grew only modestly. Desktop publishers shrank in numbers, possibly because of the rise of blogs and other Web- rather than paper-based formats. The population of customer service reps was projected to grow 32% in 10 years; the actual growth was about 10%, possibly reflecting a combination of offshoring and self-service, both phone and Web based. The need for retail salespeople was projected to grow by 12%, but the number stayed flat. Here is another example where IT, in the form of the Web and self-service, might play a role.

TABLE 14.1 2009 Layoffs and Business Closures as a Percentage of Total Sector Employment (All numbers in thousands)

Industry	Total Employment	Job Losses	Losses as % of Total Jobs
Construction	9,702	1,095	11.29%
Manufacturing	14,202	1,450	10.21%
Professional and business services	15,008	1,214	8.09%
Retail trade	15,877	829	5.22%
Information	3,239	146	4.51%
Financial activities	9,622	360	3.74%
Leisure and hospitality	12,736	448	3.52%

Data Source: Bureau of Labor Statistics.

Neither sales clerks nor customer service reps would constitute anything like a backbone of a vibrant middle class: Average annual wages for retail are about $25,000 while customer service reps do somewhat better, at nearly $33,000. The decline of middle-class jobs is a complex phenomenon: IT definitely automated away the payroll clerk, formerly a reliably middle-class position in many firms, to take one example. Auto industry union employment is shrinking, however, in large part because of foreign competition, not robotic armies displacing humans. That same competitive pressure has taken a toll on the thick management layer in Detroit as well, as the real estate market in the suburbs there can testify. Those brand managers were not made obsolete by computers.

Looking Ahead

President Obama gets the (almost) last word. In a town hall meeting in Illinois in mid-August 2011, he returned to the ATM theme:

> *One of the challenges in terms of rebuilding our economy is businesses have gotten so efficient that—when was the last time somebody went to a bank teller instead of using the ATM, or used a travel agent instead of just going online? A lot of jobs that used to be out there requiring people now have become automated.*[12]

Have they really? The impact of IT and its concomitant automation on the unemployment rate is not at all clear. The effect is highly variable across different countries, for example. Looking domestically, travel agent was never a major job category: Even if such jobs were automated away as the number of agencies dropped by about two-thirds in the decade-plus after 1998,[13] such numbers pale alongside construction, manufacturing, and, I would wager, computer programmers whose positions were offshored.

The unfortunate thing in the entire discussion, apart from people without jobs obviously, is the lack of political and popular understanding of both the sources of the unemployment and the necessary solutions. Merely saying "education" or "job retraining" defers rather than settles the debate about what is to be done in the face of the structural transformation we are living through. On that aspect, the president is assuredly correct: He has the terminology correct, but structural changes need to be addressed with fundamental rethinking of rules and behaviors rather than with sound bites and Band-Aids.

Notes

1. "Secret Sauce," *The Economist,* November 12, 2009, www.economist.com/node/14844987.
2. Diego Comin, "Total Factor Productivity," in The *New Palgrave Dictionary of Economics,* 2nd ed., ed. Steven N. Durlauf and Lawrence E. Blume (New York: Palgrave Macmillan, 2008). *The New Palgrave Dictionary of Economics Online,* www.dictionaryofeconomics.com/article?id=pde2008_T000081.
3. Ann P. Bartel, Casey Ichniowski, and Kathryn Shaw, "How Does Information Technology Affect Productivity? Plant-Level Comparisons of Product Innovation, Process Improvement and Worker Skills," *Quarterly Journal of Economics* (November 2007), www.nber.org/papers/w11773.
4. "Technology and Unemployment," Economist.com blog post, June 15, 2011, www.economist.com/blogs/democracyinamerica/2011/06/technology-and-unemployment.
5. See Robert Inklaar and J. Christina Wang, "Real Output of Bank Services: What Counts Is What Banks Do, Not What They Own," Federal Reserve Bank of Boston working paper 11-1, February 2011, www.worldklems.net/conferences/worldklems2010_inklaar_wang.pdf.
6. Zvi Griliches, "Introduction to Griliches," in *Output Measurement in the Service Sectors* (Chicago: University of Chicago Press, 1992), p. 6.
7. David M. Herszenhorn, "For Ailing Health System a Diagnosis but no Cure," *New York Times,* January 17, 2010, http://prescriptions.blogs.nytimes.com/2010/01/17/an-economist-who-sees-no-way-to-slow-rising-costs/.
8. Hal Varian, "Information Technology May Have Cured Low Service-Sector Productivity," *New York Times,* February 12, 2004, http://people.ischool.berkeley.edu/~hal/people/hal/NYTimes/2004-02-12.html.
9. Erik Brynjolfsson, "The Productivity Paradox of Information Technology: Review and Assessment," MIT Center for Coordination Science working paper, September 1992, http://ccs.mit.edu/papers/CCSWP130/ccswp130.html.
10. U.S. Census Bureau, *Statistical Abstract of the United States,* 2011, tables 619 and 634, www.census.gov/compendia/statab/2011/2011edition.html.
11. "BLS Releases 2000–2010 Employment Projections," press release, December 3, 2001, www.bls.gov/news.release/history/ecopro_12032001.txt.
12. "Obama and Travel Agents," Economist.com blog post, August 21, 2011, www.economist.com/blogs/gulliver/2011/08/obama-and-travel-agents.
13. Ibid.

Business Model Disruption

After we define the components of a business model, we examine a number of industries to see the variety of ways that technology innovation can translate into a mix of opportunities and threats to established patterns of business behavior.

CHAPTER 15

Business Model Overview

Technology changes of the sort we have examined at length represent one strand of innovation—a better mousetrap, as it were. But for technological innovation to make its way to people in the marketplace, a second factor is required: a business model. That is, there must be an organization of resources that facilitates an exchange of value, often monetary, in order that technology artifacts can find users.

For most of the mass production era, business models have involved capital-intensive factories or collections of infrastructure that generated products or services consumed by paying customers. With information goods in a digital era not necessarily requiring the same capital intensiveness, business models have proliferated: One professor who has studied Internet commerce has organized dozens of examples into nine families.[*1] Thus, (1) packaging the right technology into the right market offering (product, service, or hybrid), (2) creating a compelling exchange proposition, and (3) organizing resources to make the trades happen requires additional types and layers of innovation, capital, and management. The better mousetrap, in short, requires a mousetrap store, collective, foundation, or other arrangement to connect the product with people's needs.

---

*The nine families are advertising, affiliate, brokerage, community, infomediary, manufacturer (direct), merchant, subscription, and utility.

Definition

While the term "business model" is widely used,* I follow the definition of my previous coauthor, Henning Kagermann, the former chief executive of the German software company SAP. A business model, he and his coauthors state, consists of four interlocking elements that, taken together, create and deliver value.

1. *Customer value proposition*, including target customer, the customer's job to be done, and the offering that satisfies the problem or fulfills the need.
2. *Profit formula*, including the revenue model, cost structure, margin model, and resource velocity (lead times, turns, etc.).
3. *Key resources* to deliver the customer value proposition profitably, potentially including people, equipment, technologies, partnerships, brand, and so on.
4. *Key processes* also include rules, metrics, and norms of behavior that make repeated delivery of the customer value proposition repeatable and scalable.[2]

Let us expand on each of these dimensions.

The *customer value proposition* gets much of management's attention insofar as it's front and center at the nexus of provider and customer. Kagermann and his coauthors rightly focus on the customer as a person (potentially a person in an organizational role) with a job to do or need to be filled. This orientation can help prevent against infatuation with a technology for its own sake, a "push" orientation toward innovation.

Profit formulas have become problematic in the age of "free" as a viable price point for many digital goods. Linux and Wikipedia have business models even though they lack profit formulas. Similarly, Microsoft and the New York Times Company have been forced to reinvent their business models by the presence of free alternatives. Even in traditional for-profit businesses, the scale of digital business can alter the business model landscape. Google is estimated to deliver 34,000 search results per second; Facebook reached a half billion users in six years. Radio took 38 years to ship 50 million units; the iPod took 3 years to hit the same milestone. Each of these four technologies has a distinctive set of profit formulas to fit its context.

In addition, profit formulas typically include a time scale: are key processes enacted in tenths of a second (Google), in days (luxury resorts),

---

*A Google search on the phrase "business model" returned 6.8 million hits in late 2010.

in decades (life insurance)? Charles Fine's notion of "clockspeed"[3] has been redefined in the past decade by such developments as smartphone app marketplaces, Twitter feeds, and real-time status updates for social gaming at Sony, Microsoft, and Facebook. The speed of technology-driven change—which futurist and inventor Ray Kurzweil insists is getting faster*—stress-tests many organizations: Lucent, Sun Microsystems, and Motorola merely begin a list of companies dragged down in the vortex of rapid change.

Key resources are changing. Intellectual property, brand, and other intangibles matter in new ways (compare Amazon's patent portfolio to Xerox's), yet physical infrastructure is also scaling to new levels. For example, as we discussed, AT&T's wireless data traffic increased 5,000% in four years; few businesses have ever had to address that kind of growth at a national level. Leadership remains a scarce resource, as comparisons of Yahoo! and Google, or Microsoft pre- and post-Bill Gates's retirement show.

Key processes encompass a wide range of activities. Formal policies, informal cultural practices, operational choices, and measurement and incentive systems can each be a critical element in a venture's success. Note that repetition is listed as a goal: One-hit wonders are too often the norm in technology-driven businesses. Similarly, in an age of network effects, global reach, and cheap media, scale has become a strategic dimension in ways it might not have been in industries where growth occurred at a less frenetic pace.

Changing Minds, Changing Models

Even when the need is clear, however, changing a business model can be difficult. General Motors' template for labor costs, model changeovers, and brand management dates to the 1960s and did not adapt to new dynamics of competition, healthcare cost explosion, and consumer behavior; the company had to declare bankruptcy and rethink every aspect of its business after 2008. The music industry's bundling of songs into LP records worked for a few decades, but the model failed in the digital era, leaving the labels' economics and practices out of step with the market. Established air carriers' inattention to the low end of the market and to their own cost structures left them vulnerable to a new wave of budget airlines, such as EasyJet, Ryan Air, and Southwest.[4] American Airlines used to be a star in the

---

*Kurzweil famously contends that the rate of change is itself accelerating. See www.kurzweilai.net/the-law-of-accelerating-returns.

industry because of its pioneering use of information technology with the Sabre reservations system, but the company has struggled to turn a profit in recent years and finally declared bankruptcy in 2011.

Business models are less a strategy than a way of understanding the world and optimizing an entity's place in that world. As a cognitive "operating system," as it were, business models must be widely understood and internalized by both employees or others inside the organization and by customers or other outsiders. For example, the Zappos culture, and its maniacal focus on customer service, is inextricably connected to the business's margin structure, which is premised on minimal discounting.

Similarly, Apple's App Store model provides an illustration where an idea rapidly took hold, enabling Apple to create a textbook example of a two-sided platform. (See Chapter 5.) No technologies were considered breakthrough: iTunes had conditioned people to download content and established a micropayment storefront, and the iPhone was well established (in the United States particularly) at the device level. But the business model change in how software was innovated and delivered to customers generated an entirely new industry, altering standard assumptions about channels, pricing, and developers.[5]

Henry Chesbrough, a business school professor now at the University of California, Berkeley, has studied business models for more than a decade. When looking at the path of technologies to market, he contends that these cognitive frameworks turn out to be as important as, if not more important than, the content of the technology itself. Nowhere is this more true than in the case of new (or what Harvard professor Clayton Christensen has elsewhere called "disruptive") technologies: "[T]he technological management literature shows that firms have great difficulty managing innovations that fall outside of their previous experience, where their earlier beliefs and practices do not apply." Chesbrough continues by noting that "Authors do not agree . . . whether the roots of that difficulty lie in characteristics of the technology itself, the management processes employed to manage it, or the means used to access the surrounding resources."[6]

Disruptive Innovation

In each of the five industries discussed in subsequent chapters, at least part of the upheaval has been caused by one of Christensen's disruptive innovations. His model, which is nearly 15 years old, continues to explain parts of the technology and business landscape particularly effectively, so it is worth revisiting.

In normal times, innovations can accumulate gradually. Christensen calls this "sustaining" innovation, where the basic parameters are perhaps enhanced by a new flavor, or new packaging, or improved performance.[7] Eventually in technology markets particularly, improvements eventually can outrun the capacity of the market to exploit them (for example, the overwhelming functionality of Microsoft Word, or 3-gigahertz Intel processors for people who do word processing and e-mail, not video transcoding). This tendency toward overshoot can be accentuated by so-called lead-user analysis, taking the point of view of "power users" as representative. Sustaining innovation is also a prime candidate for the trap of focus groups, which routinely both assert that they would pay for a new feature and deny the attractiveness of features that prove to be popular in the marketplace.

Sometimes, at the same time that sustaining innovation outruns market requirements, a new offering appears in the market. Disruptive innovations "fail" when compared head to head with an incumbent: Portable ultrasound machines lack the resolution and flexibility of conventional hospital-grade units, for example. But the disruptive innovation addresses a related set of user needs, without the heavy overhead and often at a radically low price: The portable ultrasound may cost only 5% of the incumbent. ING Direct introduced online banking that began with only simple savings accounts, limited physical branch structure, and extensive self-service technologies: It "failed" on complex products, in-person customer service, and certain types of convenience and reassurance. But the low infrastructure costs allowed ING Direct to pay well-above-market interest rates, making competition difficult for providers with expensive asset bases and complex processes to administer.

The combination of ease of use, low cost, and new competitive bases often allows the disruptive innovation to gather rapid market share growth, as in the case of MP3 audio files relative to physical compact discs: Audio fidelity may have been lower, but price, convenience, selection, and speed of distribution (given Napster and similar peer-to-peer services) were all superior.

A further factor in disruptive innovation relates to scale. What start out as niche markets are unappealing to large organizations, which (1) may already market a competing incumbent product and "know" nobody would want the less powerful offering, (2) resist both distraction from "core competences" and resource drains from proven winners, and (3) set high thresholds for return on investment and market size. Under a previous leadership team, managers at one large consumer products company stated that projected markets smaller than $100 million simply weren't worth pursuing.

That firm has now revised its managers' earlier assumption and found billion-dollar markets for new, disruptive products that started below that

$100 million threshold. New technologies with (initially) small markets usually require small organizations, with tolerance for ambiguity, lean infrastructures, and low resistance to change as the business model evolves.[8]

Disruptive Innovation as Paradigm Shift

Christensen's many examples of disruptive innovation hold much in common with the cognitive transition explained by Thomas Kuhn in his landmark book, *The Structure of Scientific Revolutions.*[9] Kuhn's "normal" science parallels sustaining innovation; the breakthrough, or "paradigm shift" in Kuhn's model, occurs with a change in mind-set rather than a brilliant invention. HP's pricing of inkjet printers to lock users in to high-margin resupply purchases of ink in proprietary packaging is a classic business model innovation that originated with a lifetime view of customer profitability (as well as some historical reflection on King Gillette), not in a lab.

Kuhn's paradigm shift is a change in the collective mind of a community: "[D]uring [scientific] revolutions scientists see new and different things when looking with familiar instruments in places they have looked before. . . . [P]aradigm changes do cause scientists to see the world of their research-engagement differently."[10] The same thing happens in disruptive innovation. Facebook Photos disrupt Kodak's physical (and even digital) printing business because the problem shifts from *having* photos to *sharing* them. Unmanned aerial vehicles focus on delivering weapons and surveillance capability where they are needed instead of investing heavily in evasive maneuverability (and a pilot) as the key asset.

It is difficult to overemphasize the point that cognitive reframing of the customer value proposition and the profit formula, in particular, constitute critical elements of successful technology deployments. Online grocery, for example, was dismissed as impossible, given the low margins of traditional grocery and the high costs of personalized picking and delivery. But if compared instead to pizza delivery (characterized by 50% margins, higher with beverages and side dishes), online grocery potentially can work if the key processes are designed according to delivery-centric rather than selection-centric criteria.

Looking Ahead

Every enterprise, from a lemonade stand on up, has a business model. In rapidly changing technology-driven markets in particular, however, it is not always clear that a firm has the business model it *needs*. For all the billions of dollars spent on research and development, many patents and other innovations fail to make it to market. As we study the five indus-tries highlighted in the coming chapters, it becomes clear that mind-set and preconceptions matter decisively in most disruptions: Time and again, competitive rules of engagement, margin structures, and customer behav-ior were taken as given or as an entitlement. (The music industry resisted attempts to unbundle music from the album format, for example, even though consumers wanted songs they liked rather than a collection that included too many songs they didn't.)

To make business model change real, in addition to labs full of PhD scientists, many companies need change agents, people with flexible out-looks who can see problems from multiple perspectives. They also need to devise market solutions every bit as innovative as the hardware, mol-ecules, or user experience. Finally, these change agents must be capable of that most difficult of tasks: changing other people's minds.

Notes

1. Michael Rappa, "Business Models on the Web," http://digitalenterprise.org/models/models.html.
2. Mark W. Johnson, Clayton M. Christensen, and Henning Kagermann, "Reinventing Your Business Model," *Harvard Business Review* (December 2008): 51–59.
3. Charles Fine, *Clockspeed: Winning Industry Control in the Age of Temporary Advantage* (New York: Basic Books, 1999).
4. See Henning Kagermann, Hubert Oesterle, and John Jordan, *IT-Driven Business Models* (Hoboken, NJ: John Wiley & Sons, 2010).
5. See Dion Hinchcliffe, "The App Store: The New 'Must-Have' Digital Business Model," ZD Net blog, January 21, 2010, www.zdnet.com/blog/hinchcliffe/the-app-store-the-new-must-have-digital-business-model/1172.
6. Henry Chesbrough and Richard S. Rosenbloom, "The Role of the Business Model in Capturing Value from Innovation: Evidence from Xerox Corporation's Technology Spinoff Companies," *Industrial and Corporate Change* 11, no. 3 (2002): 529–555.
7. Clayton M. Christensen, *The Innovator's Dilemma: When New Technologies Cause Great Firms to Fail* (Boston: Harvard Business School Press, 1997), p. xv.
8. Ibid., p. 121.
9. Thomas S. Kuhn, *The Structure of Scientific Revolutions*, 2nd ed. (Chicago: University of Chicago Press, 1970).
10. Ibid., p. 111.

CHAPTER 16

Data and Communications

The business model for U.S. telephony has undergone not one but a complex series of disruptions in the past 15 years. Technological innovation was certainly a factor, but demographics, regulation, and organizational dynamics both inside and around the carriers also played their parts in the drama. With anything so vast, old, and technologically complex, it is impossible to summarize without losing important facets that often are the subject of book-length monographs in and of themselves. One example was the carriers' yellow-pages publishing business. In many ways the forerunner to Google, commercial telephone directories were a $14 billion business in 1995, bigger than the entire recording industry. Furthermore, unlike newspapers (roughly $50 billion in 2000) or music, the telecommunications sector is a sprawling, regulated, but rapidly evolving complex that is particularly difficult to change. In addition to being complicated, telecommunications companies are big, representing about 3% of the global economy.

Evolution of the Incumbent Business Model, 1877–1996

From the founding of the Bell Telephone Company, the U.S. telecommunications sector has been characterized by a combination of technological innovation (much of it still relating to Alexander Graham Bell's master patent, #174465) and creative, intensive capital formation. Once Bell Telephone was bought by AT&T in 1899, it enjoyed essentially monopoly status. Indeed, a key feature of the history of American telephony is the ongoing role played by regulators concerned about anticompetitive behavior, consumer protection, pricing, and taxation. The operating assumption from the World War I period forward was that building multiple wireline networks was infeasible; AT&T and its successor companies were treated as a "natural monopoly" for decades.

Technological innovation was intertwined with the business model from the outset. In 1913, for example, AT&T acquired the patent rights to a new type of vacuum tube that exhibited superior performance in amplifying voice signals. The technology in turn enabled AT&T to strengthen the performance and lower the cost of long-distance carriage. In 1925, AT&T created Bell Labs to formalize its commitment to research and development.

The company was exceptionally good at research, having an important claim in the invention of the transistor,[*] radio astronomy,[†] the photovoltaic cell, the laser, the UNIX operating system, and the C programming language; AT&T also commissioned the Telstar communications satellite. The record of commercialization of this research was far less distinguished, however.

The expenses for funding this prodigious lab derived from the regulated monopoly revenues: 50 state regulatory bodies and the Federal Communications Commission (FCC; for interstate commerce) set tariffs and tax rates that guaranteed the private company a comfortable return on the huge investment it had made in what eventually became nearly universal service to the vast majority of American households; U.S. wireline penetration was the highest of any major country in the world. As of 1970, for example, three times as many U.S. households had service compared to Ireland or France, measured by teledensity.

Not only was phone service universal, it was exceptionally reliable. Beginning with the leased phone and extending into the heart of the network, AT&T made its own equipment through its Western Electric subsidiary. Because competition was not an issue, there was no pressure to cut costs. Rather, equipment was engineered as an end-to-end closed system and built to higher standards than are typically available on an open market. As a result, wireline phone service in the United States had up to "six nines" availability: 99.9999% uptime means only about 30 seconds of outage per year.

Phone calls were billed on the basis of elapsed time, in minutes rounded up, and distance between calling parties, with lower prices available to consumers outside of business hours. Under circuit

---

[*]Bell Labs' John Bardeen, Walter Brattain, and William Shockley shared a Nobel Prize in physics for the discovery.
[†]Bell Labs' Arno Penzias won a Nobel Prize in physics for helping discover what later was identified as the radio remnant of the Big Bang.

switching, the same technology pioneered by Bell, two calling parties hold a physical connection for the duration of a call in much the same way that a switch closes connecting the batteries and a bulb on a flashlight. (Actually, two circuits are occupied, one for the voice transmission and one for the call setup and billing system.) For both circuits, edge devices (telephones, typically) are "dumb," and the intelligence to do things like call waiting or caller identification lies in the network. The extra value of a dedicated connection over greater distance was taken as article of faith, and since rates were set by governments and the service was a monopoly, customers could do little except complain about the power of "Ma Bell:" At its peak before the 1984 divestiture, AT&T was the biggest company on earth, employing more than one million people.

In 1974, the U.S. Department of Justice (DOJ) began antitrust proceedings against AT&T, which had only recently been forced to allow non-AT&T devices (such as early data modems) to connect to its network. In addition, and not part of the DOJ action, MCI was the first company apart from AT&T allowed by the FCC to sell point-to-point long-distance service to businesses. An agreement was reached in 1982 to break AT&T into seven Regional Bell Operating Companies (RBOCs, known shortly thereafter as R-Bocks) that provided local service, and a long-distance company retaining the AT&T name (along with the Western Electric manufacturing operation) that would compete with MCI and Sprint. The breakup occurred in 1984.

In the aftermath, AT&T reduced long distance rates by 40% over six years, though local carriers added access charges that prevented consumers from seeing all of the cost reduction. The local operating companies (led by Ameritech, beginning in the Chicago area that was home to Motorola, which helped develop the radio technology) also began offering mobile service in the 1980s after it had been developed by Bell Labs.

By 1990, packet switching (see Chapter 24) had begun to emerge as the Internet began its rapid scale-up: The data to be transmitted are broken up into packets, which are moved over a robust mesh of connections one packet at a time following different paths, and reassembled by a "smart" edge device (a computer rather than a phone) upon receipt. The transition to a "dumb" network ran completely counter to Bell engineering experience and doctrine. In addition, mobile telephony entered its modern phase in the early 1990s with so-called 2G (roughly, second generation wireless) networks. Nokia patented handset technology to sense signal strength and reduce transmission power accordingly, thereby improving battery life dramatically, which helped fuel cellular growth.

All of this helped set the stage for the Telecommunications Act of 1996. Local telecoms were ordered to supply access to their lines at a government-mandated price, enabling a vast number of upstart phone companies to compete with the RBOCs using, in many cases, Bell infrastructure, which was leased at attractive rates. The Competitive Local Exchange Carriers (CLECs, pronounced "See-Lex") proliferated, numbering 30 in 1996 and growing to more than 700 in just four years.

Business Model Disruption, 1996–2010

But a funny thing happened in the aftermath of the Telecom Act: Millions of U.S. customers stopped wanting location-dependent copper-wire voice telephony. Untethered from physical wires, the notion of a "natural monopoly" based on the perceived inefficiency of multiple connections from competing carriers no longer obtained. The very asset that was regulated from natural monopoly to shared resource began to lose its attractiveness after more than a century of becoming essential. Beginning with cellular voice, expanding to Voice over Internet Protocol (VoIP), and then in the mobile smartphone/tablet boom of the late aughts, new ways of connecting to people and information made the old universal infrastructure a liability rather than an asset.

Think of the math in a simple illustration. In 1990, say, copper phone lines pass 100 houses, and maybe 95 of those households subscribe. The costs of maintaining the physical plant, repairing it after storms, and issuing and collecting bills are shared by 95 customers. Fast forward to 2010. The physical plant is 20 years older, municipalities are taxing phone companies' physical switching offices and sometimes even phone poles, and the costs of maintaining the infrastructure are now being borne by only 45 customers. Raising the monthly charges is scarcely an option for both competitive and regulatory reasons, so the wireline operations of the Bell operating companies (the rebranded AT&T, Verizon, and Qwest) are underperforming. Most of the CLECs have disappeared.

Despite (or perhaps because of) being some of the oldest tech firms on earth, telecoms had a tumultuous decade.

- *Customers defected* from landline service at staggering rates: according to the Telecommunications Industry Association, U.S. landline subscriptions declined by more than 20 million in the five years to 2005, and perhaps another 10 million since then, as Figure 16.1 illustrates.
- *Technical developments*, such as dense wave division multiplexing, made infrastructure investments in fiber optics stretch farther, and new revenue sources—particularly texting and ringtones for the carriers' mobile operations—helped offset the wireline decline.

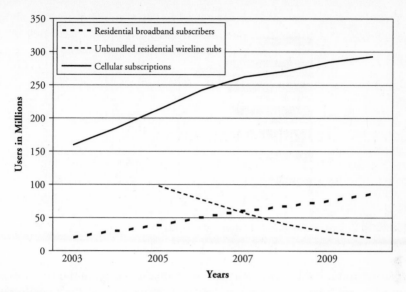

FIGURE 16.1 Alternatives to Wireline Telephony in the U.S., 2003–2009
Source: Telecommunications Industry Association, World Bank.

- Furthermore, perhaps the most troubling competitor—Skype and its 200 million users of *nearly free international calling*—was itself a major headache to eBay, which failed to monetize its original $2.6 billion investment and therefore cost chief executive Meg Whitman her job.

Three external transitions hit the industry in parallel.

First, analog switched circuits over copper gave way to digital packet-switched data applications over networks connected through air or fiber optics. Analog data transmissions (faxes, particularly internationally) were a lucrative revenue source that digital e-mail helped decimate. Voice went from being the whole of the value proposition to being just another application, and one less appealing than text for the younger demographic. (See Figure 16.2.) Networks had to be redesigned and rebuilt: Verizon bet more than $20 billion on connecting individual premises to fiber optics, a far more expensive architecture than the cable operators' coaxial cabling or AT&T's fiber-to-the-neighborhood topology, but one with much greater capacity. In rural areas with low population density, meanwhile, sale of the wireline voice infrastructure is often an attractive option to RBOCs where buyers for voice networks can be found.

Second, mobile phones began as replications of their fixed-line counterparts but rapidly evolved, with texting in particular, but also with the personalization expressed by ringtones. Having a number associated with

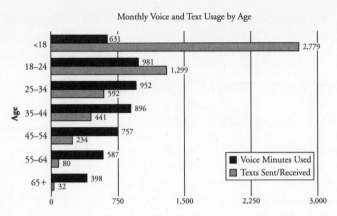

FIGURE 16.2 Text Messaging Is Dominant among the Young
Data Source: The Nielsen Company, April 2009–March 2010.

a person and not a location is a significant change. Even at the level of the country code, dialing 81 is no guarantee whatsoever that the person who answers will be in Japan. To the extent that the former monopolies had to make competitive claims after a century of regulated monopoly status, the advantages of Bell wireline service (reliability and ubiquity) were not claims that could be made for mobile service.

Finally, Bell companies went from being regulated to . . . still being regulated. On one hand, they face competition from cable operators and mobile service; at the same time, they must adhere to sometimes arbitrary decisions by state and federal regulators, using sometimes outdated logic or data, as to how to run their business. Put another way, the core competencies of being a successful regulated monopoly are not those of a battle-hardened competitive firm. Changing the organizational size, shape, and culture to be competitive, in several senses of the word, remains an ongoing challenge for AT&T and Verizon.

At the level of internal business strategy, voice telephony had both competitor businesses (particularly cable operators offering VoIP voice in a voice-video-Internet bundle as well as such providers as Vonage) and Skype, which, like Linux, could not be beaten by undercutting prices, litigation, or acquisition. Trying to preserve voice revenue, compete with Comcast and other cable operators, and deal with free as a viable price point (albeit one with some interconnect charges) made life especially difficult for the telecom firms and potential insurgents alike. To take only one example, eBay took on many attributes of a bank with the brilliant PayPal acquisition, but the connection of voice communications to off-price auctions is far less strategically obvious. Put another way, given the size, legacy, and regulatory constraints of telecoms compared to eBay, it's

difficult to see a better path forward that these far less nimble and entrepreneurial companies should have followed.

Implications of "Stupid" Networks

David Isenberg, formerly a business innovation researcher at AT&T,
helped identify what he called the "paradox of the best network" in the
Internet age. He built on an insight from the astute investment analyst
Roxane Googin, who noted in 2001 that "the perfect network is perfectly
plain, and perfectly extensible. That means it is also the perfect capital
repellant, [which] implies a *guaranteed* loss to network operators, but a
boon to the services on the 'ends.'"[1] This thinking that emerged from the
success of the Internet ran counter to most everything that had worked for
the Bell companies for a century:

- Intelligence at the edges, in computers or similar devices, relied on a
  "stupid" (Isenberg's famous word from his samizdat paper* of 1997)
  network in the middle that does only one thing: move bits.[†] Bell networks had stupid edge devices connected by a smart network that
  could bill for a call, forward that call to a preprogrammed number, or
  connect relatively conveniently to various forms of government surveillance systems.
- Intelligence at the edge allowed for innovation to proliferate. The
  people running the network core, meanwhile, were very good at their
  jobs, but this excellence precluded them from changing anything at
  all dramatically. Unsurprisingly, Bell Labs engineers "knew" that the
  Internet would not work when they were first presented with its early
  theories and bypassed an opportunity to build it.[2]
- Stupid networks do not differentiate their traffic; smart networks know
  quite a lot about the two parties on the ends as well as what is passing between them.
- Moore's law[3] meant an exponential pace of innovation in computer-
  related industries, including data networking: Dense wave division
  multiplexing, a technology for dividing light into component colors,
  each of which carries signal, allowed 16-fold improvements in the

---

*Underground transmission of officially prohibited texts, from the Russian system
of government under which transmission was common.
[†]The Internet is not really as "stupid" as it might seem: Routing algorithms have
grown quite sophisticated in analyzing optimal traffic patterns, particularly related
to extreme variation in demand.

1990s. The Bell system, in contrast, doubled in performance once a century, according to one industry wit.

Looking Ahead

Most critically for the Bell companies, losing the very things implied by a smart network—distance-based billing, or billing of any sort, for starters—challenged the business model at its essence. Recall our starting point: A business model is a cognitive commitment that makes a variety of behaviors possible in part by belief. With voice service, the legacy carriers face substantial dislocation as they confront the implications of a communications network that broke every rule that had helped build the best voice service, and the biggest company, on the planet.

Notes

1. Roxane Googin, *High Tech Observer* newsletter, September 2001, quoted at http://netparadox.com/.
2. Paul Baran interview, *Wired* 9, no. 3 (March 2001): "AT&T headquarters, with the old analog people, missed it. If a guy knew only analog, he could not comprehend what I was saying about the behavior of a digital circuit," www.wired.com/wired/archive/9.03/baran_pr.html.
3. The long-term tendency of computing power (or price/performance) to double roughly every 18–24 months due to increased density of transistors on a microprocessor chip. The observation was originally attributed to Intel co-founder Gordon Moore.

CHAPTER 17

Software Business Models

The business model disruption framework as it applies to software has multiple layers: Platforms have changed and are changing; enterprise and personal computing markets differ significantly; and the division of labor among operating systems, network services, and application software is also in flux. For our purposes, let's look at the case of Microsoft, insofar as it was a dominant player in software markets through most of the 1990s. How did Internet-related events and trends disrupt its business model?

Incumbent Model Pre-2000

Back when investors were looking for "the next Microsoft," they held certain assumptions about what a highly successful software company looked like.

Customer Value Proposition

The value proposition for Windows in the 1990s was compelling: If you want to do any of the many wonderful things computers can allow you to do, we are the only game in town. Apple was a niche provider with tiny market share and high prices because of the proprietary hardware-software relationship. For a time, IBM's OS/2 operating system had some technical advantages over Windows, but IBM never established the application ecosystem that would make its OS competitive. No other platforms were credible after the semihobbyist and cult brands of the 1980s, such as Amiga, were sufficiently marginalized.

Once you bought a computer with the Windows OS, by 1995 there were no real alternatives for office productivity applications. In this complementary market, MS Office became the default choice, for both PCs and Macs, where it held even higher market share than on the PC. (On the PC at the time, WordPerfect still had pockets of loyal customers—in law firms, for example.)

Software was available on various types of plastic discs and was sold as a tangible product directly to the user (or her employer). As product companies, software vendors cared about software functionality and performance; data as they were generated or managed by the application fell out of scope. Both desktop and laptop computers were used sitting still, plugged into a hard-wired network when they were near the correct wall jack.

Profit Formula

Software platform leadership requires the development of mechanisms for user lock-in and network effects. Word processing programs stand as an obvious example, where switching is hard and expensive once you learn to use a package, and it makes sense to be on the same product as all of your coworkers if document sharing is a priority.

Software upgrade cycles delivered sustained profitability: That locked-in user base eventually had to buy the new, improved version, particularly after support was withdrawn or new functionality (for example, Wi-Fi in which 802.11A didn't work with 802.11B) was not backward compatible. Upgrades delivered a major revenue infusion to the software seller and perhaps the wider ecosystem.

For both OSs and applications, preventing digital copying of the assets was essential to maintaining pricing power. (See Chapter 4).

Technical support costs had to be kept low or, ideally, turned into a profit center.

Key Resources

Microsoft sold software to large customer bases one consumer or one business at a time. This reality of the market implies effective management of brand, retail channels, and enterprise sales forces. Retail channels such as CompUSA, Computer City, Micro Center, and others were important points of contact (and both formal and informal training) between the big hardware and software brands and the customer. Dell's direct model grew in influence through the 1990s but did not triumph until later.

An enthusiast magazine community helped users overcome their fear of ignorance in the face of complex language, purchase criteria, and user experience. These magazines, while not belonging to Microsoft, performed important functions: The implicit user question, Which computer should I buy?, was always answered by "a machine running Windows," marginalizing the differences between, say, Toshiba and Gateway.

Strong technical teams matter: Once functionality is specified early (by market-facing product teams) in the new product development cycle, it must be hard-coded into the package. At Microsoft, feature inclusion apparently mattered more than security, stability, or reliability, but switching costs were sufficiently high, and alternatives scarce, that those drawbacks had few consequences for market share.

Key Processes

Software development was clearly essential to Microsoft's growth and continued market power. One challenge grew out of the fact of the sheer size of the code base: The Vista operating system reportedly contained 50 million lines of code. Achieving usability, debugging, consistent security architectures, and performance tuning at that scale is difficult or even impossible.

As a platform play in a heterogeneous ecosystem, Microsoft had to maintain working relationships with a wide variety of firms and organizations. Standards bodies and other forms of intercompany relationship building had to be managed to ensure the success of interoperability, brand consistency, investment effectiveness, and other objectives. Industry analysts (such as IDC) had to be kept abreast of the status of the platform; consumer product branding was insufficient to ensure enterprise adoption, particularly of server and development environments.

As big as Microsoft was (and remains), it could not address all the particular uses to which the software would be put. Building, certifying, and nurturing an independent software developer community helped put Windows systems into small businesses, corporate environments, schools, and other institutions. Developers, in turn, required tools, templates, frameworks, education, marketing materials, and many other forms of support in order to be effective.

Business Model Disruption after 1998

Whether one looks at Google—a clear challenger to Microsoft's dominance—or at Apple, Facebook, or Linux (not a company at all), many of the assumptions about the Microsoft model no longer hold true. Greatness in software now requires a lot of the old-world programming skills and positioning, plus a healthy dose of some new elements.

To set some context, Table 17.1 looks at some familiar companies listed by market capitalization and price/earnings (P/E) ratio as of late 2010 compared to 10 years before, at the end of 2000.

Note that Salesforce, the exemplar of software as a service, is valued at 20 times Microsoft's P/E ratio. Microsoft's market capitalization, meanwhile, grew less than 8% in a decade. In addition, as of 1998, anyone looking for "the next Microsoft" probably would not have looked to Viacom or Disney as models. And for good reason: The role of "pushed" content remains in transition more than a decade later. Yet so-called shrinkwrap business models emphasizing software as a physical product often sold by the number of users or "seats" are in rapid decline while the core of the media-industry model—the packaging of audiences for sale to advertisers—is fueling growth at Google, presenting both technical and cultural challenges at Yahoo!, being rewritten at Facebook, and the source of deep concern among Microsoft's top leadership.[1]

The changing of the guard is further emphasized by Microsoft's recent experience with old-school software, its Vista operating system. The product shipped three years late, with a stripped-down feature set, and effectively cost several senior executives their jobs. It never sold in large numbers, in part because enterprise buyers refused the trade-offs of cost, risk, and performance that it offered. Windows 7 sold better but garners little press recognition or industry buzz: It has many attributes of a utility or an appliance, while strong market presence and growth are the hallmarks of Facebook, Apple, and, in mobile particularly, Google. In contrast, Microsoft's mobile software platform has yet to generate momentum, although the company's landmark alliance with Nokia will certainly bear watching here.

What are the emerging dynamics for software dominance? Compared to the standards for success circa 1997, a few factors have been inverted while most still hold true, albeit with a twist.

TABLE 17.1 Selected Technology Companies' Market Capitalization and P/E Ratio

Company	2000 Market Cap	2000 P/E	2010 Market Cap	2010 P/E
Apple	$5 billion	6	$294 billion	21
Google			$189 billion	24
IBM	$144 billion	19	$180 billion	13
Microsoft	$221 billion	23*	$238 billion	12
Oracle	$125 billion	19	$153 billion	24
Salesforce.com			$18 billion	245

*2000 high was $599 billion/68.

Product versus Service

In the majority of cases, nobody wants a product for what it *is*. (Diamonds and other luxury goods are obvious exceptions.) Rather, we want the capabilities delivered by the product: Knives slice food, cars provide transportation, and cameras deliver memories. When people buy software for what it *does*, there are numerous advantages to not owning seat licenses (particularly unutilized ones), physical artifacts such as discs or manuals, physical server hardware, physical data centers, or even physical storage. At the enterprise level, Microsoft has not suffered as directly from the presence of Salesforce.com as have Oracle and SAP, but the Salesforce model is helping people change their mind-sets: Recall that a business model is in large measure a cognitive commitment rather than a written document or legal status. At the personal level, Google's search, applications, maps, and mail/storage prove their utility daily to tens of millions of users. Software as a product is getting to be a more difficult sell.

The conception of software as a service rather than a product was advanced by the open-source community in the late 1990s. Understanding the difference between the use value and the sales value of software, particularly for custom enterprise applications, helped provide intellectual legitimacy for Apache, Linux, and others. As Eric Raymond, the author of the open-source manifesto *The Cathedral and the Bazaar*, put it, "[S]oftware is largely a service industry operating under the persistent but unfounded delusion that it is a manufacturing industry."[2]

Platforms

Rather than developing for UNIX, Windows, Mac OS, Symbian, set-top boxes, and a variety of other OSs, Google and Amazon have led the way toward development of services for the Internet as a platform. Among other things, this stance greatly simplifies product distribution: The differences between today's Google Maps and a 1998 version of Rand McNally's Windows package are striking. Every time a new road was paved, or interstate exits were renamed, or a pedestrian mall was built, millions of CDs became obsolete. In contrast, Google (or NAVTEQ or whatever) makes one change to the base map and every subsequent query will be addressed with accurate information.

Getting the platform right still matters, but the definition of the term is changing from local to virtual, solitary to distributed, and product to environment. Furthermore, platform heterogeneity is a reality: Mobile devices and PCs, tablets and set-top boxes, and even automobiles are semi-integrated, so user identities, data, and preferences must move seamlessly back and forth. Google runs across platforms, following the user, perhaps better than any major software vendor, while Microsoft remains heavily desktop-centric, not to mention Microsoft-centric.

Lock-in

The lock-in aspect still concerns Wall Street analysts, particularly because switching costs can be so low. If I change from Yahoo! Finance to, say, Fidelity's investor workbench, apart from my investment in learning the old interface, there's very little to restrain me from leaving. Tim O'Reilly, who helped formulate the very notion of Web 2.0*, asserts that users should own their data in these sorts of scenarios, but the exceptions to his assertion prove that Web 2.0 is hardly the last word. A person's eBay reputational currency, iTunes preferences, and Facebook profile are neither open nor portable—by design. Google owns search history and mobile search location; Amazon owns search, review, and purchase history; cloud e-mail providers own substantial clues about identity. Data has thus become a new mode of lock-in, joining application compatibility, learning investments, and long-term licensing.

Network Effects

There's no question that successful software still exploits network effects. The more developers who code to a given platform—Facebook, Salesforce, or Google Maps—the more that standard gains authority: Note that none of those aforementioned businesses counts only as a Web site. One of the platform pioneers powerfully illustrates the point perfectly: Amazon once noted in its earnings conference call that it had 265,000 developers signed up to use its Web services, a huge number for a young technology. There are also powerful network effects among users, whether at eBay, MySpace, or such peer-to-peer content distribution services as BitTorrent: *The more people who use the service, the more valuable it becomes.* Conversely, when people defect in large numbers, the flywheel spins in reverse. Compare that one fact to consumer products, banking, automobiles, or pharmaceuticals, and we are reminded how significantly online dynamics depart from those of widget business or even most of the service sector.

---

*Web 2.0 was a notion revolving around foundational changes from a static, broadcast model for the Web to a more dynamic, people-powered environment; user-generated content is an essential component of the term. Key examples of the tendency include Flickr, Google Maps, Wikipedia, and Facebook.

Upgrade (and Therefore Revenue) Cycles

No longer is the objective to leverage a large installed base onto a new version of the product. Google makes money every hour of every day, and apart from acquisitions, we don't expect spikes in its revenues. Indeed, the escape from the cyclicality of product upgrade cycles may not yet be fully appreciated as analysts assess the new breed of software companies. The dependence of shrinkwrap software companies (that sell software as a product) on secondary revenue streams may become problematic: Oracle CEO Larry Ellison noted in an interview with *FT* that his company was collecting 90% margins on software maintenance.[3] Customers can't be, and aren't, happy with those economics, so it is likely only a matter of time until competition and/or customer resistance change the model. SAP's attempt to move into the cloud and "information appliance" markets (where it encounters Sun+Oracle products) will be interesting to watch insofar as it represents a departure from the company's legacy business model.

Selling Software as a Product, One at a Time

Google once reported quarterly revenues that represented a year-over-year improvement of 58%. Did its sales force grow by 60% in a year? Highly doubtful. Although the company offers a few software products a customer can purchase, enterprise search hardware and software, hosted applications, and geographic information system tools amount to mere drops in that $29 billion annual bucket. An important facet of the software as a service trend is that in an increasing number of cases, users don't have the software on their own devices but access a server, the location of which is irrelevant, to get something done. As a result, *the customer base (of advertisers) is dramatically smaller than the user base*, which delivers favorable sales force performance metrics.

Accordingly, software distribution channels are being completely reinvented: The old goal used to be to get your product onto a shelf and/or catalog page at Computer City, Egghead, and MicroWarehouse. Note that all of those businesses are defunct, another indication of deeper change in the industry. In a related development that sheds further light on a complicated situation, *PC Magazine* subscriptions and ad pages dropped to the point where it ceased paper publication in 2008.

Retail Channel

Because it owns neither the PC hardware layer nor a content distribution channel, Microsoft is caught in conflicting trends here. Apple's retail stores are a powerful presence for the linked hardware-software platform, bringing in about $10 billion a year. At the same time, the demise of the PC-centric format hit Microsoft particularly hard: Best Buy, with troubles of its own and where PCs are displayed alongside toasters, cannot replicate the capabilities of a CompUSA of years gone by, not to mention an Apple Genius Bar, with its nearly-ideal selling environment. Apple's App Store/ iTunes format constitutes yet another competitive front. Finally, online distribution of free applications or services serves as another way that software gets to users.

People Buy Features and Performance

There's a wonderful video that embodies this thinking perfectly: Enter "microsoft ipod" into the YouTube search bar. Microsoft apparently produced this spoof internally, illustrating the trend toward "speeds and feeds" in stark contrast to Apple's aura and powerful design sense. Just run down the standard old-school software questions in regard to Facebook or MapQuest:

- What is the recommended processor?
- How much free disk space is required?
- What is the minimum memory required?
- How many transactions per second can the application handle?
- How fast can the application render/calculate/save/etc.?

The very mention of these former performance criteria in regard to the most successful "applications" of our time highlights the discontinuity between where we are and where we were. It's critically important to note that the path from the PC-resident Lotus Organizer to Basecamp project management or the original Encarta CDs to Wikipedia involved a step-function change rather than evolutionary progression: Incremental improvements to existing products are often insufficient in times of radical innovation.

Hire the Best Technical Team

There's no question that high-caliber architects and developers matter. Look at the arms race among Microsoft, Amazon, Google, and Yahoo! to hire the giants of the industry. At the same time, Facebook is raiding Google for software engineers and managers by the hundreds. In addition, the outside-in dynamic of user-generated content also allows such sites as Twitter or Facebook to thrive. In these kinds of businesses, it's certainly imperative to get top-flight operations and data-center professionals, no question, but these folks are of a different breed compared to the breakthrough innova-tors of the sort represented by Google's Vint Cerf, Louis Monier (who spent time at AltaVista, eBay, and Google), and Gordon Bell at Microsoft.

The lowering of coordination costs facilitated by the Internet allows smart people to collaborate outside of institutions, as we saw in Chapter 9.[4] With a target on its back as the dominant firm of the previous computing regime, Microsoft thus must compete on multiple fronts:

- Apple is proprietary, high margin, and design driven, a hardware+ software and fixed+mobile platform.
- Linux is free, user driven, organically evolving, and robust but ugly.
- Google is network-centric, mobility and geography-aware, with an ad-driven revenue model.

Competitive positioning relative to three such different models of soft-ware creation and distribution stands as a truly problematic proposition.

Rows and Columns

While I don't want to oversimplify and assert that value has migrated from nodes to links, the fact remains that the structure of business, personal connections, and information is looking much more like a spiderweb than a library card catalog. As scholarship from Rob Cross at the University of Virginia and others has illustrated, informal networks of personal contacts, once exposed, often explain a corporation better than the explicit titles and responsibilities.[5] At the engineering level, the very concept of social networking behind Twitter, Flickr, and Foursquare represents a departure from a conventional relational database mentality. The world as a radial graph is a very different proposition from trying to fit reality into cells in a preordained and fixed database schema.

Looking Ahead

The corporate architectures at Microsoft, Google, and Apple mirror their varying approaches to the market. For roughly a decade Apple's share price included a healthy dose of respect for the management skill of Steve Jobs, in that particular context, to both envision and execute. Conversely, the achievement of Google, with the jury out on the model's staying power, may lie in leadership's balancing of individual brilliance at differ-ent layers of the hierarchy with financially realistic corporate objectives. Finally, Microsoft appears to be working hard to define an emerging man-agement model as the founding generation hands off to new leaders.

Taken together, these tendencies are reshaping the software business: Programming (as in putting content together on radio or television) has joined programming (as in coding) as a core competency for many kinds of businesses that fall in the gaps between computing and media. The fusion also shakes up conventional media, as we noted earlier. The purely push-based media model, used to advertise things primarily for largely unmeasurable brand impact (unmeasurable at the level of the ad, particularly), is being challenged by viewers and readers who want more participation in both the experience (what used to be called consumption)[6] and the process (formerly known as publishing or content creation). As blogs, social networks, and professional content get further jumbled, and as NewsCorp founder Rupert Murdoch seems to be intent on demonstrating, the business models of media, software, gaming, and information transport will continue to become further intermixed.

Notes

1. Ray Ozzie announced himself as Bill Gates's successor as chief software architect at Microsoft with a memo entitled "The Internet Services Disruption," dated November 9, 2005, www.zdnet.com/blog/web2explorer/page/ray-ozzie-the-internet-services-disruption/54.
2. Eric Raymond, "The Magic Cauldron,"   http://catb.org/~esr/writings/magic-cauldron/.
3. Richard Waters, "Transcript: FT Interview with Larry Ellison," *Financial Times* April 18, 2006, www.ft.com/cms/s/2/5f7bdc18-ce85-11da-a032-0000779e2340.html#axzz1QPPGvl3F.
4. Clay Shirky, *Here Comes Everybody: The Power of Organizing Without Organizations* (New York: Penguin, 2008).
5. Rob Cross, *The Hidden Power of Social Networks: Understanding How Work Really Gets Done in Organizations* (Boston: Harvard Business School Press, 2004).
6. See, for example, SocialVibe, which explicitly contracts for viewers to watch ads on their time schedule rather than on an interruption model.

CHAPTER 18

Music Business Models

The business model disruption framework as it applies to music has multiple moving pieces: Tastes change, attitudes toward intellectual property sharing differ significantly by demographic, and the place of recorded music in modern life is also in a period of deep transition. The Recording Industry Association of America (RIAA), which began as a standards body, became perhaps the most disliked lobbying group in the country by suing music lovers, which was a curious strategy, to put it charitably. Music is a small but visible industry (moving and storage was about the same size, but Mayflower never had the Grammy Awards), and it was also disrupted early in the Internet's life cycle, before telecom or newspapers, for instance. How did technology-related events and trends disrupt the music industry's business model to such an extent that its trade association felt compelled to adopt such an extreme position?

Incumbent Model Pre-2000

It is tempting to say that Napster changed everything, and peer-to-peer (p2p) file sharing is clearly a hugely important factor in the media landscape. It is not the only factor, however, and a series of services have in fact disappeared, sometimes permanently: In addition to Napster, Pirate Bay and Limewire have been subject to legal challenges. But as we will see, the music industry business model had a number of problems before the Napster watershed.

Customer Value Proposition

The goal before the Internet era was to sell physical artifacts that carry music: cassettes, long-playing (LP) records, compact discs. As platforms evolved, record companies could sell the exact same content multiple times, which was one driving impetus behind the high-resolution formats that came to market in the late 1990s: Super Audio Compact Disc (SACD) and High Definition DVD (HD-DVD). Unfortunately for the record labels, at the same time that Napster and later the iPod popularized MP3 files, the audio-buying public was viewing SACD versus HD-DVD as a reprise of VHS-Betamax: People remembered buying machines that became worthless when the other standard emerged as dominant, making software, spare parts, and resale difficult. By the time Sony's SACD format won the standards war, the market had little enthusiasm for music players that required a new form of physical media.

Profit Formula

Record companies recognized million sellers with gold records as far back as 1942, but it was in the period between 1970 and 1980 that the industry saw huge sales of LPs: A handful of efforts from Michael Jackson, Pink Floyd, Fleetwood Mac, the Eagles, and other artists sold in excess of 40 million copies over their lifetime. For a number of reasons, labels sought a 10-million-seller rather than ten 1-million-unit milestones: The industry first became album driven (in that 8 to 12 songs were bundled into a 40-minute LP rather than being sold individually), then hit driven. The profit formula also was predicated on keeping artists in a disadvantaged position with regard to contract provisions and enforcement: Senator Orrin Hatch (a Utah Republican who has written more than 300 songs) once remarked that music is the only industry in which, after you pay off the mortgage, the bank still owns the house.[1]

Key Resources

Control of physical factories was essential: While pirate physical copies of LPs then CDs were available in some foreign countries, the complexity of manufacturing helped maintain the labels as an oligopoly. The labels viewed cassette taping with alarm in the 1970s, but the audio quality of tapes was inferior in most cases, as was the quality of the cover artwork, for which the LP format was ideally suited from a graphics perspective. Finally, the artist and repertoire function of discovering new bands was essential: Much like baseball scouts, certain individuals developed a track record in discovering successful new acts.

Key Processes

In addition to the supply chain of discovering talent, packaging albums, and distributing physical media, two other processes deserve mention.

Touring was often an important tool for building support for a new release. Also, music is a prototypical information good insofar as it presents a sampling problem: The only way to know if you like a book, video game, movie, or song is to experience the artifact itself. Statistics, reviews, and word of mouth help, to be sure, but radio played a key role in solving the sampling problem for recorded music. Later, just at the dawn of the CD format, MTV pioneered the music video that performed a similar function. Getting a song onto radio and, later, cable television often made the difference between a hit and a miss. Not surprisingly, money and favors could be exchanged in this pursuit, most notoriously in the payola scandal that cost disc jockey Alan Freed (who coined the term "rock 'n' roll") his career in the 1950s, but also as recently as 2005, when then New York attorney general Eliot Spitzer settled out of court with three major labels, each of which paid a multimillion-dollar penalty.

Technology Evolution and Industry's Response: The Case of Home Taping and MTV

In the late 1970s, the labels had succeeded in making disco music a perfect fit for the mass-distribution model. The problem was that the intense focus on the genre had run the industry into a cul-de-sac: As me-too acts multiplied, the American audience's appetite for disco dropped sharply, and there were few acts of other styles in the pipeline. Despite this saturation, the industry focused its public relations, legal, and lobbying efforts on stigmatizing and if possible outlawing the practice of cassette recording. One industry campaign featured a cassette-shaped skull and crossbones with the tagline "Home taping is killing music." Rather than exploiting this new, popular technology, labels fought it. The RIAA's president claimed that for every album that was bought, another went unbought because of taping. The RIAA also claimed that 425 million hours of music were taped even though blank tape sales were only half of that total.

Record sales had fallen 11.4% in 1981 and were rumored to be headed for another double-digit decrease in 1982. That year Columbia Records alone fired 300 people from the label while such superstar acts as Blondie and Fleetwood Mac canceled tour dates.

Enter MTV, a venture launched in 1981 by Warner Communications, which sold it to Viacom in 1985. MTV introduced a new musical vocabulary including heavy doses of synthesizers

(continued)

and electronic drum machines into the American market, initially including British pop acts like Duran Duran and the Eurythmics that enjoyed huge success in the 1980s. The technology innovation of replacing or augmenting the top-40 single with a cable TV music video changed the promotion landscape dramatically and introduced fresh "inventory" into the supply side of the music pipeline. In the end, the "crisis" in the music industry was not the fault of the tapers—who did not cease and desist even as the industry subsequently logged unprecedented profits—but had to a large extent resulted from stagnation in musical innovation at the major labels.

Michael Jackson's *Thriller* LP is widely credited as the first release to consciously utilize the new MTV promotional medium (e.g., by hiring commercial directors to make music videos as mini-movies): It sold between 26 and 40 million copies, depending on who's counting. At the same time, MTV's technology further intensified the music business's blockbuster economics that are in part responsible for the current situation. Being able to pass video costs on to the performer allowed labels to avoid confronting the vast potential of the new medium while limiting risk.

Business Model Disruption Pre-Napster

The 1990s witnessed at least a dozen changes to the music industry business model that helped set the stage for the knockout punch that Napster delivered. Any one by itself was not crippling but, en masse, these changes shifted the foundations of the industry sufficiently that labels were unable to respond to the challenge of p2p, in large measure because the customer value proposition was perceived to be unfair to both consumers and artists, who continued to enjoy favorable fan response.

1. *Piracy* had become an issue. As of 2001, about a quarter of CDs sold worldwide were suspected of being counterfeit. The ease of copying CDs on personal computers was one impetus for the SACD and HD-DVD formats, which incorporated copy protection schemes that, much like the DVD, would eventually have been broken anyway. At the turn of the century, the odds were less than 50% that a given CD was legitimate in such markets as China, Russia, and Brazil.

2. As *large-format retailers* gained in scale in the 1990s, they did more to dictate what was stocked. Just as they did in other industries, Target, Best Buy, and Wal-Mart gained in power relative to their suppliers, in this case both the labels and independent "rack jobbers" who stocked mom-and-pop operations. Such music-centric chains as HMV, Tower, and Wherehouse disappeared entirely.

3. Those large-format retailers helped shift an industry institution, the top-40 or Hot 100 list, to a more *data*-driven basis. In 1991, point-of-sale data replaced editors' phone calls to a few retail buddies. Garth Brooks was an instant beneficiary: Country music was found to be seriously underrepresented in the informal lists. Market research replaced taste and intuition in signing artists, leading to a homogenization of styles around a few themes, hip-hop and country among them.

4. Another factor led to a *lack of fresh new acts*. Reselling consumers the same music they had liked years or decades earlier was profitable and easy, particularly given favorable royalty arrangements in contracts that did not anticipate emerging formats. Music industry revenue nearly doubled between 1989 and 1994, largely on the strength of back catalog sales.

5. At the same time that nonmusic retailers increased their presence, *radio was consolidating*. Clear Channel came to own 11% of U.S. broadcast outlets but controlled 20% of ad revenue. Four broadcast groups controlled 63% of stations with a top-40 format. Once again, homogenization of musical genres, rather than diversity, was one outcome.

6. Even as it struggled with its own business model, *satellite radio* challenged physical music providers for share of wallet. The extreme variety and high audio quality made Sirius and XM credible alternatives to owning a CD collection, particularly for automobile listening.

7. *MTV* shifted its programming over time to the point where it seldom played new music videos. Meanwhile, the cost of producing a single music video, often borne by the artist, climbed to potentially more than $2 million.

8. *Touring* became an attractive revenue stream, but it was also subject to industry consolidation. Eventually, the Ticketmaster-Live Nation merger of 2010 meant that venue owners confronted a powerful alliance of concert booking and ticketing entities that could dictate terms. Clear Channel also operated in this market segment, leading to charges that radio airplay was being used as a negotiating tactic with non-Clear Channel promoters.

9. Recording artists won congressional support for an overturn of work-for-hire contact language that the RIAA had previously helped codify

into *law*. The language would have had the effect of denying artists' claims to copyright, particularly as new formats emerged.

10. The *DVD*, priced at about the same $16 point for which labels sold CDs, became the fastest-selling technology in U.S. history. In the four years after the format's launch in 1998, DVD players outsold CD players 3:1.

11. In another legal setback, the labels' practice of setting *minimum advertised prices* (MAPs; very close to price fixing) was found to be illegal in 2003. Consumers were supposed to receive small checks, and the labels were supposed to donate music to nonprofit institutions. The loss was small monetarily, but at the time that the RIAA was suing its customers, the MAP verdict was further bad publicity, leading consumers to feel, rightly or wrongly, that they were being treated unfairly by the labels.

12. Retailers speak of "*share of wallet*" and fast food franchises of "share of stomach." Music's "share of ear" diminished rapidly in the 2000 time frame as cell phones grew rapidly in availability and use. Nextel, to take one example, reported that minutes per user per month increased 65% between 2001 and 2002, to 11 hours per month. Presumably some of this time had previously been spent listening to music.

13. Similarly, the DVD and *video game* occupied part of the day for those aged 16 to 24 in particular, who a generation earlier were spending more time listening to music.

14. Finally, the *Internet*, apart from its file-sharing capabilities, constituted a diversion from traditional ways of finding and listening to music.

These changes combined to create a slowdown: Compared to the doubling that occurred between 1989 and 1994, purchases of recorded music increased only an average of .4% per year between 1996 and 2002, as Figure 18.1 illustrates.

Business Model Disruption Post-Napster

Against the backdrop of so many challenges to the core business model, from stale inventory of new acts, to poor perception of the labels by consumers, to heavy overhead in the cost structure of music production and distribution, Napster hit the industry like a lightning bolt: In November 2000 alone, 1.75 billion songs were downloaded via the service. That number, annualized, projected to 21 billion songs, or about 1.5 billion CDs. In 2000, the U.S. retail channel moved about 1 billion CDs.

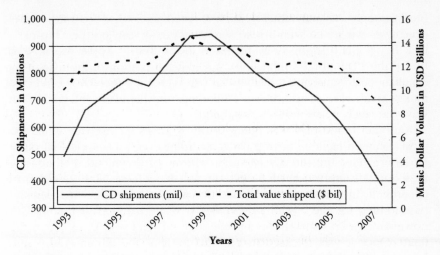

FIGURE 18.1 CD Shipments and Total Music Dollar Volume, 1993–2007
Data Source: Recording Industry Association of America.

In essence, the "inferior" technology (with a poor interface, complicated naming conventions, and obvious audio inferiority) effectively surpassed the entire retail channel as a distribution mechanism in one year. In addition, it was a highly centralized system in contrast to later file-sharing arrangements, but at its peak there were reportedly 25 million users and 80 million songs, and the system never once crashed.

With public perception of the labels already low because they were perceived to be exploiting both customers and artists, ripping off the companies was morally less complicated for college-age students than was, say, stealing books from a public library. When the labels began suing music lovers (or mistakenly suing people who did not listen to music), that perception took a further downturn. Meanwhile, the holding companies within which the labels resided were dissatisfied with their poor performance: Labels simultaneously faced pressure from artists long ill-served by standard contract practices, from listeners, from retailers that moved CD selling space to more profitable ventures, and from their bosses.

Enter Apple, a company with a substantially more positive public persona. The iPod was neither the first nor the most powerful MP3 player. It did employ systems thinking to create a seamless, easy user experience, and co-founder Steve Jobs' background in Hollywood while at Pixar gave him familiarity with the entertainment industry. Here as elsewhere, the business model was more a shift in perception rather than a technology breakthrough. As one industry analyst noted in 2002, "The music label executives we spoke with are so sure piracy is destroying their business, that they seemed strangely uninterested in the truth."[2] Apple was able to bridge the CD and MP3 models for a significant portion of the market by simultaneously satisfying the labels (in part with copy protection) and customers (with ease of use, clever marketing, and hardware integration) in ways the labels by themselves could not.

Another brand play was being made by artists themselves. While the most common tactic is buying (or rerecording) one's back catalog, other artists are releasing directly to various forms of download. Perhaps the most famous and successful episode for experiment was Radiohead's experiment in name-your-own-price downloads, which let fans (legally) pay nothing for the album *In Rainbows*. While many paid nothing (or downloaded p2p copies), the average amount paid was £4 ($5.70 at the time). Once it was released in physical formats, the album sold 3 million units in all formats; a limited edition box set of LPs and CDs with other extras sold 100,000 units at $80 apiece. Thus, the band conducted a real-world experiment in versioning information goods, letting the market segment into multiple price tiers in exchange for varying bundles of value. The experiment has also never been successfully repeated, even by the same band.

By 2010, download sales, never on the scale of physical CD sales, had stagnated.[3] Streaming services such as Pandora and Grooveshark were adding users at a rapid rate at the same time that iPod sales slowed (nearly a fifth between 2009 and 2010) in the face of smartphone and tablet adoption.

Touring remained big business: The 13 highest-grossing tours ever, each of which made more than $200 million in 2010 dollars, all occurred after 2001—in other words, *after* Napster. Significantly, nearly all (with the exception of the Backstreet Boys in 2001) were acts in their 40s or older: the Rolling Stones, U2, Cher, Madonna, the Police, and Bruce Springsteen, for example. Although so-called 360-degree deals are coming into favor (where the label helps promote, and takes a cut of, merchandise and tour revenues, for example), generally bands rather than labels keep most of the tour profit.

Because the hardware is locked down more tightly than CDs or DVDs, game platforms have generated surprising revenues for bands and labels: Inclusion of a track in a sports title or in Rock Band or another music game generates revenues, though labels typically are—unsurprisingly—unhappy with the royalty rates. In the three years after the launch of the plastic-guitar game genre, revenues were reported in the $2.3 billion range, but sales dropped rapidly when the fad passed; in 2010 Viacom sold its music-games business, which like other console games faced a major disruption of its own from low-tech social games such as FarmVille.

Looking Ahead

It's hard to imagine an industry responding much worse than the record labels did when faced with such a significant challenge. Taking profit margins almost as a birthright, most decisions—including appeals for legislation—were premised on maintenance of the status quo. Several decisions have proved crucial, most falling into the mind-set/worldview camp rather than a technology challenge per se:

- Customers resisted bundle pricing when they could emotionally identify the valuable assets in the bundle. Existing margins, however, became a baseline assumption even though Internet music distribution destroyed the logic for a physical package of multiple songs.
- Having limited contact with the consumers of their products, labels compounded the perception issue by suing users, planting corrupted files in p2p networks, clinging to unrealistic pricing ($16.99 for a physical CD), and making other profit-driven moves that detracted from the user experience.
- Continuing to think of music as a product rather than a service inhibited innovation along the lines of what worked for Apple, Pandora, Spotify, and other distributors of online music files and streams. Even in 2011, innovation came from Amazon even as EMI, one of the remaining four major labels, bounced between reluctant owners: Citicorp repossessed the label from a private equity group whose debt to the bank went unpaid, then in turn sold pieces of it at a loss to Sony and Universal (part of Vivendi).
- Managing demographics in a taste-driven business is never easy, but the quest for megahits may preclude the development of an ecosystem with varying levels of popularity (the so-called long tail) and proliferation of niches.

For the music industry to recover even partially, online distribution will need to be managed in a seamless web of actors, channels, and audiences. Live music, television, streaming, and licensing can all contribute to overall revenue. Both extreme localization and global megastars play a role in the ecosystem. Finally, the place of a music label in talent identification, content generation, and digital distribution needs to be redefined from a blank sheet. Music matters to many people, but making it profitable for the various entities in the industry remains a challenge.

Notes

1. Orrin Hatch quoted in "Rights Issue Rocks the Music World," *USA Today*, September 16, 2002, www.usatoday.com/life/music/news/2002-09-15-artists-rights_x.htm.
2. Josh Bernoff of Forrester Research quoted in Dan Bricklin, "The Recording Industry is Trying to Kill the Goose That Lays the Golden Egg," September 9, 2002, www.bricklin.com/recordsales.htm.
3. Glenn People, "Growth in Sales of Digital Downloads Slows to a Trickle," Reuters, December 10, 2010, www.reuters.com/article/2010/12/11/us-downloads-idUSTRE6BA09620101211.

CHAPTER 19

News

News is a particular kind of business. Subject to some textbook examples of information economics, newspapers at their best also enrich communities, sustain democracies by speaking truth to power, and occasionally build family dynasties. The migration from paper to the Internet has proven particularly challenging, with implications for all three of those defining characteristics.

Compared to old-school stockbrokers disintermediated by $10 trades or travel agents put out of business by online booking and electronic tickets, newspapers have been undone in other ways. The power of the traditional newspaper was its bundling, in economic terms, along two axes. First, subscriptions bundle content by time: Readers pay for daily delivery of papers whether they get read or not, for the sake of convenience. In addition, a daily paper contains bundled content that a given reader ignores: people of a certain age will remember how many hundreds of pages of a 1990s Sunday *New York Times* were thrown away untouched.

The sheer material wastefulness of the resource-intensive physical distribution model might have been an indicator that alternatives could flourish. Incumbents, not surprisingly, included smart, informed editors and publishers, many of whom were pillars of their communities. That such highly esteemed men and women could preside over a wholesale dismantling of a century-old model in a few short years provides one reason why the transition of news is such a compelling story.

Incumbent Formula Pre-2005

Daily newspaper readership had been dented badly before, by the widespread introduction of radio, then television. After the decline in the 1940s, however, demographics helped stabilize the situation: As table 19.1

TABLE 19.1 U.S. Newspaper Circulation versus Population, 1900–2010

Year	Daily Newspapers	Circulation (1,000s)	U.S. Population	Papers per Capita
1900	2,226	15,102	76,212	.198
1920	2,042	27,791	106,021	.262
1940	1,878	41,132	132,164	.311
1960	1,763	58,882	179,323	.328
1980	1,745	62,202	226,542	.274
2000	1,480	55,773	281,421	.198
2010	661	34,044	308,000	.110

Data Sources: Newspaper Association of America; U.S. Census.

shows, circulation kept rising, on the strength of population growth, even as a smaller and smaller percentage of the population bought newspapers.

Figure 19.1 graphs the data from Table 19.1. Note that the drop-off in readership rates is hidden under population-driven circulation growth for several decades. Newspapers were underrepresented in the population in the aftermath of television especially, but the essentials of the business model did not change markedly.

That model was a classic two-sided platform. (See Chapter 5.) Newspapers aggregated audiences with advertising and the things advertising could buy: foreign bureaus, improved color and layout, faster presses, and so on. Advertising-side revenue, particularly classifieds, subsidized the subscriptions (by roughly 4:1), giving readers an attractive value proposition in that they received a product that cost more to produce than what they paid.

Customer Value Proposition

Newspapers could hire reporters and editors, subscribe to wire services, and print and distribute newspapers. Barriers to entry were high, and even in multipaper towns, one paper generally took the morning while the weaker one handled the less attractive afternoon business.* Monopoly dynamics applied: For depth (baseball box scores or stock tables), radio or television couldn't compete, and newspapers were unchallenged

---

*As urban congestion worsened in the 1970s and after, getting the trucks full of papers to delivery points was much more difficult than the task of distributing newspapers at 5:00 A.M.

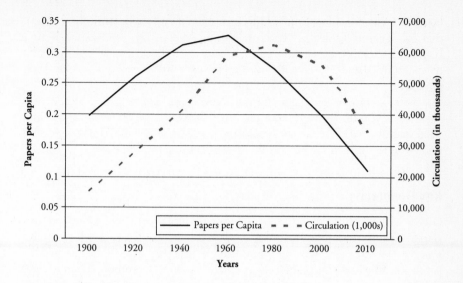

FIGURE 19.1 U.S. Newspaper Readership, 1900–2010

in some categories of news. For local matters, such as zoning or school boards, television typically found the tedium of committee meetings and report filings ill-suited for their 20 minutes at 6:00 and 11:00 p.m. From an advertiser standpoint, the infinite capacity for classified ad inventory meant that used cars, apartment listings, or job postings were much better suited to print than electronic media. This is, of course, a classic network externality: Every additional help-wanted ad, or open house, makes the platform more valuable to both advertisers (which gain strength in numbers relative to other channels) and to customers, who become more likely to solve their search needs with one-stop shopping.

Profit Formula

Time-based bundling, better known as subscriptions, helped match production to demand and generated less waste compared to more volatile newsstand sales. In cases where subscriptions were paid ahead of delivery, newspaper companies enjoyed steady revenue flows and better working capital: Ink and newsprint and reporters' salary and benefits were to some degree paid for before they were consumed.

The bundling of material into sections meant that every newspaper enjoyed the luxury of subsidies: Classified ads cost essentially nothing to produce but brought in handsome revenues, as did grocery store ads. Advertising in turn subsidized other efforts, such as foreign news bureaus, which could not afford to pay their own freight. Bundling meant that no person typically read everything every day, but every reader could find something of interest. As long as ad revenues were sufficient to maintain the editorial side of the house, profits were solid or even attractive.

Note in Figure 19.2 that for the New York Times Company, profits were steady, with a dip during the early-1990s recession, from 1984 until 2006, during which year the company took an $814 million write-down related to its Boston *Globe* and Worcester *Telegram* properties.

Key Resources

Given a newspaper's status as a two-sided platform, running a newspaper required parallel sets of resources. In fact, an article of faith among practitioners was the integrity of the separation between editorial (reader-side customers) and advertising (commercial interests) functions. Ad sales, editorial-page positioning, and overall circulation numbers were required to keep advertisers happy; quality reporting, good pictures, the right mix of syndicated comics, and heavy ad inventory in key segments (such as apartment listings or job postings) attracted readers. The more readers, the more advertising revenue. The more advertising, the more reporters and columnists, the more color pages, and the more coverage: Ideally, these enhancements led to still more readership.

Thus, the required resources were extensive, which helped raise barriers to entry: reporters, editors, layout teams, pressmen, drivers, ad sales forces, human resource functionaries to deal with large staffs, and extensive billing and customer service operations. Capital investment in presses, syndication memberships, and delivery fleets (not to mention oil-related

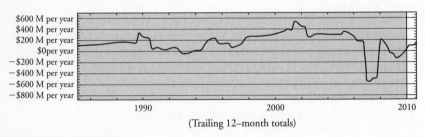

(from Dec 1984 to Sep 2010)

FIGURE 19.2 New York Times Company Net Income, 1984–2010
Source: Wolfram Alpha LLC. 2011. input="new york times company revenue"Wolfram | Alpha.

operating expenses for fuel and ink) made skilled financial management a requirement for long-term success.

Key Processes

Not surprisingly, those key resources performed obvious functions: Reporters reported and wrote, editors edited, pressmen printed, drivers delivered, sales reps sold, accountants counted. Skillful and attuned editorial leadership could drive readership with good story selection, astute newswriting, and other effects of quality; the opposite could quickly alienate a paper from its community.

Business Model Disruption

If the music industry's problem was resisting the spread of free music via the Internet, the newspapers' problem was in part caused by giving too much value away for too long. In addition, the threats came from multiple directions, in such large numbers and in such diversity that a focused strategic response was essentially impossible: As early as 1998 one consultant aptly referred to the process as "termiting." Surprisingly, a prominent newspaper industry report from 2009 preferred instead to blame a single villain.

> *Then the emergence of Google, an Internet search company that was launched without a business plan, soon blew up the content business into millions of "atomized" pieces, each piece disassociated at some level from its original context and creator. Like all the king's men, news enterprises were left to put the Humpty Dumpty of editorial and commercial content back together again, restore their original integrity, and finance the costly operation of being the trusted curator of news and transactions.*[1]

This representation is somewhat disingenuous: "Financing the costly operations" of content creation and curation is still profitable. As the Princeton historian Paul Starr points out, the average newspaper operating margin in late 2008 was 11.5%.[2] The problem, however, is that percentage represents roughly a 50% drop from only six years prior, and the decline appears to be deepening. Accordingly, investor confidence in the future of the business model is plummeting: Newspaper stocks have been battered through good times and bad since 2005 or so.

Long before Google News, however, many of the bundled facets of a newspaper were separated out by stand-alone Web businesses, each taking some segment of the readership and unbalancing the former cross-subsidies. Sports readers could go to the league sites (now with heavy video footage), television spinouts from Fox/ESPN/CNN+Sports Illustrated, fan-driven blogs and/or message board efforts, or any number of sites updating them on favorite cricket, soccer, or other international sports the metro dailies can barely cover, if at all. The local geographic monopoly was broken.

News is still primarily gathered by the usual suspects but commented on, linked to, and reaggregated by everyone from Google News, to bloggers, to ideology-driven destination sites. Daily A–Z stock charts aren't a particularly helpful way to watch the financial world, opening the door to broad distribution of previously professional-grade charting, archiving, and analytics; less professional message boards, blogs, and other mechanisms spread the wisdom (or lack thereof) of crowds.

At the same time and in a similar manner, the papers' extremely profitable ads were hit hard by multiple competitors. (See Figure 19.3.) eBay then later Craigslist took over the realm of random objects, Monster and others (including the hiring firms directly) redefined the help-wanted field, and Edmunds and Cars.com along with eBay Motors improved on the car-buying experience by improving information availability and transparency. Match.com and eHarmony improved on the user experience and inventory levels of the personal ads, while real estate agents alone and in their trade association aggregated and augmented millions of property ads with photos, maps, and video walk-throughs. Online food-related sites proliferated,

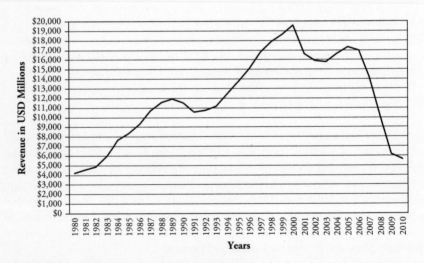

FIGURE 19.3 Classified Advertising Revenue, 1980–2010
Data Source: Business Analysis and Research, Newspaper Association of America, "Advertising Expenditures," www.naa.org/Trends-and-Numbers/Advertising-Expenditures/Annual-All-Categories.aspx.

all better at providing meal solutions than the once-a-week recipe page that accompanied the newspaper grocery ads.

In the end, most any page of a 1990s-era newspaper was challenged by an online outlet. With the readership in decline, both ad and subscription revenue spiraled downward, and the splintered nature of the competition made coordinated response impossible. Newspapers are also hampered by their physical distribution model: News is old before readers even receive their papers, petroleum-intensive physical distribution is expensive, and from an ecological perspective, newsprint is anything but green. Indeed, U.S. newsprint consumption fell by 50% between 2001 and 2009.[3] Because this figure is greater than the rate of subscriber loss, papers were getting smaller as well, indicating a steep decline in ad revenue.

In addition, the culture of "free" has affected news nearly as much as music, but far less so than books, for example. Some observers, including *The Economist*, have speculated that a Kindle or other reader might play a part in a revitalized news distribution business model. This makes sense: Books, newspapers, and magazines emerged as business opportunities following a technology disruption, so changing the technology implies change for both reading habits and business building.

Indeed, 2010 proved to be the year of the tablet following the rapid consumer adoption of the iPad. Large content companies such as Condé Nast, News Corporation, and Time Warner flocked to tablets, hoping to establish an early consumer pattern in which paying for news was a conditioned behavior. Before the device was released, industry insiders, hoping for such a state of affairs, called the iPad "the Jesus tablet."[4] Now that the category appears to be thriving, however, pricing, ergonomics, archives, the balance of still to video layouts, and many other aspects of the newspaper model remain works in progress, and no clear answer has yet emerged, profitable or not.

Looking Ahead

In parallel with the decline in newspaper readership, the advertising industry has been fundamentally challenged by targeted, interactive, and well-instrumented ads and all they imply. If tablets and other e-readers do reinvigorate the news business, this sector will need to move sure-footedly in parallel with the editorial business to regain much of the ground it has lost to Google in the past few years. In addition, while the movement away from traditional print models is highly visible, YouTube and the phenomenal rise of Internet video will also force a reshaping of television's economics. The ability of citizens armed with cameraphones to "report" on local events, as on CNN's iReports, further complicates the news business.

What If Digital News Is Inherently Unprofitable?

On the day that the Chicago *Tribune* broke the story of Illinois Governor Rod Blagojevich's arrest for allegedly peddling Barack Obama's Senate seat, the paper's parent company declared bankruptcy. The timing told a powerful story. In a time and in a world with so much up for grabs and such a pressing need for informed citizenries, the demise of the daily newsprint-driven business model raises critically important questions about accountability, about investment, and about the role of advertising.

Losing a newspaper is different from losing a travel agent or record store. Democracy is premised on public accountability, and a free, active press supports that objective, particularly through investigative journalism. A variety of efforts are under way to redefine newspaper reporting as a civic trust, potentially supported with foundation grants, National Public Radio-type donations, or a hybrid model. As Paul Starr put it,

> *If newspapers are no longer able to cross-subsidize public-service journalism and if the decentralized, non-market forms of collaboration [such as Wikipedia] cannot provide an adequate substitute, how is that work going to be paid for? The answer, insofar as there is one, is that we are going to need much more philanthropic support for journalism than we have ever had in the United States.*[5]

Yale's David Swensen and Michael Schmidt made the same point in a *New York Times* editorial just weeks earlier:

> *[T]here is an option that might not only save newspapers but also make them stronger: Turn them into nonprofit, endowed institutions—like colleges and universities. Endowments would enhance newspapers' autonomy while shielding them from the economic forces that are now tearing them down.*[6]

How big an endowment? A budget the size of the *New York Times* would cost $5 billion to endow. That's Warren Buffett/Bill Gates territory, unless Facebook's Mark Zuckerberg were to step up.

Notes

1. American Press Institute, *Paid Content: Newspaper Economic Action Plan*, May 2009, p. 7, *www.niemanlab.org/pdfs/apireportmay09.pdf.*
2. Paul Starr, "Goodbye to the Age of Newspapers (Hello to a New Era of Corruption)," *New Republic,* March 4, 2009, www.tnr.com/article/goodbye-the-age-newspapers-hello-new-era-corruption.
3. Michael Ducey, "Newsprint Demand, Production Continue Freefall," March 29, 2010, www.newsandtech.com/news/article_cac1f0dc-3b57-11df-b071-001cc4c03286.html.
4. Kenneth Li and Andrew Edgecliffe-Johnson, "Industry Awaiting 'Jesus Tablet,'" *FT,* January 28, 2010, www.ft.com/cms/s/2/cd8e6ee6-0ba3-11df-9f03-00144fe-abdc0.html#axzz1gLKodEin.
5. Starr, "Goodbye to the Age of Newspapers."
6. David Swensen and Michael Schmidt, "News You Can Endow," *New York Times,* January 27, 2009, www.nytimes.com/2009/01/28/opinion/28swensen.html?pagewanted=all.

CHAPTER 20

Healthcare

The solution seems obvious: to get all the information about patients out of paper files and into electronic databases that . . . can connect to one another so that any doctor can access all the information that he needs to help any given patient at any time in any place.
—"Special Report: IT in the Health-Care Industry," *The Economist*, April 30, 2005

There's no question that U.S. medicine is approaching a crisis. Depending on who's counting, tens of millions of Americans carry no health insurance. Between 44,000 and 98,000 people are estimated to die every year from preventable medical errors such as drug interactions; the fact that the statistics are so vague testifies to the problem. The United States leads the world in healthcare spending per capita by a large margin ($7,500 versus about $5,000 for the runners-up: Norway, Canada, and Switzerland), but U.S. life expectancy ranks twenty-seventh, near that of Cuba, which is reported to spend about 1/25th as much per capita. Information technology (IT) has made industries such as package delivery, retail, and mutual funds more efficient; can healthcare benefit from similar gains?

Any assessment of the impact of information and communications technologies on the U.S. healthcare system must consider their effects on the multiple business models already in place. Unlike, say, Napster and the music industry or even the multithreaded issues of news, publishing companies, and the Internet, U.S. healthcare is so incredibly vast, with dozens if not hundreds of business models, that there is no single "it" to be disrupted.

The farther one looks into this issue, the more tangled the questions get. Let me assert at the outset that I believe electronic medical records are a good idea. But for reasons outlined later, IT by itself falls far short of meeting the challenge of rethinking health and healthcare. At the same time, those invested in the status quo should probably not get too comfortable, given some weak signals in the area of social media in particular.

Definitions

What does the healthcare system purport to deliver? If longevity is the answer, clearly much less money could be spent to bring U.S. life expectancy closer to Australia, where people live an average of three years longer with per capita expenditures 57% lower than in the United States. But health means more than years: the phrase "quality of life" hints at the notion that we seek something nonquantifiable from doctors, therapists, nutritionists, and others. At a macro level, no one can assess how well a healthcare system works because the metrics lack explanatory power: We know, only roughly, how much money goes in to a hospital, health maintenance organization (HMO), or even economic sector, but we don't know much about the outputs.

Thinking of life expectancy, Americans at large don't seem to view death as natural, even though it's one of the very few things that happens to absolutely everyone. Within many outposts of the healthcare system, death is regarded as a failure of technology, to the point where central lines, respirators, and other interventions are applied to people who are naturally coming to the end of life. This approach of course incurs astronomical costs, but it is a predictable outcome of a heavily technology-driven approach to care.

At the other end of the spectrum, should healthcare make us even "better than well?" As the bioethicist Carl Elliott compellingly argues in his book of that name,[1] a substantial part of our investment in medicine, nutrition, and surgery is enhancement beyond what's naturally possible. Cosmetic surgery, steroids, implants, and blood doping are no longer the exclusive province of celebrities and world-class athletes. Not only can we not define health on its lower baseline, it's getting more and more difficult to know where it stops on the top bound as well.

If health is partially defined by what people ingest, why stop with vitamins and supplements? What about the less healthy inputs that can be named as contributors to pulmonary conditions, obesity, or mouth cancers? That is, do both negative and positive contributors to people's well-being get included in the accounting? Are cigarette sales factored into the healthcare accounting? As a result of the definitional issues inherent in the subject matter and the massive scale of the enterprise, trying to name the U.S. healthcare "system" invites conceptual misery.

Healthcare as Car Repair for People?

Speaking in gross generalizations, U.S. hospitals are not run to deliver health; they are better described as sickness-remediation facilities. The ambiguous position of women who deliver babies demonstrates the primary orientation. Many of the institutional interventions and signals (calling the woman a "patient," for example) are shared with the sickness-remediation side of the house even though birth is not morbid under most circumstances. Some hospitals are turning this contradiction into a marketing opportunity: Plushly appointed "birthing centers" have the stated aim of making the new mom a satisfied customer. "I had such a good experience having Max and Ashley at XYZ Medical Center," the intended logic goes, "that I want to go there for Dad's heart problems."

Understanding healthcare as sickness remediation has several corollaries. Doctors are deeply protective of their hard-won cultural authority, which they guard with language, apparel, and other mechanisms, but the parallels between a hospital and a car repair garage run deep. After Descartes philosophically split the mind from the body in the 17th century, medicine followed the ontology of science to divide fields of inquiry—and presumably repair—into discrete units.

At teaching hospitals especially, patients frequently report feeling less like a person and more like a sum of subsystems. Rashes are for dermatology, heart blockages set off a tug-of-war between surgeons and cardiologists, joint pain is orthopedics or maybe endocrinology. Root-cause analysis frequently falls to secondary priority as the patient is reduced to his or her compartmentalized complaints and metrics. Pain is no service's specialty but many patients' primary concern. Systems integration between the subspecialties often falls to floor nurses and the patient's advocate if he or she can find one. The situation might be different if one is fortunate enough to have access to a hospitalist: a new specialty that addresses the state of being hospitalized, which the numbers show to be more deadly than car crashes.

The division of the patient into subsystems that map to professional fields has many consequences. Attention focuses on the disease state rather than the path that led to that juncture: Preventive care lags far behind crisis management in glamour, funding, and attention. Diabetes provides a current example. Drug companies have focused large sums of money on insulin therapies, a treatment program that can change millions of people's lives, and more recently on obesity drugs. But when public health authorities try to warn against obesity as a preventive attack on diabetes, soft-drink and other lobbies immediately spring into action.

Finally, western medicine's claim to be evidence based contradicts the lack of definitive evidence for ultimate consequences. The practice of performing autopsies in cases of death where the cause is unclear has dropped steadily and steeply (from 19% of all U.S. deaths in 1972 to 8% in 2003), to the point where doctors and families do not know what killed a sizable population of patients. A study at the University of Michigan estimated that almost 50% of hospital patients died of a condition for which they were not receiving treatment.[2] It's potentially the same situation as storeowner John Wanamaker bemoaning that half of his advertising budget was being wasted, but not knowing which half.

Following the Money

Healthcare costs money, involves scarcities and surplus, and employs millions of people. As such, it constitutes a market—but one that fails to run under conventional market mechanisms. (For example, excess inventory, in the form of unbooked surgical times, let's say, is neither auctioned to the highest bidder nor put on sale to clear the market.) The parties that pay the most are rarely the parties whose health is being treated; the parties that deliver care lack detailed cost data and therefore price services only in the loosest sense; and the alignment of patient preference with some notion of greater social good through the lens of for-profit insurers has many repercussions.

Consider a few market-driven suboptimizations:

- Chief executives at HMOs are rewarded for cost cutting, which often translates to cuts in hospital reimbursement. Hospitals, meanwhile, are frequently not-for-profit institutions, many of which have been forced to close their doors in the past two decades.
- Arrangements to pay for certain kinds of care for the uninsured introduce further costs, and further kinds of costs, into an already complex set of financial flows.
- As the British social researcher Richard Titmuss showed more than 30 years ago in *The Gift Relationship*,[3] markets don't make sense for certain kinds of social goods. In his study, paying for blood donation lowered the amount and quality of blood available for transfusion; more recently, similar paradoxes and ethical issues have arisen regarding tissue and organ donation.

- Insurers prefer to pay for tangible rather than intangible services. Hospitals respond by building labs and imaging centers as opposed to mental health facilities, because services like psychiatric nursing are rarely covered.
- Once they build labs, hospitals want them utilized, so there's further pressure (in addition to litigation-induced defensiveness) for technological evidence gathering rather than time-consuming medical art such as history taking and palpation, for which doctors are not reimbursed.
- Many medical schools can no longer afford for their professors to do nonreimbursable things such as teach or serve on national standards bodies. The doctors need to bring in grant money to fund research and insurance money for their clinical time. Teaching can be highly uneconomical for all concerned. One reason there is a shortage of nurses, meanwhile, is that there is a shortage of nursing professors.
- As a result, conditions with clear diagnoses (such as fractures) are treated more favorably in economic terms, and therefore in interventional terms, than conditions that lack "hard" diagnostics (such as allergies or neck pain). Once again, the vast number of people with mental health issues are grossly underserved.

If the trend does not reverse soon, healthcare expenditures are projected to double as a percentage of gross domestic product (GDP) in only 25 years, according to the Congressional Budget Office. (See Figure 20.1.)[4]

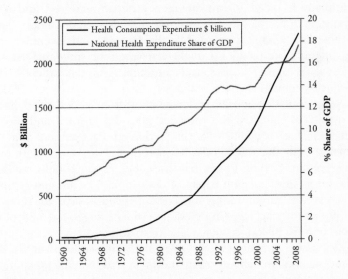

FIGURE 20.1 U.S. Healthcare Costs in Dollars and as a Percent of GDP

Source: U.S. Department of Health and Human Services.

Where Information Technology Can and Cannot Help

IT has made significant improvements possible in business settings with well-defined, repeatable processes, such as originating a loan or filling an order. Medicine involves some processes that fit this description, but it also involves a lot of impossible-to-predict scheduling, healing as art rather than science, and institutionalized barriers to communication.

IT is currently used in four broad medical areas:

1. Billing and finance
2. Supply chain and logistics
3. Imaging and instrumentation
4. Patient care

Patient registration is an obvious example of the first; waiting rooms and foodservice the second; magnetic resonance imaging (MRI) appointments, blood tests, and bedside monitoring the third; and physician order entry, patient care notes, and prescription writing the fourth. Each type of automation introduces changes in work habits, incentives, and costs to various parties in the equation.

Information regarding health and information regarding money often follow parallel paths: If I get stitched up after falling on my chin, the insurance company is billed for an emergency department visit and a suture kit at the same time that the hospital logs my visit—and, I hope, flags any known antibiotic allergies. Meanwhile the interests and incentives are frequently anything but parallel: I might want a plastic surgeon to suture my face; the insurer prefers a physician's assistant. From the patient's perspective, having systems that more seamlessly interoperate with the HMO may not be positive if that results in fewer choices or a perceived reduction in the quality of care. On the provider side, the hospital and the plastic surgeon will send separate bills, each hoping for payment but neither coordinating with the other. Bills frequently appear in a matter of days, with every issuer hoping to get paid first, before the patient realizes any potential errors in calculating copay or deductible. The amount of time and money spent on administering the current dysfunctional multipayer system is difficult to conceive: One credible estimate suggested 21% of excess spending, or $150 billion in 2008, came from administrative costs.[5]

Privacy issues are nontrivial. Given that large-scale breaches of personal information are almost daily news in 2011,[6] what assurance will patients have that a complex medical system will do a better job shielding privacy than Citigroup or LexisNexis? With genomic predictors of health—and of potential costs for insurance coverage—around the corner, how will patients' and insurers' claims on that information be reconciled?

Currently a number of services let individuals combine personal control and portability of their records. It's easy to see how such an approach may not scale: Something as trivial as password resets in corporate computing environments already involve sizable costs. In light of that complexity, think about managing the sum of past and present patients and employees as a user base with access to the most sensitive information imaginable. With portable devices proliferating, the many potential paths of entry multiply both the security perimeter and the cost of securing it.

Hospitals already tend to treat privacy as an inconvenience—witness the universal use of the ridiculous johnnie gowns, which do more to demean the patient than to improve quality of care. The medical record doesn't even belong to the person whose condition it documents. American data privacy standards, even after the enactment of the Health Insurance Portability and Accountability Act of 1996 (HIPAA), lag behind those in the European Union. From such a primitive baseline, getting to a new state of shared accountability, access, and privacy will take far more diplomacy than systems development.

Spending on diagnostic technology currently outpaces patient care IT. Hospitals routinely advertise less confining MRI machines, digital mammography, and 3D echocardiography; it's less easy to impress constituencies with effective metadata for patient care notes, for example. (Some computerized record systems merely capture images of handwritten forms with only minimal indexing.) After these usually expensive machines produce their intended results, the process by which diagnosticians and ultimately caregivers use those results is often haphazard: Many tests are never consulted or compared to previous results—particularly if they were generated somewhere else. NIH doesn't just stand for National Institutes of Health; not invented here is also alive and well in hospitals.

Back in the early days of business reengineering, when technology and process change were envisioned as a potent one-two punch in the gut of inefficiency, the phrase "Don't pave the cowpaths" was frequently used as shorthand. Given that medicine can be routinized only to a certain degree, and given that many structural elements contribute to the current state of affairs, it's useful to recall the old mantra. Without new ways of organizing the vastness of a longitudinal medical record, for example, physicians could easily find themselves buried in a haystack of records, searching for a needle without a magnet. Merely automating a bad process rarely solves any problems, and usually creates big new ones.

Change comes slowly to medicine, and the application of technology depends, here as always, on the incentives for different parties to adopt new ways of doing things. Computerized approaches to caregiving include expert knowledge bases, automated lockouts much like those in commercial aviation, and medical simulators for training students and experienced practitioners alike. Each of these methods has proven benefits but only limited deployment. Further benefits could come from well care and preventive medicine, but these areas have proven less amenable to the current style of IT intensification. Until the reform efforts such as the Leapfrog initiative to mobilize employer health insurance purchasing power can address the culture, process, and incentive issues in patient care, the increase in clinical IT investment will do little to drive breakthrough change in the length and quality of Americans' lives.

Disruptive Innovation

Apart from clinical IT, however, several potential disruptions appear to be taking shape. Brief descriptions of some of these are accompanied by potential winners and losers.

Channel Innovation

Recall that healthcare IT focused on four areas: billing and finance, supply chain and logistics, imaging and instrumentation, and patient care. If "patient care" is rephrased as "customer service," it's clear that companies already good at some of these processes might have potential in some aspect of medicine. As it turns out, such retailers as Wal-Mart, CVS, and Walgreens are putting clinics in selected stores to address routine matters that would often otherwise require an emergency department visit.[7]

Potential winners: Patients get the right level of care with extreme convenience. Payors get excellent performance for money, if the visit is reimbursed at all, since profitable economics are engineered into the self-selecting population. Retailers give customers more reason to visit. Emergency rooms should benefit by having the private market triage some low-intensity patients out of the system.

Potential losers: Hard to see any, apart from physician prestige.

Telemedicine

Particularly in the developing world, where doctors and clinics cannot meet the need in many countries, mobile phones are connecting people to medical resources in new ways. Real-time diagnostic indicators can be easily transmitted by, and often read on, mobile devices. Cameras can be used as sensors, so the mobile phone becomes a rudimentary blood lab. Text-message reminders to take necessary medication are increasing compliance and improving outcomes. Geolocation can help identify safe water, malarial ponds, and other public health resources. The list goes on, but many of these techniques will migrate from Asia and Africa to North America and Europe in a fascinating pattern of "reverse" globalization.

Potential winners: Citizens, entrepreneurs.

Potential losers: Hard to see any downside, but traditional modes of cure might see decline in prestige.

Online Communities

Imagine living alone, in a big city or a rural town, and having a serious condition, such as multiple sclerosis. Even with insurance, physician and nurse visits can only provide so many answers. What will be the sequence of the disease? How do I choose a good wheelchair? What are the side effects of a given treatment regimen? Web sites such as www.patients likeme.com have emerged to accumulate and deliver real-world advice and support to many disease communities.[8]

An important advantage of peer communities over therapeutic providers is in compliance and motivation. In weight loss, for example, having a doctor say "lose 15 pounds" does little in the way of motivation. Finding a community, perhaps one with a shared or individual goal, can make a huge difference. Individually, such behavioral motivators as stickk. com use the academic insight that small symbolic wagers and similar techniques can be highly effective in changing people's patterns. At the group level, the team of Northwestern University alums at workplaces in Chicago will work harder to lose their collective 500 pounds if a charitable donation to the United Way and bragging rights over the Illinois alumni are at stake.

Potential winners: Anyone who has felt isolated while in ill health.

Potential losers: It's hard to call this disruptive, in that most physicians won't claim to be effective motivators, but online communities do have the potential to diminish the doctor's cultural authority when shared research and motivated interest lead the group to start recommending diagnostic or treatment protocols.

Rethinking Devices

A typical ultrasound machine for sale in the United States typically costs in the range of $100,000 and is approximately the size of a washing machine.

Portable units closer to the dimensions of a laptop PC have been in various stages of development for roughly a decade and are starting to gain market traction. From the standpoint of an incumbent—GE or Siemens, for example—the new models are not a threat insofar as radiologists at major medical centers would not be satisfied with the limited flexibility and image quality of the portables, so these companies are in fact "disrupting themselves" with certain models.

But the innovation goes beyond engineering and marketing at device manufacturers. What are the implications for the business processes that the technology supports? New kinds of technicians, and training, and treatment protocols are necessary to wrap around the technology. Rather than potentially disrupting nonexistent radiologists in the developing world, the technology has the potential to create whole new "lines of business" compared to stethoscopes or other health technology alternatives.

Portable ultrasound has also been implicated in more than 100 million missing women in Asia: Because of various cultural concerns, girl babies are less desired than boys. Ultrasound imaging can give prospective parents advance notice of a fetus's sex, and gender-driven abortion is common even while illegal. While technologists cannot tell parents the sex, the ultrasound report is sometimes delivered in a pink or blue envelope, and the parents can act on the winked information.[9]

Potential winners: Hardware manufacturers, wireless carriers, patients.

Potential losers: Patient privacy could become an issue.

Checklists

Surprisingly, the simple checklist is a radical idea in healthcare and in practice is anything but simple. Much like aviation, where the concept originated, many healthcare procedures are complex, life critical, and prone to simple human error: the wrong side of the body is operated on, sponges are left inside the body, bandages and intravenous lines are not changed at the right intervals. Harvard surgeon Atul Gawande has been a leader in a worldwide effort to introduce checklists into surgery, with dramatic results.[10]

The idea of a checklist introduces multiple issues. Surgeons are known to be skilled and expected to be in charge of the proceedings, but anything as complex as surgery is a team event, and surprisingly little time is spent on improving team performance: Even the simple act of having the team members introduce themselves by name was found to make a difference. Much like business process steps that people are less inclined to perform sloppily if they hand off to a known associate as opposed to an anonymous "other," surgery goes better if the person behind the mask is a person with a name. Similarly, giving nurses the authority, and the responsibility, to stop a procedure if a critical step, such as the preoperative administration of antibiotic, is not followed shifts responsibility from the artisanal surgeon to the entire team.

Checklist formulation, however, is hard to do well. Put in too many steps, and they get skimmed or the list is disregarded. Fail to spell out, in the fewest words possible, every task, and debates begin about the intent. Include only the essentials, be they trivial or monumental, and checklists save lives: When Captain Chesley Sullenberger and his crew successfully ditched his USAirways A320 in the Hudson River in 2009, they were following checklists, not acting out heroic improvisations. Another aviation checklist includes the imperative "Fly the airplane:" Restarting an engine can become so engrossing that pilots have neglected other higher priorities, such as watching out the window.

While checklists disrupt few business models, they are improving performance, changing authority relationships, and forcing hospital administrators and doctors themselves to revisit their assumptions about the origins of improved patient outcomes. As Gawande writes:

> *[I]f someone discovered a new drug that could cut down surgical complications with anything remotely like the effectiveness of the checklist, we would have television ads with minor celebrities extolling its virtues. . . . Government programs would research it. Competitors would jump in to make better and better versions.*[11]

Looking Ahead

With so any moving parts, healthcare delivery and reimbursement in the United States is impossible to characterize except in the broadest possible terms. There will be no Napster, it is safe to say, no Skype, and no Facebook that will dominate. At the same time, changing mores about participation, about cultural differences (in both attitudes and genomes), and about cost and transparency are driving change. The current trajectory is unsustainable, the baby boom generation is entering its most expensive phase of healthcare life, and the numbers prove emphatically that the current model is broken. Fixing little corners, often quietly, will be the norm, and like a path of footsteps in the sand, we most likely will have to look back to figure out when we changed direction.

Notes

1. Carl Elliott, *Better Than Well: American Medicine Meets the American Dream* (New York: Norton, 2003).
2. Atul Gawande, *Complications: A Surgeon's Notes on an Imperfect Science* (New York: Picador, 2003), p. 67.
3. Richard Titmuss, *The Gift Relationship: From Human Blood to Social Policy* (New York: New Press, 1997 reprint).
4. "The Long-Term Outlook for Medicare, Medicaid, and Total Health Care Spending" www.cbo.gov/ftpdocs/102xx/doc10297/Chapter2.5.1.shtml.
5. See, for example, Uwe Reinhart, "Why Does U.S. Healthcare Cost So Much: (Part II: Indefensible Administrative Costs)," *New York Times* Economix blog, November 21, 2008, http://economix.blogs.nytimes.com/2008/11/21/why-does-us-health-care-cost-so-much-part-ii-indefensible-administrative-costs/.
6. Note the large number of insurers and providers with data breaches at www.privacyrights.org/data-breach#CP.
7. Gary Ahlquist, Minoo Javanmardian, and Ashish Kaura, "The Pharmacy Solution," *Strategy + Business*, February 23, 2010, www.strategy-business.com/article/10103?gko=8ec98.
8. For some leading indicators related to social media and health information, see Susannah Fox, "The Social Life of Health Information, 2011," May 12, 2011, Pew Internet & American Life Project, www.pewinternet.org/Reports/2011/Social-Life-of-Health-Info.aspx.
9. "The War on Baby Girls," *The Economist*, March 4, 2010, www.economist.com/node/15606229/.
10. This entire section relies on Atul Gawande, *The Checklist Manifesto: How to Get Things Right* (New York: Henry Holt, 2009).
11. Ibid., p. 158.

CHAPTER 21

Two Disruptions that Weren't

Two large, consumer-facing sectors have had their ups and downs over the past decade, but heretofore neither has been "disrupted" in the way that Linux, Skype, and Google News dismantled existing industries.

Retail

Despite its unquestioned status as an innovator and a leader in customer experience, Amazon historically hasn't been credited with business model disruption on the scale of Napster, Skype, or online brokerages like E*TRADE: That situation may change. While major retailers, including Target and Wal-Mart, appear to be weathering the current economy reasonably well, and many stores may be in for a wave of changes, to date retail looks a lot like it did 20 years ago.

Four overlapping forces appear to be at work to change retail, two of them moving extremely rapidly: economics, demographics, mobility, and social media. Taken together, these powerful waves of change are creating new opportunities, threats, and leaders in a well-established industry.

Economics

Consumers have less money to spend, particularly on discretionary purchases. Three main drivers come into play here.

MORTGAGE EQUITY From 2000 until 2008, Americans withdrew more than $40 billion of mortgage equity per quarter, riding an updraft in housing prices to turn that change in market value into vacations, cars, or kitchen renovations.[1] Now equity is increasing: People are investing more in their mortgages than they are pulling out. Foreclosures certainly skew this number, but the bottom line is that consumers are not converting mortgage equity into consumption at nearly the same rate as earlier.

Perhaps the most visible symbol of the transition is the change in the upscale home decor market: Home Depot's 34 Expo Design Centers closed in 2009. Interestingly, two years later, its Web site was still up. A sampling of the text illustrates the transition from the heyday of renovations, a long way from current days when dollar store and McDonald's stocks top the leaderboard:

> *EXPO Design Center offers homeowners professional design and installation services, and carries the most luxurious and innovative products picked from around the world.*
>
> *Each of EXPO's 10 showrooms features unique lifestyle vignettes so that customers can walk from one to the other, visualizing full-room scenes while pulling all of the elements of an interior design project together.*

Despite record low mortgage rates in 2011, home renting is growing while both new and existing home sales remain slow. The thought of investing in new kitchens and bathrooms for resale purposes feels out of tune with the austerity and reality of the times. That a cost-no-object home improvement palace could be viable only 10 years ago illustrates how fast and how far the pendulum has swung.

WAGES AND UNEMPLOYMENT In addition to the shutoff of mortgage equity cash withdrawals, unemployment remains high: By Gallup's poll numbers, fully one-fifth of the workforce is either without work or working part time when full time would be desired.[2] For the employed, meanwhile, wage pressure is high: According to Labor Department statistics, year-over-year wage and benefit growth has been slowing for at least the last decade. On average, a worker can expect to see his or her pay packet increase only about 1% to 2% a year. To take a slice of the population I see every day, 40% of Americans in their 20s move back in with parents, in part because expenses are high and job prospects are limited. For their part, the parents themselves may need help making the mortgage.

PRICE PRESSURE Oil prices surged since the wave of democracy movements spread across the Arab oil states. Food prices will head up because oil supplies fertilizer feedstocks and powers tractors but also because of short-, medium-, and long-term factors: climatic conditions (Russian wildfires, Chinese drought, Mexican freezes), competition for crops from ethanol production, and increased meat in the diets of the developing world.

When a family spends more for food and fuel and most likely doesn't see big raises (if they're not in the 20% of the underemployed workforce), discretionary purchases will have to shrink.

Demographics

As smartphones become more and more prevalent, distinctions based on the separation of physical retail from cybershopping are quickly disappearing. Significantly, the social couponing startup Groupon says its customers' usage overlaps heavily with smartphones: 68% of users (as of 2010) were 18 to 34 years of age, and 49% were single. Following the Groupon direction, 67% of smartphone users under 35 use smartphones while shopping, according to the research firm Chadwick Martin Bailey.[3] As fast as U.S. consumers are buying smartphones, however, they lag southern Europe. According to year-end 2010 figures from the researchers at comScore, U.S. smartphone penetration moved 50% in a year, from 17% at the end of 2009 to 27% a year later. Spain, meanwhile, leads all countries at 38% smartphone market share. Italy is growing more slowly but still ranks second to Spain at 35%.

It shouldn't be a surprise that women are more social than men, but online, they are clearly in the ascendancy.[4] Consider what these sites all share in common: Women drive 62% of Facebook activity. Sixty percent of Zynga gamers (FarmVille *et al.*) are women. Seventy-seven percent of Groupon users are women. Women follow more people and post far more than men at Twitter. Women are notably more active than men at dining-related sites, including Yelp and Opentable. Why does this matter? Women control 80% of consumer spending in the United States.

Mobility

Once people go mobile, what do they do? Among smartphone users in the United States, the overwhelming leader in shopping tasks is price comparison. eBay bought the Red Laser start-up in 2010 and quickly rolled out its capability to turn a smartphone into a barcode scanner and compare the Universal Product Code (UPC) of the physical good in the store to prices across virtual merchants. The speed and power of the services are most impressive. Nine million downloads were reported as of early 2011, and eBay has licensed the technology to more than 150 firms, including Coupons.com and Shopkick (about which, more in a moment). Amazon offers the same functionality. Some retailers are defeating the bar codes on their own merchandise (black permanent markers are quick and effective, while some chains historically have pasted proprietary bar codes over the UPC) to prevent in-store price comparison.

The logic of these merchants is easy to understand. Amazon has massive buying power, enjoys a ~6% structural price advantage because of its sharply limited exposure to state sales tax, and has built a powerful lens into various product categories with its affiliate sellers: Shop for a camera, and J&R or Adorama will likely be featured on the page, while in athletic shoes, Road Runner Sports might show up. Through these and other means, Amazon knows and likely often makes the market for a given item.

Apart from these shopping-specific applications, the power of the smartphone platform as a general-purpose computing platform is being explored at a stunningly rapid pace. As mobility becomes more powerful and more flexible, retailers will continue to be pressed to match the innovations of the smartphone. The Apple App Store, operating since 2008, has a section of about 500,000 titles; the Android platform is growing faster and has about as many apps, if not as much revenue.

Having access to such power while in motion has the effect of lowering coordination costs. Services that not long ago required a formal organization can be accomplished on a people-to-people basis. Airbnb (an air mattress in your spare room turns you into a bed-and-breakfast, hence the name) has booked a million room nights and now has launched a mobile app, for example. Square, a potentially disruptive credit card reader attachment for smartphones, allows anyone to become a merchant. Kiva has loaned more than $200 million to more than 500,000 entrepreneurs in just over five years. Zipcar operates a short-term car rental service that would be impossible without distributed wireless technology. Each of these innovations holds challenges and lessons for physical retailers.

For example, access to smartphones changes game play. Check-in games such as Foursquare and Facebook Places allow patrons to become "mayors" of businesses they frequent,or connect to other facets of identity. Shopkick, a two-year-old start-up, gives shoppers reward points simply for checking into a retail location. The service employs a proprietary radio technology that both works indoors and is more accurate than GPS. Best Buy and Sports Authority are both customers.

More recently, two-dimensional bar codes (see Figure 21.1) allow the retailer to leverage the mobile platform to raise customer service capabilities, manage promotions, and otherwise use the same smartphone to help turn the tide of price comparison and the concomitant commoditization. Home Depot launched a program using bar codes to drive in-store purchase behavior, in part through the kind of detailed product information and person-to-person reviews familiar to anyone who has shopped online. Macy's and Best Buy are also experimenting with the technology in selected markets.

FIGURE 21.1 Two-Dimensional Bar Code

Social Media

Shopkick is also significant in that it marries location/mobility with social media. Many users of Facebook and other networks are interested in social change, so Shopkick piloted with CauseApp, which was downloaded more than 500,000 times. It donated money to nonprofits based on a consumer checking into participating retailers. (SocialVibe offers similar functionality to such clients as Disney, GE, and Microsoft but not specifically on mobile.)

Apart from social causes, shopping is an inherently social activity. Groupon is an obvious example: Deals are not merely broadcast but engineered to be shared by social networks. Blippy allowed members to update each other on purchase behavior before shifting direction. LivingSocial began as a social sharing site (tell your friends what's on your bookshelf) but later launched daily coupon deals.

Back in the retail domain, shopping is taking on a social dimension as it overlaps with gaming and entertainment. Calling it "shoppertainment" isn't elegant, but the description fits. While people have long passed on news of deals to their friends (coupon-sharing sites are more than a decade old), the trend toward merging entertainment and commerce can be clearly seen in the rapid rise of one-deal-at-a-time (ODAT) sites. The granddaddy here is probably Amazon: The Gold Box was introduced in 2002 and has been expanded and refined in the years since. More recently, woot! launched in 2005, offering one deal a day, with the new product available at midnight Dallas time. The social dimension is key: Contests, blogs, and user-generated content abound. Facebook refers significant traffic. Product descriptions are written in a mock-literary tone that can be equally grating, snarky, and humorous: The FAQ expressly states they are included for entertainment purposes.

The site then expanded from its core in electronics to include parallel wine, home, T-shirt, and kids' offerings. Amazon acquired the firm in 2010.

In that same period, Gilt Groupe was getting serious publicity. The ODAT firm, founded in 2007, specializes in luxury goods, available only to members for 36 hours. Annual revenues are in the $300 million range. Given the firm's New York offices and proximity to the fashion industry, media attention has been plentiful. The firm's leaders state that it is contemplating an initial public offering in 2012.

Far from New York, another ODAT business has expanded. Backcountry.com is headquartered in Salt Lake City and carries roughly 1,000 brands. Its family of sites sell bike, snowboard, ski, and outdoor gear, sometimes at aggressive discounts. As opposed to Amazon (which hosts Gold Box deals for a few hours), woot! (24 hours), or Gilt (36 hours), Backcountry's steepandcheap site usually sells in 30-minute windows. Matching the inventory, the price, and the time is akin to television programming: Much as local stations rely on late-night comedian David Letterman to bring viewers to their 11:00 P.M. newscasts, steepandcheap and its sister sites like Bonktown (for cycling gear) need people to sit on the site for more than one bargain.

Several tools help drive Backcountry's success. First, social media and texting allow people to clue fellow enthusiasts in to new deals. Second, the site can send alerts to mobile devices, and smartphone owners can purchase from that platform. Finally, affiliate sites, some of them aggregators, also help spread the word among deal hunters. Given that these are discretionary purchases, the game elements of the presentation help provide incentive: Counters convey the number of people on the site (for the Web site version, not the app), the current inventory levels, and the time remaining. Deals may show up multiple times per day; somewhat fewer than 48 unique products are featured every 24 hours. But because of the randomness, an average of about 10,000 to 12,000 users can be watching the site during daylight hours.

The model clearly works. In one 30-minute segment, 168 Oakley sweatshirts came up at $16.99 each; 152 sold, for a net revenue of $2,582. In another block, 339 pairs of cold-weather boxer shorts sold at $14.00 apiece; that netted $4,746. Averaging those random examples gives about $3,600 per half-hour, $7,200 per business hour, or perhaps $75,000 to $100,000 per 24-hour day. Guesstimating $500,000 per seven-day week would extrapolate to $25 million a year just for one site; others, devoted to bigger-ticket items including bicycles, would have different profiles. All together, Backcountry.com is a $250 million business, according to the firm's Web site.

Adding It Up

Where is retail heading? Three overall trends appear to be mutually reinforcing:

1. *Physical and virtual shopping are becoming indistinguishable.* Shoppers can touch and compare physical items at the same moment they are accessing extensive price comparisons, researching detailed descriptions of features and benefits, and weighing word of mouth (either archived on review sites or real-time via Twitter).
2. *Retailing, particularly for discretionary purchases, must transcend price, selection, and service.* Involvement, whether through game elements (including the in-store promotions made possible with smartphone bar-code readers), user-generated content (e.g., ski videos at Backcountry), clever ad copy, or other features, is becoming more important in some categories.
3. *Price and performance pressure will not relent.* Groupon and LivingSocial are conditioning bargain hunters to expect 50% off as the baseline. Amazon's volume purchasing, supply-chain excellence, and tax-advantaged status make it difficult to beat. At the same time, its sites load fast, its mobile apps are appealing, and surveys rank it at the top of on- or offline customer service polls. Regardless of prime real estate, customer goodwill, or previous isolation from competition, local retailers cannot avoid confronting the long reach of the Seattle superstore. In addition, Amazon never stands still, constantly innovating, acquiring, and refining, making it a moving target for anyone else to benchmark, much less emulate.

Real Estate

It's hard to believe that in the 15 years since the notion of Internet disintermediation first received widespread attention in Bill Gates's book *The Road Ahead*, we're still being surprised. If you look at travel agents who formerly collected a lot of money for printing airline tickets, for example, the prophecy has come true.

Residential real estate was another field predicted to be toast. John Baen and Randall S. Guttery predicted in 1997 that jobs would be lost to automation, commissions would drop, and more sellers could sell direct.[5] The logic of the argument is strong, even in hindsight, but it doesn't hold up. Instead of being pushed aside by the Internet, real estate agents, individually and in powerful trade associations, have been aggressive in their adoption of emerging technologies. Rather than being disintermediated, the National Association of Realtors has become the subject of Federal Trade Commission and Department of Justice inquiries into price maintenance: U.S. house sellers generally pay a 6% commission while in the United Kingdom, the figure is only 2%.

What happened that the prediction could be so far off?

The picture is not unambiguously successful. Real estate agents in the United States enjoyed a year of extremely high market activity in 2004, but average commission income went down, in part because average selling prices were accompanied by a drop in the average commission to 5.1% and in part because the barrier to entry for the field is low enough that lots of new aspiring agents got their licenses. Still, this increased interest largely means that the field was a victim of its own success. Six factors appear to have helped real estate brokers avoid disintermediation:

1. *Real estate is a relationship business.* Whether an individual is hunting for scarce properties in a hot market or scarce buyers in a cool one, good real estate agents embed themselves in deep social networks. The trust required for buyers to make what is typically the biggest purchase of their lives does not translate to a browser-based form. In a tough market for house sellers, people often find their buyer through a real estate agent who had been working with her as a buyer's broker. Could a Web site, however thorough, have emulated that trust if people try to sell the property themselves?

2. *Houses aren't plane tickets.* To the extent that house purchases are deeply personal and given that every buyer is different, the matching of buyer to property requires both architectural and psychological understanding, patience, and some luck. Real estate agents spend a lot of time behind the scenes learning the market, tracking trends, and generally becoming informed as to what combinations of features will match up best with a given buyer.

3. *Control over information confers power.* A real estate transaction involves multiple layers of information: comparable sales, future uses for nearby vacant land, whether the neighborhood kids are nice and the schools good, what kind of builder put up the structure, and so on. Little of this exists in standardized databases, and it's both hard and expensive to generate in a channel outside traditional real estate firms. Where data does exist in structured form, access both to add and to view important kinds of information is tightly controlled.

4. *Organization is power.* The National Association of Realtors is large, well funded, and effective in influencing legislation. Many attempts to create alternative business models, involving less than full service but more than for-sale-by-owner behavior, have been literally

or effectively outlawed in certain states. No comparable organization exists for travel agents, for example.

5. *Real estate has embraced emerging technologies.* I can recall seeing the iPix 3-D photographic demo at a trade show in the late 1990s; now fly-throughs, often sophisticated, are a staple of real estate Web sites. Some brokers have taken to using blogs as another tool to build relationships, confer authority, and generally keep their names in play. Even so, the most powerful tool for most agents remains the mobile phone, a device and set of capabilities that the Web has a hard time replacing.

6. *Home buying is a complex transaction.* As my former Penn State colleague Steve Sawyer and his coauthors have found, it's naive to speak of disintermediation, singular, in the process of purchasing a house or condominium. The Web has clearly changed the process, but there are too many moving parts in the transaction for it to be conducted completely on line. Some business-to-business aspects are moving toward standards like XML to smooth work flows between, say, mortgage lenders and title insurers, but conceiving of the process as analogous to even car buying ignores the coordination and other roles played by a trusted party in a complicated, emotional, and large purchase. As Sawyer et al. state, "The analytic simplicity of categorizing complex transactions as either intermediated or not belies the web of connections and actions that make selling and buying real estate a multi-state and multi-step process."[6]

It's good counsel to observe as we analyze other predictions in the future.

Notes

1. http://financialinsights.files.wordpress.com/2011/02/mortgage-equity-withdrawals.jpg.
2. Dennis Jacobe, "No Improvement in Gallup's Underemployment Rate in May" Gallup Economy, June 3, 2010, www.gallup.com/poll/139346/no-improvement-gallup-underemployment-rate-may.aspx.
3. "Smartphones Lead to Greater Transparency in the Shopping Experience", Press Release, Cmbinfo.com, March 9, 2011, http://blog.cmbinfo.com/press-center-content/bid/55078/Smartphones -Lead-to-Greater-Transparency-in-the-Shopping-Experience.
4. Aileen Lee, "Why Women Rule the Internet," TechCrunch blog, March 20, 2011, http://techcrunch.com/2011/03/20/why-women-rule-the-internet/.
5. John Baen and Randall Guttery, "The Coming Downsizing of Real Estate," *Journal of Real Estate Portfolio Management* 3, no. 1 (1997) 1–18.

6. Steve Sawyer, Rolf Wigand, and Kevin Crowston, "Redefining Access: Uses and Roles of Information and Communication Technology in the U.S. Residential Real Estate Industry from 1995–2005," *Journal of Information Technology* 20, no. 4 (2005). See also Waleed Muhanna, "The Impact of e-Commerce on the Real Estate Industry: Baen and Guttery Revisited," *Journal of Real Estate Portfolio Management* 8, no. 2. 2002, pp. 141–152.

Technology Landscapes

Innovation in many domains is creating compound effects, given the shared platforms of PCs, smartphones, and the Internet. Looking briefly at a range of technologies as resources for innovation should help drive further breakthroughs.

CHAPTER 22

Code

In any world, the current situation is not inevitable; "It might have been otherwise," in the words of the American poet Jane Kenyon. Nowhere is this more true than in the world of computer code, which embeds past history, deeply buried assumptions and decisions, and future possibilities (or lack thereof). The ways in which the world is captured in code, and in which code is embedded in the world, are important to recognize if not fully comprehend.

"Code" is a wonderful word, one with many interweaving meanings. As Harvard law professor Lawrence Lessig brilliantly pointed out in his analysis of the Internet, the first meaning of the word relates to law and jurisprudence. Codes can also be systems of rules outside the law: a code of ethics. Most every child at some point gets fascinated with backward writing, letters to numbers (A=1, B=2, etc.), and other ways of transmitting secret messages: code as symbol, as in *The Da Vinci Code*. The genetic code is something else again. According to the *Oxford English Dictionary*, however, the relevant definition for our purposes is straightforward: "Any system of symbols and rules for expressing information or instructions in a form usable by a computer or other machine for processing or transmitting information." Note how rules, representation, and a system are common to all meanings of the term.

It would be impossible to discuss all the changes wrought by our digital world without talking about code itself. Doing so, however, is extremely difficult, a bit like talking about the wind: We can readily see what it *does* (move leaves) but not what it *is*. A brief digression is necessary here. Code that makes things happen (moves characters in a game, performs operations in a spreadsheet, or turns on the car radio) is typically experienced as *compiled* code: One cannot see the potentially millions of operations behind the scenes while using FarmVille or Excel or a Volkswagen. (Decompiling the code is possible, and often done for the purpose of copying the program in violation of copyright, so decompilers often operate in a legal gray area.) If one so desires, Linux and other examples of *open-source* software allow the owner/user of the software to see behind the curtain and to change the code before it runs in compiled form. Generally speaking, a small minority of people tweak code before runtime, but even they can't reprogram their car's antilock brakes or make the microwave oven sing "Happy Birthday." Most code is hidden, expert user or no expert user.

Intangibility

This quality of intangibility is a central fact of our age: For every 100 teenagers in 1961 who could understand and alter how a car ran by looking under the hood, only a handful of high schoolers today can modify a current video game or cell phone. Every car has a hood, an engine, spark plugs, wheels, a transmission, and the like. Physical laws govern the behavior of each component as well as the components' interaction. Physical senses allow an individual to see, hear, touch, and smell a properly—or improperly—running automobile.[1] Software, while exhibiting effects everywhere, remains hidden from the senses.

An exception helps prove the rule: From the early days of the World Wide Web, browsers included a control to reveal the page code, to show in a parallel window how the Web site was built.[2] The language that defined those pages was called Hypertext Markup Language, or HTML; it was lightweight and easy to learn. As the technical publisher Tim O'Reilly noted at the time, a generation of people learned to build Web sites by looking at how other people had built Web sites. HTML is a static language that describes appearance: It defines where page elements are placed, what colors appear, how big a font is, and the like. Nothing happens, unless you count crude animations. Meanings of and relationships between page elements are not specified.

For maps to slide with a mouse click, or videos to play, or payments to process, or Facebook to know friends from nonfriends, newer, more complex languages (and infrastructure such as databases, encryption, etc.) are required. With these, simple imitation will not suffice: You must be a programmer of at least modest experience to *understand* the workings of a current-day Web page, although tools exist for nontechnical people to *build* powerful sites with drag-and-drop editing. These more powerful Web pages, considered as code, have considerable implications, as we will see presently.

For the rest of us nonprogrammers, sensory appropriation does little or nothing to allow us to understand or manipulate code; no amount of baling wire or duct tape can fix a problem. For example, quantification has often been applied to programmer productivity metrics, as though mining coal or selling magazine subscriptions were similar to making computers work. "Lines of code written" proves to be a particularly bad way of judging programmer quality, as it turns out, but there are no easy yardsticks. Fred Brooks, a legend in the field of software engineering, writes of the "delight" the coder has in his materials:

> *The programmer, like the poet, works only slightly removed from pure thought-stuff. He builds his castles in the air, from air, creating by exerting the imagination. Few media of creation are so flexible, so easy to polish and rework, so readily capable of realizing grand conceptual structures.*[3]

Thus, as tempting as it is to equate code with the hardest of logic, with the unsurpassable lack of gray area implied by ones and zeros, there are ways in which code can best be understood as poetry, subject to the same loose laws of assessment, the same qualities of individual idiosyncratic genius, the same problems of meaning.

Before we leave Brooks, he makes one other salient point. Whereas progress can be assessed visually with physical media, computer code is not done when the program is complete but rather when it is tested and debugged. Inexperienced project managers regularly make this mistake, thinking of building construction when it is a dangerously misleading metaphor. Because code is invisible and people's sensory inputs do little to help them understand the extremely large numbers of potential interactions between subunits of a large system, testing and debugging are difficult tasks that require a particular discipline, sophisticated tools, and as much time as it takes to do the job—a quantity notably difficult to predict.

Fungibility

Testing and debugging also require the code to be done. For this to be accomplished, those building the system need to know what they are trying to build, then freeze the requirements. "Freezing the requirements" means saying no to people who change their mind or have new information. It also means stepping back from the essential malleability of code as well as the trait that allows it to do anything, its fungibility. These loops—of requirements, of design, of "just one more feature"—contribute to programs' being late, even before the project team faces the final task, which is finding errors, incompatibilities, and just plain mysteries that only appear at runtime.

Another fact of modern life separates us from the teenage mechanics of 50 years ago. Whereas an automobile engine, or a refrigerator compressor, could not play music, or balance the checkbook, or identify one's location, or conjure up Grandma's face and voice from either the past or the present, today's most basic digital devices can do any of these and all of these. That is, code is not only abstract and disembodied, it is ubiquitous and increasingly fungible: A GPS location becomes a social media posting becomes a mash-up becomes a song becomes a video becomes a game move.

Code Embeds Value Judgments

Broadly speaking, computer code does one of two things: It instructs some piece of hardware to do something, or it records a value (the product of having done something) for future recall and potentially manipulation. In a loose analogy, the former type of code functions as verbs; the latter is essentially nouns. During the early stages of any software project, decisions are made that determine the rules of the road for how those nouns and verbs will work together. As Kevin Kelly, an astute commentator on matters technological, has pointed out, those default assumptions are rarely discussed at their moment of inception and yet persist, in some cases for decades, imposing their will on generations of both users and tenders of the system.[4] The legal scholar Lawrence Lessig is more concise: "Code codifies values, and yet, oddly, most people speak of code as if it were just a question of engineering."[5] Once again, the meanings of the term overlap.

Can (a) a user, (b) a systems administrator, or (c) no one change the color or the logo of the home screen? How are languages built on non-alphabetical elements, such as Arabic or Korean, rendered? In the credit crash of 2008, one credit-rating firm had a risk model in which housing prices never went down: False optimism was literally engineered into the system. The lack of sensory inputs and of "user-servicable" parts makes these embedded assumptions all the more powerful insofar as they cannot even be identified, much less adjusted. Furthermore, the large number of interacting variables makes isolating the relevant ones difficult or impossible: Systems debugging is a challenge for professionals who need to make the code run, and most people who want to understand what the code *means* find this barrier too steep to challenge with any regularity.

Metadata

As for the "noun" code, better known as data, we have more to say in the chapters on analytics (Chapter 29) and security (Chapter 7). From the perspective of pure code, data is important insofar as it is defined by more data. The bits on a compact disc can play a song, for example, but the CD standard developed by Sony and Philips has no provision for the name of the song, or the artist, to be included on the disc. These facts, the data about the data, are called metadata and are phenomenally interesting in the age of extremely broad digitization and connectedness.

A digital photograph, for example, embeds information about the camera, the time and date, the lens, the exposure settings, and other optional information, such as GPS coordinates. Metadata becomes complex and political when it is located in enterprise systems (when was this document created, when was the payment logged), and we will leave those aside for the moment.

In the era of Blogger, Facebook, and Flickr, the social web has broad-reaching implications for personal data. In the early days, before computing, there was data, enumerating how many, what kind, where. Data was kept in proprietary formats and physically located: If the university library was missing the *Statistical Abstract* for 1940, or some other grad student had sequestered it, you had little chance to determine corn production in Nebraska before World War II. Even such statistics were the exception: Most data remained unpublished, in lab notebooks and elsewhere, or uncollected.

Once data migrated from print into bits, it became potentially ubiquitous, and once formats became less proprietary, more people could gain access to more forms of data. The early history of the Web was built in part on a footing of public access to data: Online collections of maps, congressional votes, stock prices, phone numbers, product catalogs, and other data proliferated.

Data has always required metadata: That table of corn production had a title and probably a methodological footnote. Such metadata typically was contributed by an expert in either the technical field or in the practice of categorizing. Official taxonomies have continued the tradition of creators and curators having cognitive authority in the process of organizing. In addition, as Clay Shirky pointed out in his essay "Ontology Is Overrated," the heritage of physicality led to the need for one answer being correct so that an asset could be found: A book about Russian and American agricultural policy during the 1930s had to live among books on Russian history, agricultural history, or U.S. history. It was arguably about any or all of those things, but someone (most likely at the Library of Congress) assigned it a catalog number that finalized the discussion: The book in question was officially and forever "about" this more than it was about that.[6]

In the past decade, the so-called read-write web (based on code that assigns *values* and *relationships* to the items on the page rather than merely describing their layout) has allowed anyone to become both a content creator and a metadata creator. Sometimes these activities coincide, as when someone tags her own YouTube video. More often, creations are submitted to a commons like YouTube or Flickr or Facebook, and the commoners (rather than a cognitive authority) determine what the contribution is "about" and if they "like" it. Rather than editors or peer reviewers judging an asset's quality before publication, in more and more settings, the default process is publication then collaborative filtering for definition, quality, and meaning.[7]

Imagine a particular propane torch for sale on Amazon.com. So-called social metadata has been nurtured and collected for years on the site. If I appreciate the way the torch works for its intended use of brazing copper pipe, I can submit a review with both a star rating and prose. Amazon quickly allowed for more social metadata as you the reader of my review can now rate my review, thus creating metadata about metadata.

Here is where the discussion gets complicated and extremely interesting. Suppose I say in my review that I use the Flamethrower 1000 for crème brûlée even though the device is not rated (by whatever safety or sanitation authority) for kitchen use. The comments about my torch review can quickly become a foodie discussion thread: the best crème brûlée recipe, the best restaurants at which to order it, regional variations in the naming or preparation of crème brûlée, and so forth. Amazon's moderators might truncate the discussion to the extent it's not "about" the Flamethrower 1000 under review, but the urge to digress has long been exhibited and will forever be demonstrated elsewhere.

Social Metadata

Enter Facebook. The platform is in essence a gigantic metadata generation and distribution system. ("I liked the concert." "The person who liked the concert did not know what she was talking about." "My friend was at the concert and said it was uneven." And so on.) Strip Facebook of attribute data and there is little left: It's essentially a mass of descriptors (including "complicated"), created by amateurs and never claimed as authoritative, linked by a twenty-first-century kinship network. Facebook's adoption in 2010 of the Open Graph protocol institutionalizes this collection of conversations as one vast, logged, searchable metadata repository.

If I "like" something, my social network can be alerted, and the Web site object of my affection will know as well.

In late 2009, the security expert Bruce Schneier laid out five categories of social networking data:

1. *Service data.* Service data is the data you need to give to a social networking site in order to use it. It might include your legal name, your age, and your credit card number.
2. *Disclosed data.* This is what you post on your own pages: blog entries, photographs, messages, comments, and so on.
3. *Entrusted data.* This is what you post on other people's pages. It's basically the same stuff as disclosed data, but the difference is that you don't have control over the data—someone else does.
4. *Incidental data.* Incidental data is data the other people post about you. Again, it's basically the same stuff as disclosed data, but the difference is that 1) you don't have control over it, and 2) you didn't create it in the first place.
5. *Behavioral data.* This is data that the site collects about your habits by recording what you do and who you do it with.[8]

What does Schneier's list look like in the aftermath of Facebook's decision in 2011 to use facial recognition to identify people in photographs as the default, without the individual's permission? A user's trail of "like" clicks makes this list, or her Netflix reviews and star ratings (themselves the subject of privacy concerns), seem like merely the tip of the iceberg. With anything so new and so massive in scale (50,000 sites adopted the "like" software tool kit in the first week), the unexpected consequences will take years to accumulate. What will it mean when every opinion we express online, from the passionate to the petty, gets logged in the Great Preference Repository in the Sky, never to be erased and forever being able to be correlated, associated, regressed, and otherwise algorithmically parsed?

Several questions follow: Who will have either direct or indirect access to the metadata conversation? What are the opt-in, opt-out, and monitoring/correction provisions? If I once mistakenly clicked a Budweiser "like" button but have since publicly declared myself a Molson man, can I see my preference library as if it's a credit score and remedy any errors or misrepresentations? What will be the rewards for brand monogamy versus the penalties for promiscuous "liking" of every product with a prize or a coupon attached?

While this technology appears to build barriers to competitive entry for Facebook, what happens if I establish a preference profile when I'm 14, then decide I no longer like zoos, *American Idol*, or Gatorade? Will people seek a fresh start at some point in an undefined network, with no prehistory? What is the mechanism for "unliking" something, and how far retrospectively will it apply?

Precisely because Facebook is networked, we've come a very long way from that *Statistical Abstract* on the library shelf. What happens to my social metadata once it traverses my network? How much or how little control do I have over what my network associates ("friends" in Facebook-speak) do with my behavioral and opinion data that come their way? As both the Burger King "Whopper Sacrifice" (defriend 10 people, get a hamburger coupon) and a more recent Ikea-spoofing scam have revealed, Facebook users will sell out their friends for rewards large and small, whether real or fraudulent.

Finally, to the extent that Facebook is both free to use and expensive to operate, the Open Graph model opens a fascinating array of revenue streams. If beggars can't be choosers, users of a free system have limited say in how that system survives. At the same time, the global reach of Facebook exposes it to a broad swath of regulators, not the least formidable of whom come out of the European Union's strict privacy rights milieu. As both the uses and inevitable abuses of the infinite metadata repository unfold, the reaction will be sure to be newsworthy.

Looking Ahead

Before we can look at GPS, or Facebook, or Amazon, it's helpful to understand that code's unique properties precondition the range of behavioral, economic, and technical possibilities. Above all, code is in its essence paradoxical. It is ephemeral yet permanent; as a colleague once said, "Digits never die." Code is malleable yet frustratingly complex. Code is both universal, particularly when defined by powerful standards, and intimately personal: A given task can typically be performed any number of ways, and programmers develop stylistic "signatures." Code can be fungible and intractable, as when a document looks different when opened on two seemingly similar PCs six inches apart.

Given these multiple layers of paradox, it is no surprise that so many facets of information, technology, and business strategy become puzzling, nonlinear, and counterintuitive as they are informed by the essential qualities of the twenty-first-century's lingua franca. Expect the situation to get more complicated, scarier, and farther reaching in the coming years as smartphones define more of everyday life.

Notes

1. For an extended meditation on code, including a better comparison to automobiles, Neal Stephenson's essay "In the Beginning Was the Command Line" is essential reading. http://artlung.com/smorgasborg/ C_R_Y_P_T_O_N_O_M_I_C_O_N.shtml.
2. Tim O'Reilly, "The New Age of Infoware: Open Source and the Web" (Summer 1999), http://tim.oreilly.com/archives/mikro_age_of_infoware.pdf.
3. Frederick P. Brooks, Jr., *The Mythical Man-Month: Essays on Software Engineering* (Boston: Addison-Wesley, 1995), p. 7.
4. Kevin Kelly, "The Power of the Default," The Technium blog, June 22, 2009, www.kk.org/thetechnium/archives/2009/06/triumph_of_the.php.
5. Lawrence Lessig, *Code and Other Laws of Cyberspace* (New York: Basic Books, 1999), p. 59.
6. Clay Shirky, "Ontology Is Overrated: Categories, Links, and Tabs," Clay Shirky's Writings about the Internet (Spring 2005), www.shirky.com/writings/ ontology_overrated.html.
7. Clay Shirky, *Here Comes Everybody: The Power of Organizing Without Organizations* (New York: Penguin, 2008), pp. 81 ff.
8. Bruce Schneier, "A Taxonomy of Social Networking Data," Schneier on Security blog, November 19, 2009, www.schneier.com/blog/archives/2009/11/ a_taxonomy_of_s.html.

CHAPTER 23

Sensors

Sensors are critically important building blocks of the digital world yet in their ubiquity are often invisible. Not only are they worth appreciating for the elegance and cleverness of their engineering, but also sensors are on their way to generating a truly unimaginable proportion of the planet's information. What held true for code is doubly true of sensors: Value judgments, future possibilities, and economic interests are represented in architectures that typically operate beneath the threshold of human consciousness.

Historical Roots

To understand the current sensor landscape, let us step back for a moment to see its antecedents. Originally, a variety of sensors were invented to augment human senses. Examples include the telescope, microscope, ear trumpet, hearing aids, and other devices. With the advent of electro-optics and electromechanical devices, new sensors could be developed to extend the human senses into different parts of the spectrum (e.g., infrared, radio frequencies, measurement of vibration, underwater acoustics, etc.). Where they were available, electromechanical sensors:

- Stood alone
- Measured one and only one thing
- Cost a lot to develop and implement
- Had inflexible architectures: They did not adapt well to changing circumstances

Let's discuss each of these points in turn. Sensors traditionally stood alone because networking them together was expensive and difficult. Shared technical standards were rare, so if one wanted a network of, say, offshore data buoys, the system of connections would be uniquely engineered to a particular domain. Someone connecting sensors of a different sort (such as surveillance cameras) would have to start from scratch, as would anyone monitoring road traffic.

In part because of their mechanical componentry, sensors rarely measured across multiple yardsticks. The oven thermometer measured only the oven temperature and displayed the information locally, if at all. The electric meter only counted watt-hours. Now it's common for a consumer Global Positioning System (GPS) unit, for example, to tell location, altitude, compass heading, and temperature, along with providing weather radio.

Sensors were not usually mass-produced, with the exception of common items, such as thermometers. Because supply was limited, particularly for specialized designs, the combination of monopoly supply and small order quantities kept prices high.

The rigid architecture was a function of mechanical devices' specificity. A vibration sensor was different from a camera was different from a humidistat. Humidity data, in turn, was designed to be moved and managed in a particular analog domain (a range of zero to 100%), while image recognition in the camera's information chain typically featured extensive use of human eyes rather than automated processing.

Ubiquity

Changes in each of these four facets combine to help create today's emerging sensor networks, which are growing in scope and capability every year. The many examples of sensor capability accessible to (or surveilling) the everyday citizen shows the limits of the former regime:

- Computers, which sense their own temperature, location, user patterns, number of printer pages generated, and so on.
- Thermostats, which are networked within buildings and now remotely controlled and readable.
- Telephones, the wireless variety of which can be understood as beacons, bar-code scanners, pattern-matchers (the Shazam application names songs from a brief audio sample), and network nodes.
- Motor and other industrial controllers, including drive-by-wire throttle linkages, automated tire-pressure monitoring, and airbags' accelerometers and high-speed actuators.

- Vehicle components, often including an on-board diagnostics module, a toll pass, satellite devices on heavy trucks, and theft recovery services such as LoJack, not to mention the inevitable mobile phone.
- Surveillance cameras (of which there are over 10,000 in Chicago alone, and more than 500,000 in London, England).[1]
- Some hotel door handles and many minibars, which are instrumented and generate electronic records of people's and vodka bottles' comings and goings.
- Physical sensors, whether embedded in animals (radio-frequency identification [RFID] chips in both household pets and racehorses) or gardens (the EasyBloom plant moisture sensor connects to a computer via USB and costs only $50), or affixed to pharmaceutical packaging.

Note the migration from heavily capital-intensive or national-security applications down-market. A company called Vitality has even developed a monitoring system for something as simple as a pill bottle: If the cap is not removed when medicine is due, an audible alert is triggered or a text message could be sent.[2]

A relatively innovative industrial deployment of vibration sensors illustrates the state of the traditional field. In 2006, BP instrumented an oil tanker with "motes," which integrated a processor, solid-state memory, a radio, and an input/output board on a single two-inch-square chip. Each mote could receive vibration data from up to 10 accelerometers, which were mounted on pumps and motors in the ship's engine room. The goal was to determine if vibration data could predict mechanical failure, thus turning estimates—a motor teardown every 2,000 hours, to take a hypothetical example—into concrete evidence of an impending need for service.

The motes had a decided advantage over traditional sensor deployments in that they operated over wireless spectrum. While this introduced engineering challenges arising from the steel environment of ships as well as the need for batteries and associated issues (such as the fact that the lithium in some batteries is a hazardous material), the motes and their associated sensors were much more flexible and cost effective to implement compared to hard-wired solutions. The motes also communicate with each other in a mesh topology: Each mote looks for nearby motes, which then serve as repeaters en route to the data's ultimate destination. Mesh networks are usually dynamic: If a mote fails, the signal is routed to other nearby devices, making the system fault-tolerant in a harsh environment. Finally, the motes could perform signal processing on the chip, reducing the volume of data that had to be transmitted to the computer where analysis and predictive modeling was conducted. This blurring of the lines between sensing, processing, and networking elements is occurring in many other domains as well.[3]

All told, there are dozens of billions of items that can connect and combine in new ways. The Internet has become a common ground for many of these devices, enabling multiple sensor feeds—traffic camera, temperature, weather map, social media reports, for example—to combine into more useful, and usable, applications.

A popular term for this state of affairs is "the Internet of Things."[4] As we saw earlier, network effects and positive feedback loops mean that considerable momentum can develop as more and more instances converge on shared standards. While we will not discuss them in detail here, it can be helpful to think of three categories of sensor interaction:

1. *Sensor to people.* The thermostat at the ski house tells the occupants that the furnace is broken the day before they arrive, or a dashboard light alerts the driver that the tire pressure on the car is low.
2. *Sensor to sensor.* The rain sensor in the automobile windshield alerts the antilock brakes of wet road conditions and the need for different traction-control algorithms.
3. *Sensor to computer/aggregator.* Dozens of cell phones on a freeway can serve as beacons for a traffic-notification site, at much lower cost than helicopters or "smart highways."

Current Examples

Less abstractly, the most mundane, low-tech activities of daily life are being transformed. Here are three: housecleaning, running, and parking.

Vacuuming

The Roomba robotic vacuum cleaner (see Figure 23.1) was introduced in 2002 by iRobot, an MIT spinout that got its start building military robots for cargo hauling and mine sniffing. Roombas randomly cover an area, sensing walls and furniture, before retreating to a predefined dock for recharging. They are not particularly powerful but do spare people the drudgery of one of housecleaning's least rewarding tasks. As of 2010, more than 5 million household robots had been sold, primarily the Roomba but also sibling units for floor washing, gutter cleaning, and other tasks.

The device found a ready audience as befits a classic disruptive innovation: It underperformed the existing market on traditional standards, such as suction or dust-bag capacity, but introduced an entirely different axis of competition: freedom from drudgery and an acceptably clean floor with zero effort. The Roomba quickly became a popular item on wedding registries.

FIGURE 23.1 Roomba Robotic Vacuum Cleaner
Photo courtesy of iRobot Corporation.

Once customers obtained their Roombas, a funny thing started happening: Many people named the appliances and described them in human terms. Seventy percent of people in a survey reported giving their robot a name, a gender, and a place in the family hierarchy. Broken robots were known to be "hospitalized." The device does require maintenance: Fine dust can clog the sensors, for example, but people far preferred "grooming" their robots to using a traditional appliance.

People reported adjusting both their habits (picking up more carefully the day before a scheduled run) or rearranging furniture in response to the device. One person threw away a shag rug because the Roomba was "getting frustrated" trying to clean it. Promotion was common: Owners would take the Roomba to their parents' house to show it off, for example, but felt protective of the device because of the hazards of a new, not-yet-optimized environment.[5]

The outcome is counterintuitive: These robots, which are in essence a bunch of sensors and actuators networked through computing, evoke emotional responses in people far more than the Roombas can sense anything about the people. To oversimplify, the inanimate watcher/doer becomes an emotional presence in the human environment. The phenomenon is not new: Many people name their Roomba R2D2, others the Terminator, evoking robotic movie characters that generated large followings. In other cases, the vacuum becomes secondary: iRobot also sells educational robot programming kits, essentially Roombas without the primary functionality.

Running

Most people's everyday experience with mobile wireless data originated with smart devices like a BlackBerry pager or iPhone or an OnStar telematics system. The running of the Boston Marathon illustrates another scenario. Ever since 1996, each of up to 40,000 runners had a transponder about the size of a quarter on his or her shoe. Hardwired sensor mats keep track of runners' progress and prevent cheating. More recently, the system sends automatic e-mails to prearranged addresses, notifying fans of their friend's progress and projected finish time.[6]

In 2008, Nike teamed with Apple to link an accelerometer in the shoe (that counted footstrikes) to an iPod via a short-range wireless connection. (This arrangement was conceptualized as a PAN, or Personal Area Network. Bluetooth headsets are a classic example that uses the same technology as the Nike+.) The iPod supplies workout music and also provides audio feedback on time and distance markers, congratulations from Nike celebrity endorsers, and cumulative statistics. Maintaining personal fitness data became simpler, and then the sensors—more technically, the sensors' home PCs—became networked, enabling people from different cities to "race" against each other or simply to compare their personal performance on different days. As of mid-2011, Nike+ surpassed 425 million cumulative miles logged. The feedback provided by the electronic sensor is of an entirely different quality compared to a pedometer, paper mileage log, or other traditional device. In addition, the solitary activity becomes social; virtual teams compete to hit goals or beat other teams, often in conjunction with an actual event, such as a major marathon.

Parking

Parking meters* are hardly glamorous and rarely connote particularly advanced technology, but networking them together provides unexpected benefits and consequences. A pilot deployment in San Francisco addresses many issues.

REAL-TIME INFORMATION San Francisco's population can nearly double in a normal weekday, from 700,000 to 1.3 million. Up to 30% of automobile traffic is estimated to be generated by people cruising, looking for an open spot. GPS sensors that record arrivals and departures for each spot are connected via wireless network to the city's parking authority,

---

*The technology that allows a car to automatically parallel park operates on a different, but no less interesting, set of sensors and controllers. See, for example, the Lexus system at http://bit.ly/480EvM.

where the information is posted to a Web site: all of the available spots are mapped, and inventory levels are current.

SUPPLY AND DEMAND   Given accurate, up-to-date knowledge of available inventory, the city then prices parking in such a way as to maintain 15% of all spots open at a given time. High prices will deter some drivers, while heavy fines for overstaying one's meter might shorten visits.

PAYBACK   The sensor technology is clearly expensive to install, but so too are the millions of person-hours wasted each day. Variable congestion pricing has been implemented in other cities, such as Stockholm and Singapore, but only at toll stations and/or bridges. Moving the locus of congestion pricing to the extended parking infrastructure eliminates a choke point and theoretically can dynamically adjust pricing to reflect current supply and demand.[7]

Phones as Sensors

Several factors make the rapid deployment of "smart" phones (that get smarter every year) a powerful force for change. We have more to say about these devices in other Chapters 12 and 27, but purely from a sensor point of view, eight factors are relevant:

1. *Massive deployment.* On a planet of roughly 7 billion, there are more than 5 billion mobile phones in use.
2. *Networked.* For every camera, every accelerometer, and every geolocator in these phones, there is a radio transmitter inches away.
3. *Powered.* Getting power to a sensor network can be remarkably complicated. Those 5 billion sensor platforms are each attached to a human who presumably takes time to charge the device regularly.
4. *Human deployed.* Imagine having to build a network of surveillance cameras to cover miles of freeway or hundreds of city blocks. The cost is considerable, and the odds of having a major event occur out of coverage remain high. With humans in a subway explosion, or near an accident site, or in the presence of a strange odor, people will reach for mobile devices and start generating images, coordinates, and other information immediately.
5. *A shared platform.* Every mobile phone in the world can theoretically, if not economically, connect to any other.* No other sensor platform

---

*Subject to the technical and economic limits on the number of possible combinations imposed by the various network layers.

in history has been so big and so interconnected. Thermometers, speedometers, scales, radar—all of these stood alone.

6. *Read/write*. In addition to sensing motion, or light, or bar codes, or sound, mobile phones can display results, processed versions of the input, authentication tokens, time/date stamps, and many other aspects of sensor-related information. Whereas a vibration sensor on a fence, for example, can send only what it measures, a camera that photographs a suspicious person or activity is connected to a display of image-recognition results, mug shots, or other relevant information.

7. *Metadata enabled*. Not only can a cameraphone record and display a picture, it can encode and decode information about the current and past photos of the same attraction or person, announcing who or what the subject of the photo is. Facebook photo recognition and augmented reality apps such as Word Lens (which translates text of signs) are familiar examples.

8. *Mobile*. Fixed sensor deployments required often highly sophisticated modeling to determine the location of sensors, networking infrastructure, power, security considerations, and other factors. Allowing the sensors to move can create gaps in coverage but also makes possible new kinds of approaches to data collection.

Looking Ahead

The whole planet is being instrumented from the bottom up—Weather Underground's network of more than 30,000 volunteer weather stations is a long-standing example—with help from some very expensive top-down infrastructure in the form of GPS along with open-access satellite and aerial imagery on Google Earth and elsewhere. Inexpensive and often redundant hardware, running on mobile and wireless platforms, creates new possibilities for discovery, for convenience, and also for the invasion of privacy. Given the speed of deployment and innovation, we will be seeing more questions than answers in the coming years.

When Social Meets Sensors

At ski areas operated by Vail Resorts, visitors who want to share photos with their Facebook network have a new option. The EpicMix app launched in 2010 with an RFID tag inside the lift ticket (commonly used at many resorts to deter fraud) and a location-aware social network much like Foursquare. By passing through reader-equipped portals, skiers could track their vertical footage skied and compete with their friends as well as complete tasks for Foursquare-like badges.

For 2011, EpicMix added photo sharing. According to Vail Resorts' chief executive, Rob Katz, "There's a lot of research out there that shows that the anticipation of a vacation, and the memories of it, are actually more valuable than the vacation itself. Photos are an important part of the memory aspect."[8] Here's how it works: Professional photographers are stationed at key locations across the resort taking shots of skiers, who can have their tags scanned by the camera operator. The app automatically uploads a low-resolution image to the skier's social network, free of charge. Higher-resolution images are available for purchase.

Given that high-definition helmet cameras are readily available for rental and that people more and more routinely opt for camera-phone images, the fact that the resorts give away professional images does not really cannibalize an existing revenue stream. The service builds goodwill with the resorts, improves the quality of the vacation memories, and shares the moment with the customer's friends— a useful variety of word of mouth. Given the differences between a ski area and an amusement park where roller coaster riders can buy photos at the ride, the sensor capabilities deliver location awareness and seamless identification of customers in a broad geographic area.

Notes

1. Brian Palmer, "Big Apple Is Watching You," Slate, May 3, 2010, www.slate .com/id/2252729/.
2. Llinca Nita, "Pill Bottle Caps to Call You via AT&T and Remind You to Take Your Medication," Unwiredview.com, October 8, 2009, www.unwiredview .com/2009/10/08/pill-bottle-caps-to-call-you-via-att-and-remind-you-to-take-your-medicine/.
3. Tom Kevan, "Shipboard Machine Monitoring for Predictive Maintenance," *Sensors Mag*, February 1, 2006, www.sensorsmag.com/sensors-mag/shipboard -machine-monitoring-predictive-maintenance-715?print=1.
4. Inge Gronbaek, "Connecting Objects in the Internet of Things (IoT)," Telenor Research & Innovation Research Report (June 2008), *www.telektronikk.com/ volumes/pdf/2.../Tel_2-08_Page_109-120.pdf* www.telenor.com/en/innovation/ research/publications/reports/2008.

5. Ja-Young Song, Lan Guo, Rebecca E. Grinter, and Kenrik I. Christensen, "'My Roomba Is Rambo': Intimate Home Appliances," in J. Krumm, G. D. Abowd, A. Seneviratne, and Th. Strang (eds.), *Ubicomp 2007*, (Berlin, Germany: Springer-Verlag, 2007), pp. 145–162.

6. Fred O'Connor, "RFID Helps the Boston Marathon Run," *InfoWorld*, April 9, 2007, www.infoworld.com/t/networking/rfid-helps-boston-marathon-run-441.

7. Lisa Camner, "Car Talk," *Atlantic Monthly* blog, May 24, 2010, www.theatlantic.com/personal/archive/2010/05/car-talk/56983/.

8. Joe Lindsey, "EpicMix Lets You Get Your Hero On," Wired.com, August 31, 2011, www.wired.com/playbook/2011/08/epicmix-lets-you-get-your-hero-on/.

CHAPTER 24

The Internet and Other Networks

The Internet is both an engineering marvel, as much at the management layer as in its silicon and glass, and a powerful precursor to many of the possibilities we examine in this book: Whether we consider eBay, or Web video, or globally coordinated social protest, the way the Internet was designed and built establishes the limits of possibility for much of the modern world.

History has been made by a long series of networks. The Nile, the Euphrates, the Ruhr. England's navy and colonies. The railroads. Wires for electricity and for communications. Eisenhower's interstate highways. In the United States, first three then an explosion of television networks. FedEx's air freight system. Wal-Mart's trucks, marketing and supply-chain algorithms, and distribution centers.

These networks were built at particular times for particular purposes: The interstates could not haul rail cars and in fact helped drive U.S. passenger rail essentially out of business. Electric wires could not carry information. The scale of capital investment often made network owners, whether in the public or private sectors, expand into adjoining economic niches: Railroads often owned hotels, while AT&T not only completed telephone calls, it made both the customer premise and capital equipment necessary to do so. These complementarities were typically physical, and logical extensions of the core service.

These networks had clearly visible hubs: London for the British Empire, Chicago for American rail, New York's Broad Street for transatlantic telephone cables, the Strategic Air Command's headquarters near Omaha, Memphis for FedEx, and Louisville for UPS.

To sum up, until the Internet, most major physical (as opposed to social) networks had several defining characteristics:

- A network had a single purpose, or at most two, depending on the level of abstraction: The British used sea power to protect and conduct maritime trade as well as to project military power.
- Networks were expensive to build and operate, so they often became (or were treated as) natural monopolies.
- Networks were physically and geographically delimited. Interconnection (as with airline routes or intercountry phone calls) was possible but typically mapped on a 1:1 basis, with extensive negotiation and customization for each pairing.
- Networks had visible centers of gravity, hubs where multiple links converged.

Legacy Telecom Network Principles

For roughly a century, these characteristics were tangibly embodied by AT&T and its equivalents around the world. Speaking specifically of communications networks, three facts were often taken as axiomatic before the Internet:

1. *Networks, whether AT&T's premise equipment or British Telecom's transatlantic assets, were closed.* U.S. wireline companies in particular controlled their networks with notoriously tight standards, helping ensure reliability at the cost of innovation.
2. *Because one company, or a tightly linked consortium, had control, network engineering was conducted under known operating assumptions.*
   - Latency, or systemic delay in signal transmission, was highly predictable.
   - Similarly, the parameters of available bandwidth, or carrying capacity, were known with great reliability within the network operations center or its equivalent.
   - The location of network elements and their respective characteristics—the overall topology—was known with certainty.
   - Network assets were closely administered, in locked-down facilities, by technicians with highly standardized training. If X happened in any facility, the correct response was almost always known to be Y.
3. *Given these factors, operating costs were reasonably well understood for such a complex system.* At the corporate level, however, costs were only semirelevant because revenues were set by regulators in most every country.

Defense Origins of the Internet

The Internet grew from origins in the U.S. defense community in the early 1960s. It was built to solve the problem of survivable communications: Given the amount and broad dispersal of nuclear weaponry, ground troops, naval assets, and so on, the commander in chief needed to get messages to all relevant parties extremely quickly no matter what and then those various resources had to be able to coordinate.

Two key technologies define the Internet's topology. First, information is digital, chopped into binary elements of 1s and 0s rather than a continuous analog representation. Whether a pixel in an image, a slice of a musical waveform, or a digital representation of a keyboard character, bits can be moved more robustly than analog signal, which degrades with multiple re-amplifications. A Xerox of a Xerox of a Xerox gets successively less legible; a bit is much more likely to survive multiple handoffs intact.

Second, the links in the network were made redundant. If each node has three or more possible short pathways available and bits can be handed off repeatedly without degradation, a system of multiple short-hop pathways can route around the fact of any given node being unavailable.

Given these two design decisions, Paul Baran of the RAND Corporation went to work:

> I figured there was no limit on the amount of communications that people thought they needed. So I figured I'd give them so much communications they wouldn't know what the hell to do with it. Then that became the work—to build something with sufficient bandwidth so that there'd be no shortage of communications. The question was, how the hell do you build a network of very high bandwidth for the future? The first realization was that it had to be digital, because we couldn't go through the limited number of analog links.
>
> For redundancy to be cost effective, the cost of the components had to drop. This was a direct contradiction of AT&T doctrine, in which very expensive, highly engineered pieces at each step of the circuit-switched infrastructure were the norm. Unfortunately, the "star" topologies of such systems provided little redundancy and very vulnerable targets at the network core.

Baran continued:

> You can build very, very tough networks—by tough I mean a high probability of being able to communicate if the two end nodes survive—if you had a redundancy level of about 3. The enemy

*could destroy 50, 60, 70 percent of the targets or more and it would
still work. It's very robust. That was the thing that struck me. . . .*

*If you were going to build a network with redundancy, that
tells you right there how many paths you need. There's no choice.
At the same time, you don't have to use high-priced stuff anymore.
Because in the analog days both ends of the connection had to
work in tandem, and the probability of many things working in
tandem without failing was so low that you had to make every part
nearly perfect. But if you don't care about reliability any more,
then the cost of the components goes way down.[1]*

The net result is a *more* reliable network based on cheaper, *less reliable*
components: The idea of inexpensive redundancy as opposed to overen-
gineered single-path fault-tolerance has taken hold elsewhere in computer
science, in the areas of cloud computing and disc storage, for example.

Baran's resulting conceptual picture (Figure 24.1) clearly indicates the
robustness of the distributed topology.

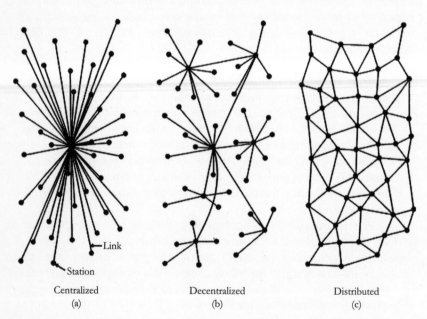

Centralized   Decentralized   Distributed
(a)   (b)   (c)

FIGURE 24.1 Paul Baran's Original Conceptual Drawing of a Distributed Network
Topology
Source: Paul Baran, "On Distributed Communications. I. Introduction to Distributed
Communications Networks," RAND Corporation memorandum RM-3420-PR (August 1964),
available at www.rand.org/pubs/research_memoranda/RM3420.html.

Internet Principles

The global Internet that resulted from the work of Baran and other pioneers stood in nearly total contradiction to any network ever built. Its closest antecedent, the telephone system, did not prepare anyone for what would soon become possible after the National Science Foundation released it to commercial use in the early 1990s. The Internet was new in several important ways.

- The Internet was *open*. Anyone could serve content with minimal investment in infrastructure and a simple, nonproprietary naming convention. Viewing and receiving information was free: Every computer connected to the Internet can in theory connect to any other, independent of distance.
- Because of the robust network engineering underlying the Internet, engineering assumptions that held true in the Bell era had to be rethought. Because no one company could build a network of the Internet's scale, it is properly considered as *a network of networks*.
  - Accordingly, any given interaction could traverse numerous transporting entities. Latency cannot be predicted.
  - Throughput (often confusingly called bandwidth) varies, sometimes considerably. If one is on a cable modem, for example, that household is sharing resources with about 150 other homes. After work, network traffic can surge when people log on, download movies, or whatever, and available bit rate can drop. Similar phenomena occur at other layers in other networks.
  - The topology of any given communication is both ad hoc and inconsistent. Packets of information are sent through available pathways; the routing decisions for any given packet are made in millionths of a second, so multiplying the number of packets times the number of "hops" will generate a truly large number for a load the size of a movie, for example. The packets seldom arrive in the order they are sent, so reconstructing the coherence of a human voice, for example, can be more technically challenging than, say, stapling together an e-mail. The location of the desired content relative to its intended recipient thus becomes an important consideration.
  - The Internet is not "administered" but rather held together by working understandings and more or less formal technical standards. When things break, finding the source and solution can be difficult, as in denial-of-service and other attacks on universities, governments, and infrastructure.

■ The economics of an essentially self-administered network of networks led to considerable *business model challenges*. In the words of Internet observers David Isenberg and David Weinberger, building on the insight of telecommunications analyst Roxane Googin, "[T]he best network is the hardest one to make money running."[2]

The truth of this paradox can be found in the difficult path of delivering high-speed Internet access to large numbers of people. Creating the right mix of incentives and protections has been difficult in the United States, which lags most of its peers in deployment, in network speed, and in price. According to OECD data shown in Figure 24.2, the results are consistently disappointing.[3] The United States has consistently slow speeds, low penetration, and high prices relative to other developed countries.

Defenders of the status quo point to population density, but Iceland's is lower than the United States yet it leads the world in deployment. Proponents of government policy point to Korea, a country roughly the size of New Jersey and with a much more homogenous culture. Japan has very fast connections, but its economy

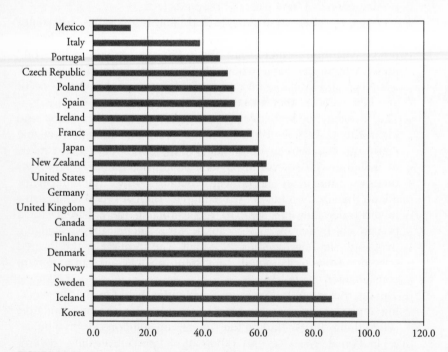

FIGURE 24.2 Wireline Broadband Internet Access, Percent of Households, 2009
Data source: OECD.

has not obviously benefited from broadband leadership. Finland, however, has made broadband a legal right of citizenship and promises 100 megabits per second connections by 2015.[4] The paradox of the best network is alive and well, as the share prices of Internet carriers attest: No carrier has beaten the Standard & Poor's 500 index in the last five years.

Consequences of Internet Principles

We are still in the midst of discovering and understanding all of the many implications of an open, global, digital network of networks. A few of these follow:

- The vast *quantity of innovation* that resulted from this open position is still stunning, even in retrospect. Without rules or assumptions about how the Internet might be used, people created a vast array of techniques, services, archives, data sets, and other resources.
- The *speed of innovation* can be understood through analogy. Consider many different railroad companies, each working independently with tracks of slightly different gauges. Network effects are not as strong as they could be, and any innovation is stranded on its isolated network. With the Internet riding on its single set of standards, all innovation can build on the shoulders of giants and spur still more innovation. The history of search engines in the 1990s is a case in point, as commercial advances in information retrieval far outpaced academic theory. Facebook's leapfrogging of MySpace serves as another case in point.
- *Vulnerabilities* can be truly frightening in their scale. Bots, trojans, and viruses can move at ridiculous speeds. Compromised computers from all over the world are mobilized by remote control, out of sight of antivirus software, to invade people's privacy, steal their money, and disable their civic and technical infrastructure. Simple human error—a mistyped command into the wrong computer—can bring entire systems down.
- Once *everything becomes bits*, the Internet does a superb job of moving them. Telephone networks transported voice then fax. Radio stations broadcast music and voice. Television carried video, but in a different way from movie theaters. Now the same edge device (a PC or smartphone, for example) can access vast quantities of news, or music, or stock trades, or books, or photographs, or maps, or geographic coordinates. Furthermore, those *many information types can be readily intermingled.*

- *Business models* for the Internet are particularly tricky. Traditional control of choke points and toll gates, whether through patents, geography, brand, or other means, can be difficult to enact and to enforce. Because the network of networks is inherently robust, it routes around choke points as a matter of course.
- It sounds obvious, but the Internet supports phenomena with *strong network effects*. E-mail (and spam), social networking of the LinkedIn or Facebook sort, large-scale distributed self-organization (e.g., Wikipedia), and eBay are all examples of phenomena that could not have taken hold on any prior network structure.
- *Place and space diverge.* The physical location of a resource seldom matters for information purposes, as long as one knows its virtual whereabouts. While Facebook or Google operate huge data centers, their physical locations matter little to the services' users.

Looking Ahead

Despite the issues with wired broadband access, in the United States in particular, the rapid rise of the wireless high-speed Internet promises broader access, more innovation, and new unintended consequences. The science of networks, both social and technical, is advancing rapidly with developments in economics, physics, biology, and sociology.[5] Routers* get bigger and faster, fiber-optic cables are still being steadily deployed, innovations in optics mean increased performance and carrying capacity from the core infrastructure, and innovations in business models mean more people can do more things, connected to more people, each year. For all of its paradoxes, challenges, and vulnerabilities, the Internet remains a cultural and engineering marvel, in many ways the salient fact of modern life in many parts of the world.

Notes

1. Stewart Brand, "Founding Father," *Wired* (March 2001), www.wired.com/wired/archive/9.03/baran.html?pg=1&topic=&topic_set=. Reproduced with permission.
2. David Isenberg and David Weinberger, "The Paradox of the Best Network," n.d., www.netparadox.com/.

---

*The big, expensive specialized computers that forward packets across the Internet.

3. OECD Broadband Portal, www.oecd.org/document/54/0,3343,en_2649_34225_ 38690102_1_1_1_1,00.html.
4. "Finland Makes Broadband a 'Legal Right,'" BBC News, July 1, 2010,www.bbc .co.uk/news/10461048.
5. See, for example, Albert-Laszlo Barabasi, *Linked: The New Science of Networks* (New York: Perseus, 2002).

CHAPTER 25

Location Awareness

Even though they're sometimes overlooked in relation to spectacular growth rates (50-fold increases in wireless data carriage), successful consumer applications (nearly a billion Facebook users), and technical achievement (at Google, Amazon, Apple, and elsewhere), location-based technologies deserve more attention than they typically receive. The many possible combinations of wired Internet, wireless data, vivid displays, well-tuned algorithms running on powerful hardware, vast quantities of data, and new monetization models, when combined with location awareness, have yet to be well understood.

Digital location-based services arose roughly in chronological parallel with the commercial Internet. In 1996, General Motors introduced the OnStar navigation and assistance service in high-end automobiles. Uses of Global Positioning System (GPS, which, like the Internet, was a U.S. military invention, as Figure 25.1 shows) and related technologies have exploded in the intervening years, in the automotive sector and, more recently, on smartphones. The widespread use of Google Earth in television newscasts is another indicator of the underlying trend.

Sales of handheld GPS units continue to double every year or two in the North American market. As the technology is integrated into mobile phones, the social networking market is expected to drive far wider adoption. Foursquare, Facebook Places, numerous other start-ups, and the telecom carriers are expected to deliver more and more applications linking "who," "where," and "when." Powerful indications of this tendency came when Nokia bought NAVTEQ (the "Intel inside" of many online mapping applications) for $8.1 billion in 2007, when Facebook integrated location services in 2010, and when the rapid adoption of the iPhone and other

FIGURE 25.1 A New Generation of GPS Satellites Began Deployment in 2010
Source: U.S. Air Force.

smartphones amplified the market opportunity dramatically. Location-based services (whether Skyhook geolocation, Google Maps and Earth, GPS, or others) have evolved to become a series of platforms on which specific applications can build, tapping the market's creativity and vast quantities of data.

In the process, the evolution of location relates to significant questions:

- Who am I in relation to where I am? That is, what are the implications of mapping for identity management?
- Who knows where I am, when I'm there, and where I've been? How much do I control the "information bread crumbs" related to my movements? Who is liable for any harm that may come to me based on the release of my identity and location?
- Who are we relative to where we are? In other words, how do social networks change as they migrate back and forth between virtual space (Facebook) and real space (Mo's Bar)? What happens as the two worlds converge? That is, as a person walks down the street and an everyday smartphone can capture his or her face, the connection of the face to its data can happen pretty much instantaneously. Few people are comforted by this scenario.

Variations on a Theme

While location often seems to be synonymous with GPS, location-based data services actually come in a variety of packages. Some examples follow.

Indoor Positioning Systems

For all of the utility of GPS, there are numerous scenarios where it doesn't work: Mobile X-ray machines or patient gurneys in hospitals, people in burning buildings, work-in-process inventory, and specialized measurement or other tools in a lab or factory all need to be located in sometimes vast and often challenging landscapes, usually within minutes. GPS signals may not penetrate the building, and even if they can, the object of interest must "report back" to those responsible for it. A variety of wired and wireless technologies can be used to create what is in essence a scaled-down version of the GPS environment.

Optical

Such well-known firms as Leica and Nikon have professional products to track minute movements in often massive structures or bodies: dams, glaciers, bridges. Any discussion of location awareness that neglects the powerful role of precision optics, beginning with the essential surveyor's transit, would be incomplete. As they merge with other precision technologies such as lasers, optical instruments become more accurate still.

Wi-Fi Mapping

The worldwide rise of Wi-Fi networking is very much a bottom-up phenomenon. Two consequences of that mode of installation are: often lax network security and considerable coverage overspill. Driving down any suburban or metropolitan street with even a basic wireless device reveals dozens of residential or commercial networks. Such firms as Google have systematically mapped those networks, resulting in yet another overlay onto a growing number of triangulation points. The privacy implications of such mapping have yet to be resolved.

Cellular

Wireless carriers can determine the position of an active (powered-up) device through triangulation with the customer's nearby towers. Such an approach lacks precision when compared to approaches (most notably

GPS) that reside on the handset rather than in the network. In either case, the carrier can establish historical location for law enforcement and potentially other purposes.

Skyhook

A start-up based in Boston, Skyhook has built a database of 250 million Wi-Fi physical coordinates then added both GPS and cellular components, making it most precise (inside or near buildings) where GPS is weakest. A software solution combines all available information to create location tracking for any Wi-Fi–enabled device, indoors or out. Skyhook powers location awareness for devices from Apple, Dell, Samsung, and other companies and is now generating secondary data based on those devices.

Landmarks

Noting a few historic transitions and innovations in the history of location-based services reveals the scale, complexity, and wide variety of applications that the core technologies are powering.

OnStar

With roughly 5.5 million subscribers as of mid-2010, OnStar has become the world's largest remote vehicle-assistance service. In addition to receiving navigation and roadside assistance, subscribers can have doors unlocked and gain access to certain diagnostic data related to that particular vehicle. The service delivers important information to emergency response personnel: When extricating occupants from a damaged vehicle, knowing which airbags have deployed can help keep emergency medical technicians, police, and firefighters safe from the explosive force of an undeployed device that might be inadvertently tripped. Knowing the type and severity of the crash before arrival on the scene can also help the teams prepare for the level of damage and injury they are likely to encounter.

The service was launched as a joint venture. General Motors brought the vehicle platform and associated engineering, Hughes Electronics managed the satellite and communications aspects, and Electronic Data Systems, itself being spun out from GM in OnStar's launch year, performed systems integration and information management.

GPS

The history of GPS is even more compelling when considered alongside its nearly contemporary stablemate, the Internet. GPS originated in 1973, the Internet's DoD predecessor ARPANET in 1969. Ronald Reagan allowed GPS to be used for civilian purposes after a 1983 incident involving a Korean Air Lines plane that strayed into Soviet airspace. The Internet was handed off from the National Science Foundation to commercial use in 1995; Bill Clinton ordered fully accurate GPS (20-meter resolution) to be made available May 1, 2000. Previously, the military had access to the most accurate signals while "Selective Availability" (300-meter resolution) was delivered to civilian applications. If an object was big enough (a ship or aircraft), multiple receivers could be networked to generate higher resolution: 1-meter accuracy in 2000. Twenty-four satellites orbit the earth to provide the service.

Since 1990, GPS has spread to a wide variety of uses: recreational hiking and boating, commercial marine navigation, cell phone geolocation, certain aircraft systems, and of course vehicle navigation. Heavy mining and farming equipment can be steered to less than inch tolerances. Vehicles (particularly fleets) and even animals can be "geofenced," with instant notification if the transmitter leaves a designated area. In addition to latitude and longitude, GPS delivers highly precise time services as well as altitude.

Trimble

Founded by Charles Trimble and two colleagues from HP in 1978 (the first year a GPS satellite was launched), Trimble Navigation has become an essential part of geolocation history. From its base in Silicon Valley, the company has amassed a portfolio of more than 800 patents and offers more than 500 products. Much like Cisco, Trimble has made acquisition of smaller companies a core competency, with many merger-and-acquisition moves in the past 10 years in particular. A measure of Trimble's respect in the industry can be seen in the quality of its joint-venture partners: Both Caterpillar and Nikon have gone to market jointly with Trimble.

The company has a long history of firsts: the first commercial scientific-research and geodectic-survey products based on GPS for oil-drilling teams on offshore platforms, the first GPS unit taken aboard the space shuttle, the first circuit board combining GPS and cellular communications. The reach of GPS can be seen in the variety of Trimble's product offerings: agriculture, engineering and construction, federal government, field and mobile worker (including both public safety and utilities applications), and advanced devices, the latter indicating a significant commitment to research and development.

Location, Mobility, and Identity

Issues of electronic identity and mobility have been playing out in quiet but important ways. Each of several instances is a classic case of social or economic problems being tangled up with a technology challenge. To see only one side of the question is to create the possibility of unintended consequences, allow hidden agendas into play, and generally confuse the allocation of sometimes-scarce resources. At the same time, seeing the issues holistically requires time, perspective, and often resources: For example, Americans take the 911 system for granted but seldom realize how complex and fragile the infrastructure actually is. Each of these examples hints at forthcoming challenges and opportunities.

Social Networking Goes Local

Whether through Dodgeball (a New York start-up that was bought by Google in 2005 then left unexploited), Foursquare, or Facebook Places, the potential for the combination of virtual and real people in virtual or real places is still being explored. Viewed in retrospect, the course of the Dodgeball acquisition raises the revenue questions familiar to watchers of social networks dating from Friendster et al. onward: Who will pay for what, and who collects, by what mechanism? Who owns my location information, and what aspects of it do I control? Much like my medical records, which are not mine but rather the doctor's or hospital's, control appears to be defaulting to the collector rather than the generator of digital bread crumbs, at least in the United States: In Europe, privacy laws and attitudes generally favor the citizen.

The Breakdown of 911

After a series of implementations beginning in 1968, Americans on wireline voice connections could reliably dial the same three-digit emergency number anywhere in the country. As the Bell System of the twentieth century fades farther and farther from view, the presumption of 911 reliability declines proportionately with the old business model even as demand increases: The United States generates about 250 million calls a year to 911. The problem comes in two variants.

First, a number of Voice over Internet Protocal (VoIP) customers with life-threatening—and as it turned out, life-ending—emergencies could reach only a recording at Vonage saying to call 911 from another phone. The Texas attorney general raised the question after a 911 call failed during a home invasion in Houston. A baby's death in Florida in 2005 was blamed on a Vonage 911 failure. According to the *Wall Street Journal*, "In a letter to Florida's Attorney General, [the mother] said the Vonage customer-service representative laughed when she told her that Julia had died. 'She laughed and stated that they were unable to revive a baby.'"[1]

For their part, Vonage and the cable operators include bold-print instructions for manual 911 mapping during the sign-up process, but it's been estimated by the U.S. Department of Education that between 14 and 22% of the U.S. population is functionally illiterate.[2] In addition, one feature of VoIP is its portability: Plug the phone into an Internet connection anywhere and receive calls at a virtual area code of the customer's choice. Children are also a key 911 constituency. Taken collectively, these overlapping populations raise dozens of tricky questions. At the infrastructure level, the Federal Communications Commission and other agencies face the substantial challenge of determining the fairest, safest set of technical interconnection requirements incumbent on the Regional Bells and VoIP carriers.

From the Bell perspective, 911 obviously costs money to implement and maintain, and declining wireline revenues translate to declining 911 funds. Connecting 911 to the Internet in a reliable, secure manner is nontrivial—network attacks have used modems to target the service in the past—and until contractual arrangements are finalized, the Bell companies are reluctant to subsidize the same firms that present themselves as full wireline replacements.

In addition, 911 isn't just a VoIP problem: Cellular users represent nearly 75% of emergency callers, but math and economics conspire to make finding them difficult or impossible. In rural areas, cell towers often follow roads, so attempting to triangulate from three points in a straight line can limit precision. Some states have raided 911 tax revenues for budget relief, limiting funds for further refinement.

Cell Phone Tracking

Wireless carriers offer a variety of services that give a relative (often a parent or an adult child of a potentially confused elder) location information generated by a phone. The service also has been used to help stalkers and abusive spouses find their wives in hiding. Women's shelters routinely strip out the tracking component of cell phones; according to the *Wall Street Journal*, a Justice Department report in 2009 estimated that 25,000 adults in the United States were victims of GPS stalking every year.[3] In addition to the carriers, tracking capability is being developed by sophisticated PC users that spoof the behavior of a cell tower. Keystroke- and location-logging software is also available; one package, called Mobile Spy, costs under $100 per year.

Looking Ahead

As the telephone system migrates from being dominated by fixed lines, where identity resided in the phone, to mobile usage, where identity typi- cally relates to an individual, location is turning out to matter a lot. Mobile number portability was an unexpectedly popular mandate a few years ago, for example. Given the global nature of some of these questions, not to mention numerous issues with global governance over IP addresses and domain naming conventions, the discussions and solutions will only get more complicated. As the examples illustrate, getting social arrangements to keep pace with technology innovation, is if anything, more difficult than the innovation itself.

Notes

1. Shawn Young, "Internet Calling's Downside: Failing to Link Callers to 911," *Wall Street Journal,* May 12, 2005, http://online.wsj.com/article/ SB111585619278031205.html.
2. National Center for Education Statistics, "National Assessment of Adult Literacy (NAAL)," http://nces.ed.gov/naal/kf_demographics.asp.
3. Justin Scheck, "Stalkers Exploit Cellphone GPS," *Wall Street Journal,* August 3, 2010. http://online.wsj.com/article/SB10001424052748703467304575383522318 244234.html.

CHAPTER 26

Clouds

Given extensive and ever-faster connections over both air and fiber optics, the location of computing power relative to the user of said horsepower has become negotiable. Because of the need to do hard things in the service of a smartphone, the awareness of massive inefficiencies in the power consumption of fixed computers, and the cost and complexity of the systems that support a given server, offloading some of the infrastructure to a specialized provider that operates at a huge scale makes sense in ways it did not in the era of the *personal* computer and *local* area network.

The proliferation of so-called cloud computing platforms has been rapid. Because there is so much material available that defines the phenomenon (see Figure 26.1), we'll move here to an examination of some of the unexpected consequences and complicated implications of moving some or all of a computing environment to offsite, third-party environments. We will find that the impact of the Internet, as a conduit for both communications and computing, extends far beyond the data center.

To get the problematic and inevitable definitional question out of the way, here is one from *Information Week*'s John Foley: "Cloud computing is on-demand access to virtualized IT resources that are housed outside of your own data center, shared by others, simple to use, paid for via subscription, and accessed over the Web."[1]

There are of course other contending definitions, but Foley's is mercifully brief. Even so, it begs the questions of private clouds, of how small a cloud can be before it starts being something else, and how individual uses of clouds (many people don't own a data center but satisfy most of Foley's other conditions) vary from and overlap corporate ones. It does get us started in more or less the right direction.

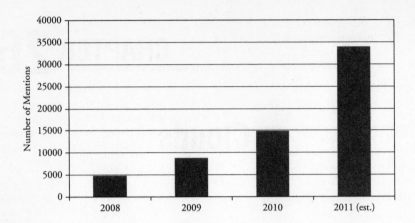

FIGURE 26.1 Media Mentions of the Phrase "Cloud Computing," 2008–2011
Data source: Google News archives.

Both Technical and Economic Innovation

It's important to note that cloud computing is as much, or more, a matter of economics than of processing cycles: Who invests capital? What products or services are bought and sold or produced and consumed? HP and IBM have long made boxes that created compute capacity; Amazon and Google now sell computing capacity without the box. The end user's business need has not changed—calculating a complex model, recognizing revenue, analyzing transaction histories—but the way resources are organized to meet that need can be radically different.

According to one of the few canonical documents on the topic, a technical report from the University of California at Berkeley, these economic differences are expressed in hardware in three main ways:

1. *The illusion of infinite computing resources available on demand,* thereby eliminating the need for cloud computing users to plan far ahead for provisioning.
2. *The elimination of an up-front commitment by cloud users,* thereby allowing companies to start small and increase hardware resources only when there is an increase in their needs.
3. *The ability to pay for use of computing resources on a short-term basis as needed* (e.g., processors by the hour and storage by the day) and release them as needed, thereby rewarding

conservation by letting machines and storage go when they are no longer useful.[2]

The rapid pace of change in this area is such that we must add to that list. Marc Benioff is chief executive officer of Salesforce.com, which helped pioneer important aspects of software as a service, a progenitor of modern cloud computing. He further differentiates Amazon, Google, IBM, and other first-generation cloud providers from YouTube, Twitter, and Facebook, all of which, as home to new kinds of applications, serve as cloud providers of a different sort.

As Benioff notes, first-generation clouds were notably low in cost, fast at the compute level, and easy to use. The benefits of the second generation are different: They include collaboration, mobility, and real-time capabilities.[3] Thus, the blurring line between hardware (cloud support of lightweight mobile devices such as tablets, e-readers, and smartphones) and people-powered benefits, including incredibly rapid information dissemination and mass collaboration, becomes difficult to trace but important to monitor.

Cloud Computing and the Enterprise

Those large-scale social network cloud behaviors generally are limited to the consumer market, for the moment anyway. Let's return to enterprise computing: As various analysts and technology executives assess the pros and cons of cloud computing, two points of consensus appear to be emerging:

1. Very large data centers benefit from extreme economies of scale.
2. Cloud success stories generally are found outside of the traditional IT shop.

Let us examine each of these in more detail, then probe some of the implications.

Advantages of Scale

Whether run by a cloud provider or a well-managed enterprise IT group, very large data centers exhibit economies of scale not found in smaller server installations. The leverage of relatively expensive and skilled technologists is far higher when one person can manage between 1,000 and 2,000 highly automated servers, as at Microsoft, as opposed to one person being responsible for between 5 and 50 machines, which is common.

In addition, the power consumption of a well-engineered data center can be more efficient than that of many traditional operations. Yahoo! built a new facility in upstate New York, for example, that utilizes atmospheric cooling to the point that only 1% of electricity consumption is for air-conditioning and related cooling tasks.[4] Having people with deep expertise in cooling, power consumption, recovery, and other niche skills on staff also helps make cloud providers more efficient than those running at smaller scales. The engineering challenges at this scale are themselves new and often fascinating.

Also, large data centers benefit from aggregation of demand. Assume facility A has 10,000 users of computing cycles spread over a variety of different cyclical patterns while facility B has fewer users, all with similar seasonality for retail, quarterly closes for an accounting function, or monthly invoices. Facility A should be able to run more efficiently because it has a more "liquid" market for its capabilities while facility B will likely have to build to its highest load (plus a safety margin) then run less efficiently the majority of the time. What Amazon Distinguished Engineer James Hamilton calls "non-correlated peaks" can be difficult to generate within a single enterprise or function.[5]

IT Organizations Have Yet to Reap the Cloud's Benefits

For all of these benefits, external cloud successes have yet to accrue to traditional IT organizations. At Amazon Web Services, for example, of roughly 200 case studies, none is devoted to traditional enterprise processes such as order management, invoicing and payment processing, or human resources.[6]

There are many readily understandable reasons for this pattern; here is a sample of four. First, legal and regulatory constraints often require a physical audit of information handling practices to which virtual answers are unacceptable. Second, the laws of physics may make large volumes of database joins and other computing tasks difficult to execute off-premise. In general, high-volume transaction processing currently is not recommended as a cloud candidate.

Third, licenses from traditional enterprise providers, such as Microsoft, Oracle, and SAP, are still evolving, making it difficult to run their software in hybrid environments (wherein some processes run locally while others run in a cloud). In addition, only a few enterprise applications of either the package or custom variety are designed to run as well on cloud infrastructure as they do on a conventional server or cluster. Fourth, accounting practices in IT shops may make it difficult to know the true baseline costs and benefits to which an outside provider must compare: some chief information officers never see their electric bills, for example.

The Cloud Will Change How Resources Are Organized

For these reasons, among others, the conclusion is usually drawn that cloud computing is a suboptimal fit for traditional enterprise IT. However, let's invert that logic to see how organizations have historically adapted to new technology capability. When electric motors replaced overhead drive shafts driven by waterwheels adjoining textile mills, the looms and other machines were often left in the same positions for decades before mill owners realized the facility could be organized independently of power supply. More recently, word-processing computers from the likes of Wang initially automated typing pools (one-third of all U.S. women working in 1971 were secretaries); it was not until 10 to 20 years later that large numbers of managers began to service their own document-production needs and thereby alter the shape of organizations.[7]

Enterprise IT architectures embed a wide range of operating assumptions regarding the nature of work, the location of business processes, clock speed, and other factors. When a major shift occurs in the information or other infrastructure, it takes years for organizations to adapt. If we take as our premise that most organizations are not yet prepared to exploit cloud computing (rather than talk about clouds not being ready for "the enterprise"), what are some potential ramifications?

- *Organizations are already being founded with very little capital investment.* For a services- or knowledge-intensive business that does not make anything physical, free tools and low-cost computing cycles can mostly be expensed, changing the fundraising and indeed organizational strategies significantly.
- *The perennial question of "who owns the data?"* enters a new phase. While today USB drives and desktop databases continue to make it possible to hoard data, in the future, organizations built on cloud-friendly logic from their origins will deliver new wrinkles to information-handling practices. The issue will by no means disappear: Google's Gmail cloud storage is no doubt already home to a sizable quantity of enterprise data.
- *Smartphones, tablets, and other devices built without mass storage can thrive in a cloud-centric environment, particularly if the organization is designed to be fluid and mobile.* Coburn Ventures in New York, for example, is an investment firm comprised of a small team of mobile knowledge workers who for the first five years had no corporate office whatsoever: The organization operated from Wi-Fi hotspots, with only occasional all-hands meetings.
- *New systems of trust and precautions will need to take shape as the core IT processing capacity migrates to a vendor.* It's rarely consequential to

contract for a video transcoding or a weather simulation and have it be interrupted. More problematically, near-real-time processes such as customer service likely will need to be redesigned to operate successfully in a cloud or cluster of clouds. Service-level agreements will need to reflect the true cost and impact of interruptions or other lapses. Third-party adjudicators may emerge to assess the responsibility of the cloud customer that introduced a hiccup into the environment relative to the vendor whose failover failed.

Practical Considerations

Because the cloud model introduces innovations in both economics and technology, making educated purchasing and deployment questions requires new metrics, models, and potentially skills.[8] Some practical questions illustrate the complexity of changing organizational, operational, physical, legal, and computational models on the fly:

1. *From the buyer's perspective, what is a vendor's profit path?* What can be differentiated and thus generate margins? Compared to the conventional model of data centers, which is often measured in $10,000 or $100,000 increments, cloud computing usage at Amazon is measured in dimes.

2. *Related to point 1, how does cloud lock-in vary from existing software (à la classical Microsoft) or hardware (the vintage IBM model) variants?* And let's return to that initial Berkeley document: When resources are "released" for other users, where does my data go? If it is in the cloud, the resources can't all be released for other purposes, and if the data moves out of the cloud back to my premise, we both lose cloud advantages (such as power management) and introduce security considerations: Who validates the hard-disk scrub when I retreat from the shared resource?

3. *How will incumbents respond?* If company A has an established business selling hardware as capital expenditure, and a competing model shifts compute power to an operating-expense model, presumably company B doesn't stand still. How do buyers hedge risk with such a dynamic vendor environment?

4. *As with so much of the world's infrastructure, what is the incentive to invest in "pipes" when the value-add lies elsewhere, or nowhere?* The robust, high-speed networks upon which the cloud providers rely cannot simply be assumed.

5. *If for legal or other reasons the buyer needs performance, security, and/or reliability guarantees, how are these delivered if the buyer cannot see or physically access her assets?*

6. *There are no free lunches: who bears risk?* Every one of the Web's elite destinations has suffered from major outages at some point.[9] In light of that history, what does a fault-tolerant cloud environment look like, require, and cost? As with so many networked scenarios, the price of failure goes up: When Amazon suffered a cloud outage in 2011, it took dozens of companies without backup down with it.

7. *How does optimization work in a cloud?* The vendor may be managing to power consumption, say, while customer A wants stable (not necessarily fast, but predictable) transaction times for a shopping-cart scenario. Customer B needs fast compute capability despite big and frequent reads and writes to disc. How can all three parties go home happy at the end of the day?

8. *How can virtual, hybrid environments be tested before major real-world events: a quarterly close, a consumer promotion, a currency meltdown?* While there will be some pure cloud successes, a big question relates to how well clouds can integrate with existing data centers and other assets. (What constitutes unit testing in a cloud?)

9. *What can a customer ask for by way of customization?* Who can and will provide it, and at what costs in money and performance? The price points reflect commodity economics, but sooner or later most buyers stumble on needs that surpass plain vanilla.

10. *Which standards are open and which are proprietary?* The PC architecture flourished in part because of its interoperability: someone could choose a big Maxtor hard drive or a faster Seagate, a Dell flat-panel or Sony Trinitron display, and the hardware maker could buy the cheapest CD drives, memory, and power cords on a given day. USB made the platform more flexible yet. By comparison, once buyers choose a cloud provider, how must they choose an Internet service provider, a system management vendor, a billing system? In short, what are the dependencies introduced by a cloud instance?

11. *How fast is fast enough?* Cloud computing is a coherent-sounding phrase, but computing has many facets. Think about the different time scales relating to
    - Network latency
    - The laws of physics regarding hard drive access
    - The laws of physics regarding hard drive failure
    - Core competency versus utility workload allocation
    One size clearly cannot fit all.

12. *Who guarantees precision?* Speaking of laws of physics, all microprocessors are not created equal. Some highly precise calculations, out to many decimal points, might run slightly differently on two different computing cores. How does the user of a given scientific calculation, for example, know that his or her result will be consistent across

computing instances, across different clouds, or across brands of processor?

At the end of the day, orchestrating all of those sets of events, each with its own timescape, in a virtual world is a really, really tough technical and managerial problem. Getting the systems to work doesn't even scratch the questions of profitability, liability, audit and related requirements, and so on.

Looking Ahead

For all of those substantial challenges, the question is not whether cloud computing will happen but rather how this tendency will unfold and how organizations, regulators, and other actors will respond. Until the rhetoric and more important the base of experience moves beyond the current state of pilots and vaporware, the range of potential outcomes is too vast to bet on with any serious money. Those problems are soluble. The larger implications are already becoming visible. As cloud computing reallocates the division of labor within the computing fabric, it will also change how managers and, especially, entrepreneurs organize resources into firms, partnerships, and other formal structures. Once these forms emerge, the nature of everything else will be subject to reinvention: work, risk, reward, collaboration, and indeed value itself.

Notes

1. John Foley, "A Definition of Cloud Computing," *InformationWeek* Plug Into the Cloud blog, September 26, 2008,www.informationweek.com/cloud-computing/blog/archives/2008/09/a_definition_of.html.
2. Michael Armbrust et al. "Above the Clouds: A Berkeley View of Cloud Computing," Electrical Engineering and Computer Sciences, University of California at Berkeley technical report # UCB/EECS-2009-28, February 10, 2009, www.eecs.berkeley.edu/Pubs/TechRpts/2009/EECS-2009-28.pdf.
3. Marc Benioff, "Welcome to Cloud 2," Google Latitude conference presentation, April 14, 2010.
4. Rich Miller, "Yahoo Computing Coop: Shape of Things to Come?" Data Center Knowledge, April 26, 2010, www.datacenterknowledge.com/archives/2010/04/26/yahoo-computing-coop-the-shape-of-things-to-come/.
5. James Hamilton, "Private Clouds Are Not the Future," Perspectives blog, January 17, 2010, http://perspectives.mvdirona.com/2010/01/17/PrivateCloudsAreNotTheFuture.aspx.
6. Amazon Web Services Web site, http://aws.amazon.com/solutions/case-studies/.

7. See also Erik Brynjolfsson, Paul Hofmann, and John Jordan, "Cloud Computing and Electricity: Beyond the Utility Model," *Communications of the ACM* 53, no. 5 (May 2010): 32–34, doi 10.1145/1735223.1735234.

8. See "Let It Rise: A Special Report on Corporate IT," *The Economist*, October 25, 2008, esp. pp. 13–17, www.economist.com/node/12411882.

9. See, for example, Craig Labovitz, "The Great GoogleLapse," Arbor Networks Web site, May 14, 2009, http://asert.arbornetworks.com/2009/05/the-great-googlelapse/, and "EBay Apologizes for Web Site Glitch," CNN Tech, November 23, 2009,http://articles.cnn.com/2009-11-23/tech/ebay.outage_1_ebay-glitch-search?_s=PM:TECH.

CHAPTER 27

Wireless

The path to today's smartphone has many branches: the Bell system, for certain, but also large government contracts, a grassroots networking protocol, and many clever architects and programmers. These developer communities can either be independent or in the service of the computing giants: Adobe, Google, Microsoft, and of course Apple. The iPhone proved to be a breakout device for many reasons.

While we talk about cell phones with the emphasis on "phones," the smartphone is far from being an extrapolation from Bell's original device. The iPhone's naming convention makes a certain amount of sense, but it's not really a phone: Person-to-person voice communication is maybe a fifth of its value. Calling it an ultraportable computer would not have worked; I defer to the marketing genius behind this extraordinarily successful product. But the fact remains that the smartphone has much more to do with computing than with traditional voice.

Precedents

Even the term "smartphone" needs to be defined carefully. The original Amazon Kindle, for example, allowed only rudimentary Web access, eschewing the Swiss Army knife approach in favor of intense concentration on one core activity: reading. Amazon is routinely secretive about competitive issues and thus has given no firm indication of how many readers are out there. Given the massive software sales—Kindle titles outsell all print editions on the earth's biggest bookstore—hardware sales have to be robust. The Kindle is, in point of fact, a single-purpose mobile device, with the Sprint wireless network utilized to facilitate the instant downloads of new purchases on the airport tarmac, for example. Broadband access costs are bundled into some combination of hardware (including ad revenue from the low-price variant) and book revenue, invisible to the customer but a mobile data transaction nevertheless.

The Apple iPad presents similar definitional issues. Lacking a hard drive and a hardware keyboard/mouse, it's not really a laptop, yet it duplicates considerable functionality. At the same time, it can't make voice calls or send and receive text messages unless the user jumps through some hoops. For our purposes, the iPad counts as a large smartphone rather than a small computer; most of the factors in this section work to explain the tablet's success.

The following trends, some coming from unrelated domains, converge in the contemporary smartphone.

Miniaturization

In the 1950s, the IBM RAMAC featured a 5-megabyte hard drive (drum storage) that weighed about 1,000 pounds and was the size of a large washing machine. Fifty-plus years later, solid-state memory gets smaller and faster at a predictable rate, to the extent that 64 gigabytes (about 10,000 times more) had shrunk to a package weighing about 1.5 ounces, or 10,000 times smaller. Combined, that's improvement by a factor of 100 million—not to mention the cost, which has declined by a slightly smaller factor.

Most any component of a smartphone has been miniaturized, if not by such a dramatic multiple (see Figure 27.1, which shows Nokia's progress in this regard). GPS units used to be carried in backpacks; they now fit in a pocket. High-resolution color displays were formerly built from cathode-ray tubes; the LCD then OLED* display (and the miniaturization thereof) is an often-overlooked part of the smartphone's success. Batteries, antennas, even speakers—the list goes on.

Usability

Cramming all the functionality of a contemporary smartphone into a tiny package is an engineering accomplishment, to be sure, but what's even more noteworthy is how the market has been "trained" to accept the trade-offs that come with the packaging. Voice quality, for example, remains an issue, as does wireless data coverage. Dropped calls, which rarely happened on traditional wirelines, are met with the shrug of a shoulder: Expectations have been downsized in that particular domain.

---

*Organic Light-Emitting Diode technology is brighter and uses less power than LEDs, among other benefits.

FIGURE 27.1 Nokia's First Car Phone and First Mobile Phone Compared to Current Products
Source: Nokia.

Ringtones, however, are customizable, which generated substantial revenue for the carriers in the period from 2004 to 2007 particularly.

Texting is another area where the carriers were surprised when a secondary piece of capability emerged as a major market in its own right. Originally a kludgey workaround on GSM* networks in the 1990s, Nordic and some Asian teens used the Short Messaging Service (SMS) as a way to avoid the heavy voice tariffs that were designed to capture revenue from the rapidly increasing base of users. Uptake has been nearly universal on every continent, moving from the original strictly text-based service to include sound, photo, and video variants as bandwidth and device capability improve.

The Apple iPod trained people to dock their devices to a computer and, later, to buy content from an online storefront. As the form of that content migrated from songs to movies to software, users could take small steps up a ladder of increasing complexity. Experiments with a stylus, on

---

*Global System for Mobile Communications, originally *Groupe Spécial Mobile,* denoted the standards used for second generation (2G) wireless telephony in European markets.

the Palm Pilot and Apple Newton, in the mid-1990s helped pave the way for full touch-screen operation, a step that Nokia and BlackBerry are finding it difficult to take. One factor in the smartphone's success, then, is the development of native mobile operating systems that gracefully support the wide range of functionality in an on-the-move context. Early versions of Windows CE and Windows Mobile, meanwhile, treated the smartphone as a small desktop, down to file folder metaphors, which newer designs have resisted.

Fungibility of Sound, Voice, Video, Text

Not that long ago, digital communications was format specific: Reading a magnetic stripe card, playing a compact disc, taking a digital photograph, or watching digital video each required its own piece of equipment. In the smartphone, voice bits can move over a cellular carrier or over Skype; video can be recorded, edited, uploaded, and/or consumed; still images go to Flickr or Facebook; e-reader applications duplicate the function of the book or newspaper; and MP3 files can play through the earphones just as easily as any other kind of sound. Not only can the smartphone manage all those different media types, the Internet can move them with equal ease and low cost.

GPS

As we saw in Chapter 25 and elsewhere, GPS has become essential for both consumer way-finding and industrial applications as well as military coordination. The migration of location awareness into the smartphone involves GPS, to be sure, but also the Wi-Fi mapping efforts of Google Maps and such services as Skyhook. On top of the U.S. government's core system, such private-sector players as NAVTEQ (now part of Nokia) and TomTom along with Google's powerful Maps and Earth tools combine to offer extensive geographic capability to smartphones and tablets.

Radio

As much as the iPhone has stressed the cellular network, the picture would be far worse if Wi-Fi had not picked up so much of the load. According to comScore, 47.5% of iPhone traffic is handled by Wi-Fi; Google Android smartphones move 78% of their data over cellular networks, while iPads are 92% Wi-Fi centric.[1] The role of Wi-Fi in the success of the smartphone is all the more important for two reasons: These are ad hoc networks that were not built with a government stimulus package, a spectrum purchase, or a conscious deployment plan; and every trans-action over Wi-Fi spares the often-overtaxed cellular system, which was deployed at great cost. This offloading of bandwidth explains the steady variation in mobile pricing plans: As video gains in importance and more people carry smartphones (now estimated to be about a third of the U.S. market), unlimited plans become less attractive to carriers.

The importance of a robust wireless data network is obvious to any-one who has tried to download even simple content over slow con-nections. The tens of billions of dollars spent by U.S. carriers alone on spectrum licenses, tower rights and real estate, and networking equipment can at times be overlooked, but like electricity, it's painfully obvious in its absence.

After Wi-Fi and cellular, the third radio in their smartphone that few people think about much belongs to Bluetooth, the close-range protocol used mostly for headsets but also for printing and keyboards. Named for a Scandinavian king from the tenth century who united warring tribes, the standard fills an important gap for which higher-power (and battery-depleting) protocols would be undesirable. After the Bluetooth special interest group (a common factor in technology platform development) was formed in 1998, the standard was rapidly adopted and only six years later could be found in 250 million different devices. At its 10-year anni-versary, 2 billion devices had been shipped.[2]

Software Developers

More than 15 billion pieces of software had been downloaded to iPhones as of mid-2011. Amazing as that number is, Apple has a log of every single one, even the free ones, through its App Store ERP* backbone. As good as its design and hardware might be, the iPhone's success relies in large measure on Apple's reinvention of the global software market in only a few years. A vast ecosystem of software developers has created more than 500,000 approved applications for the iPhone, and Android developers have been essentially as busy. One indication of the primacy of the "ecosystem" is the separation of Android and Apple from the rest of the smartphone market: The Nokia and BlackBerry hardware might be superior, in theory, but app selec-tion is severely lagging. Because platform dynamics are in force (see Chapter 5), developers and customers flock to the market leaders, fur-ther marginalizing the laggards: Feedback loops and network effects can be powerful at this global scale.

---

*Enterprise Resource Planning.

On the handset front, meanwhile, Apple confronts the question of how to reach the next 50 million users and the next 50 million after that, given that many of those people will be using non-alphanumeric languages, such as Chinese and Arabic. Stand-alone hardware companies scramble for software partners: Motorola is being acquired by Google, HTC and Samsung debate how safe it is to stay on Android, and Nokia is betting on its alliance with Microsoft. Each combination brings a distinctive package of strengths and weaknesses to the table as they fight for market share in a global contest for hardware supremacy in a new order. Whatever happens, we will be confronted by growth rates the likes of which no manager (or capital market) has ever seen, each with its own raft of unintended consequences.

The Breakthrough

The Apple iPhone was not the first or the most technologically capable smartphone. (IBM introduced a prototype in 1992.) Why, then, did it break through to broad market success? Not to enter the realm of Apple hagiography, but Steve Jobs presided over five defining moments[*] in the history of computing. Getting lucky could explain one, or even two, successes, but the overall pattern must be recognized: Jobs understood something about the power of great design and smooth user experience that led to a no-prisoners demand for easy-to-use, and even fun-to-use, products in a way no other U.S. tech executive has been able to deliver on a consistent basis.

Jobs and Apple got a lot of little things, along with some big ones, close enough to right to make the iPhone the standard-bearer for a critical phase of the smartphone's market development. Google's Android platform has since done extremely well, but surprisingly, given the powerful global players in competition—Samsung, Motorola, Research In Motion, Nokia, and Microsoft—it is currently a two-horse race. How did Apple jump into a segment as an outsider and proceed to set the agenda for an entire industry?

- Apple managed the price curve. $499 (which AT&T was not allowed to discount from the outset) yielded an estimated 50% margin, according

---

[*]The five products were the original Macintosh with graphical user interface and unboxed hardware design; Pixar computer animation; and the iPod, iPhone, and iPad since 2001. Apple's share price multiplied thirty-eight-fold in the 10 years following the iPod announcement.

to iSupply, which does market research on bill-of-materials costs. That profitability, however, allowed Apple to cut the price after the early adopters paid a premium, and economies of scale dropped the cost of the inputs. Even after other touch-screen smartphones came to market, Apple could charge premium prices. In part, this relates to Apple's supply-chain effectiveness, which shows up in procurement, logistics (inbound, outbound, and product returns), manufacturing quality, and on-time launches.

- The form factor works. Other smart devices with rich visual interfaces have failed to translate well as handsets for conversations: The BlackBerry is great from the thumbs' point of view but less attractive to mouth and ears. Looking at global markets, many young SMS users can text blindfolded. The iPhone's smooth screen doesn't allow this kind of typing, yet the drawback hasn't been a major factor in sales. Dispensing with the stylus, judged as risky at the time, proved to be a very smart decision.

- Apple understood the Swiss Army knife factor. All-in-one devices reduce footprint, but few chefs rely on a red pocket knife to slice cheese, bone meat, and dice carrots. And who's ever used the saw for anything? The point here is that the iPhone's range of capabilities is good enough to make it acceptable for nearly any relevant activity. Digital camera and video camera sales are falling; the iPhone is the most commonly used camera by people who upload images to Flickr.[3] The GPS functionality of smartphones is hurting the share prices of TomTom, Garmin, and their kin. Apart from e-readers such as the Kindle and Nook, few portable electronic devices are stand-alone any longer—Apple's own falling iPod sales testify to the trend. Even game consoles are expected to be surpassed by smartphones in the coming years.[4]

- The device works. Apart from some issues with the iPhone 4 antenna/case, Apple has made the product sufficiently reliable and robust to survive the rigors of tens of millions of users' many habits, abuses, and extremes of environment. Battery life, overall durability, voice quality, and data security are all good enough for most of the market, and usability apparently is more important than any single aspect of functionality.

- Apple has masterfully built a partner network. Ranging from Foxconn, which does assembly in China, to FedEx, to component suppliers, to the developer network, and to movie studios and record labels, the Apple extended ecosystem is big, capable, and on-task. Significantly, Apple seized control of the handset from the wireless carriers, whose earlier gatekeeper role had allowed them to set much of the mobile agenda. By creating must-have hardware, Apple forced AT&T and then other carriers to accede to terms and conditions no other handset manufacturer had been able to win. Customer service is Apple's, high-margin extended warranty revenues are Apple's, advertising is approved by Apple, and pricing is set by Apple. Compare the Windows 7 smartphone launch in 2010, in which AT&T was offering two handsets for the price of one just weeks after the product came to market.

- The retail channels for the iPhone are important. Apple has massive foot traffic—74.5 million in the fourth quarter of 2010, more than all of Major League Baseball and more than how many visited a Disney theme park—into its own stores. There the product education function of the heavily scripted Genius bar experience helps introduce nontechnical buyers who might lack a family Mac-head to get them started. At more than $5,600 in sales per square foot, Apple stores measure nearly double the rate of Tiffany, the traditional leader in that metric.[5]

- Launching into a mature mobile market with powerful incumbents, high capital intensity, and well-defined roles, Apple elevated its level of execution. In contrast to the music market into which the iPod launched in 2002, which was characterized by tumbling share prices at the labels, distribution of the capital base (recording studios and pressing plants) to millions of PC owners, and few megaselling titles, the wireless industry has consolidated to a small number of global network operators, equipment manufacturers, and handset firms. The scale of wireless is almost unfathomable: At the time of the iPhone launch, Apple had sold about 100 million iPods in five years, which is a huge number in the PC industry. In the fourth quarter of 2006, Nokia all by itself sold 102 million handsets.

- Design-wise, Apple invented a new category of device, learning from previous failures. In the music player case, Apple integrated a far superior music management software application with its version of the MP3 player and implemented copy protection to satisfy the labels that their 99-cent songs would not be copied indefinitely. In the iPhone case, Apple took a variety of lessons from Motorola's ROKR music player+phone, which had its iPod/iTunes license pulled. Rather than being a follow-up to the extremely successful RAZR phone, the ROKR is essentially the answer to a trivia question.

- Apple once again used superior industrial design, elevated to the level of art, to create unsurpassed "cool" factor in a category. The microscopic attention to coherence and detail in the iPod, from marketing, to packaging, to peripherals, to product endorsers, created an emotional appeal found in few electronic devices, and the iPhone built on that foundation. Few other companies have that kind of precedent to live up to and to build from.

- As venture capitalist John Doerr noted, Apple has a vast army of users trained to sync their device with a computer.[6] It's an installed base of user behavior that gave the iPhone a jump-start in adoption.
- The iPhone captured momentum amidst industry disruption, and with its success consolidated several trends. As mobile broadband emerged from competing standards and platforms, the iPhone dominated a multiradio niche just at the moment that heterogeneous coverage became a reality. Working at the office? Going abroad? Working in a Starbucks hotspot? Surfing on a train in the Northeast Corridor? Customers found that having a unified device to maintain connectivity across access technologies proved extremely valuable.
- Unlike many previous successes, the iPhone is not powered by a single "killer application." In the case of the iPod, it was clearly iTunes music management and legal downloads. With the iPhone, voicemail is handy, but fewer people rely on voice communications. Texting and typing support is good; the BlackBerry and in some cases Android devices are better. Maps and way-finding are excellent, but days or weeks might go by between uses if the device owner is on her home turf. The point is that as compared to the spreadsheet for the early PC, for example, or Internet access for 1990s laptops, the device supports whatever the user requires: Major League Baseball's At Bat app is great, but that doesn't explain the iPhone's success. Facebook and social games play well, but not for everybody. Weather and news can be viewed through many handy services.

Looking Ahead

As we saw in Chapter 12, the mobile phone is having extended implications across the world, and not only in the realm of entertainment and convenience. Once the majority of the world's technology users connect to the Internet through a smartphone or related device, we will see even broader changes: What does it mean never to have to be captive to a wire for any form of information retrieval? What does it mean to have the phone become your date book, your wallet, the window to your music "collection" (whatever that term will come to mean), your photos, and so many other defining artifacts? After Apple built on the achievements of Palm, of Nokia, of Trimble, of Samsung, and of Research In Motion, so now will Google and perhaps Nokia/Microsoft attempt to leapfrog the iPhone franchise. Ultimately, the winner in such a high-stakes competition among powerful firms will be a whole new generation of customer who will be less and less tolerant of any sense of limits on the power of what could be the twenty-first century's defining device.

Power and Portability

Wireless telephony is in many ways a challenge to basic physical laws. Miniaturization proceeds apace as manufacturing techniques and materials science advance. Signal quality and availability improve with advances in radio. The final frontier may be batteries, subject as they are to the laws of chemistry and ultimately physics.

Until the early 1990s, nickel-cadmium batteries were used in most portable electronics applications. Nickel is obviously heavy, however, and cadmium is environmentally toxic. In contrast, lithium is extremely light and holds more energy per unit of weight than any other metal. It is, however, unstable and thus dangerous. Lithium ion batteries, introduced by Sony in 1991, actually have no lithium metal, being made instead of cobalt, carbon, copper, and iron. Accordingly, the U.S. government classifies lithium ion batteries as a nonhazardous waste stream. But because all the metals involved are common, there is little economic incentive to recycle them. As of 2006, American threw away an estimated 2 billion lithium ion batteries per year.[7]

Current research into battery innovation focuses on weight (or energy density) and recharging time. Refinements of the lithium ion model appear feasible, but no breakthrough replacement appears to be imminent. In addition, recharging using body motion is being investigated, as is wireless transmission of power (currently at very short range). Recharging pads for mobile devices are commercially available, and similar technology is used on electric toothbrushes, which are used in wet environments where open electrical contacts could be dangerous.

Notes

1. http://readerszone.com/facts/comscore-traffic-by-device-may-2011-report-ipad-is-winner.html.
2. www.bluetooth.com/Pages/History-of-Bluetooth.aspx.
3. www.flickr.com/cameras/.
4. James Brightman, "John Carmack: 'Unquestionable' That Mobile Will Surpass Current Consoles," *IndustryGamers*, July 7, 2011, www.industrygamers.com/news/john-carmack-unquestionable-that-mobile-will-surpass-current-consoles/.
5. Jordan Kahn, "Apple Ranks #1 in Retail Sales per Square Foot among Retailers," 9to5Mac.com, August 23, 2011, http://9to5mac.com/2011/08/23/apple-ranks-1-in-retail-sales-per-square-foot/.
6. Dan Farber, "Churchill Club: 9th Annual Top Ten Tech Trends," Zdnet.com, April 3, 2007, www.zdnet.com/blog/btl/churchill-club-9th-annual-top-ten-tech-trends/4779.
7. Robert L. Mitchell, "Lithium Ion Batteries: High-Tech's Latest Mountain of Waste," Computerworld, August 22, 2006, http://blogs.computerworld.com/node/3285.

CHAPTER 28

Search

While widespread availability of search technology is only about 15 years old, its implications continue to accumulate. Work and commerce, medical care and mate finding, crime and education all are being reshaped by an effectively infinite base of information made usable by various types of search, indexing, and related technologies. In addition, search is closely related to substantial changes in how knowledge is generated, stored, and distributed.

It remains to be seen how the search era will be positioned in the grand sweep of human intellectual progress. In the short term, several interrelated facets of search should be noted: context, value, impact, and future constraints.

Why Search Matters: Context

Search is in many ways the defining tool of the Internet age. Digital data is ever easier to generate, more of our entertainment takes digital form, globally dispersed actors can find each other and coordinate, and the number of sources of information continues to multiply. As we saw in Chapter 6, the long tail of content production requires search and other matching technologies (including word of mouth and algorithmic "if you liked this you might like that" matching).

Information Volume Is Multiplying

Many sources of information have been separated from their location. Compare the Internet to national and university research libraries, which required dozens or hundreds of years to assemble, cost millions of dollars to sustain and maintain, and employed large staffs of experts in such specialties as acquisitions, cataloging, bookbinding, and archival management. Early search technologies used text-string matching, but Google's major breakthrough was in hyperlink analysis: Links were, in essence, votes on a given site's value. In the past decade, metadata matching and semantic analysis (does the searcher mean "field" as in wheat, magnetic, or career?) have made strides. As a result, technology has made billions of megabytes of information available to billions of people. Those people can be anywhere and in any number, so information access is no longer restricted by physical presence. In addition, the virtual resource can be used by as many people as need it at a given instant, unlike physical books or microfilms.

Furthermore, raw data can be consumed and transformed without traveling to physical laboratories or research stations. Weather satellite data, Web-based laboratories for remote experimentation, virtual shared instruments, and worldwide access to webcams or data buoys are only a few examples of shared data sources. National and international statistical authorities are further sources of information that scholars can transform into more formalized outputs.

Finally, repositories of knowledge have different gatekeepers. Books and paper journals are no longer the definitive word in some fields, given how long editorial review and publishing can take. Blogs, e-mails, and videos can find a worldwide audience in just hours, not months or years. As a result, formal cataloging systems for books and journals are not necessarily the authoritative taxonomies of a given field.

Search Changes Information Access

In some ways, access to knowledge has been democratized—many tools, formerly restricted to researchers at a relatively few well-endowed research institutions, including search engines themselves, are now widely available. One example would be LexisNexis licenses, which cost tens of thousands of dollars.*

At the same time, however, literacy is not universal, and search literacy requires a particular form of skill and discernment that is not equally distributed. Search results frequently lack context and in many instances do not speak for themselves. Knowing what one is looking for can be surprisingly difficult, notwithstanding the simplicity implied by the clean input screen. Finally, search results are not objective, yet the results imply

---

*One published figure quoted $300 per hour.

an algorithmic ranking in order of fitness, accuracy, or popularity that cannot be assumed yet is difficult to consciously override.

Search Technologies Reinforce Economic Trends

Search has long been recognized as a stage in many transactions, but Google-scale digital search also plays a role in several broad-based economic tendencies.

- Search costs factor into nearly every economic transaction: As buyers and sellers both need to discover each other, compare needs and capabilities, and coordinate, search engines have facilitated easier matching of parties to a transaction.[1]
- Although many people casually speak of an "information economy," Stanford professor Paul Romer developed an academic formulation for it around 1990. Commonly known as new growth theory, the Romer theory asserts that land, labor, and capital are no longer the building blocks of a modern economy. Instead, he asserts that *ideas* create a significant fraction of an economy's value. Conventional economics would portray the end of the petroleum era as implying the end of transportation. But in Romer's view, human innovation will develop new fuel sources and economically viable technologies for utilizing them, then harvest market rewards for doing so.[2] In such an environment, search technologies become essential for making an information economy run.
- In Thomas Friedman's formulation, "the world is flat" insofar as certain kinds of value creation become physically removed from their consumption.[3] Nurses have to be in the same room as their patients to give injections or take temperatures, but equity analysts or radiologists can be thousands of miles away from the user of their knowledge. Search is both a cause and an outcome of the flattening process as it makes both formal and informal knowledge accessible to anyone with an Internet connection at any time.
- Information is no longer distributed only by broadcast methods. Two influential books—Chris Anderson's *The Long Tail*[4] and Nassim Nicholas Taleb's *The Black Swan*[5]—both analyze how power-law distributions explain increasing numbers of events. In the physical world, distributions of height must absolutely fall on a Gaussian distribution, and all examples are within 1 order of magnitude: Every human stands between 1 foot tall and 10 feet tall. In contrast, information landscapes, most obviously the World Wide Web, see billions of page views on a fat-tail distribution where about 1% of Web sites receive roughly 50% of all traffic.[6] The remaining half is spread over billions

of pages, some with tiny audiences, the so-called long tail of the power-law distribution. Here there are no barriers as to who can serve as editorialist, editor, or publisher. To navigate online auction sites, bookstores, or music services, search becomes an essential service. To perhaps oversimplify, there would be no long tail of content without search engines, and the world would have less need for search without long tails.

Search Changes the Rules of Information Assembly

For thousands of years, assembling information has conferred many benefits, including strategic or tactical advantage, prestige, and erudition. Because books were so valuable, many titles were chained to the shelves in Greek libraries and later in the Sorbonne and elsewhere.[7] The invention of the public circulating library was closely connected to the realm of political organization: Benjamin Franklin was intimately involved in both the development of public libraries and the American Revolution. Such a connection separates him from many political figures, regardless of era.

Over the centuries, the emphasis of libraries migrated from assembly (as at Alexandria) to classification. The most notable example of the latter was the French encyclopedists, including Denis Diderot, but the U.S. Library of Congress system stands as another significant milestone. In the Internet period, assembly, such as at the Internet Archive, has fallen to a lower priority, given the power and ubiquity of search. Because Google and its peers render both classification and assembly less important, *finding* information, rather than owning or organizing it, is often the predominant task.

The Wide Reach of Search

Because search has so rapidly become part of the pattern of everyday life for so many people, remembering how life was transacted *before* AltaVista, Excite, Google, and Bing can be difficult. A brief list suggests some of the many domains that have already been reshaped by this transformative technology. Each of these is at least a $100 billion industry in the United States; Google is less than 15 years old, making the transformations that much more remarkable.

Media

While Google obviously reinvented the advertising model, other media industries have been deeply affected. YouTube (part of Google) helped change video viewing habits from scheduled to searched. MP3 files are routinely searched online rather than scanned in physical bins. Google News assembles stories with algorithms rather than editors. Such resources as the Internet Movie Database (IMDb), owned by Amazon, figure prominently in search results. Finally, search and matching technologies are at the core of the success of Netflix relative to its physical competitors.

Retail and Secondary Markets

Finding used auto parts, or rare baseball cards, or any of the other millions of items on Craigslist or eBay would be impossible without search. Amazon invested so heavily in its A9 search service that it competed head-to-head with Google for a brief while. Extensive comparison shopping based on price, quality, or location becomes a matter of mouse clicks rather than hours or days of work.

Healthcare

According to the Pew Internet and American Life Project, 80% of Internet users (or 59% of all U.S. adults) search for medical information online.[8] This has significant implications for the entire healthcare industry, from the doctor-patient relationship to sellers of niche (and potentially ineffective) remedies.

Employment

People born before 1980 will remember requesting friends to mail the Sunday help-wanted ads from remote cities, which would then arrive the following Thursday, so that application letters could be mailed to post office boxes. In a very short time, the entire process of job hunting has been transformed, largely by search.

Automobiles

From a situation where information asymmetry was extreme (see Chapter 3), and buyers greatly mistrusted both new- and user-car sellers, the Internet has helped bring about greater transparency into both vehicle pricing and used-car history.

Travel

In some ways, search leveled the playing field between small hotels and megachains as do-it-yourself trip planning replaced visits to a travel agent or supplemented branded toll-free reservations systems. Air fares get easier to compare every year, in part by the addition of new features to the major search engines. In multiple ways, search helped alter and diminish the role of the travel agent.

Hospitality

As with lodging, millions of online word-of-mouth recommendations for restaurants have reshaped the industry. With mobile search, finding "Chinese restaurants near me" becomes a simple matter, complete with directions.

Real Estate

While real estate agents have not been disintermediated (see Chapter 21), the search technologies available at a range of sites have reshaped the house-hunting and rental process. Once again, the combination of search and location-based technologies proves to be particularly powerful.

Valuing Search

Even before the Web, according to Kevin Kelly, the founding editor of *Wired**, U.S. searches added up to 111 billion a year, most of them directory assistance telephone calls, but he also counted librarian queries. After the invention of free search engines, people appear to be asking more questions: The measurement firm comScore estimated 3 billion searches per day at Google alone. Twitter serves more than 1.5 billion searches per day. The list goes on.

In Kelly's rough estimate, an unnamed Google employee hypothetically and unscientifically values these searches as follows. Here are his assumptions in a thought exercise:

1/4 of all searches are really easy ones (like 'american airlines') that save the user maybe 30 seconds;
    1/4 are a little hard and save maybe 5 minutes;
    1/4 are just wasting time, and
    1/4 are hard ones that lead to substantial savings—like diagnosing your serious disease, or choosing the right college, or the right vacation destination.

---

*A full-color magazine created in San Francisco that is now owned by Condé Nast and has been publishing stories about technology and related topics since 1993.

Suppose it takes 10 searches on average to get one of these "hard" answers, but when you get it, you've saved maybe 3 hours. That averages out to 6 minutes saved/search. Figure average income of $25,000/year, or $12.50/hour. So we get a value of $1.25/search by this metric.[9]

Assuming the U.S. audience as 2 billion searches per day at that $1.25 per search, and Google's market share of roughly 65%, that would mean that Google creates $584 billion of value for its U.S. users per year.

Given these unofficial numbers and that this is only a thought experiment, even if the numbers are off by a factor of 5, it still means that Google creates 25 cents of value with the average search, at a cost to serve in the range of 0.2 cents. That would represent a hundredfold ratio of customer well-being to cost, a stunning value proposition by any measure.

A more rigorous valuation was performed by the McKinsey Global Institute.[10] Again, the numbers get very large. Moving beyond the conventional metrics for search valuation—time savings, price transparency, and increased awareness—the McKinsey study instead proposes a model with nine inputs:

1. Better matching of information to need
2. Time savings
3. Increased awareness
4. Price transparency
5. Long-tail access
6. People matching
7. Problem solving
8. New business models
9. Entertainment

Building from these disparate categories, the study estimated global measurable value created by search at $780 billion. Importantly, some of this fails to register in gross domestic product: Increased consumer surplus from getting a better deal, for example, or from saving time as in the previous example, is not counted. In any event, the magnitude of these sources of value, economic and otherwise, will only grow in the coming years.

Looking Ahead

In the past decade, search has facilitated the broadly decentralized production of information. Finding one's way among a continually growing volume of data and information will be shaped in part by three current forces:

1. *The growth of hidden data.* Online but hidden databases (for example, an airline reservation system behind a search screen and firewall) are known as the "deep Web." Because they are hidden, search engine crawls discover only a tiny fraction of online information.[11] Deep Web information is hidden for a reason, often because it is proprietary and a source of competitive advantage.[12]

2. *Generation of semantic metadata.* Organizing information often relies on metadata, which is handled in two basic ways. In the top-down approach, semantics (systems of meaning) are built to coordinate data, especially for machine-to-machine transactions, such as financial transactions. These formal semantic maps, known as ontologies, tend to be extensive, labor intensive, and rigid. There are definitely some circumstances in which they are essential; in other situations, ontologies can be little more than a nuisance, particularly if they are implemented but not maintained.

   Several ambitious efforts are under way to build a "semantic Web," utilizing semantics to power database-like Internet queries rather than text-string-based searches.[13] George W. Bush attended Yale University and later was elected president of the United States. Asking "How many U.S. presidents attended Yale University?" of a search engine would not work, but querying a database of U.S. presidents would be trivial. Freebase (which is now part of Google) is an attempt to organize information (such as the whole of Wikipedia) with sufficient disambiguation and classification to make queries possible. Other semantic Web efforts focus on scientific publishing, situations in which a working vocabulary is potentially easier to define and organize.

3. *Human-assisted tagging.* In contrast to ontologies imposed from the top down, tagging works from the bottom up. It is the practice of site visitor's attaching metadata to an item, commonly a news story or a photo, based on a personal view. There is no effort made to reconcile conflicting terminology; there are no authoritative answers. Instead, simple visualizations such as tag clouds (see Figure 28.1) show popularity of various tags. In the absence of an abstract, tags work well for both image data and text as cost-effective first approximations: They do a "good enough" job of answering a simple question: What is this picture or blog post about?[14]

Finally, a major question for search in the future concerns "following the money:" How does the escalating competition between search engines questing for better results and largely invisible search engine optimization (SEO) providers affect how information is organized, found, and distributed? Before they founded Google, Sergey Brin and Larry Page stated:

11:56 AM global business model innovation **September 2011 Early Indications: The Innovation Moment?** SteepandCheap they are

clearly in the ascendancy ▼ **Email This** Home July **Gilt Groupe** skip to sidebar

September Early Indications May 2011: Firms, Ecosystems, and Collaboratives story Early Indications July 2011: Place, Space, and Tim... **$4 billion in 2011 revenue.** March 2011 Early Indications: Reinventing Retail June Kiva **Share to Facebook** human-centric information fusion Backcountry.com BlogThis! Chadwick MartinBailey 2:57 PM **Posts (Atom)** according to the Journal rhetoric 8:57 PM

► 5:51 PM **7:17 PM 1:37 PM** Older Posts **April 2011 Early Indications: The iPad as a Teaching Tool** 2011 Early Indications July 2011: Place, Space, and Time **Early Indications August 2011: Paradoxical Product...** Atom Gallup's numbers John M. Jordan Early Indications August 2011: Paradoxical Productivity woot! September 2011 Early Indications: The Innovation M... View my complete profile Early Indications June 2011: Identity and privacy 6:38 PM Square Americans withdrew more than $40 billion of mortgage equity per quarter August Share to Twitter Shopkick **skip to main** Facebook delivers 31% of the 1.1 trillion ads

FIGURE 28.1 Tag Cloud Indicating Relative Popularity of Terms at the Author's Blog Page

> *[From] historical experience with other media, we expect that advertising funded search engines will be inherently biased towards the advertisers and away from the needs of the consumers. Since it is very difficult even for experts to evaluate search engines, search engine bias is particularly insidious.[15]*

Because search has become the organizing and access mechanism for the majority of online information, Google in particular is making significant decisions behind the scenes as to what people can and cannot find easily, what is important, and what will be commercially valuable to Google. (See Figure 28.2.) The power that comes from "organizing the world's information," to quote Google's mission statement, means that the company also has a disproportionate influence on what the world knows. Algorithms may seem impersonal, but as we saw in Chapter 22, code is highly political. Google, Microsoft, and InterActive Corp (with Ask) both reflect and shape economic and cultural power with their results, and their users would be wise to bear economic motives in mind when reviewing the apparently objective results.[16]

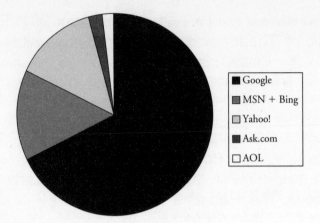

FIGURE 28.2 Search Engine Market Share, August 2010
Source: Nielsen.

Frontiers of Search

Text-string searching continues to get better, and mobility brings with it geographic facets of context sensitivity: Typing "pizza" in Tampa brings up nearby restaurants. Type-ahead or auto-fill sometimes can shorten the process. Other innovations in search are making their way into commercialization:

- Video search, of both the images and the audio.
- Mobile search, which includes more precise geolocation input than is available from most PC searches.
- Queries, which build on structured data, as opposed to the free-text nature of search engines. An example might be "tell me all books about roses written in German" or "list the winners of the Best-Actress Oscar who have children."
- Social search, finding things my friends liked.
- Natural-language questions and answers, which allow people (not machines) to ask and answer complex, nuanced questions: "what car should I buy?" or "where should I go on vacation?" Services including Quora have significant potential in this direction.
- Image search, which involves teaching computers to see the difference between a cat and a fish without a human naming the file or tagging the photo.

- Item search, using cell phone cameras to generate queries, such as "what is this part, or building, or person?" or "where am I standing?"
- Personalized search, which knows my particular uses of certain terms, the sources I routinely reject, and the times of day or of the week that I want certain kinds of responses.

Notes

1. An early paper identified this dynamic, which has obviously scaled and grown more complex in the intervening decade. See John Lynch and Dan Ariely, "Wine Online: Search Costs Affect Competition on Price, Quality, and Distribution," *Marketing Science* 19, no. 1 (Winter 2000): 83–103.
2. David Warsh, *Knowledge and the Wealth of Nations: A Story of Economic Discovery* (New York: Norton, 2006).
3. Thomas Friedman, *The World Is Flat: A Brief History of the Twenty-First Century* (New York: Farrar Strauss & Giroux, 2005).
4. Chris Anderson, *The Long Tail: Why the Future of Business Is Selling Less of More* (New York: Hyperion, 2006).
5. Nassim Nicholas Taleb, *The Black Swan: The Impact of the Highly Improbable* (New York: Random House, 2007).
6. In 1997, 1% of sites attracted 70% of traffic; 2003 figures reaffirmed the hypothesis with weblog data. See Jakob Nielsen, "Zipf Curves and Website Popularity," www.useit.com/alertbox/zipf.html, and Jason Kottke, "Weblogs and Power Laws," February 9, 2003, http://kottke.org/03/02/weblogs-and-power-laws.
7. Foster Stockwell, *A History of Information Storage and Retrieval* (Jefferson, NC: McFarland, 2001), p. 35.
8. Susannah Fox, "The Social Life of Health Information, 2011," Pew Internet & American Life Project, May 12, 2011, http://pewresearch.org/pubs/1989/health-care-online-social-network-users.
9. Kevin Kelly, "The Value of Search," October 16, 2007, www.kk.org/thetechnium/archives/2007/10/the_value_of_se.php.
10. Jacques Bughin et al., "The Impact of Internet Technologies: Search," McKinsey & Company (July 2011), www.mckinseyquarterly.com/Measuring_the_value_of_search_2848.
11. Alex Wright, "Exploring a 'Deep Web' That Google Can't Grasp," *New York Times*, February 22, 2009, www.nytimes.com/2009/02/23/technology/internet/23search.html?th&emc=th.
12. Gerry Smith, "Yale Social Security Numbers Exposed In Latest Case of 'Google Hacking'," HuffingtonPost.com, August 24, 2011, www.huffingtonpost.com/2011/08/24/yale-social-security-numbers-google-hacking_n_935400.html.

13. See Toby Segaran, Colin Evans, and Jamie Taylor, *Programming the Semantic Web* (Sebastapol, CA: O'Reilly, 2009).

14. Gene Smith, *Tagging: People-Powered Metadata for the Social Web* (Berkeley, CA: New Riders, 2008).

15. Sergey Brin and Lawrence Page, "The Anatomy of a Large-Scale Hypertextual Web Search Engine" (1998), http://infolab.stanford.edu/~backrub/google.html.

16. For more on this topic, see Eli Pariser, *The Filter Bubble: What the Internet Is Hiding from You* (New York: Penguin, 2011).

CHAPTER 29

Analytics

Thanks in part to vigorous efforts by vendors (led by IBM) to bring the idea to a wider public, analytics is coming closer to the mainstream. Whether in ESPN ads for fantasy football, or election-night slicing and dicing of vote and poll data, or the ever-broadening influence of quantitative models for stock trading and portfolio development, numbers-driven decisions are no longer the exclusive province of people with hard-core quantitative skills backed by expensive, often proprietary infrastructure.

Not surprisingly, the definition of "analytics" is completely problematic. At the simple end of the spectrum, one Australian firm asserts that "[a]nalytics is basically using existing business data or statistics to make informed decisions."[1] Confronting market confusion, Gartner market researchers settled on a similarly generic and less elegant assertion: "Analytics leverage data in a particular functional process (or application) to enable context-specific insight that is actionable."[2]

To avoid terminological conflict, let us merely assert that analytics uses statistical and other methods of processing to tease out business insights and decision cues from masses of data. In order to see the reach of these concepts and methods, consider a few examples drawn at random:

- The "flash crash" of May 2010 focused attention on the many forms and roles of *algorithmic trading of equities*. While firm numbers on the practice are difficult to find, it is telling that the regulated New York Stock Exchange has fallen from executing 80% of trades in its listed stocks to only 26% in 2010, according to Bloomberg.[3] The majority occurs in other trading venues, many of them essentially "lights-out" data centers; high-frequency trading firms, employing a tiny percentage of the people associated with the stock markets, generate 60% of daily U.S. trading volume of roughly 10 billion shares.

- In part because of the broad influence of Michael Lewis's best-selling book *Moneyball*,[4] *quantitative performance analysis* has moved from its formerly geeky niche at the periphery to become a central facet of many sports. MIT holds an annual conference on sports analytics that draws both sell-out crowds and A-list speakers. Statistics-driven fantasy sports continue to rise in popularity all over the world as soccer, cricket, and rugby join the more familiar U.S. staples of football and baseball.
- *Social network analysis*, a lightly practiced subspecialty of sociology only two decades ago, has surged in popularity within the intelligence, marketing, and technology industries. Physics, biology, economics, and other disciplines all are contributing to the rapid growth of knowledge in this domain. Facebook, al Qaeda, and countless start-ups all require new ways of understanding cell phone, GPS, and friend-/kin-related traffic.

Why Now?

Perhaps as interesting as the range of its application are the many converging reasons for the rise of interest in analytics. Here are ten, from perhaps a multitude of others:

1. Total quality management and six sigma programs trained a generation of production managers to value rigorous application of data. That six sigma has been misapplied and misinterpreted there can be little doubt, but the successes derived from a data-driven approach to decisions are informing today's wider interest in statistically sophisticated forms of analysis within the enterprise.
2. Quantitative finance applied ideas from operations research, physics, biology, supply chain management, and elsewhere to problems of money and markets. In a bit of turnabout, many data-intensive techniques, such as portfolio theory, are now migrating out of formal finance into day-to-day management.
3. As Google CEO Eric Schmidt said in August 2010, we now create in two days as much information as humanity did from the beginning of recorded history until 2003. That's measuring in bits, obviously, and as such the estimate is skewed by the rise of high-resolution video, but the overall point is valid: People and organizations can create data far faster than any human being or process can assemble, digest, or act

on it. Cell phones, seen as both sensor and communication platforms, are a major contributor, as are enterprise systems and image generation. More of the world is instrumented, in increasingly standardized ways, than ever before: Bar codes and radio-frequency identification (RFID) tags on more and more items, Facebook status updates, GPS, and the ZigBee technical specification and other "Internet of things" efforts merely begin a list.

4. Even as we as a species generate more data points than ever before, Moore's law and its corollaries (such as Kryder's law of hard discs, which have periods of intensive growth without the long-term stability of microprocessor improvement[5]) are creating a computational fabric which enables that data to be processed more cost-effectively than ever before. That processing, of course, creates still more data, compounding the glut.

5. After the reengineering/ERP push (which generated large quantities of actual rather than estimated operational data in the first place), after the Internet boom, and after the largely failed effort to make services-oriented architectures a business development theme, technology vendors are putting major weight behind analytics. It sells services, hardware, and software; it can be used in every vertical segment; it applies to every size of business; and it connects to other macro-level phenomena: smart electrical grids, carbon footprints, healthcare cost containment, e-government, marketing efficiency, lean manufacturing, and so on. In short, many vendors have good reasons to emphasize analytics in their go-to-market efforts. Investments reinforce the commitment: SAP's purchase of Business Objects was its biggest acquisition ever, while IBM, Oracle, Microsoft, and Google have also spent billions buying capability in this area.

6. Despite all the money spent on ERP, on data warehousing, and on "real-time" systems, most managers still cannot fully trust their data. Multiple spreadsheets document the same phenomena through different organizational lenses, data quality in enterprise systems inconsistently inspires confidence, and timeliness of results can vary widely, particularly in multinationals. Executives across industries have the same lament: For all of our systems and numbers, we often don't have a firm sense of what's going on in our company and our markets.

7. Related to this lack of confidence in enterprise data, risk awareness is on the rise in many sectors. Whether in product provenance (e.g., Mattel), recall management (Toyota, Cargill, or CVS), exposure to natural disasters (Allstate, Chubb), credit and default risk (anyone), malpractice (any hospital), counterparty risk (Goldman Sachs), disaster management, or

fraud (Enron, Satyam, Société Général, UBS), events of the past decade have sensitized executives and managers to the need for rigorous, data-driven monitoring of complex situations.

8. Data from across domains can be correlated through such ready identifiers as GPS location, credit reporting, cell phone number, or even Facebook identity. The "like" button, by itself, serves as a massive spur to interorganizational data analysis of consumer behavior at a scale never before available to sampling-driven marketing analytics. What happens when a "sample" population includes 100 million individuals?

9. Visualization is improving. While the spreadsheet is ubiquitous in every organization and will remain so, the quality of information visualization has improved over the past decade. This may result primarily from the law of large numbers (1% of a boatload is bigger than 1% of a handful), or it may reflect the growing influence of a generation of skilled information designers, or it may be that such tools as Mathematica and Adobe Flex are empowering better number pictures, but in any event, the increasing quality of both the tools and the outputs of information visualization reinforces the larger trend toward sophisticated quantitative analysis.

10. Software as a service (SaaS) can put analytics into the hands of people who lack the data sets, the computational processing power, and the rich technical training formerly required for hard-core number crunching.

Some examples follow.

Successes, Many Available as SaaS

- *Financial charting and modeling* continue to migrate down-market: Retail investors can now use Monte Carlo simulations and other tools well beyond the reach of individuals at the dawn of online investing in 1995 or thereabouts.
- *Airline ticket prices* at Microsoft's Bing search engine are rated against a historical database, so purchasers of a particular route and date are told whether to buy now or wait.
- *Customer segmentation* can grow richer and more sure-footed as data quality and processing tools both improve. Bananas have, in recent years, been the biggest-selling item at Wal-Mart, for example, so their merchandising has evolved to reflect market basket analysis: Seeing that bananas and breakfast cereal often showed up together, the chain experimented with putting bananas (as well as other items) in multiple locations—adding a display in the cereal aisle, for example.
- *Wolfram Alpha* (Figure 29.1) is taking a search-engine approach to calculated results: A stock's price/earnings ratio is readily presented

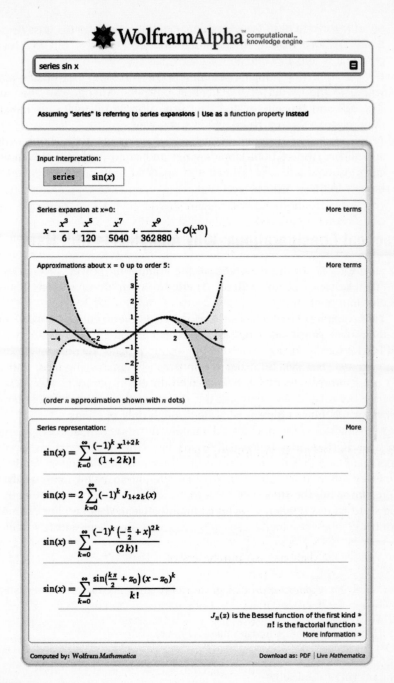

FIGURE 29.1 Wolfram Alpha Delivers a Computation Rather than a Search Engine Interface

Source: Wolfram Alpha LLC.

on a historical chart, for example. Scientific calculations currently are handled more readily than natural-language queries, but the tool's potential is unbelievable.

- *Google Analytics* brings marketing tools formerly unavailable anywhere to the owner of the smallest business: Anyone can slice and dice ad- and revenue-related data from dozens of angles, as long as they relate to the search engine in some way.
- *Fraud detection* through automated, quantitative tools holds great appeal because of both labor savings and rapid payback. Health and auto insurers, telecom carriers, and financial institutions are investing heavily in these technologies.

Practical Considerations: Why Analytics Is Still Hard

For all the tools, all the data, and all the computing power, getting numbers to tell stories is still difficult. There are a variety of reasons for the current state of affairs.

First, organizational realities mean that different entities collect data for their own purposes, label and format it in often-nonstandard ways, and hold it locally, usually in Excel but also in e-mails, or pdfs, or production systems. Data synchronization efforts can be among the most difficult of a chief information officer's tasks, with uncertain payback. Managers in separate but related silos may ask the same question using different terminology or see a cross-functional issue through only one lens.

Second, skills are not yet adequately distributed. Database analysts can type SQL* queries but usually don't have the managerial instincts or experience to probe the root cause of a business phenomenon. Statistical numeracy, often at a high level, remains a requirement for many analytics efforts; knowing the right tool for a given data type, or business event, or time scale takes experience, even assuming a clean data set. For example, correlation does not imply causation, as every first-year statistics student

---

*Structured Query Language is the language of database interrogation: An example would be
UPDATE a
SET a.[updated_column] = updatevalue
FROM articles a
JOIN classification c
ON a.articleID = c.articleID
WHERE c.classID = 1

knows, yet temptations to let it do so abound, especially as electronic scenarios outrun human understanding of ground truths.

Third, odd as it sounds in an age of assumed infoglut, getting the right data can be a challenge. Especially in extended enterprises but also in extrafunctional processes, measures are rarely sufficiently consistent, sufficiently rich, or sufficiently current to support robust analytics. Importing data to explain outside factors adds layers of cost, complexity, and uncertainty: Weather, credit, customer behavior, and other exogenous factors can be critically important to either long-term success or day-to-day operations, yet representing these phenomena in a data-driven model can pose substantial challenges. Finally, many forms of data do not readily plug into the available processing tools: Unstructured data, such as e-mails or text messages, is growing at a rapid rate, adding to the complexity of analysis.

Fourth, data often relates to people, and people may not willingly give it up. Loyalty-club bar codes have been shared (often by cashiers), smart electrical metering is being viewed as a privacy invasion in some quarters,[6] and tools for online privacy (cookie blockers, adware removers, etc.) are increasingly popular.

In certain situations, the algorithmic sensemaking available in common analytical tools is useful in uncovering and providing relevant information, wherever it may have originated. The cost and availability of such information are improving: In oil and gas, for example, information technology has helped drop the cost of a three-dimensional seismic map of the subsurface from $8 million per square kilometer in 1980, to $1 million in 1990, to $90,000 in 2005. But even the best analytics cannot reliably replace the human intelligence needed to draw the right conclusions from the information. Furthermore, not every quantitative question has a calculable answer.

Looking Ahead

Getting numbers to tell stories requires the ability to ask the right question of the data, assuming the data is clean and trustworthy in the first place. This unique skill requires a blend of process knowledge, statistical numeracy, time, narrative facility, and both rigor and creativity in proper proportion. Not surprisingly, such managers are not technicians and are difficult to find in many workplaces. For the promise of analytics to match what it actually delivers, the biggest breakthroughs will likely come in education and training rather than algorithms or database technology.

Notes

1. www.onlineanalytics.com.au/glossary.
2. Jeremy Kirk, "'Analytics' Buzzword Needs Careful Definition," Infoworld, February 7, 2006, www.infoworld.com/t/data-management/analytics-buzzword-needs-careful-definition-567.
3. "NYSE May Merge With German Rival," Bloomberg News, February 10, 2011, www.fa-mag.com/fa-news/6815-nyse-may-merge-with-german-rival.html.
4. Michael Lewis, Moneyball, (New York: W.W. Norton & Company, 2011)
5. "Kryder's Law," MattsComputerTrends.com, www.mattscomputertrends.com/Kryder%27s.html.
6. "PG&E Smart Meter Problem a PR Nightmare," smartmeter.com, November 21, 2009, www.smartmeters.com/the-news/690-pgae-smart-meter-problem-a-pr-night mare.html.

CHAPTER 30

Information Visualization

Because it is now easier to create visually pleasing graphics, because there is so much data to manage and understand, and because tools such as spreadsheets have finite limits in their ability to convey meaning, information visualization is a rich area, particularly linked as it usually is with ideas of information analytics. The ultimate challenge is less technical than cognitive: What is the creator trying to say, and what can he or she assume the reader will bring to the task of understanding both the data and its representation?

Over the past 30 years or so, the field of information visualization has evolved rapidly. Several factors help explain this development: supply, demand, and the audience. Today, each of these elements is changing rapidly, with broad consequences.

Supply

Both the quantity of information that needs to be processed (at both human and organizational levels) and the quality of the tools for managing and displaying it are increasing. To process this information, humanity makes increasing use of larger and higher-resolution displays as well as faster computing in devices not technically called computers: Sony PlayStations are wonders of graphics processing, for example.

Demand

More and more processes are being driven by digital information. Text and numbers gave way to pictures and sounds, then to video, and now to three dimensions. Where sailors once relied on stars and sun to navigate, differential GPS deliver resolution to a few meters nearly anywhere on earth.

Audience

With the numbers of people accessing Internet and other information growing rapidly, translation into countless languages is often difficult. Visual displays, while not culturally universal, can help bridge across audiences that may be divided by language. Audiences are also expecting information in visual forms. In the United States, such expectations were traditionally set with election-night reporting; network news organizations often revealed new quantitative tricks to help hold audiences.

Definition and Purpose

For our purposes, a simple definition of visualization should suffice: "the use of computer-supported, interactive visual representations of data to amplify cognition."[1] "Cognition" is a word with its own definitional issues: Do I want information to enlighten me about something I did not know (much in the manner of *USA Today*'s random daily graphics), to answer a question I already have, or to provide context for some future action? The need is acute: According to a 2006 Harris survey, 75% of respondents said they had made a flawed business decision because of flawed data.[2]

Different visualizations serve different purposes. In the 1980s and 1990s, for example, graphics workstations were widely deployed in television studios as an arms race of weather-casting helped advance the state of the field. The weather people can boast results: Many more people can understand a Doppler radar image than can grasp binomial distributions, bid-ask spreads, or genetic mutations. As we shall see, geospatial information can bring with it built-in tools for understanding: Many people can find north on a map, while other cultures have yet to invent the concept of a map at all.

Historically, many visualizations have resulted from individuals who wanted to change their world: Florence Nightingale's striking maps relating conditions in military hospitals after the Crimean War helped persuade Queen Victoria to initiate broad reforms in public sanitation. More recently, the tools built by Hans Rosling and his colleagues at Gapminder are clearly aimed at increasing public awareness of international economics and other social issues. His visualizations have made this Swedish public health expert an Internet celebrity based on his TED* videos.[3]

Implicitly or explicitly, all visualizations answer roughly the same set of questions:

- How are similarity and difference conveyed?
- Is time static, as in a pie chart, or dynamic, as in many line graphs or slider-bar tools?
- How much granularity is sacrificed for "glanceability," and how much does comprehension require investments of time and skill to deliver details?
- Is causality intended to be conveyed? Can it be unreasonably inferred?
- How does space function in the representation? Do proportions relate to some ground truth?
- What do the colors convey? Are colors used in standard (green = proceed safely; red = danger) or nonstandard ways?
- How are the reliability, timeliness, accuracy, precision, and other attributes of the underlying data represented in the visualization?[4]
- Computer visualizations, unlike paper ones, can be interactive. How easily can users learn to reposition, zoom in, reset a baseline, and otherwise get the visualization to respond to their actions?
- How likely is ambiguity? Why might the display be read three different ways by three different people?
- Independent of the graphical tool(s) chosen, does the visualization ask appropriate questions of the data?

Current State

There's no shortage of activity in the field of information visualization, samples of which can be experienced at Flex.org, VisualComplexity.com, or IBM's Many Eyes. Some work is truly stunning, and global centers of design leadership are emerging. Even so, the fundamental tension quickly becomes evident: Words like "galleries" suggest that we are viewing works of art, and in many instances the work should be in museums. But art by definition is unique; visualization has yet to be brought to the masses of managers, citizens, and students who have something to say but lack

---

*Originally founded by Richard Saul Wurman and now under the direction of Chris Anderson, TED (Technology Entertainment and Design) is a global set of conferences intended to disseminate "ideas worth spreading." Free online videos of the conference talks are available at YouTube.

the tools, grammar, and training to create the beautiful. In short, the task of helping high levels of information visualization migrate from the artist to the worker remains unaccomplished. Three categories of work can be broadly identified: business intelligence tools, physical data visualization, and nonspatial data.

Business Intelligence Tools

As part of an ongoing trend toward consolidation of the enterprise application software market, visualization vendors have been incorporated into broader package or service offerings. In 2007, for example, Oracle bought Hyperion, IBM acquired Cognos, and SAP bought Business Objects. Combined with a strong offering from Microsoft, these players dominate the market, leaving only SAS and MicroStrategy as leading stand-alone contenders. Business intelligence (BI) software, while not particularly expensive or difficult to use, sometimes requires extensive cleanup work on the data to be analyzed. Between standardization on format and nomenclature, explication of assumptions across operating units, and shared storage and access at the enterprise level, the data warehousing and data mining components of a BI effort can run into millions of dollars before a single report is generated.

Executive dashboards have become common, but as noted visualization pioneer Edward Tufte notes, the metaphor itself introduces issues, as do words like "cockpit" or "command center." As Tufte wrote in 2003, three basic questions must be addressed:

1. What are the intellectual problems that the displays are supposed to help with? *The point of information displays is to assist thinking; therefore, ask first of all: What are the thinking tasks that the displays are supposed to help with?*
2. How much can I trust the underlying information? *It is essential to build systematic checks of data quality into the display and analysis system. For example, good checks of the data on revenue recognition must be made, given the strong incentives for premature recognition. Beware, in management data, of what statisticians call "sampling to please"—selecting, sorting, fudging, choosing data so as to please management.*
3. What is the underlying business or other process I am managing? *For information displays for management, avoid heavy-breathing metaphors, such as the mission control center, the strategic air command, the cockpit, the dashboard, or Star Trek. As Peter Drucker once said, good management is boring. If you want excitement, don't go to a good management information system.*[5]

Physical Data Visualization

In 1931, Alfred Korzybski, a little-known philosopher, stated that "the map is not the territory."[6] Visualizations of physical phenomena are by definition abstractions, which means that interpretation, selection, and representation issues confront both makers and viewers of these visualizations. Compared to nonphysical phenomena, such as beliefs and risk, physical data is more straightforward, but significant considerations still inform the craft of visualization in the physical domain.

A tangible example is provided by Harry Beck's classical visualization of the London Underground first completed in 1931 and revised thereafter.[7] Compared to the predecessor map, which is unremarkable, Beck's elegant abstraction was much more readable. It does suffer, however, from factual errors: Stations on different lines that are only a few hundred meters apart are shown as far away, leading riders to make two transfers and walk down long tunnels when, had they been aboveground, they could have seen how physically close the stations were.

Beck was an electrical draftsman by training, so the convention of a grid, allowing only 90- and 45-degree angles, was familiar to him from circuit diagrams. This artifice largely eliminated topography from the design brief, enabling him to concentrate instead on relative location along a given line: Distances between stations on different lines are often vastly out of proportion. Other key elements of the map's success—use of white space, color-based simplification, and modern design cues, including typography and limited symbolism—came from Frank Pick, the design-minded head of publicity for the London Underground. Weighing the importance of usability for the task at hand against the physical reality being represented is a key step, and the importance of Beck's contribution, as well as its limitations, is reflected in London Transport's decision to call the aid not a map but a Journey Planner.

Nonspatial Data

The task of conceptual data visualization is particularly difficult because good displays must create spatial representations of nonspatial data. While the concept of geographic information displays is relatively straightforward (using one or more variations of a map and presenting overlaid information on it), representation of nonspatial data can be more challenging. This is not new: Linear representations have conveyed time for millennia, and pie charts have become handy shorthand for subsets of a whole. Good maps remain the gold standard but enjoy the advantage of being a spatial representation of space rather than something less tangible. Consult a UK Ordnance Survey map or a fine nineteenth-century sample from any number of countries, and compare the quality to the nonspatial representations we encounter every day: *USA Today* visuals, executive dashboards, or owner's manuals. In most cases, the antique remains superior to the modern.

A powerful visualization known as a tree map has proven very useful for nonphysical data. Smart Money's Map of the Market,[8] which visualizes daily stock market performance, is probably the best-known tree map. Information domains are formed of rectangles, each of which includes component entities, sized proportionately to population, market capitalization, risk, or other variables and available for inspection by mouse roll-over. The visualization provides at-a-glance awareness of the state of the entire domain, a given sector, or individual components.

As the field evolves, information architects are challenged to create readable, repeatable conventions for such abstractions as risk, intellectual property (patents are a poor proxy for human capital, for example), and attitudinal information, such as customer satisfaction or confidence in government. Search and visualization have much to offer each other: Semiarbitrary lists of text-string matches remain hard to make visual. (Concepts are notoriously difficult to map spatially, in contrast to the elegance of the periodic table of the elements, to take a classic example.) Static social network maps, especially those of large social graphs, such as Facebook, quickly grow useless at their enormous scale. Attempting to show a dynamic social network using a graph (e.g., showing individuals as nodes in a two-dimensional graph and social interconnections as links between nodes) is a common representation but may not be satisfying because of limitations in showing the character of the social links (e.g., type of connection, strength, duration, interactions among multiple people, etc.) and other factors.

Looking Ahead

Some precedents may be useful. The history of sailing and shipping is rich with examples of various parties agreeing on conventions (port and starboard do not vary in different countries the way rules for automobiles do) and solving problems of conveying information. Shipping containers interlock regardless of carrier while being handled at countless global ports.[9] The Beaufort wind scale arose from the need for agreed-on metrics for measuring wind aboard a ship, a matter of great practical importance. Even today, with satellites and computerized navigation systems, a Beaufort 0 ("Calm; smoke rises vertically") is the same around the world, while a 12 ("Air filled with foam; sea completely white with driving spray;

visibility greatly reduced") spells disaster no matter how fast the hurricane winds are actually blowing.[10]

Musical notation presents another relevant example. Easily transportable, relatively impervious to language, and yet a representation (rather than a reproduction) of a performance, scores have the kinds of conventions that information visualization for the most part still lacks. At this point, good visualizations are featured in "galleries"—as befit works of art. They are created by artists and artisans, not by people who merely have something to say. At the risk of a strained analogy, we are at the stage where latter-day monks painstakingly hand-letter sacred texts, still awaiting both Gutenberg and the typewriter.

In his book *Envisioning Information,* Tufte suggests five tactics for increasing information density and "escaping flatland"—conveying more than two dimensions of meaning on paper. These are:

1. Micro/macro readings (relating both wholes and parts as distinct entities)
2. Layering and separation (often by use of color and graphic weight, as in a technical drawing)
3. Small multiples (to show often-subtle differences within elements of a system: A good lunar chart is an example)
4. Color and information (sensitivity to the palette as color labels, measures, represents reality, and enlivens)
5. Narratives of space and time (compressing the most powerful human dimensions onto flatland).[11]

For all of the wisdom in these suggestions and the beauty of Tufte's examples—it's no accident that he's both a statistician and a working artist—good information visualizations remain rare. For information to convey meaning in standard, predictable ways, we need tools: "tools" as in grammars and lexicons rather than more widgets. Somewhat paradoxically, the path to better visualizations will be paved not with software but with words.

Notes

1. S. K. Card, J. Mackinley, and B. Schneiderman (eds.), *Readings in Information Visualization—Using Vision to Think* (San Francisco: Morgan Kaufmann, 1998).
2. Business Objects press release, "Information Workers Beware: Your Business Data Can't Be Trusted," June 26, 2006, www.sap.com/about/newsroom/businessobjects/20060625_005028.epx.

3. Hans Rosling, www.ted.com/speakers/hans_rosling.html TED talks; www.ted.com/talks/hans_rosling_shows_the_best_stats_you_ve_ever_seen.html.

4. S. Deitrick and R. Edsall, "Making Uncertainty Usable: Approaches for Visualizing Uncertainty Information," in M. Dodge, M. McDerby, and M. Turner, *Geographic Visualization: Concepts, Tools and Applications* (Hoboken, NJ: John Wiley & Sons, 2008), pp. 277–291.

5. Edward Tufte, "Ideas for Monitoring Businesses and Other Processes," July 11, 2003 blog post at edwardtufte.com; www.edwardtufte.com/bboard/q-and-a-fetch-msg?msg_id=0000bx.

6. Alfred Korzybski, "A Non-Aristotelian System and Its Necessity for Rigour in Mathematics and Physics," paper presented at the American Mathematical Society at the New Orleans, Louisiana, meeting of the American Association for the Advancement of Science, December 28, 1931. Reprinted in *Science and Sanity* (1933): 747–761.

7. K. Garland, *Mr. Beck's Underground Map* (London: Capital Transport Publishing, 1994).

8. www.smartmoney.com/map-of-the-market/.

9. M. Levinson, *The Box: How the Shipping Container Made the World Smaller and the World Economy Bigger* (Princeton, NJ: Princeton University Press, 2006).

10. S. Huler, *Defining the Wind: The Beaufort Scale, and How a 19th-Century Admiral Turned Science into Poetry* (New York: Three Rivers Press, 2004).

11. Edward Tufte, *Envisioning Information* (Cheshire, CT: Graphics Press, 1990).

SECTION V

Some Big Questions

While such questions as personal identity, social relationships, and physical existence may seem outside the scope of a business book, the breadth of change being facilitated by the communications and computing fabric of our time has implications for many areas of life.

CHAPTER 31

Identity and Privacy

As people's identities migrate into the ether of digital representation, all manner of questions emerge: Rights, responsibilities, and risks all can be thought of in significantly different terms than they were 20 years ago.

With the launch of Google Plus in 2011, it's an opportune time to think about digital privacy, insofar as Google is explicitly targeting widespread user dissatisfaction with Facebook's treatment of their personal information. The tagging feature, for example, that was used to build a massive (hundreds of millions of users) facial recognition database has important privacy implications. In standard Facebook fashion, it's turned on by default, and opting out once may not guarantee that a user is excluded from the next wave of changes. If a government did that, controversy would likely be intense, but in Facebook's case, people seem to be resigned to the behavior.

According to a 2010 poll of customer satisfaction developed at the University of Michigan, Facebook scored in the bottom 5% of providers—in the range of cable operators, airlines, and the Internal Revenue Service. Even as Facebook is rumored to be holding off user-base announcements for 100-million intervals since a billion is in range, users are defecting. While the service is said to be closing in on 750 million users globally, reports of 1% of that population in the United States and Canada defecting in one month were not confirmed by the company, but neither were they denied. A Google search on "Facebook fatigue" returned nearly 100,000 hits. At the same time, Facebook delivers 31% of the 1.1 trillion ads served in the United States each quarter (Yahoo! is a distant second at 10% share); those ads are expected to represent $4 billion in 2011 revenue.[1]

Privacy

With the Facebook initial public offering still pending, the questions about privacy take on more urgency as the firm is being scrutinized. What, really, is privacy? It's clearly a fundamental concept, typically conceived of as a human or civil right. According to the *Oxford English Dictionary* (OED), privacy is "the state or condition of being alone, undisturbed, or free from public attention, as a matter of choice or right; seclusion; freedom from interference or intrusion." It's an old word, dating to the fourteenth century, that is constantly being reinvented as times change.

Being left alone in a digital world is a difficult concept, however, given the sheer number of connections. Here, New York University's Helen Nissenbaum is helpful: "What people care most about is not simply *restricting* the flow of information but ensuring that it flows *appropriately*."[2] Thus, she does not wade further into the definitional swamp but spends a book's worth of analysis on the issue of how people interact with the structures that collect, parse, and move their information.

Through this lens, the listed artifacts cannot be judged as public or private, good or bad, acceptable or unacceptable, but they can be discussed and considered in the context of people's values, choices, and autonomy: When I use X, is my information handled in a way that I consent to in some reasonably informed way? The digital privacy landscape is vast, including some familiar tools, and for all the privacy notices I have received, there is a lot I don't know about the workings of most of these:

- Loyalty card programs
- Google streetview
- Toll-pass radio-frequency identification (RFID) tags
- Surveillance cameras
- Transportation Security Administration (TSA) no-fly lists
- Facebook data and actions
- Credit-rating data
- Amazon browsing and purchase history
- Google search history
- Foursquare check-ins
- Digital camera metadata
- Expressed preferences, such as star ratings, Facebook "likes," or eBay seller feedback
- Searchable digital public records, such as court dates, house purchases, or bankruptcy
- Cell phone location and connection records
- Medical records, electronic or paper
- Gmail correspondence

- TSA backscatter X-ray
- Item-level billing systems, as used at telecom firms and many others

Does such lack of knowledge mean that I have conceded privacy or that I am exposing aspects of my life I would rather not? Probably both. In addition, the perfection of digital memory—handled properly, bits don't degrade with repeated copying—means that what these entities know, they know for a very long time. The combination, therefore, of lack of popular understanding of the mechanics of personal information and the permanence of that information makes privacy doubly suspect.

Scale

Given the climate of the past 10 years in relation to privacy, the events of 9/11 have conditioned the debate to an extraordinary degree. The U.S. government was reorganized, search and seizure rules were broadened, and rules of the game got more complicated: Not only were certain entities ordered to turn over information related to their customers, they were legally obligated to deny that they had done so. More centrally, the Federal Bureau of Investigation's well-documented failure to connect the dots spurred a reorganization of multiple information silos into a vast and possibly suboptimally sprawling Department of Homeland Security.

Governments have always wanted more information than people typically want to give them. Given the new legal climate along with improvements in the technologies of databases, information retrieval, and image processing, for example, more is known about U.S. individuals than at any time heretofore. (Whether it is known by the proper people and agencies is a separate question.) At the 2000 Super Bowl, for example, the entire crowd was scanned and matched against an image database. Note the rhetoric employed even *before* the terrorist attack on the twin towers and the Pentagon:

> *[Tampa detective Bill] Todd is excited about the biometric crimestopper aid: The facial recognition technology is an extremely fast, technologically advanced version of placing a cop on a corner, giving him a face book of criminals and saying, Pick the criminals out of the crowd and detain them. It's just very fast and accurate.*[3]

Note that the category of "criminals" can be conveniently defined: the definition in Yemen, Libya, or Pakistan might be debatable, depending on one's perspective. In Tampa, civil liberties were not explicitly addressed, nor was there judicial oversight:

> *Concerned first and foremost with public safety, the Tampa police* *used its judgment in viewing the images brought up on the monitor.* *Although the cameras permitted the police to view crimes captured* *by the cameras and apprehend suspects for pick-pocketing and* *other petty crimes, their real goal was to ensure crowd safety. The* *Tampa police were involved in forming the database and deter-* *mining by threat level who was added to the database. (Emphasis* *added.)*

Letting a police force, which in any given locality may have corruption issues, as in large areas of Mexico, use digital records to figuratively stand on a corner and pick "the criminals out of the crowd" without probable cause is scary stuff. Also in the news, a major story concerns an FBI agent who protected his informant (Whitey Bulger) from murder charges. And police officers might not be corrupt: Mexican drug gangs are now being said to threaten U.S. law enforcement officers with harm. Once the information and the technology exist, they will be abused: The issue is how to design safeguards into the process.

Consider RFID toll passes. According to a transportation industry trade journal, the first instance of electronic toll record tracking may have occurred in September 1997,

> *when the New York City Police Department used E-Z Pass toll* *records to track the movements of a car owned by New Jersey* *millionaire Nelson G. Gross who had been abducted and mur-* *dered. The police did not use a subpoena to obtain these records* *but asked the Metropolitan Transportation Authority and they* *complied.[4]*

Again, the potential for privacy abuse emerged before protections did. In 2010, there were nearly 21 million E-ZPass transponders in use, roughly half of the U.S. total number of toll passes: They were read about 2.4 billion times.[5] As only one in a number of highly revealing artifacts attached to a person's digital identity, toll tokens join a growing number of sensors of which few people are aware. The on-board diagnostics system in a car, expanded from a mechanic's engine diagnostic, has become a "black box" like those recovered from airplane crashes. Progressive Insurance is experimenting with data logging from the devices as a premium-setting tool. Significantly, its tool does not include GPS information; the firm discontinued a GPS-based experiment in 2000.

Invisibility

In its excellent "What They Know" investigative series in 2010, the *Wall Street Journal* concluded that "they" know a lot. Numbers only scratch the surface of the issues:

- Dictionary.com installed 234 tracking cookies into a browser in a single visit. WSJ.com itself came in below average, at 60. Wikipedia.org was the only site of 50 tested to install zero tracking software files.
- When Microsoft relaunched Internet Explorer in 2008, corporate interests concerned about ad revenue vetoed a plan to make privacy settings persistent. Thus, users have to reset the privacy preferences with every browser restart, and few people are aware of the settings console in the first place.
- The Facebook "like" button connects a behavior (an online vote, a pursuit of a coupon, or an act of whim) to a flesh-and-blood person: The Facebook profile's presumably real name, real age, real sex, and real location. Again according to the *Journal*:

  > For example, Facebook or Twitter know when one of their members reads an article about filing for bankruptcy on MSNBC.com or goes to a blog about depression called Fighting the Darkness, even if the user doesn't click the "Like" or "Tweet" buttons on those sites. For this to work, a person only needs to have logged into Facebook or Twitter once in the past month. The sites will continue to collect browsing data, even if the person closes their browser or turns off their computers, until that person explicitly logs out of their Facebook or Twitter accounts, the study found.[6]

- Few people realize how technologies can be used to follow them from one realm to another. The giant advertising firm WPP recently launched Xaxis, which, according to the *Wall Street Journal* (in a story separate from its "What They Know" series),

  > will manage what it describes as the "world's largest" database of profiles of individuals that includes demographic, financial, purchase, geographic and other information collected from their Web activities and brick-and-mortar transactions. The database will be used to personalize ads consumers see on the Web, social-networking sites, mobile phones and ultimately, the TV set.[7]

- A team at Carnegie Mellon University combined off-the-shelf facial recognition software, large cloud computing databases, and readily available social networking data to identify strangers and gain their personal information. According to the lead researcher, "When we share tagged photos of ourselves online, it becomes possible for others to link our face to our names in situations where we would normally expect anonymity."[8] Given that none of these technologies is particularly difficult to obtain, the results suggest that anonymity might be a soon-to-be obsolete notion.

In each of these examples, it's pretty clear that all of these companies ignored, or at least lightly valued, Nissenbaum's notion of contextual integrity as it relates to the individual. Given the lack of tangible consequences, it makes economic sense for them to do so.

Identity

Given that digital privacy seems almost to be a quaint notion in the United States (Europeans live and are legally protected differently), a deeper question emerges: If that OED sense of freedom from intrusion is being reshaped by our many digital identities, who are we and what do we control? Ads, spam, nearly continuous interruption (if we let ourselves listen), and an often-creepy sense of "how did they know that?" as LinkedIn, Amazon, Google, Facebook, and Netflix hone in our most cherished idiosyncrasies—all of these are embedded in the contemporary connected culture. Many sites, such as Lifehacker, recommend frequent pruning: E-mail offers, coupon sites, Twitter feeds, and Facebook friends can multiply out of control, and saying no often requires more deliberation than does joining up.

Who am I? Not to get metaphysical, but the context for that question is in flux. My fifth-grade teacher was fond of saying "Tell me who your friends are and I'll tell you who you are." What would he say to today's fifth grader, who may well text 8,000 times a month and have a public Facebook page?

Does it matter that a person's political alignment, sexual orientation, religious affiliation, and zip code (a reasonable proxy for household income) are often now a matter of public, searchable record? Is her identity different now that some many facets of it are transparent? Or is it a matter of Mark Zuckerberg's vision—people have one identity, and transparency is good for relationships—being implicitly shared more widely across the planet? Some reviews of Google Plus argued that people don't mind having one big list of "friends," even as Facebook scored poorly in customer satisfaction indexes year after year.

Indeed, one solution to the privacy dilemma is to overshare: If nothing can possibly be held close, secrets lose their potency, perhaps. (For an example, see the story of Hasan Elahi and his Tracking Transience Web site in the May 2007 issue of *Wired* magazine and in Albert-László Barabási's book *Bursts*.) The recent spread of YouTube pregnancy-test videos is fascinating: One of life's most meaningful, trajectory-altering moments is increasingly an occasion to show the world the heavy (water) drinking, the trips to the pharmacy and the toilet, and the little colored indicator, followed by the requisite reaction shots. (For more, see Marisa Meltzer's piece on *Slate*, wonderfully titled "WombTube."[9])

The other extreme, opting out, is difficult. Living without a mobile phone, without electronic books, without MP3 music files, without e-mail, and of course without Facebook or Google is difficult for many to comprehend. In fact, the decision to unplug (usually temporarily) frequently goes hand in hand with a book project about "My Six Months Offline," so unheard-of is the notion.

At the same time, the primacy of the word represented by these massive *information* flows leaves out at least 10% of the adult U.S. population: Functional illiteracy, by its very nature, is difficult to measure. One shocking statistic, presented without attribution by the Detroit Literacy Coalition, pegs the number in that metro area at a stunning 47%. Given a core population of about 4 million in the three-county area, that's well over 1 million adults who have few concerns with Twitter feeds, Google searches, or allocating their 401(k) portfolio.

Looking Ahead

Between the extremes of oversharing and opting out, where most Americans now live, there's an abundance of gray area. As "what they know," in the *Journal's* words, grows and what they can do with it expands, perhaps the erosion of analog notions of privacy will be steady but substantial. Another possibility is some high-profile, disproportionately captivating event that galvanizes reaction. The fastest adoption of a technology in modern times is not GPS, or DVD, or even Facebook: It was the U.S. government's Do Not Call registry. Engineering privacy into browsers, cell phones, and very large data stores is unlikely; litigation is, unfortunately, a more likely outcome: In 2011, a U.S. federal judge refused to halt a class-action suit against Google's practice of using its Street View cars for Wi-Fi sniffing. The story of privacy, while old, is entering a fascinating, and exasperating, new phase, and much remains to be learned, tested, and accepted as normal.

Are Private Planes Private?

Every aircraft has a unique tail number that identifies the hardware, the owner, the manufacturer, and other registration information. A number of flight-tracking Web sites, such as FlightAware, have emerged, allowing anyone to type in a tail number, find the current location of the plane, and see who owns it. (At least one tail number is used as a branding opportunity, even though no logo appears on the Gulfstream G-V: N1KE.)

People who own or fly private planes were given the opportunity to block their registration from being used for tracking purposes. Some owners claimed competitive reasons: Negotiations to acquire a company could quickly become public if corporate jets were found traveling to the target's headquarters. Paparazzi clearly could use the data for their purposes. Others claimed that the safety of the passengers depended on privacy.

In 2011, the *Wall Street Journal* built a database of corporate planes.[10] Shareholders in public companies could see the benefit to executives who may not have broken out the jet in compensation figures, particularly when the destinations were not business related. Nonshareholders could indulge their curiosity: It is simple to see the destinations included in the travels of the Bombardier BD-700 Global Express, tail number N54SL, registered to Harpo, Inc., more readily identified with Oprah Winfrey.

In 2008, the National Business Aviation Association (NBAA), a lobbying group of business aircraft users, filed suit to have the Federal Aviation Administration (FAA) block tail-number information if the owner so requested. A court ruled against the NBAA in 2010, and, in 2011, the FAA declared it would shut down the blocking program. According to Secretary of Transportation Ray LaHood, "This action is in keeping with the Obama administration's commitment to transparency in government. Both general aviation and commercial aircraft use the public airspace and air traffic control facilities, and the public has a right to information about their activities."[11] Preliminary indications were that operators who could show a "verifiable threat," including death threats or kidnapping, would qualify for the blocking, but final rules have yet to appear and some information remains blocked.

Notes

1. Stephanie Reese, "Quick Stat: Facebook to Bring In $4.05 Billion In Ad Revenues This Year," emarketer.com, April 26, 2011, www.emarketer.com/blog/index.php/tag/facebook-ad-revenue/.
2. Helen Nissenbaum, *Privacy in Context: Technology, Policy, and the Integrity of Social Life* (Palo Alto, CA: Stanford Law Books, 2010), p. 2.
3. Jeanne Bonner, "Looking For Faces In The Super Bowl Crowd," SecuritySolutions.com, May 1, 2001, http://securitysolutions.com/mag/security_looking_faces_super/.
4. "Electronic Toll Records Are Watching You, "FleetOwner.com, December 12, 2003, http://fleetowner.com/news/fleet_electronic_toll_records/.
5. E-ZPass Group, Statistics, www.e-zpassiag.com/about-us/statistics.
6. Amir Efrati, "'Like' Button Follows Web Users," *Wall Street Journal*, May 18, 2011, http://online.wsj.com/article/SB10001424052748704281504576329441432995616.html#ixzz1QhgQ8FEj.
7. Emily Steel, "WPP Ad Unit Has Your Profile," *Wall Street Journal*, June 27, 2011, http://online.wsj.com/article/SB10001424052702304447804576409562922859314.html#ixzz1Qhf7pHeS.
8. Carnegie Mellon News, "Face Recognition Software, Social Media Sites Increase Privacy Risks, Says New Carnegie Mellon Study," Press Release, August 1, 2011, www.cmu.edu/news/stories/archives/2011/august/aug1_privacyrisks.html.
9. Marisa Meltzer, "Wombtube," Slate.com, March 14, 2011, www.slate.com/id/2286434/.
10. http://projects.wsj.com/jettracker/.
11. John Croft, "FAA Guts Block Aircraft Registration Programme," Flightglobal.com, June 2, 2011, www.flightglobal.com/articles/2011/06/02/357399/faa-guts-block-aircraft-registration-programme.html.

CHAPTER 32

Communications and Relationships

It's reasonably obvious that the state of a society's communications tools will shape the size, nature, and intensity of potential interpersonal relationships within that society, and vice versa. Cave painting, orally transmitted legends, tabloid newspapers, and telephones each support different kinds of social networks. Smartphones and the Internet are no different: The changing state of our tools is altering how we relate, and new ways of relating feed back into the evolution of the tool sets. Those evolving relationships have implications for work: Is your boss your Facebook friend? What do you do when a coworker's profile appears on Match.com? These new relationship patterns are shifting the nature of entrepreneurship: Why build a physical widget when you can write an app? Finally, there are huge commercial questions: Will Apple, Facebook, Google, or some other entity profit from being the same kind of force AT&T was in the heyday of the telephone as the dominant communications platform?

Three layers of the relationship questions merit attention. First, we consider the changing nature of our connections. Second, we examine what kinds of networks emerge from those connections. Finally, we see what creative possibilities emerge from the changes in the ways we relate and communicate with each other.

Connections

People of a certain age will remember what it was like to have two phone numbers, one for the workplace and one for home. If you were near one of them, you could be reached; if not, you might be hard to find. In some ways, the mobile phone simplifies matters: If a voice connection is desired, one number follows you 24 hours a day, across oceans, in some tunnels, in national parks and crowded urban canyons. But what if one doesn't want to be reached for soccer league purposes during preparation for an important meeting? What are the limits of when a coworker can call on the weekend? One number for everything forces such issues out of the infrastructure into the realm of interpersonal rules of engagement.

But for more and more people, a voice-to-voice connection is not necessarily the objective. A picture may be important or merely entertaining but has capabilities of its own. Skype makes video calling cheap and easy; so does Apple's iChat, but each requires a bit of setup and coordination. Text messaging has soared in popularity in the United States in less than a decade. Maybe a Facebook message, or a Google chat, or a Twitter direct message is the right tool for the job.

Given so much multitasking, not even counting "productivity" applications such as Word or Excel, it's hard not to wonder about distractedness. In the early years of the Internet boom, Linda Stone, who at the time was at Microsoft, saw multitasking as "continuous partial attention:" People were sort-of tuned in to multiple windows, maybe earphones, and perhaps a television nearby.[1] Now that people can interact with others so quickly and at such scale, at least one blogger has raised the issue of "continuous partial affection," the notion that we can be sort-of connected to a whole bunch of people but not really attend on an emotional level.[2]

Multimedia, especially on the move, deserves attention: As we saw in relation to innovation, being able to see techniques, read facial and other physical cues, or situate a person or group in physical context enriches the conversation. Putting a teleconference rig on a simple robot changes the dynamic of a remote meeting: The outsider can inject nuance, follow the conversation into the hallways or to the lunch table, and generally be more present.[3] The tagline at YouTube, meanwhile, reads "Broadcast Yourself." The implications of hundreds of millions of people doing just that have yet to be fully plumbed, but the transition from wireline voice to mobile multimedia is happening extremely fast. Just what will change as a result will be fascinating to see—literally.

Thus, the first problem is determining what kind of interaction I want to initiate. Then I need to think of the recipient's patterns, and then the identity problem enters in: Facebook simplifies this by using a real name, but it's common for a single individual to have multiple phone numbers, aliases, avatars, and other naming conventions. Many of us are in a similar position to the Bell system's "telephone ladies," the young women who patched callers together at early-twentieth-century switchboards. Particularly at work, when colleagues of different generations are involved, the task of management is complicated by the multiplicity of platforms, each with ill-defined conventions for its use.

In a world of so many connections, everybody is on some information grid, whether in a spy satellite's photo, a digitally facilitated social network, a photograph, or any number of economic transactions. Even Osama bin Laden had (delayed) access to e-mail in his compound, relying on what old-timers refer to as "sneakernet," the process of hand-carrying first floppy drives and later USB sticks (100 of which were seized in the 2011 commando raid in which bin Laden was killed) from computer to computer.[4]

Online Dating

Love and work are the cornerstones of our humanness.
—Sigmund Freud

How have the technological changes of the recent past affected these two facets of our existence? In terms of love, we have seen misplaced romantic e-mail damage the careers of public figures, including chief executives and a governor. Finland may show us the wave of the future: In 2006, the prime minister met a woman through an online dating service, then broke up with her via text messaging a few months later, stating economically "Että se" ("that's it").

Structured dating services such as Match.com or eHarmony have become huge businesses, not counting the vast amount of flirting within the big social networks: Paid online dating sites had become essentially a billion-dollar industry in 2008, according to Forrester Research, putting it ahead of pornography and making the industry slightly more than half as big as digital music and gaming. eHarmony's 2010 ad budget was estimated at $90 million.[5] Harris Interactive estimates an average of 542 eHarmony users got married—every day—as of 2009. Match.com, part of InterActiveCorp, was recognized in 2004 as the largest dating site in the world and reported 20 million members worldwide as of 2011.

Countries around the world are getting involved: In Japan, dating sites must register with the police, and more than 1,600 such companies did so in the first month of the requirement. According to *New Media Age*, UK traffic to online dating sites grew 13% between September 2008 and February 2009: Total visitors to the leading site

(continued)

currently number about 5 million, reaching 13% of the total UK online population. Australia represents a hot new market, with both Match.com and eHarmony advertising aggressively.

Online matchmaking has many variations. One can search for potential spouses, for religiously or culturally similar partners, for friends, for same-sex prospects, for uncommitted physicality, or, at Toronto's Ashley Madison, be guaranteed an extramarital affair—or your money back. The various market segments each have multiple providers, varying by geography, matching method, and revenue model. Based only on online comments from users rather than any personal experience, claims of differentiation between different sites' matching accuracy and inventory may be inflated: Many people use multiple sites and find the same people matching their profile. Furthermore, the basic model misaligns incentives: Sites do not get paid for good matches.[6]

As we saw in Chapter 19, when the American Press Institute convened a meeting of newspaper executives to discuss the state of their industry, they placed substantial blame on Google for being the "atom bomb" to the news industry even as ESPN.com, Monster, Realtor.com, and dozens of other sites were eroding newspaper readership long before Google News.[7] Personal ads are clearly a part of this erosion: Match.com, eHarmony, and the rest did not cannibalize all of that $957 million in U.S. revenue from newspapers, but clearly papers have lost some of their mojo in that department. Some independent newspapers maintain a strong singles presence, as witness the *Chicago Reader* or *The Onion*. Mainstream papers, meanwhile, take a variety of approaches. Boston.com (the *Globe*'s online operation) franchises singles from Yahoo! The *LA Times* points readers to eHarmony. Many papers, including the *New York Times* and *Dallas Morning News*, have no personal ads.

Why is the Internet a good singles market? The decoupling of physical location from the search process is a very big deal for market "thickness," not to mention the overall sense of romance and adventure in the process. If you live in a small town, the online services broaden your mating horizon.

In addition, the use of algorithmic matching tools is enhancing the matching process: eHarmony's "scientific" survey instrument includes 400 questions, far more than most people ever answer on any unsuccessful first date. As we will see, however, the comprehensiveness of the surveys has many implications. At Match.com, the core algorithm trades off 1,500 variables. According to the engineer who manages the search process, it's a lot like Netflix, which uses a similar matching algorithm to suggest movies you might like—"except that the movie doesn't have to like you back."[8]

Not surprisingly, the online dating phenomenon has generated sometimes-hilarious commentary in the form of vast numbers of blog entries and a few books. Such titles as *MatchDotBomb: A Midlife Journey through Internet Dating*, *Millions of Women Are Waiting to Meet You: A Memoir*, and numerous how-to volumes (including a Dummies guide) testify to the pervasiveness of this cultural phenomenon.

The unintended consequences are fascinating to watch:

- Is it ethical for pay sites to count nonpaying (former) participants in a match panel?
- How sustainable are the various business and operational models? Might one technology, celebrity endorsement, or other factor prove decisive in a particular market?
- What happens to a profile after the user quits the service, either because it worked or because it failed? What rights does the user have to his or her profile on either free or paid services (1) after a month, (2) after a year, or (3) after the company goes bankrupt or gets acquired?
- What are the de facto (when people meet in person) and de jure (in court) standards for truthfulness? eHarmony, for example, insists that applicants be single: Legally separated individuals are excluded and can be banned if they lie to get on. "Truth in advertising" has many nuances in this domain.
- What exactly are people paying for? What are the guarantees, warranties, or lack thereof?
- How can and will various systems be gamed? Some services have been accused, without proof, of employing "ringers" (professional first-daters) to exaggerate the quality of available singles.
- What will the profile be used for? Cross-selling opportunities, for example, are numerous and more than a little spooky, given the extensive questionnaires and behavioral tracking.
- While the nightmare blind date has become a cultural stereotype, the prospect of meeting truly dangerous people online is more than a little scary, as the Boston Craigslist murders suggest. It's also possible for bad first encounters to facilitate stalking. A colleague whose "thanks for coffee" and the implied "have a nice life" after a public, "safe" meeting drove the unsuccessful dating candidate to look her up using available search methods. He later turned up on her doorstep unannounced. Match.com was sued by a woman raped by a convicted sex offender the service set her up with; Match.com announced it will now screen for convictions of this sort.

(continued)

The role of such civic institutions as churches, service clubs, and bowling leagues in the wake of suburbanization, television, and more women in the workplace has changed slowly but significantly over the past 50 years. The matchmaking process has changed as well, and the state of online dating businesses will bear watching. In addition, the place of Facebook in 20-somethings' lives is undoubtedly generating its own set of changes to courtship.

Networks

Given the characteristics of today's social communications tools, networks of kinship, association, and other types of ties are evolving as well. Before looking more closely at Facebook and Twitter, a fundamental question relates to how big a person's meaningful network actually can be: Just because technology makes "friend" lists of thousands of individuals possible, can a person actually relate to that many contacts in any meaningful way?

Robin Dunbar teaches anthropology at Oxford. He compared brain sizes for various primates with the size of their social circles and hypothesized that, based on brain size, humans should be able to manage social networks of 147.8 people (within a wide error margin).[9] What about Facebook lists measured in thousands? Research is ongoing, but based on address books and other measures, most people interact in meaningful, sustained ways with a much smaller number of friends: As of 2009, Facebook's own measures suggested that an "average" man who has about 120 friends replies to wall posts of about 7 people; women responded regularly to about 10 friends' posts. Even people with big (greater than 500) friend counts left comments for 17 people (men) and 26 people (women).[10]

This conceptualization is useful as far as it goes. But in an age of "six degrees of separation," measuring the power of a network is not a matter of counting friends, defined in whatever way. Beginning with a seminal paper by Mark Granovetter in 1973,[11] networking science has investigated the power of weak ties, not only primary ones: The question is not who do you know but whom can your network reach. Richard Bolles popularized the notion in his job-hunting guide, *What Color Is Your Parachute?* In the book, Bolles emphasizes that people seldom know the person who will hire them when they begin the job search. *Parachute* first appeared in 1970 and has since sold more than 10 million copies worldwide.[12]

Making Social Networks Visible: The Case of 9/11

The next article was published in newsletter form on September 13, 2001, long before the advent of Facebook or Twitter, tools that would have changed the way that fateful day unfolded.

This week's attacks and the subsequent deaths are being painfully felt. Everybody, it seems, knows someone who knows someone who died or was injured. Here in Boston, the odds of being connected are especially high, while our hearts go out to the New Yorkers living with so much uncertainty and dread. At this time of tragedy, the phenomenon known as "six degrees of separation" feels different. Each of us connects to the computer network administrators, or the daughters, or the fire fighters, or the air travelers for some personal reason: I've flown American 11 to LA probably a dozen times, for example, and everyone has some similar story that connects him or her to some facet of the tragedy. In this moment, rather than talk about cell phone antennas or Internet slowdowns or American government digital snooping efforts to gather clues, I wanted to point to some fascinating research that shows some weird and wonderful aspects of networks that underlie this dynamic of personal involvement.

The story begins with a distinguished Hungarian mathematician, Paul Erdős, who died in 1996 with an academic body of 1500 research papers. For years after, however, unpublished work came out. Erdős' eminence, combined with academics' love of the obtuse, spawned an ongoing conversation among math professors about their "Erdős number"—how many links connect any given professor with Erdős as a co-author. The lower one's number (1 if co-author with Erdős, 2 if a co-author with a 1, etc), the presumably higher one's own reputation. As of 2000, the number of people 1 remove from Erdős was 507. What's interesting, apart from the traction of the exercise, is Erdős' influence: 60 Nobel prize winners have relatively low Erdős numbers (Watson's and Crick's are 7 and 8, respectively, despite their field's distance from pure math), while 42 winners of the profession's Fields medal (the highest honor in mathematics) have low Erdős numbers—most four or less, with all under 6.

(*continued*)

We then move outside mathematics, in 1967, to Stanley Milgram, the same psychologist responsible for the "we do as we're told" experiment in which subjects rather willingly administered fictional (but apparently real) electric shocks to other people under orders of an authority figure. Along a different research direction he created an experiment to see how social networks actually behave. He asked people in Kansas and Nebraska to get letters to people in Boston by sending the letters to people the Kansans and Nebraskans thought might know the recipients personally. The recipients did the same thing, forwarding the notes and notifying Milgram of their participation. The letters took from 2 to 10 hops to arrive, with the average being five. Why Milgram termed the phenomenon six degrees of separation remains a mystery, but the small number of intermediaries poses a riddle.[13]

If, as sociologists estimate, each American knows about 300 people, and there are about 270 million Americans, simple math suggests that it would take on average about a million handshakes to connect any given person to any other one. The problematic assumption here, however, is that the networks are evenly distributed. If all the people I know only know each other, it's a closed community. At the other extreme, according to Steve Strogatz of Cornell, if I know 100 people, and each of them knows 100 people, I'm two hops from 10,000 people, three from 1 million, and five degrees from the entire planet— but that assumes zero overlap, that each of 100 people has 100 more friends not already in the network.

It is the middle ground between closed order and complete randomness that Strogatz and his graduate student Duncan Watts investigated. This story made headlines in 1997 and 1998 when the six degrees of Kevin Bacon game was resonating with many people's experience with the Internet. Whether in terms of web links or e-mail communities, many people found that they knew someone who knew someone who could answer their question or procure a desired item. (In fact, Lada Adamic at Xerox PARC showed that within a large percentage of the Web, any webpage was an average of four hyperlinks from any other.)

Watts and Strogatz found that only a tiny—1%—increase in randomness had orders of magnitude implications for reducing the number of intermediaries between points A and B.

What's interesting is that redoing those few connections doesn't change the clustering within the network—most of your friends still know each other. The other factor here is that the connections are extremely unevenly distributed: everyone knows someone who's always sending along e-mail jokes or industry buzz. His or her e-mail friend network will have far more one-degree connections than average. At the same time, there are info-hounds who are the recipients of many feeds but the spreaders of few. Marketing experts like Seth Godin are looking at the network problem from this perspective.

Back to Watts and Strogatz, this is when the story gets weird: the same network structure, ordered with a tuned amount of randomness, explains not only Kevin Bacon's movie career but the western U.S. electric power grid topology and the neural structure of a worm called a nematode. The implications of this incredible finding are only beginning to be exhausted. Two business school professors found that small world networks, as they're called, explain the ownership structure of over 500 large German companies: any one firm is connected to any other by only four intermediaries. The fact that consciously engineered systems, natural systems, and cumulative patterns of behavior all can be represented by the same graphical model is truly stunning.

So in the midst of our public and private grief, the feeling of connection to the victims relate to a powerful phenomenon—one still mysterious even to experts like Watts and Strogatz, who speak with a certain reverence about it. What tragedies do is activate our sense of our networks: none of us goes around asking our coworkers if they have a friend or relative who works in, say, Miami or Milan unless there's some reason to wonder. One we identify end points—the lists of the dead or the stories of survival—then the network of human connection emerges, and from there we cry, or give thanks, or give blood, or do any of the other myriad of things people have done for millennia to heal each other in times of suffering.[14]

The question of how big a social network can or should be remains open. Google's Plus service, designed to compete with Facebook, allows multiple types of friend and acquaintance networks called circles. Path, a start-up photo-sharing site, caps one's network at 50 people, presumably to maintain intimacy. Twitter's follower model provides an alternative to

Facebook: A person's broadcasting persona can be managed more straight-forwardly than in Facebook, where reciprocity is more the norm among individuals. For celebrities, Twitter gives the person an alternative to media spin, and more than once a rumor has been corrected by the subject. At the same time, numerous high-profile athletes have been done in by their own words; ethnic and homophobic slurs are, unfortunately, common.

At the same time that people try to understand the size of digital social networks, the qualitative issues also give pause. The things that people share are not universally appreciated: A recent trend is YouTube videos of one's pregnancy tests, as we saw in Chapter 31. Facebook's ever-shifting definitions of user privacy defaults frustrate many users. Finally, some of the implicit Facebook narratives, especially among women, are problem-atic: About a third of women surveyed in 2011 complained about people who "bragged about seemingly perfect lives." Two-thirds of the survey population complained about complainers; "drama queens" and political evangelists also were common targets.[15]

Creation

There's a debate in some academic circles over what are called "gen-erative" technologies. According to Jonathan Zittrain, a law professor at Harvard, examples include:

> *Technologies like personal computers that have the capacity to produce unprompted, user-driven change. For example, on a PC any person can write code, run that code on a variety of platforms, and share that code with anyone who might want it. In general, generative technologies are useful for performing tasks, adaptable, easy to master, permission-free, and share-able. In the name of security consumers are increasingly moving away from generative technologies like the PC and towards tethered ones like the iPhone.[16]*

In point of fact, very few people could write code on PCs, Microsoft controlled much of the innovation of the platform, and PCs were not (and still are not) "easy to master." While the Apple mobile platforms are cer-tainly more locked down than the Apple IIs of the 1980s and Wintel PCs of the 1990s, meanwhile, the trade-off in ease of use means that smartphones are arguably generative in that they create change far beyond the blueprint of the inventors. Text messaging is a great example. Locality-based social networking is another. Mobile cameras and video are nothing if not creative.

At the level of the Internet, mash-ups are easier to create than PCs were to code. The availability of resources for artistic, informative, and social/political expression are vast, and the long tail of user-generated content means that more people than ever before can find an audience. Resources (maps, music, news, calculators, and data), tools, and distribution have all become free. The staggering growth of mobile and then other forms of app stores is also significant: Whereas "any person" could write code for the PC, theoretically, the wealth of creativity unleashed by the economic promise of the iPhone and Android to software developers is not to be dismissed.

At the enterprise level, another facet of creativity bears mentioning. Whereas the buzzphrase of the late 1990s was "knowledge management," one doesn't hear that much anymore. Rather than building expensive, rigid hierarchical systems for managing knowledge, there's a much greater awareness of the social context in which innovation, or good customer service, or effective marketing can emerge. Thus, enterprise tool makers, including SAP, and vendors, including IBM, are building Facebook-like infrastructure for companies that seek to unleash the brainpower and networks of employees, suppliers, partners, and customers.

Procter & Gamble (P&G) is one case in point: By opening its famously homogeneous corporate culture to external partners in the Connect and Develop program launched in 2001, new product introductions, cross-licensing agreements, and, most crucially, revenues have grown after stagnating in the 1990s.[17] The company's Old Spice brand enjoyed record growth in 2010 after an enormously clever social media/broadcast campaign featuring an entertainingly articulate spokesmodel. The degree of trust between ad agency, other partners, and the P&G team was noted at the time as being exceptional, and it is likely not an accident that the changing technology landscape coupled with the conscious shift in attitudes and behaviors across P&G helped to create that positive chemistry.[18]

Looking Ahead

At the level of individuals, families, tribes, and formal organizations, changes to the connective tissue are reshaping both the interpersonal connections and the nature of the group. Liking someone, or some topic, or some item or product is not the same proposition it was 20 years ago. The artifacts of a personal connection have also changed, with consequences for relationships, for law, and for commerce. The definitional distinctions between relationships, networks, and markets are fuzzy. All told, people's relationships are more complicated, more documented, and richer with possibility than ever before. Those relationships are set in physical contexts that themselves are in transition, and it is to that topic to which we turn next.

Notes

1. http://lindastone.net/qa/continuous-partial-attention/.
2. Gene Smith, "Continuous Partial Attention," atomiq.org, March 13, 2007, http://atomiq.org/archives/2007/03/continuous_partial_affection.html.
3. www.willowgarage.com/pages/texai/overview .
4. Dean Takahashi, "Bin Laden Relied on Thumb Drive Couriers to Evade Email Detection," VentureBeat, May 12, 2011, http://venturebeat.com/2011/05/12/bin-laden-relied-on-thumb-driver-couriers-to-evade-email-detection/.
5. Steve Mcclellan, "eHarmony Connects with OMD," *Adweek*, January 18, 2011, www.adweek.com/news/advertising-branding/eharmony-connects-omd-126250.
6. Nick Paumgarten, "Looking for Someone," *The New Yorker*, July 4, 2011, www.newyorker.com/reporting/2011/07/04/110704fa_fact_paumgarten?current Page=all.
7. American Press Institute, "Paid Content: Newspaper Economic Action Plan" (May 2009), www.niemanlab.org/pdfs/apireportmay09.pdf.
8. Paumgarten, "Looking for Someone."
9. Matt Ridley, "How Many Friends Can Your Brain Hold?" *Wall Street Journal*, February 12, 2011, http://online.wsj.com/article/SB10001424052748704422204576130602460527550.html.
10. "Primates on Facebook," *The Economist*, February 26, 2009, www.economist.com/node/13176775.
11. Mark Granovetter, "The Strength of Weak Ties," *American Journal of Sociology* 78, no. 6 (May 1973): 1360–1380.
12. Richard N. Bolles, *What Color Is Your Parachute: A Practical Manual for Job-Hunters and Career-Changers* (Berkeley: Ten Speed Press, 2011).
13. Stanley Milgram, "The Small World Problem," *Psychology Today* (May 1967): 60–67.
14. Not available on line or in print. Later issues are at http://earlyindications.blogspot.com/.
15. "Eversave Survey Reveals Secret Facebook Opinions and Habits of Women," Business Wire, March 30, 2011, www.businesswire.com/news/home/20110330005284/en/Eversave-Survey-Reveals-Secret-Facebook-Opinions-Habits.
16. Jonathan Zittrain, Glossary of The Future of the Internet and How To Stop It, http://futureoftheinternet.org/glossary.
17. Henning Kagermann, Hubert Oesterle, and John Jordan, *IT-Driven Business Models: Global Case Studies In Transformation* (New York: Wiley, 2010), pp. 74–77.
18. Marshall Kirkpatrick, "How the Old Spice Videos Are Being Made," Read Write Web, July 14, 2010, www.readwriteweb.com/archives/how_old_spice_won_the_internet.php.

CHAPTER 33

Place, Space, and Time

What does it mean to be "someplace"? What does it mean to exist independently of physical constraints? How fast is fast? When is "right now"?

For millennia, geography has defined human civilizations. As our communications capability increases, as measured by technical specifications if not necessarily emotional ones, the need to be physically located in a certain place to do a job, support a social movement, or complete a business transaction is becoming less of an absolute constraint. Mobile phones, cloud computing, and other tools (such as lightweight project management software or online social networks) allow people and resources to be organized without physical contact; this might be called the emerging domain of space, as in "cyber." People can put up virtual storefronts on eBay, let Amazon be their supply chain, rent computing from Google to run code written in India, and let PayPal be their treasury system. Salesforce.com keeps track of customers and prospects; ADP runs payroll once enough employees sign on. Thus, the actual "business" could physically be the size of a laptop computer.

As place becomes negotiable, so does time. Asynchronous television viewing, for example, is reshaping the cable TV landscape. Comcast bought NBC Universal, which in turn was part of the Hulu joint venture. Apart from sports, college students watch very little television at its scheduled time, or over its traditional channel for that matter. Shopping has also become time-shifted: One can easily walk into Sears, shop at a kiosk, and have the item delivered to a physical address, or else shop online and drive to the store for faster pickup than FedEx can manage. At the other end of the time spectrum, tools like Twitter are far faster than TV news, not to mention print newspapers. Voicemail seems primitive now that it's roughly 30 years old, a time-shifting capability now taken for granted.

Place and time increasingly interconnect. Real-time package track-ing for a routine Amazon purchase contrasts dramatically with a common scene at automobile dealerships: A customer saw a vehicle on the Web site earlier in the week and none of the salespeople knows what happened to it. UPS can track more than 15 million packages per day while a car dealer can lose a $15,000 two-ton vehicle, one of a few dozen, from a fenced concrete lot. Customer expectations are set by the former experience and are growing increasingly intolerant of the latter.

The corollary of that place/time flexibility, however, is being tracked: Everybody with digital assets is plugged into some kind of informa-tion grid, and those grids can be mapped. Sometimes it's voluntary: Foursquare, Shopkick, and Facebook Places turn one's announced location into games.* More often, though, Big Brother's watch is without consent: London's security cameras are controlled by the same police department accused of using official assets in the service of the Murdoch newspapers' snooping on innocent citizens. As we have seen, the entire idea of digital privacy, its guarantees and redresses, for bad guys and for everyday folk, is still primitive.

Examples are everywhere: Google Street View has proved controver-sial in Europe and Germany in particular. Local "open records" laws have yet to be rethought in the age of instant global access: It's one thing for the neighbors to stop by town hall to see how much the new family paid for their house but something else entirely (we don't really know what) when tens of millions of such transactions are searchable—especially within overlays of Street View, Bing's bird's-eye aerial (as opposed to sat-ellite) imagery, and other potentially intrusive mechanisms.

In 2009, a *Wired* magazine reporter attempted to vanish using a com-bination of physical disguises and digital trickery: prepaid cell phones, proxy servers for Internet Protocol address masking, cash-purchased gift cards. He was found though a combination of old-fashioned detective work and sophisticated network analysis: He was signing on to Facebook with an alias, and the alias had few real friends, making his identity an anomaly. Tellingly, the Facebook group he was lurking in was comprised of people trying to find him.[1] Elsewhere, fraudsters are creating synthetic identities from publicly gleaned information: Any given detail checks out with a real person, but the composite whole is fake. The intersections of place and space are growing more curious every year.

---

*Getting people's actual location information can be tricky: A clever hacker made himself mayor (in Foursquare terms) of the North Pole and sparked a fascinating discussion. Such gamesmanship will increase as the stakes get higher; see www .krazydad.com/blog/2010/02/mayor-of-the-north-pole/.

Virtuality

From its origins as a network perimeter tunnel (virtual private networks gave people the ability to see computing resources inside the firewall while being physically remote from the corporate facility), virtualization has become a major movement within enterprise computing. Rather than dedicating a piece of hardware to a particular piece of software, hardware becomes more fungible. In a perfect virtual world, people with applications they need to run can schedule the necessary resources (possibly priced by an auction mechanism), do their work, then retreat from the infrastructure until they next need computing. In this way, the theory goes, server utilization is improved: All the downtime associated with captive hardware can go offline, freeing computing to be used to the current work, whatever its size, shape, or origin.

Once again, physical presence (in this case, big computers in a temperature-controlled facility with expensive redundant network and power connections, physical security, and specialized technicians tending the machines) is disconnected from data and/or application logic. In many consumer scenarios, people act this way without thinking twice: looking at Google Maps instead of Rand McNally, using the online version of TurboTax, or even reading Facebook is "virtual": No software package resides on the user's machine, and the physical location of the actual computing is both invisible and irrelevant.

From the world of computing, it's a short hop to the world of work. People no longer need to go to the physical assets if they're not doing work on somebody else's drill presses and assembly lines: Brain work, a large component of the services economy, is often independent of physical capital and thus of scheduled shifts. "Working from home" is commonplace, and with the rise of the smartphone, work becomes an anytime/anywhere proposition for more and more people. What this seamlessness means for identity, for health, for family and relationships, and for business performance has yet to be either named or sorted out.

Another dimension of virtuality is personal. Whether in Linden Labs' Second Life, World of Warcraft, or any number of other venues, millions of people play roles and interact through a software persona. As processing power and connection quality increase, these avatars will get more capable, more interesting, and more common. One fascinating possibility relates to virtual permanence: Even if the base-layer person dies or quits the environment, the virtual identity can age (or, like Bart Simpson, remain timeless) and can either grow and learn or remain blissfully unaware of change in its own life or the various outside worlds.[2]

Practical applications of virtualization for everyday life seem to be emerging. In South Korea, busy commuters can shop for groceries at transparencies of store shelves identical to those at their nearby Tesco Homeplus store; the photos of the products bear two-dimensional bar codes which, when scanned and purchased, generate orders that are bundled together for home delivery. Picking up ingredients for dinner on the way home from work is a time-honored ritual; here, the shopper chooses the items but never touches them until arriving at his or her residence.[3]

Cisco is making a major play toward virtual collaboration in enterprise videoconferencing; its preferred term, "telepresence," hasn't caught on, but the idea has. Given the changes to air travel in the past 10 years (longer check-in times, fewer empty seats, higher fares), compounded by oil price shocks, many people dislike flying more than they used to. Organizations on lean budgets also look to travel as an expense category ripe for cutting, so videoconferencing is coming into its own at some firms. Cisco reports that it has used the technology to save more than $800 million over five years; productivity gains add up, by its math, to another $350 million.[4]

Videoconferencing is also popular with individuals, but it isn't called that: In July 2011, Skype's chief executive said that users make about 300 million minutes of video calls per month, which is about the same as pure voice connections. The point for our purposes is that rich interaction can facilitate relationships and collaboration in the absence of physical proximity, at very low cost in hardware, software, and connection. As recently as 2005, a corporate videoconference facility could cost more than a half million U.S. dollars to install; monthly connection charges were another $18,000, or $216,000 annually.[5] In 2011, many tablets and laptop computers include cameras, and Skype downloads are free.

Organizations

Given that vertical integration has its limits in speed and the cost of capital investment (both in dollars and in opportunity costs), partnering has become a crucial capability. While few companies can emulate the lightweight, profit-free structure of Linux, a hacker's collective like Anonymous, or Wikipedia, neither can many firms assume that they control all necessary resources under their own roof. Thus, the conventional bureaucracy model is challenged to open up, to connect data and other currencies to partners. Whether it involves sharing requirements documents, blueprints for review, production schedules, regulatory signoffs, or other routine but essential categories of information, few companies can quickly yet securely vet, map, and integrate a partner organization. Differences in nomenclature, signing authority or span of control, time zones, language, and/or currency, and any number of other characteristics complicate the interaction. So-called onboarding—granting a partner appropriate data access—can be a months-long process, particularly in secure (aerospace and defense) or regulated settings. Creating a selectively permeable membrane to let in the good guys, let out the proper information, turn off the faucet when it's not being used, and maintain trade secrets throughout has proven to be nontrivial.[6]

Automata

What would happen if a person's avatar could behave independently? If an attractive bargain comes up at Woot, buy it for me. If someone posts something about me on a social network, notify me or, better yet, correct any inaccuracies. If the cat leaves the house through the pet door and doesn't return within two hours, call the pet sitter. Who would bear responsibility for the avatar's actions: the person on whose behalf it is "working"? the software writer? the environment in which it operates?

Once all those avatars started interacting independently, unpredictable things might happen, the equivalent of two moose getting their antlers stuck together in the wild or of a DVD refusing to play on some devices but not others because of a scratch on the disc. Avatars might step out of each other's way or might trample each other in mobs. They might adapt to new circumstances, or they might freeze up in the face of unexpected inputs. Some avatars might stop and wait for human guidance; others might create quite a bit of havoc given a particular set of circumstances.

It's one thing for a person's physical butler, nanny, or broker to act on his or her behalf but something else quite new for software to be making such decisions. Rather than being a hypothetical thought experiment, these scenarios are already real. Software "snipers" win eBay auctions with the lowest possible winning bid at the last possible moment. Google Alerts can watch for Web postings that fit my criteria and forward them.

More significantly, Wall Street transactions generated by the jacketed floor traders waving their hands furiously are a dying breed. So-called algorithmic trading is a broad category that includes high-frequency trading (HFT), in which bids, asks, and order cancelations are computer-to-computer interactions that might last less than a second (and thus cannot involve human traders). By itself, HFT is estimated to generate more than 75% of equities trading volume; nearly half of commodity futures (including oil) trading volume is also estimated to be computer-generated in some capacity.[7] The firms that specialize in such activity are often not brand names, and most prefer not to release data that may expose sources of competitive advantage. Thus, the actual numbers are not widely known.

What is known is that algorithms can go wrong, and when they go wrong at scale, consequences can be significant. The May 6, 2010 "flash crash" is still not entirely understood, but the source of the New York Stock Exchange's biggest, fastest loss (998 points) in history lies in large measure in the complex system of competing algorithms running trillions of dollars of investment. The longtime financial fundamentalist John Bogle—founder of the Vanguard Group—pulled no punches in his analysis: "The whole system failed. In an era of intense technology, bad things can happen so rapidly. Technology can accelerate things to the point that we lose control."[8]

Artifacts of the algorithmic failure were just plain weird. Apple stock hit $100,000 a share for a moment; Accenture, a computer services provider, instantaneously dropped from $40 to a cent only to bounce back a few seconds later. Circuit breakers, or arrangements to halt trading once certain limits are exceeded, were tripping repeatedly. (For example, if a share price moves more than 10% in a five-minute interval, trading can be halted for a five-minute break.) A bigger question relates to the HFT firms that, in good times, provide liquidity but that can withdraw from the market without notice and in doing so make trading more difficult. Technically speaking, the exchanges' information systems were found to have shortcomings: Some price quotes were more than two seconds delayed, which represents an extreme lag in a market where computer-generated actions measure in the millions per second.

Implications

What does it mean to be somewhere? As people sitting together in college cafeterias both text other people while dining face to face, what does it mean to be physically present? What does it mean to "be at work"? Conversely, what does it mean to be "on vacation"? If I am at my job, how is my output or lack thereof measured? As discussed, counting lines of code proved to be a bad way to measure software productivity, but alternatives are not simple. How many jobs measure performance by the *quality* of ideas generated, the quality of collaboration facilitated, the quality of customer service? These are difficult to instrument, so industrial-age measures, including physical output, remain popular even as services (which lend themselves to extreme virtualization) grow in importance and impact. In most organizations, *activity* measures (e.g., phone calls answered) are more common than *outcome* measures such as how many callers left satisfied.

What is a resource? Who creates it, gets access to it, bears responsibility for its use or misuse? Where do resources "live"? How are they protected? What is obsolescence? How are out-of-date resources retired from service? Enterprise application software, for example, often lives well past its useful life; ask any chief information officer how many zombie enterprise applications she has running. Invisible to the naked eye, software can take on a life of its own, and once another program connects to it (the output of a sales forecasting program might be used in human resource scheduling or in marketing planning), the life span likely increases: Complexity makes pruning more difficult since turning off an application might have dire consequences at the next quarterly close, the next annual performance review, or the next audit. Better to err on the side of safety and leave things running.

What does it mean for information to be weightless, massless, and infinitely portable? Book collections are becoming a thing of the past for many readers, as Kindle figures and Google searches can attest: Having a reference collection near the dining room used to be essential in some academic households, to settle dinnertime contests. Photographs, either organized into albums or collected in shoe boxes, were heavy. Music used to weigh a lot, in the form of LP records. Compact discs were lighter, but the plastic jewel box proved to be a particularly poor storage solution. MP3 downloads eliminated the software but still needed bits to be stored on a personal hard drive. Now that's changing, to the point where physical books, newspapers, music, and movies all share a cloud-based solution. The result is a dematerialization of many people's lives: Book collections, record collections, sheet music—artifacts that defined millions of people—are now disappearing, for good ecological reasons but with as-yet-undetermined ramifications for identity, not to mention decorating. It also puts the network in a position where it *must* work, yet bandwidth and backup are often less than robust.

What does it mean to bear personal responsibility? If software operating in my name does something bad, did I do anything? What if I wrote code that did bad things? If I am not physically present at my university, my workplace, or my political organization, how loosely or tightly am I connected to the institution, to its people, to its agenda? Harvard sociologist Robert Putnam worried about the implications of the decline in the number of American bowling leagues; are Facebook groups a substitute for, or an improvement on, physical manifestations of civic engagement?[9] If so, which groups, and which forms of engagement? In other words, at the scale of 700-plus million users, saying anything about Facebook is impossible, given the number of caveats, exceptions, and innovations: Facebook today is not what it will be a year from now, whereas bowling leagues have been pretty stable for decades.

Looking Ahead

The fluidity of (physical) place, (cyber) space, and time has far-reaching implications for getting work done, for entrepreneurial opportunity, and for personal identity. As with so many other innovations, the technologists who are capable of writing code and designing and building breakthrough devices have little sense of what those innovations will *mean*. The sailing ship meant, in part, that Britain could establish a global empire; the first century of the automobile meant wars for oil, environmental degradation, new shapes for cities, the postwar rise of Japan, and unprecedented personal mobility, to start a very long list. What barely 30 years of personal computing, 20 years of the commercial Internet, and a relatively few months of smartphones might mean is impossible to tell so far, but it looks like they could mean a *lot*.

Notes

1. Evan Ratliff, "Writer Evan Ratliff Tried to Vanish: Here's What Happened," *Wired*, November 20, 2009, www.wired.com/vanish/2009/11/ff_vanish2.

2. See Jim Blascovich and Jeremy Bailenson, *Infinite Reality: Avatars, Eternal Life, NewWorlds, and the Dawn of Virtual Revolution* (New York: William Morrow, 2011).

3. Martina Zavagno, "Tesco's Subway Virtual Store," Adverblog, June 23, 2011, www.adverblog.com/2011/06/23/tescos-subway-virtual-store/.

4. Eric Wesoff, "Cisco: Network as 4th Utility in Smart Cities," Greentechmedia, April 22, 2011, www.greentechmedia.com/articles/read/Cisco-Network-as-4th-Utility-in-Smart-Cities/.

5. Matthew Yi, "HP Introduces State-of-the-Art Video Conferencing System," *San Francisco Chronicle* December 13, 2005, http://articles.sfgate.com/2005-12-13/business/17404591_1_conferencing-system-video-conferencing-forrester-research.

6. I'm indebted to my student Stephanie Ramsey for her research into this phenomenon.

7. David Sheppard, "NYMEX Oil Trade 45 Percent Computer-Driven," Reuters, March 3, 2011, www.reuters.com/article/2011/03/03/us-finance-summit-nymex-volume-idUSTRE7225RV20110303.

8. Tom Lauricella and Scott Patterson, "Legacy of the 'Flash Crash': Enduring Worries of Repeat," *Wall Street Journal*, August 6, 2010, http://online.wsj.com/article/SB10001424052748704545004575353443450790402.html.

9. Robert Putnam, *Bowling Alone: The Collapse and Revival of American Community* (New York: Simon & Schuster, 2000).

CHAPTER 34

Conflict

As the basis for daily life, first-world economies, and much of the world's innovation moves into the world of information and communications, it's inevitable that bad guys and bad actions migrate there as well. The term "information warfare" doesn't really mean anything specific, so it's worth looking at a few of the ways computing and communications are reshaping crime and conflict. These areas might represent business opportunities for some, risks for others, and points of departure: Innovation is occurring on the dark side as well as in the light.

The intersection of technology, economics, politics, and violence that occurred in the summer of 2011 was nothing short of a milestone. When young people used Facebook and Twitter to organize riots in London, the social media tools were frequently blamed for the violence. Given the wide scale of the events of August and the diversity of participants, such an explanation is insufficient. Certainly, communications tools including BlackBerry Messenger were used to coordinate sometimes-professional criminals who were looting from prearranged lists. Other violence was copycat, undoubtedly fueled in part by hot summer temperatures, high unemployment, and political alienation. Once more, the superb effectiveness of mobile and Internet technologies in facilitating group behavior was on display, in the service of various ends: After the damage was done, the most popular Twitter term over the four days of rioting was "riotcleanup."[1]

Warfare between Nation-States

As the United States formalizes its military posture relative to electronic intrusions and attacks, the relationship between cyberattacks and physical responses is being weighed carefully. Off the record, one "military official" reserves the right to respond to code with explosives: "If you shut down our power grid, maybe we will put a missile down one of your smokestacks."[2] On the record, the initial formulation of cyberstrategy emphasizes preparedness and effective defense: "By sharing timely indicators about cyber events, threat signatures of malicious code, and information about emerging actors and threats, allies and international partners can increase collective cyber defense." Other elements of the strategy fall under the category of common sense: "Most vulnerabilities of and malicious acts against DoD [Department of Defense] systems can be addressed through good cyber hygiene," such as strong passwords, limited use of USB drives in secure facilities, and regular antivirus sweeps and updates.[3] The formulation and execution of cyberwarfare strategy is only beginning, and much remains to be determined.

The lack of "fingerprints," for example, means that the origin of attacks can be difficult to trace. Networks of infected computers around the world can be rented to serve in so-called botnets that launch spam, denial-of-service attacks, or malware such as keystroke loggers or phishing e-mails. A nation-state actor can just as easily employ (or appear to employ) such a resource as could a criminal enterprise. The United States and Korea have been subjected to sophisticated attacks at scale in both 2009 and 2011, and while North Korea is an obvious suspect, definitive evidence was not immediately available.[4]

The debate over "missiles down smokestacks" is a recent manifestation of longer-running debate in military circles: What is the relationship between information and action? One answer can be found in a recent theory of battlefield strategy. Designed by an Air Force colonel named John Boyd, the inelegantly named (and never really explained*) OODA loop seeks to attack the opponent's decision-making faculty rather than its armament.[5] Observation, orientation, decision, and action are the stages of tactical behavior, according to the doctrine, but not in a rote life-cycle sense. According to one interpretation, "Orientation—how you interpret a situation, based on your experience, culture, and heritage—directly guides decisions, but it also shapes observation and action. At the same time, orientation is shaped by new feedback." For Boyd, effective warriors watch for "mismatches between his original understanding and a changed reality. In those mismatches lie opportunities to seize advantage."[6]

Given that reality is ceaselessly changing, continuous adaptation is required; as the German field marshall Helmuth von Moltke is said to have proclaimed in the late nineteenth century, "No battle plan survives contact

---

*Boyd's preferred mode of transmitting the idea was an in-person 14-hour presentation of overhead transparencies.

with the enemy." Given the inevitable chaos, Boyd wrote, "We must continue the whirl of reorientation, mismatches, analyses/synthesis over and over again ad infinitum." In short, as the opponent seeks to ground himself on something, anything familiar, the aggressor can capitalize on the newness of the actual situation.

Boyd's ideas gained traction in peculiar ways, as befits the stubborn iconoclast who generated them. His home service disregarded the OODA loop, whereas the Marine Corps, operating as it does on lean resources and speed rather than mass and scale, seized on the concept. The highly successful design of the attack on Iraq in the early 1990s was classic Boyd: Move fast, disorient the enemy, paralyze their responses. Fifteen Iraqi divisions surrendered to two divisions of U.S. Marines. When asked how this had happened, Brigadier General Richard I. Neal, the U.S. military spokesman, said on national television: "We kind of got inside their decision cycle."[7]

A blunter attempt to disrupt an opponent's information environment can be seen in the Chinese launch of an antisatellite missile in 2007. By knocking down one of its own aging weather satellites that orbits at the same altitude as U.S. intelligence birds, China sent a strong signal. As *Foreign Affairs* put it:

> *With the United States now depending so heavily on assets in space for real-time communications, battlefield awareness, weapons targeting, intelligence gathering, and reconnaissance, the Chinese rocket launch may have been an attempt to show Washington how Beijing can overcome its handicap in a relatively simple way.*[8]

As the evolving cyberwarfare doctrine illustrates, the response to such a strike has yet to be determined: If China damages a U.S. military satellite, either with missiles or lasers (which cannot down a satellite but can impair the optics of imaging systems), is it an act of war, even though no U.S. territory or American citizens were breached or harmed? Someday a commander in chief may have to answer that question.

Non-Nation-State Actors

Iraq's open-field battles were the last of their sort for quite a while. Battling loose networks of insurgents in what is called asymmetric warfare has been the primary order of business for more than a decade. In such conflicts, heavy weapons can be a liability, or at least are neutralized insofar as the opponent typically cannot be attacked, bombed, or sunk by conventional means. Information thus plays a central role in both the insurgencies and in nation-states' response to them. Al Qaeda in Iraq (a spinoff group of the original "brand"), for example, routinely videotapes improvised explosive device (IED) detonations for use as recruiting and motivational tools on various Web sites.[9]

Other forms of digital warfare are emerging. The lack of traceability of cyberwarfare means that nation-states can get software to do work for which missiles or bombs might be ill-suited politically. Such was apparently the case in 2010 when a software virus called Stuxnet was targeted extremely specifically: It attacked Siemens industrial devices, specifically the centrifuges at Iran's nuclear enrichment facility. With extreme sophistication, the virus embedded itself in the SCADA (supervisory control and data acquisition) system that controlled the industrial apparatus, then sent false signals to the monitoring system, indicating that devices were operating properly. Once the centrifuges spun up in an erratic manner, some were damaged, with the effect of slowing Iran's nuclear program. Official responsibility has never been claimed, but several strong clues point to the United States and Israel being involved.[10] Stuxnet is the first documented episode of an attack on industrial control systems; similar systems control power plants, chemical facilities, and military installations.[11]

Another theme in information-age conflict revolves around secrets: The entire life cycle of intelligence gathering is sensitive, including not just the facts (country X has 100 missiles aimed at country Y) but also who asked, who told, and who took notice. WikiLeaks gained considerable attention in 2010 when it published roughly 480,000 documents related to the U.S. war in Afghanistan, then made another release of 250,000 U.S. State Department diplomatic cables that compromised both sources and diplomats. The Web site's architecture is impossible to conceive of in any age before the current one, in which control of media outlets has widened. WikiLeaks' founder, Julian Assange, calls it "an uncensorable system for untraceable mass document leaking and public analysis."[12] To remove content from WikiLeaks, an entity would have to "practically dismantle the Internet itself," in the words of an analysis in *The New Yorker* from 2010.[13] While technology protects the openness of the secrets, human traits—pride, vices, carelessness, and ideological commitments—made them available in the first place.

The mission of this powerful medium is spelled out in noble terms:

> *WikiLeaks is a non-profit media organization dedicated to bringing important news and information to the public. We provide an innovative, secure, and anonymous way for independent sources around the world to leak information to our journalists. We publish material of ethical, political, and historical significance while keep-*

*ing the identity of our sources anonymous, thus providing a uni-
versal way for the revealing of suppressed and censored injustices.[14]*

With its robust, distributed servers and an international legal system
ill-equipped for this type of approach, WikiLeaks confronts established
governments and corporations with a challenge to the basic need for
secrets: "Publishing improves transparency," the Web site asserts,

*and this transparency creates a better society for all people. Better
scrutiny leads to reduced corruption and stronger democracies in
all society's institutions, including government, corporations and
other organisations. A healthy, vibrant and inquisitive journalistic
media plays a vital role in achieving these goals. We are part of
that media.[15]*

The rhetorical sleight of hand here is significant. Aligning WikiLeaks
with media as opposed to treason or espionage puts secret holders on the
defensive insofar as WikiLeaks has published verifiable material: The site's
record of veracity has not been seriously questioned. But it is not entirely
clear whether the site's objective is to bring truth to light (i.e., a quasi-
journalistic stance) or to cripple the operations of institutions it deems ille-
gitimate. Such governance is by Assange's definition conspiratorial; it is
generated by people in "collaborative secrecy, working to the detriment of
a population."[16] Much like Boyd, Assange argued that when an institution's
communication connections are disrupted, the information flow among
conspirators drops, to the point that the conspiracy becomes unsustainable. As *The New Yorker* analysis summarized, "Leaks were an instrument
of information warfare."[17]

While the role of founder Julian Assange may change as he sorts out
multiple legal problems, the basic model of WikiLeaks will likely persist,
even if its current incarnation is shut down by financial, legal, or personal-
ity issues. Digital secrets are too easy to find, to move, and to distribute
for this genie to be put back into its bottle. WikiLeaks has inspired other
similar projects, and in 2011 an even more diffuse, distributed effort was
devoted, in part, against the very concept of security.

Whereas WikiLeaks has a public spokesman, a vetting procedure, and
a fundraising component, the loose hacker collectives of 2011 have fanci-
ful names, occasional manifestos, and apparently some skilled technologists. The identities of the people associated with Anonymous, LulzSec,
and imitators are as-yet unknown, though some arrests have been made
in the United States and United Kingdom. The targets range from the silly
to the deadly serious; Rupert Murdoch's fictitious death was splashed on

the cover of one of his newspapers while e-mail addresses and passwords for Arizona public safety personnel were published in response to that state's anti-immigration posture, which the group regards as racist.[18]

Anonymous gained prominence in 2010 when it attacked PayPal and MasterCard after the payment sites cut off donations made to WikiLeaks. The group quickly multiplied its efforts. When Sony sought to sue a hacker who made it possible to run Linux on PlayStations (as the original PlayStation did), Anonymous attacked the PlayStation Network, but at an organizational level (such as it is) denied the roughly simultaneous leaking of 100 million Sony user accounts that turned out to have been particularly poorly protected.* Other targets of 2011 included the North Atlantic Treaty Organization (NATO), the Public Broadcasting System, and the U.S. Senate Web site; affiliated groups claimed to have attacked the government of Brazil. Government sites in Turkey were attacked in response to attempted Internet censorship. Booz Allen Hamilton, an information services provider to the U.S. government, had 90,000 e-mail accounts and encrypted passwords for sensitive military clients breached. Affiliated vandals posted a Twitter message from Fox News falsely stating that President Obama had been shot.

The variety of targets, and the apparently whimsical motivations for their inclusion, aligns with a leaderless collective; the agenda is opportunistic, though the skills involved in the military breaches suggest that some members possess sophisticated knowledge. At the same time, the range of targets and the scale of the breaches suggest a deeper problem: Information security is not being well practiced. While hacking for the laughs out loud (LulzSec) appears apolitical, other actions exhibit some degree of geopolitical awareness: Certain NATO documents were kept quiet, and other materials that might have compromised the *News of the World* newspaper scandal investigation in England were also claimed to be withheld. Arrests may impair the group's efforts, but Anonymous claims to be an idea rather than an organization:

> *Your threats to arrest us are meaningless to us as you cannot arrest an idea. Any attempt to do so will make your citizens more angry until they will roar in one gigantic choir. It is our mission to help these people and there is nothing—absolutely nothing—you can possibly to do make us stop.*[19]

---

*According to a Purdue University computer scientist testifying before a congressional subcomittee, Sony had no firewall protecting its networks and its Apache Web server software was an outdated version with known vulnerabilities. See www .eweek.com/c/a/Security/Sony-Networks-Lacked-Firewall-Ran-Obsolete-Software-Testimony-103450/.

Emerging Offensive Weapons

Given that an estimated 2,000 U.S. companies (that aren't talking about it very much) have been attacked by various Web assaults of sufficiently high degrees of sophistication to rule out so-called script kiddies looking mostly for bragging rights, countermeasures are increasing in intensity.[20] Google, for example, openly accused China of cyberattacks and changed its operating procedures in response. The security vendor RSA had the algorithm behind SecureID tokens stolen; 40 million of the key-fob-size devices have been shipped to serve as a third factor of authentication for secure systems. The defense contractor Lockheed Martin had to shut off its virtual private network until new tokens with uncorrupted "seeds" that generate a fresh six-digit number every 60 seconds could be distributed.[21] For a global company with sensitive data, such a scenario was troubling indeed.

So far, targets have been both civilian, including defense contractors, and military: 24,000 files were stolen in March 2011 from an unnamed contractor by "foreign intruders."[22] The new class of targets are strategic, outside the military and diplomatic sphere: power grids, drawbridges, hospital monitoring, and patient-care systems. While defensive measures are essential and sometimes effective, nation-states seek to arm themselves offensively. As the Stuxnet virus showed, software attacks can be strategically effective while being politically palatable, given the considerable legal gray area.

But where does a government buy the ability to shut down Moscow's subways, for example, or turn oil refineries in a given rogue nation into chaos? A new generation of software company, operating very quietly, is emerging to do for paying governments what skilled coders can be recruited to do in less democratic societies. Such companies as KEYW, Endgame Systems, and HBGary Federal map vulnerabilities and offer software assets for sale: What kind of computers are running where, doing what, relative to a target? How can those computers be protected, compromised, disabled, or simply monitored? For about $6 million, reportedly, a buyer gets what one article called "cyber warfare in a box."[23] Seeing the market, IBM bought Internet Security Systems (ISS) for $1.3 billion in 2006. One of ISS's key differentiators was the X-Force network-vulnerability mapping service; Endgame's founders were X-Force alumni.

Unlike the Cold War's reliance on deterrence—we know what you have and, if you utilize it, we will pay you back—cyberwar is marked by high degrees of misdirection and deniability. In addition, once a capability is shown, countermeasures can be taken in ways that were impossible with nuclear warheads, for instance: A cyberweapon has a shorter shelf life after being deployed than when it is secret. With Stuxnet, the software covered its tracks and told nuclear facility operators the centrifuges were operating normally when in fact they were spinning fast enough to destroy themselves, but now that it is known, the virus no longer can be used in a surprise attack.[24]

Such software could be written in only a handful of countries, but given the ease of triggering a virus or even an army of dormant compromised computers as compared to moving nuclear warheads across the world, cyberwarfare will not follow the pattern of exclusivity that was the hallmark of the nuclear club of known or strongly suspected regimes. To illustrate the complexity of the situation, consider the origin of the price list for vulnerability mapping, rootkits*, and even e-mail and Web addresses. In such a sensitive domain, how did Endgame's wares find their way into unclassified, public sources? An outside party hacked into HBGary Federal in 2011 and leaked the relevant e-mails. Who was that party? Anonymous, the hacker alliance that has no known geographical headquarters, appointed leader, or physical infrastructure: The group's publicity tools include press releases and YouTube videos, which can be close to untraceable, but otherwise it works pretty much invisibly.

Looking Ahead

Cyberwar, in short, differs from conventional warfare in just about every significant dimension:

- The attacker can be thousands of miles away from the target, and the attack can be timed to launch weeks or months after the decision is made.
- The identity and location of the attacker can be virtually impossible to determine.
- The attacking parties' motivation can be invisible, ad hoc, or highly developed, and different aligned parties likely will be acting in the service of different agendas.
- Some participants may be unaware of the existence or nature of their participation.

---

*A rootkit is a collection of software tools that give an individual administrator-level access ("root," as in the root directory) to a computer. Access usually comes from either a known vulnerability or intercepting or otherwise compromising a password. After the rootkit is installed, an attacker can mask his or her intrusion and commandeer the basic operations of the computer or network.

- The identity of the attacker can be hidden to make it look like the work of someone else or the work of no one in particular.
- The ultimate target may not be immediately obvious, given the dense interconnection of so many computers.
- The intent may be to deprive the target's host of a capability, to send a political message, to cause economic disruption, or to cause bodily harm, either specifically (a particular pacemaker or insulin-delivery pump) or generally (a water supply). In short, cyberattacks can be very specifically aimed.
- Cyberattacks cost far less to mount than conventional attacks.
- For many reasons, targets are readily available: Few assets are completely secure.

As the number of Internet connections and computerlike devices ascends past the 4 billion mark, thinking about such notions as authentication, perimeter security, and trust will be increasingly problematic. If the risks get severe enough, might the many benefits of interconnection and mobility be overwhelmed by the dangers, or by the precautions[25] insisted on by those charged with the protection of critical assets? That is, will the behaviors of the cyberwarriors, both official and unaligned, force substantial changes in the open, relatively low-cost, and heterogeneous environment people have come to expect?

Notes

1. John Burn-Murdoch, Paul Lewis, James Ball, Christine Oliver, Michael Robinson and Garry Blight, "Twitter Traffic During the Riots," *The Guardian*, August 24, 2011, www.guardian.co.uk/uk/interactive/2011/aug/24/riots-twitter-traffic-interactive.
2. Siobhan Gorman and Julian E. Barnes, "Cyber Combat Can Count as Act of War," *Wall Street Journal*, May 31, 2011, http://professional.wsj.com/article/SB10001424 052702304563104576355623135782718.html?mod=googlenews_wsj&mg=reno-wsj.
3. Noah Shactman, "Pentagon Makes Love, Not Cyber War," CNN, July 15, 2011, http://edition.cnn.com/2011/TECH/innovation/07/15/pentagon.cyber.war .wired/.
4. Siobhan Gorman and Evan Ramstad, "Cyber Blitz Hits U.S., Korea," *Wall Street Journal*, July 9, 2009, http://online.wsj.com/article/SB124701806176209691.html.
5. See Robert Coram, *Boyd: The Fighter Pilot Who Changed the Art of War* (New York: Back Bay Books, 2004).
6. Keith H. Hammonds, "The Strategy of the Fighter Pilot," *Fast Company*, May 31, 2002, www.fastcompany.com/magazine/59/pilot.html?page=0%2C0.
7. Coram, *Boyd*, p. 425.
8. Bates Gill and Martin Kleiber, "China's Space Odyssey: What the Antisatellite Test Reveals About Decision-Making in Beijing," *Foreign Affairs* (May/June 2007),

www.foreignaffairs.com/articles/62602/bates-gill-and-martin-kleiber/chinas-space-odyssey-what-the-antisatellite-test-reveals-about-d.

9. James Kennedy Martin, "Dragon's Claws: The Improvised Explosive Device (IED) as a Weapon of Strategic Influence," Master's thesis, Naval Postgraduate School, March 2009, www.dtic.mil/cgi-bin/GetTRDoc?Location=U2&doc=GetTRDoc.pdf&AD=ADA496990.

10. John Markoff, "Malware Aimed at Iran Hit Five Sites, Report Says," *New York Times*, February 11, 2011, www.nytimes.com/2011/02/13/science/13stuxnet.html.

11. Robert McMillan, "Siemens: Stuxnet Worm Hit Industrial Systems," *Computerworld*, September 14, 2010, www.computerworld.com/s/article/print/9185419/Siemens_Stuxnet_worm_hit_industrial_systems?taxonomyName=Network+Security&taxonomyId=142.

12. Raffi Khatchadourian, "No Secrets: Julian Assange's Mission for Total Transparency," *The New Yorker*, June 7, 2010, www.newyorker.com/reporting/2010/06/07/100607fa_fact_khatchadourian#ixzz1Smlo05Nd.

13. Ibid.

14. http://wikileaks.org/About.html.

15. Ibid.

16. Julian Assange, "Conspiracy as Governance," December 3, 2006, p. 1, finemrespice.com/files/conspiracies.pdf.

17. Khatchadourian, "No Secrets."

18. Alexia Tsotsis, "LulzSec Releases Arizona Law Enforcement Data, Claims Retaliation for Immigration Law," TechCrunch, June 23, 2011, http://techcrunch.com/2011/06/23/lulzsec-releases-arizona-law-enforcement-data-in-retaliation-for-immigration-law/.

19. Miles Doran, "Hacker Says Anonymous Still Downloading NATO Data," CBS News, July 22, 2011, www.cbsnews.com/8301-503543_162-20081635-503543.html.

20. Michael Riley and Ashlee Vance, "Cyber Weapons: The New Arms Race," *Bloomberg Businessweek*, July 20, 2011, www.businessweek.com/printer/magazine/cyber-weapons-the-new-arms-race-07212011.html.

21. Robert McMillan, "After Hack, RSA Offers to Replace SecureID Tokens," *PCWorld*, June 6, 2011, www.pcworld.com/businesscenter/article/229553/after_hack_rsa_offers_to_replace_secureid_tokens.html.

22. Chris Lefkow, "24,000 Files Stolen from Defense Contractor: Pentagon," Physorg.com, July 15, 2011, www.physorg.com/news/2011-07-stolen-defense-contractor-pentagon.html.

23. Riley and Vance, "Cyber Weapons."

24. Ibid.

25. See, for example, Scott Bradner, "Cyberwar and Cyber-Isolationism," NetworkWorld, July 12, 2011, www.networkworld.com/columnists/2011/071211-bradner.html.

CHAPTER 35

Innovation

"Innovation" is a word that veers into the realm of motherhood and apple pie: It's good because it's good. If innovation is in fact essential to the American future, however, it must move beyond personal idiosyncrasy, magic, and luck. Merely because innovation does not result from relatively rote application of algorithms does not mean it cannot be learned, measured, or codified. Two examples, among many others, may serve as inspiration going forward.

Amazon

After more than 15 years on the Web, Amazon.com remains a pioneer in online commerce. From the days when its peers were E*TRADE and Dell, then through the periods of iPod and Google ascendency, Amazon is the one company that can claim a consistent leadership position on the Web. It serves as an information-age exemplar because of its combination of innovation and execution, and especially its mastery of platform economics. Today, Amazon continues to help define the Internet as a consumer environment, with rules, limits, and opportunities often different from those experienced in physical channels. Operating under assumptions at variance with conventional businesses, and a survivor of the 2000 dot-com bubble, Amazon is a harbinger of successful business practices in a connected economy. (See Figure 35.1.)

Amazon.com opened for business in July 1995 as an exclusively Internet-based effort. After books, Amazon initially expanded into books on tape, videotapes, and sheet music. It then moved into compact discs, becoming the top Internet music merchant in its first quarter of operation. In late November 1998, Amazon announced that it was temporarily

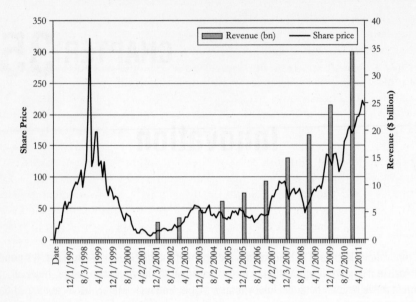

FIGURE 35.1 Amazon.com Share Price and Revenue Performance
Data source: Yahoo! Finance, Standard & Poor's.

expanding into holiday gifts, including electronics, toys, gadgets, and games. This move, while expected, came earlier than most observers predicted, providing another instance where Amazon acted proactively and forced other industry players to respond. Such expansion established a pattern that has persisted: Amazon moves unexpectedly and faster than conventional wisdom would dictate. More than once, actions that were judged as rash in the investment and business press—such as moving into tools and hardware, or the Amazon Prime prepaid two-day shipping plan—turned out to be successful.

The business was started by Jeff Bezos, who studied computer science and electrical engineering at Princeton before working in investment banking until 1994. His interest in the Internet as a consumer environment began when he saw the growth rate of World Wide Web traffic in the spring of 1994. As Bezos recalled in an interview:

> I came across a statistic that the growth rate of Web usage was 2,300 percent a year. . . . It turned out that, though you couldn't measure the baseline usage, you could measure growth rate. And things rarely grow that quickly. . . . Just anecdotally, I could tell that the baseline was nontrivial. And therefore it looked like the Web was going to get very big very fast.[1]

Bezo's immediate business goal—"Get big fast"[2]—reflects an understanding of power-law economics, the driving force in the software industry that is Amazon's main progenitor. Indeed, the story of how Bezos came to choose books as his domain has become part of Internet folklore. In the summer of 1994, he intensively researched different products to sell online, then chose books from among 20 different candidates. He and his wife moved to Seattle in part to capitalize on the area's large supply of talented computer programmers and focused on the opportunities presented by the fact of books being information goods, by the fragmentation of both supply and demand, and by the demanding inventory needs of a book retailer being easier to meet with connections to distributors' warehouses than with in-house stock. In his analysis, Bezos anticipated Chris Anderson's insight into the long tail of power-law distributions: Vast selection meeting sparse demand in an online marketplace is a formula that defines multiple sectors that Amazon has entered.

It is important to note that, from the outset, Amazon operated on a business model built to exploit the online environment rather than from the standpoint of a product focus. This perspective directly contradicts conventional business wisdom that urges executives to set business goals and then to "enable" those goals with technology. Bezos, like FedEx's Fred Smith and other visionaries, instead studied a set of emerging technological capabilities and wrapped a business around them.

How Amazon Delivers Value

Amazon has consciously built a fourfold value proposition, each dimension of which directly relates to an understanding of the leverage uniquely generated by the online medium:[3]

1. *Convenience.* The Internet is open for business all the time, across time zones. The Amazon Web site offers multiple paths to a given item: via reviews, categorical browsing lists, multiple dimensions of search capability, referral from a previous search, e-mail notification, a variety of recommendation engines, or personalized messages on the Web interface. The Web site is designed to minimize download time, and the mobile applications are similarly user-centric. (While the site was initially designed for home shoppers, before mass broadband was deployed Amazon would log significant traffic bursts at lunch hour as customers connected over their employers' corporate networks). Through its alliance with Sprint, Amazon can nearly instantly download a Kindle book anywhere there is a Wi-Fi or Sprint cellular signal.
2. *Selection.* No matter what the retail category, Amazon delivers unprecedented selection: New and used items, physical and virtual

TABLE 35.1 Item Selection Comparison across Online Retailers

Item	Amazon	Target	Specialty Store	Specialty Example
Can openers	18,509	33	55	Bed Bath & Beyond
Gas grills	11,492	52	135	Home Depot
HDTVs	48,343	200	378	Best Buy
Kitchen knives	48,310	48	337	Williams Sonoma
Multivitamins	9,639	35	50	CVS
Women's running shoes	10,123	2	283	Dick's Sporting Goods

information goods (book, movie, and music downloads), and international presence begin a list of ways in which Amazon has redefined retail. The virtualization of inventory—affiliates hold many stock-keeping units (SKUs), reducing Amazon's risk while delivering selection—was pioneered early in the company's history, then expanded. Table 35.1 shows the scale of the selection advantage compared to category leaders.

3. *Price.* Amazon owns inventory for a much shorter time than physical retailers. As a result, Amazon can sell for less because it is on the right side of debt interest (see below). Labor contributes less to selling price: Amazon's revenue per employee is more than $1 million versus roughly $200,000 for Target. Even with shipping added to an order under $25 (which many shoppers mentally discount as the cost of convenience), Amazon comes out to be roughly 8% to 15% cheaper than a physical retailer, in large measure because it aggressively avoids exposure to sales tax.

4. *Customer service.* Amazon has a call center but keeps the phone number well hidden. Customers are trained to self-service their accounts online, and the company's customer service metrics are exceptionally high even with the lack of human touch. The company's network of warehouses sets the industry standard for fast delivery, even with the large SKU count.

Execution

Amazon's extraordinary performance on some traditional measurements indicates some benefits of its business model. The foremost of these may be cash flow: Amazon's operating cycle—the time from payment to suppliers until payment from customers—is in fact negative. Given that credit card companies typically pay Amazon within 24 hours of an order's receipt, and given that Amazon pays its suppliers 46 days after receipt of goods, the firm has use of the customers' money for several weeks before bills come due. At Best Buy, in contrast, inventory is held, on average, for 74 days, or 30 days *after* the supplier was paid.

Other metrics are similarly revealing of best-in-class execution:

- Amazon scores extremely high grades on the American Customer Satisfaction Index, not just in its sector but compared to many business categories.[4] Other rankings, including those from ForeSee[5] and BIGresearch,[6] also rank Amazon on top.
- The customer base is in the range of 75 million people, with offerings customized for each individual who logs in.
- Google has indexed more that 107 million Amazon pages, which provides a rough estimate of SKU count. Because those pages are heavily viewed, Google ranks them highly in core search results, meaning that Amazon needs to spend less on paid search advertising.
- Amazon processes 24 orders per second.[7]
- Eighty-one million people visit per month, ranking Amazon in the top 20 of Web destinations worldwide.

Innovation

In keeping with the hypothesis that superb execution is necessary but no longer sufficient for business success, Amazon (like Apple) excels at innovation. The firm is responsible for several developments that are now part of the online landscape:

- From early in the company's history, Amazon has utilized user-generated content in the form of product reviews and reviews of the reviews. Amazon, in short, utilized social media before anyone called it that.
- In addition to user recommendations, Amazon helped customers navigate its large product selection with specialized search (after its A9 service did not dent Google in head-to-head competition in 2005) as well as collaborative filtering of the sort used at Netflix: People who liked this item also liked that one. All three forms of navigation are essential to making long-tail product selection work.
- The shopping-cart metaphor and one-click shopping both came from Amazon.
- Opening up Amazon's distribution network to competitors or merely third parties of any sort turned Amazon from a store into a commerce platform.

- Turning its expertise with Web-based customer service and very large data centers into a profit center, Amazon made another platform play with Amazon Web Services, a pioneering cloud computing offering.
- While Amazon has digitized many forms of media (including music and television), its Kindle book platform is reinventing the entire publishing industry. Physical bookstores, publishers, and authors all find themselves reacting to Amazon's Kindle moves. In late 2011, Amazon expanded from e-readers into tablets, with the intent of tightening the link to the shopping experience rather than confronting the Apple iPad as a general-purpose device.
- Amazon is reinventing the publishing value chain, integrating most every function from writer acquisition, self-publishing, branding (for example signing the self-help author Timothy Ferriss to Amazon's own Imprint, bypassing the conventional publisher's role), print-on-demand, and audiobook publishing as well as used-book selling.
- Amazon pioneered the Gold Box, the predecessor of one-deal-at-a-time sites such as Gilt Groupe and woot!
- In 2005, Amazon launched Prime, its prepaid free two-day shipping membership.
- The Amazon smartphone app, including instantaneous bar-code scanning, helped lead the way to hybrid local–mobile commerce. One form of this model essentially turns any physical retailer into an Amazon showroom.

Lessons from Amazon

Given its long history, its large scale, its inability to be categorized, and its operational excellence, Amazon is a hard company to copy. That said, four lessons may be applicable in other efforts:

1. *Focus on the customer.* Amazon's share price has been volatile in part because the company is not afraid of big bets (whether in warehouse networks, server farms, or now hardware device development). The company is also hard for analysts to value because it has no peers that share its key operational components. Thus, rather than managing to Wall Street expectations, Amazon manages to customer behavior.
2. *Identify inefficiencies, then invent ways to reduce or eliminate them.* Nowhere is this truer than in Amazon's redefinition of book publishing. Several layers of intermediaries find themselves cut out of the extended Kindle ecosystem.
3. *Try things, collect data, and adjust.* Amazon relentlessly innovates. Not every experiment pays off, as when the site presented variable prices for DVDs in 2000.[8] The tabbed model for different product

departments did not scale well, so the site was redesigned to put more emphasis on customization for the individual shopper than on the store's many product categories. The Kindle reader has evolved rather than being assumed to be perfect upon release: Other companies put usability issues on the customer whereas Amazon continually tweaks, monitors, and alters.

4. *Watch the platform.* Amazon's logistics system, opened to affiliates from an early date in the company's history, is one platform. Cloud computing is another. The reading Kindle is a third major platform, with the color Kindle Fire potentially a fourth. Going forward, Amazon (which already offers a credit card) could move into mobile payments. The merchant could expand its footprint in digital media. The point is that platform plays require entrepreneurial initiative, deep pockets, a wide web of relationships, and an engaged customer base. Amazon has all of the above. As winners from IBM, Microsoft, and Google have shown, the stakes of platform plays can be lucrative indeed. There is little reason to doubt Amazon's chances of extending its track record.

Crowds

The Internet, particularly its mobile variant, dramatically lowers coordination costs, as we have seen repeatedly. The possibilities for crowds to mobilize to solve problems are multiplying, providing a second rich resource for innovation.

Tools

Several examples might point the way to other possibilities.

- InnoCentive utilizes a challenge model to pose hard problems to groups of people who, often from different disciplinary perspectives, contribute insights. Sponsor companies pay only for results. On top of money, participants get the intrinsic rewards of being self-directed, creative, and recognized for making a difference.
- As we saw in Chapter 11, Foldit turns protein folding into an online game and has begun to crack long-standing scientific problems.
- A key stage in innovation is need identification. With geographic mapping tools such as Ushahidi (see Chapter 12), London Potholes (http://yourpotholes.crowdmap.com/), or Safecast (which tracks Japan's radiation levels), ground truth is easier to obtain.
- Using tools of mass sentiment, including Facebook and Twitter, as well as Google Trends (see Figure 35.2), mass behavior can be mined

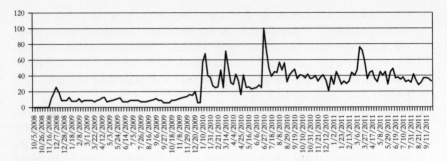

FIGURE 35.2 Google Trends Data for Interest in Search Term "Ushahidi"
Data source: Google Trends.

to generate insight on needs, if not to generate solutions. The analytics and visualization tools noted in Chapters 29 and 30 are highly relevant here.

Video

To illustrate a different angle on the crowd dynamic, I'd like to discuss a video by TED producer Chris Anderson.[9] In it he looks at the proliferation of online videos as tools for mass learning and improvement. Starting with the example of self-taught street dancers in Brazil, Japan, Los Angeles, and elsewhere, he argues that the broad availability of video as shared show-and-tell mechanism spurs one-upmanship through imitation and then innovation. The level of TED talks themselves, Anderson argues, provides home-grown evidence that cheap, vivid multimedia can raise the bar for many kinds of tasks: futurist presentations, basketball dunks, surgical techniques, and so on.

Five factors relative to usability are important in the case of Web video being radically accessible.

1. *The low barrier to entry for imitator/innovator #2 to post her contribution to the discussion may inspire, inform, or infuriate imitator/innovator #3.* Mass media did some of these things (in athletic moves, for example: Watch a playground the week after the Super Bowl or a halfpipe after the X games). The lack of a feedback loop, however, limited the power of broadcast to propagate secondary and tertiary contributions.
2. *Web video moves incredibly fast.* The speed of new ideas entering the flow can be staggering once a video goes viral, as its epidemiological metaphor would suggest.

3. *The incredible diversity of the online world is increasing every year, so the sources of new ideas, fresh thinking, and knowledge of existing solutions multiply as well.* Credentials are self-generated rather than externally conferred: A dance video gets views not because its creator went to Julliard but because people find it compelling and tell their friends, followers, or colleagues.

4. *Web video is itself embedded in a host of other tools, both social and technical, that are also incredibly easy to use.* Do you want to tell someone across the country about an article in today's paper newspaper? Get out the scissors, find an envelope, dig up his current address, figure out correct postage (pop quiz: how much is a first-class stamp today?), get to a mailbox, and wait a few days. Want to recommend a YouTube or other Web video? There are literally hundreds of tools for doing so, essentially all of which are free and have short learning curves.

5. *Feedback is immediate, in the form of both comments and views counters.* The reputational currency that attaches to a "Charlie bit my finger" or "Evolution of dance" is often (but not always) nonmonetary, to be sure, but emotionally extremely affecting nonetheless.

With such powerful motivators, low barriers to participation, vast and diverse populations, rapidity of both generation and diffusion, and a rich ancillary toolset relating to online video, Anderson makes a compelling case for the medium as a vast untapped resource for problem solving on multiple fronts. In addition, because video involves multiple senses, the odds that a given person will grasp my ideas increases as the viewer can hear, watch, or read text relating to the topic. In the face of an urgent need to innovate, the tool set is, fortunately, powerful and accessible.

Looking Ahead

Innovation has never been more needed—one study suggests that innovation per capita peaked well over 100 years ago—or more possible. Open platforms, starting with the Web itself, allow the harvesting of more effort. Wireless hardware puts tools in the hands of millions more people every year. Distributed sensors, radios, and geographic information can be cleverly combined in ways never before possible. Perhaps most important, harvesting the "people power" of good questions, good ideas, and good challenges recalibrates the investment model of many categories of innovation. As the MIT response to the DARPA balloon challenge illustrated (see Chapter 3), getting the incentive model right to drive the right people to participate was more important than any algorithm or piece of code.

Notes

1. Dickson Louie and Jeffrey F. Rayport, "Amazon.com: Portrait of a Cyber-corporation," *Electronic Commerce Advisor* (September/October 1997): 5.
2. Doreen Carvajal, "The Other Battle Over Browsers: Barnes & Noble and Other On-Line Booksellers Are Poised to Challenge Amazon.com," *New York Times*, March 9, 1998, www.nytimes.com/1998/03/09/business/other-battle-over-browsers-barnes-noble-other-line-booksellers-are-poised.html.
3. Bezos spells out the value proposition in an interview in William C. Taylor, "Who's Writing the Book on Web Business?" *Fast Company* (October 31, 1996), www.fastcompany.com/magazine/05/starwave2.html.
4. www.theacsi.org/index.php?option=com_content&view=article&id=206:acsi-scores-february&catid=14&Itemid=259.
5. "Top 100 E-Retailers: ForeSee Results Quantifies Relationship Between Customer Satisfaction and Purchase Intent," ForeSeeResults.com, May 10, 2011, www.foreseeresults.com/news-events/press-releases/top-100-e-retailers-satisfaction-predicts-intent-spring-2011-foresee.shtml.
6. www.bigresearch.com/.
7. Linda Bustos, "10 Reasons Not to Copy Amazon," GetElastic.com, July 9, 2010, www.getelastic.com/10-reasons-not-to-copy-amazon/.
8. Craig Bicknell, "Online Prices Not Created Equal." *Wired*, July 9, 2000, www.wired.com/techbiz/media/news/2000/09/38622.
9. Chris Anderson, "How Web Video Powers Global Innovation," TED Talks, September 2010, www.ted.com/talks/chris_anderson_how_web_video_powers_global_innovation.html.

CHAPTER 36

Information, Technology, and Innovation

The implications of such a massive transformation are obviously impossible to catalog, much less predict. What follows are some selected areas of business impact resulting from the shifts in the computing, communications, and social infrastructure over the past 20 years or so.

Macro Issues

Business will continue to come in multiple shapes and sizes, and the diversity is important to recognize: Construction or agriculture will always behave differently from banking or health care, but, nevertheless, each sector will see instances of what Carlota Perez described as "synergy" in Chapter 1. The speed of innovation, adoption, and transformation of technologies by their users will continue to accelerate, and, as we have seen, retail might now be facing what music confronted more than a decade ago: a sea of change in customer expectation and behavior with far-reaching consequences for the entire industry.

That said, there are three developments to watch.

1. *Mobile payments are a logical consequence of rapid smartphone deployment.* Smartphone penetration in the United States is at 33% in 2011, up from 20% in 2010. Making the smartphone into a wallet (as in Japan) or a bank branch (as in Kenya) is possible, but the question is whether the technology solves a problem that isn't a problem: Credit cards have a broad installed base in the United States, and a smartphone

is more easily lost. Merchants might be hesitant to install more terminals after already paying handsomely for the current device. That said, other countries might see different patterns of adoption, as was the case with text messaging prior to 2005.

2. *Business will become more "social."* Well beyond putting up a Facebook "like" button, companies will be faced with workers, recruits, partners, and customers who seek more nuanced interactions than are typically provided by a Web site or toll-free call center. Whether it is collaboration to solve a problem, genuine excitement over some happy outcome, prepurchase or preemployment research, or concern over product safety, people want to interact in rich, rapid, personalized ways. This might involve product promotion (Groupon), way-finding (Foursquare), social networking (Facebook Places), or other forms of involvement (Kickstarter or Shopkick). The trend toward social commerce often takes the form of games, and we can expect this tendency to become more pronounced.

3. *Innovation will be a competitive requirement in more and more sectors.* Whether it is the evolution of microfinancing and peer-to-peer lending in financial services, person-to-person coordination for overnight stays (Airbnb), or something as simple yet powerful as Craigslist, established entities can no longer assume the same barriers to entry from previous decades will continue to be effective.

Globalization

While it's difficult to quantify globalization, the fact that there will soon be 4 billion mobile phones in circulation points to a more connected future for every country, save the occasional North Korea or Somalian exception—and in Somalia, the pirates are equipped with an impressive information infrastructure, so the connection is of a different sort.[1] As we have seen, the creative uses of the technology for good and for ill are most impressive, and as learning spreads faster on that infrastructure, the cycle of experimentation, innovation, and diffusion will only get faster. Consider that the iPhone was launched in the United States in 2007 and promptly redefined the technology landscape; by 2011, it was available in 105 countries and looks to become popular among China's 700 million mobile phone subscribers now that Apple has distribution partners. This speed is completely unprecedented.

It's also useful to bear in mind the differences in adoption patterns: The mobile phones that are transforming life in Africa, for example, are not doing so with Angry Birds or Facebook but with election fraud monitoring, medical innovations, and banking. At the same time, in the developed world, those "serious" applications have enormous potential even while entertainment, "grooming" (flirting), and social coordination remain important.

A final facet of globalization relates to evolving notions of property rights. When intellectual property, such as songs, movies, and books, can be digitally copied and distributed globally for little cost, maintaining property rights obviously becomes problematic. As we saw with regard to copy protection in Chapter 4, technologically locking down bits in software form has yet to be a long-term solution: People working in pursuit of a shared (possibly illegal) objective can coordinate too easily, and the Internet is too good at moving bits for this to be viable.

An alternative conception of property rights helps Linux work. The General Public License (GPL) is the license protocol that ensures that any programmer's contribution to the software will be recognized as building on the free software with which he or she began. That is, unlike other free software licenses (such as Berkeley Software Distribution (BSD)), the GPL ensures that the free software that is modified cannot have more restrictive conditions imposed as it is redistributed after the changes are contributed. The notion is known as copyleft, or the opposite of copyright in that it protects the freedom of the artifact and the freedom of programmers to add to the code base rather than the property rights of a person or commercial entity.[2]

Wikipedia uses similar licensing. The result is a substantial public commons that is legally protected from commercial exploitation: People who contribute to a free public good know it will remain free and public and not get commercialized for private gain. At global scale, for certain kinds of goods, this kind of licensing encourages innovation, as Ushahidi (Chapter 12) shows. At the same time, it gives people in developing countries an alternative to the license fees collected by an Apple or Microsoft. Copyleft does not work very well for private goods, however, so the issue of maintaining property rights to movies, for example, remains difficult, especially given the size of the markets involved.

Strategy

While the firm remains a key element in strategic thinking, larger and more fluid entities are also increasing in importance. Technology platforms, human and organizational networks, and even coordinated individuals without corporate identity can alter the strategic landscape.

Platforms

Perhaps more than other industry, the computing and communications sector is characterized not only by product or brand competition (Ford versus Toyota or Pepsi versus Coke) but by platform competition. Platforms imply standards, often-complex ecosystems of suppliers, influencers, content partners, and third-party software developers. Microsoft won one round of platform competition in the 1990s, to be sure, but today the primary contenders appear to be Apple and Google (including allies such as HTC and Motorola) in smartphones, with Nokia and Microsoft a potentially interesting combination. Google dominates search-related advertising; Facebook is similarly strong in demographically targeted display ads. SAP and Oracle control the majority of enterprise software, with various open-source options getting more plausible every year. HP and IBM control a substantial portion of infrastructure, but "platform as a service" cloud vendors, including Amazon, are rewriting the entire book on data centers. Facebook's surge in revenue coincided with the popularity of social gaming supported by the likes of Zynga, the company behind FarmVille and other popular titles. One estimate from the University of Maryland pegs the Facebook app ecosystem employment at roughly 150,000 people, drawing about $15 billion in wages.[3]

In each of these cases, there is no winner of market share differentiated only by price or performance. Instead, the number of existing users leads to network effects that can be decisively high, as at Facebook (compared to MySpace in particular). Apple's quality of design and user experience matter, to be sure, but Google's Android platform, while notably less elegant, has more users. Instead, the customer weighs the totality of the system, which can include many other entities outside the primary vendor. This breadth and dynamism means that platform builders must walk the fine line between defining a coherent vision and not locking down the potential for the market to take the platform in new directions. Apple did not design the iPad as a teaching tool for children with autism, for example, but it excels in that role thanks to some clever applications expertly designed by people addressing those particular needs.

One way of thinking about this platform dynamic is a shift in emphasis from nodes (centers of mass, or assets) to links: connections. The force driving that transformation is the growth of networks—superficially, digital data conduits and, more crucially, the new possibilities for human connection that ride on those links. Networks and their implications have historically overturned existing rules of business strategy, whether the network was comprised of ships (England), wires (AT&T), or distribution centers (Wal-Mart). In each of these historical revolutions, the definitions of who was competing, what they were competing for, and what constituted an advantage shifted in ways that rendered many conventional strategic choices ineffective or even dangerous. We are at another such juncture today.

Consider an example of one way networks alter strategy. Just as al Qaeda has no intention of invading New York, neither does BitTorrent seek to become a record label or movie studio. In such unconventional confrontations, the insurgent doesn't want what the incumbent wants—market share, profitability, or whatever—but its goals may impede or deny the corporate pursuit of these goals. This particular asymmetry of objectives makes business strategy much harder to set; once an actor no longer contends with an outside party with either identical or mirror-image objectives, definitions of success and failure can become much more difficult to identify or counter.

Listening to the Warriors

As business strategy in the past has borrowed from military strategy for insight, we can benefit from current thinking about fighting new kinds of adversaries. In an article in the *Washington Post*, defense analyst John Arquilla put matters succinctly. "It takes a tank to fight a tank. It takes a network to fight a network," he said, quoting his own book, *In Athena's Camp*.[4] That book, cowritten with David Ronfeldt, makes several compelling arguments about what the editors call "netwar," a fight among networked components. Significantly, this is not necessarily fought on the Internet; that notion they usefully distinguish as "cyberwar." The entire concept of netwar carries directly into the field of business strategy, helping define new guidelines for achieving advantage in a networked environment.

When Arquilla and Ronfeldt speak of the great powers and say "Look around. No 'good old-fashioned war is in sight,'"[5] they could easily be describing key aspects of the corporate landscape. While geopolitical combat can pit nonstate actors (whether nongovernmental organizations, religious sects, or terrorist organizations) against nation-states, businesses confront constraints from such noncorporate entities as AARP, Napster and then Grokster, and Linux, not to mention governments in their standard-setting and regulatory capacities. Arquilla and Ronfeldt point out that in these types of conflict, "disruption may often be the intended strategic aim rather than destruction."[6]

Summing up, Arquilla and Ronfeldt contrast chess, the old strategy archetype, with Go, a fascinating emblem of the new (at least in the West). Go, they assert,

> is more about distributing one's pieces than massing them. . . .
> It is more about developing web-like links among nearby stationary pieces than about moving specialized pieces in combined operations. It is more about creating networks of pieces than about protecting hierarchies of pieces.[7]

This extended analogy serves nicely as a thought exercise for aspiring network strategists. Corporate strategy has often been a pursuit of mass, an exercise premised on given rather than malleable industry structure, an exercise in vertical integration rather than horizontal connection. As our networks reach deeper and future innovations take increasing advantage of the dominant network models, we will see more and more business dynamics that, for better and worse, parallel what we are seeing as a new chapter in military strategy.

One Path from Military Strategy to Business Management

To understand the contours of classic business strategy, it is helpful to discern its western military heritage: Competitors are seen as enemies and the marketplace is typically a battleground. The similarities are more than rhetorical. Modern business strategy's kinship with military theory dates primarily to the mid-nineteenth century, when a cadre of graduates of the U.S. Military Academy at West Point came into positions of authority. West Point trained the first of America's engineers, who went on to design such key infrastructure as railroad bridges in the Civil War. The ability to impose one's will across time and distance required lines of authority and communication that transcended physical proximity. The West Point training emphasized the importance of written orders, similar to business memoranda. Later, war veterans played key roles in the growth of commercial railroads, which employed the engineering point of view both in how they operated and, more subtly, in the organizational design necessitated by the first distributed, coordinated national enterprises.

What are the key tenets of classic business strategy that emerged from these military origins? In its simplest form, an organization or military operation should resemble a pyramid: Power and intelligence are concentrated at the top and trickle down to the wide bottom of the hierarchy, where both power and intelligence are presumed to be minimal. The ultimate goal is the familiar "command and control," which necessitates getting subordinates to do what you want while preventing them from doing what you don't. The obvious drawback to such an objective is the chaotic nature of combat, the aptly named fog of war that limits commanders' knowledge of cause and effect as well as their ability to either command or control distributed, self-organized (and to some degree self-interested) forces.

By the 1990s, military strategists like U.S. Marine Lieutenant General Paul K. Van Riper became aware that this advantaged position mentality would not serve in the new battlefield. No longer was his the rhetoric of command and control; instead, Van Riper granted that "warfare is uncontrollable once you unleash it, so the best you can do is control your use of force within the phenomenon itself." The new battlefields of war and work were more fluid, dynamic, and interconnected, and thus called for new strategic agility. "Commander's intent"—what needed to be done—came from the top; plans of action—how to do it—were now left to units closest to the action. Pyramids were out; natural phenomena like swarms were in. But the transition from models to operations was rarely simple. Both military and business leaders have learned that networks shape competition in complex ways, and devising strategic frameworks to cope with those complexities has been far more difficult than expected.

U.S. military strategy, meanwhile, is being reshaped by multiple forces:

- The notion of the "three-block war" in which armed insurgents are battled in one city block, peacekeeping is the mission next door, while in the third sector, armed forces deliver humanitarian aid
- Insurgents who blend in with local populations, as in Afghanistan
- The rise in the use and effectiveness of improvised explosive devices, often detonated by mobile phones

Challenging Porter

Today, one still hears echoes of old military thinking in the work of business strategists like Michael Porter, whose body of work dominates MBA curricula and strategy consulting methodologies alike. Porter explores the ways in which proper corporate strategy defends advantageous business positions. Although this classic perspective holds some valuable lessons, Porter's strategic orientation misses the explosive dynamics typical of network behavior. His new theory of shared value, meanwhile, has yet to take hold with the power of the still-canonical five forces, which have held sway since 1979.[8]

Strategic thinking, in his formulation, occurs within a context of these forces: those exerted by customers, suppliers, competitors, potential competitors, and product substitutes. Several events of the past decade, however, challenge that perspective. It was particularly easy in 1999 to say that networks change everything, and Porter (in a March 2001 article in *Harvard Business Review*) was correct to assert that overenthusiasm led some managers and investors to forget the basics that don't change, profits being foremost.

But three examples of networked challenges to existing businesses would seem to break Porter's model and confirm the disruptive power of the new models, particularly ones that deny the ability of corporations to create "unique sustainable competitive advantage" through coercive or other forms of consumer lock-in.

The three entities are Napster, Linux, and ecoterrorist cells. In each case, a networked entity is not competitor, or supplier, or customer. Even so, the entity poses a formidable challenge to incumbents' definitions of business as usual. These entities fail to respond to conventional interventions, such as price cuts, market exit, or merger and acquisition activity. Further, none of the three entities is a business, and as such none plays by the same rules as businesses. The disrupters are something more significant than competitors, insofar as they don't threaten market share as much as they challenge the foundational assumptions of an entire economic (and often social or cultural) sector. Networks have the potential not only to compete with firms but to transform entire markets that constituent firms take largely as given.

The facts of the music industry are for the most part well known: Napster grew to 20 million users in about a year, the sum of whom downloaded the equivalent of 1.5 to 2 times the entire U.S. volume of compact discs sold in 2000. Napster was not conceived as a business but as a guerilla technology, so it did not need to profit to succeed. At the same time, neither did it treat the existing music industry with much respect. The incumbents used their lobbying power to render Napster illegal, and it effectively ceased operations in 2001. It's noteworthy that, contrary to the labels' complaints, CD sales in fact *decreased* after the service was shut down by court order. Porter's landscape has no place for Napster in the music industry, and his advocacy of lock-in tactics was confronted by an open network that explicitly denied the industry's right to charge upward of $12 to $15 for a collection of songs when only one was going to be played.

Linux is built by a much smaller online community of thousands of technologists, but the distribution channel is similar to Napster's. Even though Microsoft lacked full copyright control over someone else's intellectual property the way record labels did, it responded in much the same way as the music industry by trying to brand the operating system and the principles it was built on as "un-American."[9] This tactic appeared to backfire even as Microsoft was tightening its grip on users through means both technical (usually involving Internet Explorer, as when RealNetworks sued Microsoft over the use of bundling with Windows Media Player) and economic (new enterprise software licensing terms). One mistake might be to take a Porterian view of Linux the software distribution as a *product* substitute when in fact Microsoft's far bigger concern is presumably with the network of *users and developers* who connect with each other in a completely new way—Linux the idea and network that once again exist entirely outside the Porter five forces.

Tom Malone of MIT's Sloan School nailed the point in his *Harvard Business Review* article. He states that Linux is more than a science-fair project of supersmart programmers, more than "a neat *Wired* magazine kind of story:" "This interpretation, while understandable, is shortsighted. What the Linux story really shows us is the power of a new technology—in this case, electronic networks—to fundamentally change the way work is done."[10]

A final example is a hazy and more troubling one. At the outset, I should make clear that I am not applauding this group's activities but rather analyzing the implications of its organization. A band of radical environmental activists, operating most visibly in America's Pacific Northwest, utilizes a cell structure to avoid detection and resist infiltration. Each group is autonomous, sharing only broadly defined goals within a loosely defined movement. The groups use a variety of methods, most illegal and some life-threatening, to interrupt logging and bioengineering. Political insurgents have operated in cells for millennia (the groups in the Bible certainly weren't the first), but what's new is the Internet's ability to connect today's groups, and to spread their messages, while preserving anonymity. As their Web site states: "The Earth Liberation Front (ELF) is an international underground organization that uses direct action in the form of economic sabotage to stop the exploitation and destruction of the natural environment."[11]

The ELF is not a group but an extremely loose network. There is no centralized authority, no membership list, no physical headquarters. Where do these groups fit on, for example, Weyerhaeuser or Boise Cascade's Porterian radar? Rather than competing with these and other timber companies, at their most extreme the ELF and similar groups deny the right of the businesses even to exist in the first place. What is an appropriate, or even feasible, strategic response? Porter's battlefield is cleanly defined (in large measure by a highly visible and fairly rigid industry structure), resembling, as many have said, a chess board. The real world is far messier as the ELF and other groups move the competition and disruption into culture and politics.

Speaking of the three challenges to Porter, members of the World Economic Forum, MBA faculties, and other business-political groups have been struggling both to understand and to respond to these new types of phenomena that utilize distributed and loosely coupled networks to disrupt and even disable various forms of centralized and tightly defined hierarchies. In conventional economic terms, there is no set model: The ELF destroys economic value, Linux creates it, and Napster redistributed it. The three examples confirm that even if it doesn't change literally everything, the Internet is redefining the competitive landscape in ways that extend far beyond what current businesses have had to confront.

Organizations

The firm, while still important, is no longer the default model for organizing resources to get work done. Similarly, the record label and publishing house are challenged by direct-to-market content distribution models. As both examples (Wikipedia) and tools (Ushahidi) get better and more recognized, it seems unlikely that organizational innovation will slow. An example can be found in Barack Obama's 2008 presidential campaign: Utilizing grassroots fundraising methods building on candidate Howard Dean's 2004 breakthrough, along with social media tools including Web video, text messaging, and a Facebook-like MyBarackobama.com infrastructure, the campaign set records for fundraising and participation. The same methods are expected to contribute to the first billion-dollar presidential campaign in 2012.

Regardless of the shape of the organization, today's tools mean that talent matters significantly: Even with high unemployment overall, the role of difference makers in government, nonprofits, start-ups, and of course the corporate sector relates heavily to the information and technology landscapes. Whether it is Apple design chief Jonathan Ive, Wieden+Kennedy social media account executive Iain Tait (who spearheaded the Old Spice campaign that more than doubled sales), Facebook chief operating officer Sheryl Sandberg, or Silicon Valley green technology investor Vinod Khosla, talented individuals are in high demand.

New organizational forms are emerging in many sectors.

- *Mobile virtual network operators (MVNOs) are basically mobile phone companies that rent infrastructure from other parties.* Virgin Mobile was among the first of these. Bringing a brand but not needing to buy wireless spectrum or build networks or billing systems, MVNOs are quite common: More than 500 were in operation as of 2011, though not all of these will survive. Amazon's Whispernet distribution service on the Kindle reader is an MVNO.
- *The one-deal-at-a-time retailers we saw in Chapter 21 merge shopping, social networking, and entertainment.* Supply chains, accounting, merchandising, and customer service all need to be reinvented for such companies as Gilt Groupe, Backcountry.com, and Amazon's woot! unit.
- *Athletic conferences, professional sports leagues, and select individual franchises are reinventing what it means to be a television network.* The University of Texas is undertaking the newest experiment in

revenue-generating content distribution: It signed a $300 million, 20-year deal with ESPN in 2011.

Marketing

Given the primacy of the traditional four Ps of the field—product, price, promotion, and placement—when price goes to zero for several categories, it's newsworthy. The music and news industries are visible examples, but other industries that formerly capitalized on expertise and relationship management have seen the price for those services drop to zero: Ask a stockbroker or travel agent about the transition. Maps, online education (but not certification), and international voice telephony are other settings where up to billions of dollars—in the case of telecoms—of revenue have vaporized.

The emergence of free stuff means responding in some industries or capitalizing in others. Some musicians have responded to free downloads with heavy touring schedules: The Dave Matthews Band earned more than $500 million over 10 years on the road.[12] Television networks found success with Hulu but appear to be unsure what to do with it, given that the revenue model does not mirror that of cable networks. Thousands of start-ups run on Skype; many companies post assembly instruction videos free on YouTube; Asus computers uses peer-to-peer networking provided by BitTorrent to help distribute software downloads. Free is hard to compete with, to be sure, but it presents ample opportunities as well.

Another key marketing dynamic is transparency. As social media empowers conversations among customers and between customers and a brand, the one-size-fits-all model or corporate branding—"Built Ford Tough!"—is being joined by a more human dimension in which the customers' voices are incorporated into the brand. The Skittles Web site color is dictated by the number of social media mentions, which are incorporated into the site, along with, at times, user-generated content, such as videos. Transparency is tricky, however, since it requires a corporate culture to show through to the world. Managing this process remains among the most challenging aspects of the current environment.

Transparency can also be a fluke: The U.S. raid that killed Osama bin Laden was being tweeted in real time by an information technology contractor who wondered why all the helicopters were converging on his small, out-of-the-way village. China's earthquake in 2008 was live on Twitter before the U.S. Geological Survey had anything. Apple has had photos of iPhone prototypes make their way onto the Web via such sites as Gawker, Gizmodo, and the like.

Valuing Global Sports Brands

It's a familiar business school discussion. "Let's talk about powerful brands," begins the professor. "Who comes to mind?" Usual suspects emerge: Coke, Visa, Kleenex. "OK," says the prof, "what brand is so influential that people tattoo it on their arms?" The answer is, of course, Harley-Davidson.

There is another category of what we might call "tattoo brands," however: sports teams. Measuring sporting allegiance as a form of brand equity is both difficult and worth thinking about, both because sports can be seen as information goods and because technology is changing the fan experience.

For a brief definition up front, *The Economist's* statement will do:

Brand equity is the value of the brand in the marketplace. Differentiation demonstrates unique value to customers, and how this is communicated is important to building brand equity. Brands that have a meaningful point of difference are more likely to be chosen repeatedly by consumers and ultimately have a much higher potential for growth than do other brands.[13]

That is, people think more highly of one product than another because of such factors as word of mouth, customer satisfaction, image creation and management, track record, and a range of tangible and intangible benefits of using or associating with the product.

Our focus here will be limited to professional sports franchises, which generally have three primary revenue streams:

1. Television rights
2. Ticket sales and in-stadium advertising
3. Licensing for shirts, caps, and other memorabilia

Of these, ticket sales are relatively finite: A team with a powerful brand will presumably have more fans than can logistically or financially attend games. Prices can and do rise, but for a quality franchise, the point is to build a fan network beyond the arena. Television is traditionally the prime way to do this. National and now global TV contracts turn viewership into advertising revenue for partners up and down the value chain from the leagues and clubs themselves. That Manchester United and the New York Yankees can have fan bases in

China, Japan, or Brazil testifies to the power of television and, increasingly, various facets of the Internet in brand building. Twitter is a prime example.

Sports fandom exhibits peculiar economic characteristics. Compared to, say, house or car buying, fans do not research various alternatives before making a presumably "rational" consumption decision: Team allegiance is not a "considered purchase." If you are a Boston Red Sox fan, your enthusiasm may or may not be relevant to mine: Network effects and peer pressure can come into play (as at a sports bar) but are less pronounced than in telecom, for example. If I am a Cleveland Cavaliers fan, I am probably not a New York Knicks fan: A choice in one league generally precludes other teams in season. Geography matters, but not decisively: One can comfortably cheer for San Antonio in basketball, Green Bay in football, and St. Louis in baseball. At the same time, choice is not completely independent of place, particularly for ticket buying (as compared to hat buying).

Finally, switching costs are generally psychic and only mildly economic (as in having to purchase additional cable TV tiers to see an out-of-region team, for example). Those psychic costs are not to be underestimated: Just because someone lives in London with access to several soccer clubs, allegiances are not determined by the low-price or high-quality provider on an annual basis. Allegiance also does not typically switch for reasons of performance: Someone in Akron who has cheered, in vain, for the Cleveland Browns is not likely to switch to Pittsburgh even though the Steelers have a far superior championship history. All in all, sports brand equity is unlike most products'.

Given the vast reach of today's various communications channels, it would seem that successful sports brands could have a global brand equity that exceeds the club's ability to monetize those feelings. I took five of the franchises ranked highest on the *Forbes* 2010 list of most valuable sports brands and calculated the ratio of the estimated brand equity to the club's revenues. If the club were able to capture more fan allegiance than it could realize in cash inflows, that ratio should be greater than 1. Given the approximations I used, that is not the case.

For a benchmark, I also consulted Interbrand's list of the top global commercial brands and their value to see how often a company's image was worth more than its annual sales. I chose six companies from a variety of consumer-facing sectors (thus ruling out IBM, SAP, and Cisco), and the company had to be roughly the same as the brand (the Gillette brand is not the parent company of Procter & Gamble).

(*continued*)

Three points should be made before discussing the results, which are summarized in Table 36.1.

1. Any calculation of brand equity is a rough estimate: No auditable figures or scientific calculations can generate these lists, as Interbrand's methodology makes clear.[14]
2. *Forbes* and Interbrand used different methodologies. We will see the consequences of these differences shortly.
3. Corporate revenues often accrued from more brands than just the flagship: People buy Minute Maid apart from the Coca-Cola brand, but the juice revenues are counted in the corporate ratio.

All told, this is not a scientific exercise but rather a surprising thought-starter.

TABLE 36.1 Ratio of Brand Equity to Revenues for Selected Brands, 2010

Brand	Brand Equity*	Revenues*	Ratio
Louis Vuitton	21,120	2,434	8.68
Coca-Cola	68,734	31,000	2.22
Harley-Davidson	4,337	4,290	1.01
New York Yankees	328	375	0.87
Dallas Cowboys	208	280	0.74
Nokia	34,864	50,381	0.69
Nike	13,179	19,176	0.69
Manchester United	285	418	0.68
Real Madrid	240	491	0.49
FC Barcelona	180	449	0.40
Apple	15,433	42,905	0.36
Amazon.com	7,868	24,509	0.32

*All figures in millions U.S. dollars.

The stunning 8:1 ratio of brand equity to revenues at Louis Vuitton is in part a consequence of Interbrand's methodology, which overweights luxury items. Even so, six conclusions and suggestions for further investigation emerge:

1. The two scales do not align. The New York Yankees, the most valuable sports brand in the world, is worth 1/24 that of Amazon. One or both of those numbers is funny.

2. Innovation runs counter to brand power. New Coke remains a textbook failure, while Apple's brand is worth only about a third of its revenue. Harley-Davidson draws its cachet from its retrograde features and styling, the antithesis of innovativeness.

3. Geography is not destiny for sports teams. Apart from New York and Madrid, the cities of Dallas, Manchester, and Boston (not included here but with two teams in *Forbes'* top 10) are not global megaplexes or media centers; London, Rome, and Los Angeles are all absent.

4. Soccer is the world's game, as measured by brand: Five of the 10 most valuable names belong to European football teams. The National Football League has 2 entries, and Major League Baseball 3 to round out the top 10 list. Despite the presence of more international stars than American football, and their being from a wider range of countries than MLB's feeders, basketball and hockey are absent from the *Forbes* top 10.

5. Assuming for the sake of argument that the Interbrand list is overvalued and therefore that the *Forbes* list is more accurate, the sports teams' relatively close ratio of brand equity to revenues suggests that teams are monetizing a large fraction of fan feeling.

6. Alternatively, if the *Forbes* list is undervalued, sports teams have done an effective job of creating fan awareness and passion well beyond the reach of the home stadium. Going back to our original assumption, if tattoos are a proxy for brand equity, this is more likely the case. The question then becomes: What happens next?

As more of the world comes online, as media becomes more participatory, and as the sums involved for salaries, transfer fees, and broadcast rights at some point hit limits (as may be happening in the National Basketball Association), the pie will continue to be reallocated. The intersection of fandom and economics, as we have seen, is anything but rational, so expect some surprises in this most emotionally charged of markets.

Supply Chains

When things went wrong in the past, customers might not know for months, if ever. As systems interconnect and social media tools give anyone access to a global audience, bad news now travels fast and sometimes widely: A wave of suicides at Foxconn, a contract electronics manufacturer, made global front-page news in part because of the company's highest-profile customer: Apple. Procurement managers now have the challenge of competing with nonindustry speculators who invest purely for profit; corn is one such commodity that has been transformed by interconnected global markets and the supercharged electronic trading systems that accompany such networks.

Apart from the speed of bad news, there's the long tail: Stock-keeping unit counts at Amazon, Netflix, and eBay are staggering. Managing inventory in such a world is an entirely different exercise compared to traditional retail. Given the primacy of search, matching technologies, and social word of mouth in connecting dispersed communities of buyers with unique tastes with big, dispersed inventories, supply chains can be challenging. Even Redbox, the kiosk-based DVD rental company, has had to be extremely clever about getting discs from where they're returned to the next available machine: College students will rent in Ann Arbor, for example, then drive south for spring break, returning DVDs at various locations down I-75. Standard planning software cannot accommodate such unpredictable behavior at a micro level; thinking more broadly, however, spring break is a predictable event, and algorithms can "learn" over time.

The IT Shop

The long evolution from the days of centralized, predictable tasks on mainframe computers—the heyday of the data processing group—to highly distributed, user-driven environments has entered a new phase in many companies. Three trends bear brief mention: clouds, consumerization, and "deperimeterization."

1. Cloud computing is by no means the answer to everything, but it is greener, more capital-efficient, and more responsive to changing circumstances than many on-premise hardware solutions. Finding how and where clouds make sense, and finding risk-mitigated ways to build them, will continue to be a priority for the industry.
2. What Doug Neal at IT services vendor CSC has called "consumerization" will continue to accelerate. Employees will experience mobility, data analytics, and real-time responsiveness in consumer settings, then bring their expectations to the corporate computing world. The information technology organization as a controlling gatekeeper is in some companies evolving to the concierge-like role: The chief information officer at the enterprise software vendor SAP says his goal is to become device-agnostic, given the pace of innovation in smartphones and tablets.[15]

3. Keeping information secure is harder in a mobile environment. Whereas a firewall metaphor was useful for a time, the untethering of so much of the infrastructure means that boundaries between inside and outside, and between us and them, are dissolving. It's a clumsy word, but the enterprise has become deperimeterized. That tendency pushes security from an enclosure project (keep our stuff safe and the bad guys out) to a much more complex task of education, prevention, and risk management.

Implications

The consequences of these and the other trends discussed in this book are not simple or easily summarized. At a broad level, five clusters of issues emerge.

1. *Change happens fast.* More than once executives have expressed exasperation that the world is moving too fast for their company's internal processes, cultural comfort, and planning cycles. In addition to the impracticality of slowing the world down, getting companies to move faster can be impossible. The stakes are high indeed.
2. *The worlds of technology and information are increasingly dominated by platforms and systems, which require different levels of strategy and execution compared to product-centric environments.* System thinking is difficult to coax from a single organization; from an ecosystem of self-interested optimizers, it is, again, nearly impossible. Platform strategies, when executed well, are powerful indeed: Think of Intel, or PayPal, or Facebook.
3. *Organizations are challenged to find the right size and shape from which to address their constituencies.* This is no less true of militaries, governments, and nonprofits than it is of traditional businesses. Lower costs of coordination, faster customer and competitor behaviors, and lightweight infrastructure mean that jobs, tasks, roles, and supervisory relationships are all changing.
4. *One facet of the organizational question relates to physical place as it relates to cyberspace.* Where are physical assets, face-to-face collaboration settings, and backup resources located? At the same time, place/space is reshaping personal identity, relationships inside and away from work, and the range of possibilities for convening problem solvers, fans, concerned parties, or bad guys for that matter.
5. *Finally, risk is, well, riskier in a more connected world.* Whether in financial markets, organized crime, or just random events, the web of interconnection puts entities into the position of feeling effects

generated far away. In addition, the speed of connection accelerates: The AIDS virus was spread by a flight attendant who worked on airplanes flying a reasonably fast 500 miles per hour. Cyberviruses move at two-thirds the speed of light, or about 120,000 miles per second. That's a factor of about 124,000 times faster. Are decision processes and reaction times accelerating in parallel? Hardly. And with more information comes more noise. Therein lies the challenge in a nutshell: In a time of extreme speed and scale, how do human decisions and processes keep up?

The Last Word . . .

Is innovation. If information technology is to have broad social impact—and if, as Carlota Perez suggests, we are in the phase of economic history in which information technologies are absorbed into a multitude of everyday artifacts and processes—businesses, governments, and other institutions must move beyond the straightforward practice of optimizing existing practices. All of these organizations must innovate, in more domains, at deeper levels. Such processes as education, death and dying, and career management are ripe for reconceptualization and reinvention.

That need for innovation is also reflected in the realities of the workplace, wherever it might be located. To generate the required number of new jobs and to address the negative outcomes of past decisions (whether environmental damage, certain forms of discrimination, or public health issues), innovation needs to be the human mandate, rather than a deterministic technological outcome, of the information age.

Notes

1. Neal Ungerleider, "Somali Pirates Go High Tech," *Fast Company*, June 22, 2011, www.fastcompany.com/1762331/somali-pirates-go-high-tech.
2. GNU General Public License, Version 3 June 29, 2007, www.gnu.org/copyleft/gpl.html.
3. "UMD Study Finds Facebook Applications Create More Than 182,000 New U.S. Jobs Worth $12.19B+," University of Maryland, news release, September 19, 2011, www.rhsmith.umd.edu/news/releases/2011/091911.aspx.
4. John Arquilla and David Ronfeldt, *In Athena's Camp: Preparing for Conflict in the Information Age* (Santa Monica, CA: RAND Corporation, 1997).
5. Ibid., p 1.
6. Ibid., p. 3.
7. Ibid., p. 11.

8. "Oh, Mr. Porter," *The Economist,* March 10, 2011, www.economist.com/node/18330445.

9. The head of Microsoft's operating systems group stated: "Open source is an intellectual-property destroyer. . . . I can't imagine something that could be worse than this for the software business and the intellectual-property business. I'm an American; I believe in the American way. I worry if the government encourages open source, and I don't think we've done enough education of policymakers to understand the threat." Andrew Leonard, "Life, Liberty and The Pursuit of Free Software," Salon.com, February 15, 2001, www.salon.com/2001/02/15/unamerican/.

10. Thomas Malone and R Laubacher, "The Dawn of the E-lance Economy," *Harvard Business Review* 76, no. 5 (September/October 1998): 144–152.

11. http://earth-liberation-front.org/.

12. Annie Lowrey, "In a dying industry, Dave Matthews Band has found its niche – and big money," Washington Post, January 8, 2011, www.washingtonpost.com/wp-dyn/content/article/2011/01/08/AR2011010804596.html.

13. http://going-global.economist.com/blog/2011/04/08/the-value-of-brand-equity/.

14. www.interbrand.com/en/best-global-brands/best-global-brands-methodology/Overview.aspx.

15. Bob Evans, "Global CIO: Inside SAP: 2,500 iPads Are Only the Beginning," *Information Week,* January 13, 2011, www.informationweek.com/news/global-cio/interviews/229000630.

About the Author

John Jordan is a clinical professor in the Department of Supply Chain & Information Systems at Penn State University. In a decade away from academia, he directed Internet research at the Ernst & Young Center for Business Innovation, then served in Capgemini's Office of the Chief Technology Officer. His consulting experience extends across industries and geography, with engagements on four continents. John holds a PhD from the University of Michigan as well as a master's from Yale University, and graduated magna cum laude from Duke University. He has won teaching awards at Michigan, Harvard, and Penn State.

Index